HISTORICAL DICTIONARIES
OF WAR, REVOLUTION, AND CIVIL UNREST
Edited by Jon Woronoff

1. *Afghan Wars, Revolutions, and Insurgencies*, by Ludwig W. Adamec. 1996. *Out of print. See No. 30.*
2. *The United States–Mexican War*, by Edward H. Moseley and Paul C. Clark Jr. 1997.
3. *World War I*, by Ian V. Hogg. 1998.
4. *The United States Navy*, by James M. Morris and Patricia M. Kearns. 1998.
5. *The United States Marine Corps*, by Harry A. Gailey. 1998.
6. *The Wars of the French Revolution*, by Steven T. Ross. 1998.
7. *The American Revolution*, by Terry M. Mays. 1999.
8. *The Spanish–American War*, by Brad K. Berner. 1998.
9. *The Persian Gulf War*, by Clayton R. Newell. 1998.
10. *The Holocaust*, by Jack R. Fischel. 1999.
11. The United States Air Force and Its Antecedents, by Michael Robert Terry. 1999.
12. *Civil Wars in Africa*, by Guy Arnold. 1999.
13. *World War II: The War against Japan*, by Anne Sharp Wells. 1999.
14. *British and Irish Civil Wars*, by Martyn Bennett. 2000.
15. *The Cold War*, by Joseph Smith and Simon Davis. 2000.
16. *Ancient Greek Warfare*, by Iain Spence. 2002.
17. *The Vietnam War*, by Edwin E. Moïse. 2001.
18. *The Civil War*, by Terry L. Jones. 2002.
19. *The Crimean War*, by Guy Arnold. 2002.
20. *The United States Army, a Historical Dictionary*, by Clayton R. Newell. 2002.
21. *Terrorism, Second Edition*, by Sean K. Anderson and Stephen Sloan. 2002.
22. *Chinese Civil War*, by Edwin Pak-wah Leung. 2002.
23. *The Korean War: A Historical Dictionary*, by Paul M. Edwards. 2002.
24. *The "Dirty Wars,"* by David Kohut, Olga Vilella, and Beatrice Julian. 2003.
25. *The Crusades*, by Corliss K. Slack. 2003.

Historical Dictionary of the Arab–Israeli Conflict

P R Kumaraswamy

*Historical Dictionaries of War,
Revolution, and Civil Unrest, No. 32*

The Scarecrow Press, Inc.
Lanham, Maryland • Toronto • Oxford
2006

SCARECROW PRESS, INC.

Published in the United States of America
by Scarecrow Press, Inc.
A wholly owned subsidiary of
The Rowman & Littlefield Publishing Group, Inc.
4501 Forbes Boulevard, Suite 200, Lanham, Maryland 20706
www.scarecrowpress.com

PO Box 317
Oxford
OX2 9RU, UK

British Library Cataloguing in Publication Information Available

Library of Congress Cataloging-in-Publication Data

Kumaraswamy, P R
  Historical dictionary of the Arab–Israeli conflict / P R Kumaraswamy.
    p. cm. — (Historical dictionaries of war, revolution, and civil unrest; no. 32)
  Includes bibliographical references.
  ISBN-13: 978-0-8108-5343-0 (hardcover : alk. paper)
  ISBN-10: 0-8108-5343-4 (hardcover : alk. paper)
  1. Arab–Israeli conflict—Encyclopedias. I. Title. II. Series.

DS119.7.K85 2006
956.04—dc22

2006010134

To
my friend, philosopher, and guide
Appa
and
to the memory of
Amma

Contents

Editor's Foreword

One of the most intractable conflicts of the modern period, the Arab–Israeli conflict has been around in its more acute form for more than half a century. It has envenomed relations not only between Israel and its Arab neighbors but also much further afield, afflicting the Middle East and Muslim world as a whole and seriously complicating relations with the United States and the West in general. Over this long period, repeated attempts have been made to resolve it, with only limited success thus far, and the hopes that arise are frequently and sometimes brutally crushed one after the other. Thus the possibilities that opened up after the death of Yasser Arafat, the new leadership of the Palestinian Authority, and the partial withdrawal by Israel were quickly reversed with the electoral success of Hamas and friction among the Palestinians, which only paralleled the division within Israel. No one knows what will happen next, and all sorts of scenarios are possible aside, it seems, from a satisfactory solution.

Whatever the future may bring, it is always helpful to have a good guide to the past, and although others exist, *Historical Dictionary of the Arab–Israeli Conflict* will certainly be useful for those who want to better understand the situation. The chronology traces the many twists and turns, marking the most decisive steps. The introduction places the conflict in its broader context and helps explain just why it is so intractable. The list of acronyms, too, should be helpful in reading not only this but any other book on the topic. But it is the dictionary section that is obviously most important, providing hundreds of entries on the military, political, economic, and social aspects of the situation in Israel and its rival nations, and also among the Palestinians as well as the outside countries that have sought to resolve or destabilize the situation. These entries include the major wars and lesser actions, terrorism and assassinations, political parties and resistance organizations, countless plans and proposals along with those who supported or blocked them, and faits accomplis on the ground. The bibliography then offers further reading on a dispute that is among the most studied and written about ever.

This book was not written by an Arab, nor an Israeli, nor a Westerner, but by an Indian—one with considerable familiarity with the subject and the region. P R Kumaraswamy studied international relations at the School of International Studies, Jawaharlal Nehru University in New Delhi. There he specialized in Middle Eastern studies, and not political science, which is probably also to the good. After graduation, Kumaraswamy worked as a research fellow at, among other places, the Truman Institute of the Hebrew University in Jerusalem. In recent years, he has taught at his alma mater and written articles and books on the conflict and Israel's relations with Asia. In a field in which bias is almost impossible to avoid no matter how hard one tries, there are advantages to relative neutrality, and this book does a better job than most in presenting the facts as facts, showing the good and bad points of the various participants, and leaving it up to the reader to draw conclusions.

Jon Woronoff
Series Editor

Preface

With the contentious Arab–Israeli conflict being the most widely written-about subject in the world, why another dictionary? As an outsider to the Middle East, I have approached the whole conflict with sympathy to none and compassion to all. There is no overall bias in favor or against any party to the conflict. For example, I see and recognize the city of Jerusalem—where most of the dictionary was compiled—as holy and sacrosanct to all three major religions of the region: Judaism, Christianity, and Islam.

I primarily see the conflict—especially the Israeli–Palestinian conflict—as two intense rival nationalisms fighting over the same piece of territory. Aware of my ethno-cultural baggage, I have sought to present an outsider's view of the conflict and tried to avoid any value judgment or prescription.

Some might question the selection of entries or the choice of expression. With each passing day, a dictionary like this would have to accommodate new entries, data, and at times new interpretations. While most of the entries are contemporary in nature, the dictionary traces as the major milestone the Jewish immigration to Palestine, the *Aliya* that began in the late 19th century.

Military operations undertaken by Israel are referred to here by their specific titles because they are widely known and present a better understanding. Thus for example, "Operation Peace for Galilee" rather than "Israeli Invasion of Lebanon." At the same time, neutral expressions are used to refer to specific Arab–Israeli wars; for example, the "Arab–Israeli War of 1947–1948," as opposed to the "War of Independence" or "al-Naqba" as it is commonly known among Israelis and Palestinians, respectively. With sufficient cross-references, the entries have been kept reasonably short. The basic idea is to provide the reader, scholar and layman alike, with a ready reference on the basic aspects of the conflict.

Any dictionary, this one included, can hardly be the endeavor of a single individual. My understanding of the complexities was enhanced by pioneering similar dictionaries by Avraham Sela, Bernard Reich, Dilip Hero, Philip Mattar, Susan Hatis-Rolef, and Yaacov Shimoni. The historical dictionary series of Scarecrow Press was also of immense help.

In the late 1980s, I came across a passage in *Jews of Islam* where Bernard Lewis observed: "It may be emotionally satisfying, but it is intellectually dishonest to compare one's theory with the other's practice. It is equally misleading to compare one's best with the other's worst." I have tried to remember this in pursuing my understanding of the Middle East.

Acknowledgments

It is my guru, Professor M. S. Agwani, who, in his own intimidating style, made me a better student of the Middle East. Since the late 1980s, I have enjoyed stimulating intellectual exchanges with my peers, Avraham Sela and C. Raja Mohan.

For nearly two decades, my friend D. Shyam Babu remained a source of inspiration, intellectual honesty, and professionalism. With tireless dedication, he has spent weeks and months in going over many of my academic writings.

I have had the good fortune of interacting with innumerable scholar-friends, including A. H. H. Abidi, Alan Dowty, Ashok Kapur, Avraham Altman, Barry Rubin, Ben-Ami Shillony, Ben-Sanders, David Menashri, David Shulman, Edy Kaufman, Efraim Inbar, Efraim Karsh, Eli Joffe, Gabi Sheffer, Gerald Steinberg, Hamid Ansari, Hillel Frisch, Irene Eber, K. R. Singh, M. L. Sondhi, Mark Heller, Manmohan Agarwal, Moshe Ma'oz, Moshe Yegar, Naomi Chazan, Nissim Rejwan, Reuven Kahane, Sreeradha Datta, Steve Cohen, V. Narayana Rao, Walter Eytan, Yaacov Shimoni, Yezid Sayigh, Yitzhak Galnoor, Yitzhak Shichor, and Ze'ev Sufott.

The library staff of the Harry S. Truman Research Institute for the Advancement of Peace at the Hebrew University of Jerusalem, especially Amnon Ben-Aryeh, gave me a good working environment. Much of the work was conceived while I was a fellow at the institute. The acrimonious debates in the Institute for Defence Studies and Analyses, New Delhi, where I briefly worked, influenced my thinking on contemporary Middle East developments. I also benefited from my discussions with colleagues and friends such as Rajesh Rajagopalan, G. V. C. Naidu, Sreedhar Rao, and Dipankar Sengupta.

My graduate students at Jawaharlal Nehru University gave me comfort and stimulation and often enabled me to sharpen my understanding of the conflict. Special mention is reserved for Stuti Bhatnagar, a doctoral candidate, who spent long hours in clarifying many of the discrepancies in the earlier draft. On numerous occasions, my colleagues, especially Professor Girijesh Pant, gave me a helpful hand. In my periodic sojourns to Jerusalem, my colleague Professor P. C. Jain had to endure the administrative responsibilities of my students.

My editor Jon Woronoff needs a special mention. He so meticulously went through my hard copy for one additional reason: he started using the Internet only toward the closing stages of the project. His speed is second only to his professionalism, and he often put up with my missed deadlines.

Professor Lin Shizhong, my late father-in-law, who was the first compiler of a Chinese-English dictionary after the Cultural Revolution, has been a source of inspiration. My mother-in-law, as well as Lin Xiaozhong and Lin Tong, have been generous with their kindness and affection.

All my life, I have enjoyed the love and affection of Jayanti and Sreedhar. Ever since I first met her in Jerusalem in the summer of 1988, my wife Lin Qian has smilingly endured my eccentricities and unending demands.

And finally my friend, philosopher, and guide Appa has been my Rock of Gibraltar, to whom I humbly dedicate this work.

24 December 2005

Acronyms and Abbreviations

AHC	Arab Higher Committee
ALA	Arab Liberation Army
ALF	Arab Liberation Front
AOLP	Active Organization for the Liberation of Palestine
APG	All Palestine Government
BWC	Biological Weapons Convention
CENTO	Central Treaty Organization
CNG	Committee for National Guidance
CTBT	Comprehensive Test Ban Treaty
CWC	Chemical Weapons Convention
DFLP	Democratic Front for the Liberation of Palestine
DoP	Declaration of Principles
DP	Displaced Person
EEC	European Economic Community
EU	European Union
FRC	Fatah Revolutionary Council
GCC	Gulf Cooperation Council
Hamas	*Harakat al-Muqawama al-Islamiyya*
IAEA	International Atomic Energy Agency
IBRD	International Bank for Reconstruction and Development
ICC	International Criminal Court
IDF	Israel Defense Forces
MAC	Mixed Armistice Commission
MENA	Middle East and North Africa
MFO	Multinational Force and Observers
MK	Member of the Knesset
MNF	Multinational Force
MoU	Memorandum of Understanding
NPT	Nuclear Nonproliferation Treaty

NRP	National Religious Party (Israel)
OIC	Organization of the Islamic Conference
PCC	Palestine Conciliation Commission
PDFLP	Popular Democratic Front for the Liberation of Palestine
PFLP	Popular Front for the Liberation of Palestine
PFLP-GC	Popular Front for the Liberation of Palestine–General Command
PLA	Palestine Liberation Army
PLC	Palestinian Legislative Council
PLF	Palestine Liberation Front
PLO	Palestine Liberation Organization
PNA	Palestinian National Authority
PNC	Palestinian National Council
PNF	Palestine National Front
PNIF	Palestinian National and Islamic Forces
PNSF	Palestine National Salvation Front
POW	Prisoner of War
PPP	Palestine People's Party
PSF	Popular Struggle Front
RCD	Regional Cooperation for Development
SLA	South Lebanese Army
TIPH	Temporary International Presence in Hebron
UDI	Unilateral Declaration of Independence
UNDOF	United Nations Disengagement Observer Force
UNEF	United Nations Emergency Force
UNIFIL	United Nations Interim Force in Lebanon
UNLU	Unified National Leadership of the Uprising
UNRWA	United Nations Relief and Works Agency
UNSCOP	United Nations Special Committee on Palestine
UNTSO	United Nations Truce Supervision Organization
USSR	Union of Soviet Socialist Republics
WZO	World Zionist Organization

Chronology

1869 Opening of the Suez Canal.

1882 First *Aliya* to Palestine.

1888 Constantinople Convention signed.

1894 Alfred Dreyfus trial in France.

1896 Theodore Herzl publishes *Der Judenstaat* (*The Jewish State*).

1897 The First Zionist Congress is held in Basel, Switzerland.

1915–1916 **July through March:** Hussein–McMahon correspondence.

1916 **May:** Sykes–Picot Agreement. **June:** Arab Revolt against the Ottomans begins.

1917 **2 November:** Balfour Declaration. **9 December:** British forces led by General Allenby entered Jerusalem.

1920 **March:** Arab Congress in Damascus proclaims Faisal king of Syria. **April:** Nabi Musa riots in Hebron and Jerusalem. San Remo Conference assigned mandate for Palestine to Great Britain. **December:** *Histadrut* labor federation is formed.

1921 **March:** Britain appoints Faisal king of Iraq. Emirate of Transjordan is formed with Abdullah as head. **May:** Formation of Haganah. Arab riots in Jaffa against Jewish population.

1922 **June:** Churchill White Paper proclaimed. **24 July:** League of Nations ratifies Palestine mandate.

1929 **August:** Western Wall riots in Jerusalem, which soon spread to other parts of Palestine.

1930 **21 October:** Passfield White Paper proposed to limit Jewish immigration into Palestine.

1936 **April–October:** Arab general strike in Palestine and beginning of Arab Revolt.

1937 **7 July:** Peel Commission recommends partition of Palestine.

1938 **5 January:** Woodhead Commission recommends partition of Palestine.

1939 **17 May:** MacDonald White Paper restricts Jewish immigration and land purchase. **1 September:** Outbreak of World War II.

1942 **11 May:** Biltmore Program recommends an end to British mandate and calls for the founding a Jewish Commonwealth.

1945 **22 May:** Arab League formed in Cairo.

1946 **22 March:** Transjordan gains independence. **1 May:** Anglo-American Committee recommends admitting 100,000 Jewish refugees into Palestine.

1947 **2 April:** Britain requests a special session of the United Nations General Assembly to consider future government of Palestine. **15 May:** General Assembly establishes a UN Special Committee on Palestine (UNSCOP). **1 September:** UNSCOP issued a majority report recommending partition of Palestine with an internationalized Jerusalem and a minority report recommending a federal scheme. **29 November:** General Assembly votes to partition Palestine and to establish, by 1 October 1948, independent Jewish and Arab states and recommended international status for Jerusalem.

1948 **19 March:** United States proposes the suspension of Partition Plan and calls for a special session of the General Assembly to discuss trusteeship for Palestine. **1 April:** Security Council calls for truce in Palestine and a special session of the General Assembly to reconsider future of Palestine. **9 April:** Large number of Palestinian civilians killed by Jewish groups Irgun and Lehi in Deir Yassin massacre. **13 April:** Medical convoy to Jerusalem's Hadassah Hospital ambushed and massacred in retaliation for the Deir Yassin Massacre. **14 May:** State of Israel proclaimed. **15 May:** Armies of Egypt, Iraq, Lebanon, Transjordan, and Syria invade the newly formed State of Israel. **20 May:** General

Assembly committee appoints Count Folke Bernadotte as mediator for Palestine. **11 June:** Four week Arab–Israeli truce commences. **22 June:** *Altalena* Affair. **18 July:** Second Arab–Israeli truce begins. **16 September:** Bernadotte Plan. **17 September:** Count Bernadotte assassinated by Stern Gang in Jerusalem. **22 September:** All Palestine Government forms. **16 November:** Security Council calls for armistice talks. **1 December:** Jericho Congress asks the Hashemite king to take over the West Bank. **11 December:** UN General Assembly establishes Palestine Conciliation Commission, reaffirms decision on Jerusalem, and recognizes Palestinian refugees' right to return to their homes or to be paid compensation (Resolution 194).

1949 **24 February:** Israel and Egypt sign the Armistice Agreement. **10 March:** Israeli army reaches Eilat on the Red Sea. **23 March:** Israel and Lebanon sign the Armistice Agreement. **3 April:** Israel and Jordan sign the Armistice Agreement. **11 May:** Israel admitted to the United Nations. **20 July:** Israel and Syria sign the Armistice Agreement.

1950 **24 April:** Jordan annexes West Bank, including East Jerusalem. **25 May:** United States, Great Britain, and France issue Tripartite Declaration on Middle East.

1951 **20 July:** King Abdullah of Jordan assassinated at the Al-Aqsa Mosque in Jerusalem.

1953 **15 October:** U.S. president Dwight Eisenhower appoints Ambassador Eric Johnston to help establish a regional water development project based on the Jordan River. Qibya raid.

1954 **July:** Lavon Affair. **28 September:** Bat Galim Affair begins. **October:** Anglo-American Alpha Plan aimed at securing a comprehensive Egypt–Israeli peace is put in place.

1955 **24 February:** Baghdad Pact comes into force. **28 February:** Gaza Raid. **31 August–1 September:** Khan Yunis raid. **27 September:** Egyptian–Czechoslovak arms deal announced. **11 October:** Arab League rejects Eric Johnston's Jordan River plan. **11 December:** Kinneret Operation.

1956 **20 July:** United States and Great Britain back out of their pledge to provide financial aid for Egypt's Aswan High Dam. **26 July:** Nasser announces nationalization of Suez Canal. **16 August:** 22 nations meet in London on Suez Canal crisis. **23 October:** Sèvres Conference. **29 October:** Israel launches the Suez War. **29 October:** Kfar Kassem massacre. **2 November:** UN General Assembly calls for a cease-fire in the Suez War. **5 November:** General Assembly establishes the United Nations Emergency Force (UNEF). **7 November:** General Assembly calls on Britain, France, and Israel to withdraw from Sinai and Suez Canal zone. **21 December:** Last British and French troops leave Egypt. **24 December:** Israel begins its withdrawal from the Sinai Peninsula.

1957   10 March: Israel completes its withdrawal from the Sinai Peninsula and the Gaza Strip. **23 March:** Suez Canal reopened.

1959 Formation of *Fatah*. **24 March:** Iraq withdraws from the Baghdad Pact. **18 August:** Baghdad Pact renamed Central Treaty Organization (CENTO).

1964   13 January: First Arab Summit held in Cairo. **29 May:** Palestine Liberation Organization (PLO) established at a conference held in East Jerusalem. **13 September:** Second Arab Summit held in Alexandria, Egypt.

1965   18 May: Eli Cohen hanged in Damascus for spying for Israel. **18 September:** Third Arab Summit held in Casablanca, Morocco.

1967   19 May: At Egypt's request, the United Nations Emergency Force (UNEF) withdraws from the Sinai Peninsula. **22 May:** Egypt reimposes naval blockade on the Strait of Tiran. **1 June:** National unity government forms in Israel with Moshe Dayan as defense minister. **5 June:** Israel launches a preemptive air strike against Egyptian, Syrian, and Iraqi air bases; later in the morning, Jordan joins the war. **6 June:** Israel Defense Forces (IDF) make advances in Sinai, the West Bank, and Jerusalem. **7 June:** Israel captures East Jerusalem as well as the West Bank and Gaza Strip. **8 June:** Israel completes the capture of the Sinai Peninsula; Egypt accepts a cease-fire. **10 June:** Israeli offensive on the Syrian front captures the Golan Heights. **19 June:** U.S. president Lyndon Johnson outlines his five-point peace plan for the Middle East. **28 June:** Israel annexes East Jerusalem. **July:** Israeli minister Yigal Allon outlines his plan for the occupied territories. **1 September:** Arab summit conference in Khartoum adopts three *no*'s: no peace, no recognition, and no negotiations with Israel. **22 November:** UN Security

Council adopts Resolution 242; Gunnar Jarring appointed special representative of the secretary-general.

1968   28 December: Israel conducts a raid on Beirut international airport, destroying 13 airliners in retaliation for the attack on an El Al plane in Athens by the Popular Front for the Liberation of Palestine (PFLP).

1969   6 January: France announces a ban on arms supplies to Israel. **23 April:** War of Attrition between Israel and Egypt begins. **21 August:** An Australian Christian tourist sets fire to the Al-Aqsa mosque in Jerusalem. **9 December:** Rogers Plan announced for Israel–Egypt peace settlement.

1970   7 August: Israeli–Egyptian cease-fire comes into effect along the Suez Canal. **September:** Civil war–like situation erupts in Jordan; King Hussein proclaims martial law and orders a military crackdown on the Palestinian militia. **27 September:** Gamal Abdel Nasser mediates an agreement to end hostilities in Jordan. **28 September:** Nasser dies of cardiac arrest; Anwar Sadat takes over as president of Egypt.

1971   26 February: Failure of the Jarring mission. **6 October:** Israel and Egypt reject the Rogers proposals. **28 November:** Jordanian premier Wasfi Tal assassinated in Cairo by Palestinians.

1972   30 May: Lod massacre. **18 July:** Sadat expels Soviet military advisers from Egypt. **5 September:** Eleven Israeli athletes are murdered by the Black September Organization during Munich Olympics. **1 November:** USSR agrees to supply limited quantities of air defense systems to Egypt.

1973   6 October: Egypt and Syria launch a surprise attack on Israel and the October War breaks out. **8 October:** Israeli counteroffensive in Sinai fails. **10 October:** Israel launches a successful attack against the Syrian forces on the Golan Heights. **15 October:** Massive American arms airlift to Israel begins. **15 October:** Israeli forces cross the Suez Canal and establish a bridgehead on the western banks. **17 October:** Arab oil-producing states introduce an oil embargo against the United States and the Netherlands. **22 October:** UN Security Council adopts Resolution 338 calling for a cease-fire. **25 October:** U.S. president Richard Nixon orders worldwide nuclear alert due to fears of Soviet military intervention on behalf of Egypt. **25 October:** Security Council establishes the United Nations Emergency Force (UNEF) II to supervise cease-fire. **21 November:** Israel appoints the Agranat Commission to inquire into intelligence failure prior to the October War. **21 December:** Geneva Middle East Peace Conference begins.

1974 18 January: Israel–Egypt Separation of Forces Agreement signed. **18 March:** Arab states lift their oil embargo against the United States. **1 April:** Agranat Commission publishes its interim report. **10 April:** Israeli prime minister Golda Meir resigns owing to Agranat Commission report; Yitzhak Rabin replaces her as prime minister. **11 April:** Kiryat Shmona Massacre. **13 May:** Ma'alot Massacre. **31 May:** Israel and Syria sign Separation of Forces Agreement. **14 October:** UN General Assembly resolves by 105 votes to 4 to invite the PLO to participate in the debate on the "Palestine question." **26–30 October:** Rabat Arab summit recognizes the Palestine Liberation Organization (PLO) as the "sole and legitimate representative" of the Palestinian people. **13 November:** PLO chairman Yasser Arafat addresses the UN General Assembly. **22 November:** General Assembly grants observer status to the PLO and recognizes the right of the Palestinians to self-determination.

1975 30 January: Agranat Commission publishes its final report. **5 June:** Suez Canal reopens for navigation. **1 September:** Israel–Egypt Interim Agreement signed. **10 November:** UN General Assembly adopts Resolution 3379 equating Zionism with racism.

1976 27 June: Air France airliner from Tel Aviv to Paris is hijacked and flown to Entebbe, Uganda. **4 July:** Israeli commandos raid the Entebbe airport and free the hostages.

1977 9 November: President Sadat announces his readiness to come to Jerusalem to address the Knesset if that would promote peace. **19 November:** Sadat arrives in Israel and holds discussions with Prime Minister Menachem Begin in Jerusalem. **20 November:** Sadat addresses the Knesset. **5 December:** Egypt severs diplomatic relations with Syria, Iraq, Libya, Algeria, and South Yemen in retaliation for their decision to suspend relations with Egypt in protest against Sadat's initiative. **13 December:** Prime Minister Begin outlines his autonomy plan for the occupied territories. **25 December:** Begin and Sadat meet in Ismailia for a summit. **28 December:** Israel Knesset approves the Begin Plan.

1978   11 March: Palestinian commandos hijack a bus on the Haifa–Tel Aviv road; in the ensuing Israeli rescue mission, 37 civilians are killed and scores of others injured. **13 March:** Israel launches Litani Operation, invading Lebanon. **19 March:** UN Security Council adopts Resolution 425 establishing United Nations Interim Force in Lebanon (UNIFIL). **11 April:** Israel Defense Forces (IDF) begins withdrawal from Lebanon. **13 June:** IDF completes withdrawal from Lebanon but hands over control of southern Lebanon to South Lebanese Army (SLA). **6–17 September:** At the initiative of U.S. president Jimmy Carter, Begin and Sadat meet at the presidential retreat at Camp David; on the 17th, both signed an Israel–Egypt peace treaty and a framework agreement for autonomy for Palestinians in the occupied territories. **27 October:** President Sadat and Premier Begin are awarded the Nobel Peace Prize.

1979   26 March: Peace Treaty officially signed between Israel and Egypt.

1980   2 June: Mayors of Nablus and Ramallah are seriously wounded in terrorist attacks carried out by Jewish underground. **13 June:** European Economic Community heads issue the Venice Declaration. **30 July:** Knesset approves the Jerusalem Law; protesting against this move, countries that have their legations in Jerusalem shift them to Tel Aviv.

1981   7 June: Israeli raid destroys the Osiraq nuclear reactor near Baghdad. **7 August:** Crown Prince Fahd of Saudi Arabia outlines his peace plan. **6 October:** President Sadat assassinated in Cairo. **14 December:** Knesset approves the Golan Heights Law.

1982   25 April: Israel completes its withdrawal from the Sinai Peninsula. **3 June:** Israel's ambassador to London, Shlomo Argov, is shot and gravely wounded by a Palestinian gunman belonging to an anti-Arafat faction. **6 June:** Israel launches Operation Peace for Galilee and invades Lebanon. **4 July:** IDF begins besieging West Beirut, cutting off power and water supplies. **1 August:** Israel Defense Forces (IDF) occupies Beirut's international airport. **1 September:** U.S. president Ronald Reagan unveils Middle East peace plan. **1 September:** Palestine Liberation Organization (PLO) completes its evacuation from Lebanon and relocates to Tunis. **6 September:** Arab Summit in Fez endorses a modified version of the Fahd Plan. **14 September:** Lebanese president-elect

Bashir Gemayel is murdered in the Phalange headquarters in Beirut. **16–18 September:** With Israeli knowledge, if not connivance, Phalange forces enter the Palestinian refugee camps of Sabra and Shatila and massacre scores of Palestinian civilians, including women and children; Israel is accused of being indirectly responsible for the crime. **20 September:** Protesting against the Sabra and Shatila massacre, Egypt recalls its ambassador from Tel Aviv. **28 September:** Following widespread public outcry, the Israeli government agrees to establish a commission of inquiry into the massacre, headed by the president of the Supreme Court, Justice Yitzhak Kahan. **29 September:** Israel completes its withdrawal from West Beirut. **28 December:** Israel–Lebanon negotiations open in Khalde.

1983 8 February: Kahan Commission issues its final report, concluding that Israel was indirectly responsible for not anticipating the consequences of the Phalange entry into the camps and recommending the removal of Defense Minister Ariel Sharon and a number of senior officers from their posts. **13 February:** Sharon resigns from his office but remains in the cabinet as minister without portfolio. **18 April:** Islamic Jihad launches a suicide attack against the U.S. embassy in West Beirut, killing 49 people. **17 May:** Israel–Lebanon agreement signed in Khalde and Kiryat Shmona. **23 October:** Hezbollah launches a suicide attack against the Lebanon headquarters of U.S. Marines, killing 241 soldiers.

1984 5 March: Under intense Syrian pressures, Lebanon abrogates the 17 May 1983 Israel–Lebanon agreement.

1985 14 January: Israel's National Unity government decides to redeploy the Israel Defense Forces (IDF) in Lebanon in three stages to be completed by June. **11 February:** Arafat and King Hussein meet in Amman to coordinate their moves. **20 May:** Israel releases 1,150 Palestinians belonging to Ahmed Jibril's group in return for the release of three Israeli soldiers held by the group. **24 June:** Israel releases 31 Lebanese detainees in an effort to secure the release of passengers of a TWA airliner held hostage in Beirut. **1 October:** Israel bombs the headquarters of the Palestine Liberation Organization (PLO) and Force 17 in Tunis. **5 October:** An Egyptian soldier kills seven Israeli civilians touring in the Ras Bourka area in Sinai. **8 October:** *Achille Lauro* Affair. **28 December:** Terrorists attack El Al counters in the Rome and Vienna airports, killing 15 innocent bystanders.

1986   13 January: Israel's inner cabinet decides to resolve the dispute over Taba through international arbitration; Egypt agrees to the return of its ambassador in Tel Aviv.

1987   11 April: Israeli foreign minister Shimon Peres and King Hussein of Jordan conclude the London Agreement. **17 April:** Hindawi Affair. **13 May:** Israel's inner cabinet fails to approve the London Agreement. **9 December:** The outbreak of the Intifada in the occupied territories.

1988   4 March: U.S. secretary of state George Shultz outlines his peace plan. **31 July:** King Hussein announces the severance of all legal and administrative links with the West Bank. **1 August:** Israel expels eight leaders of the Intifada to Lebanon. **15 November:** In Algiers, the Palestinian National Council proclaims the establishment of an independent Palestinian state that would coexist with Israel. **7 December:** Stockholm Declaration. **14 December:** President Reagan authorizes a U.S.–Palestine Liberation Organization (PLO) dialogue.

1989   1 January: Israel deports 15 Intifada activists to Lebanon. **20 January:** Defense Minister Yitzhak Rabin outlines his peace plan. **15 March:** Israel returns Taba to Egyptian sovereignty. **14 May:** Israel unveils a four-point peace initiative. **29 June:** Israel deports eight Intifada leaders to Lebanon. **29 July:** Israeli forces kidnap Sheikh Obeid, Hezbollah's spiritual leader, from his village in southern Lebanon. **15 September:** Egypt outlines a 10-point peace plan for elections in the occupied territories. **6 October:** U.S. secretary of state James Baker unveils a five-point peace plan.

1990   30 May: Two motorboats manned by members of the Palestine Liberation Front (PLF) try to attack a beach in central Israel but are nabbed before they can carry out any attacks. **20 June:** Failure of the Palestine Liberation Organization (PLO) to condemn the PLF attack results in the suspension of the U.S.–PLO dialogue. **2 August:** Iraq invades Kuwait. **6 August:** UN Security Council imposes economic sanctions on Iraq. **8 August:** Iraq annexes Kuwait. **12 August:** Iraqi president Saddam Hussein links his withdrawal from Kuwait to the Israeli withdrawal from the occupied territories. **8 October:** Rioting and subsequent firing by Israeli police results in the killing of 21 Arabs on the Temple Mount/*Haram al-Sharif* in Jerusalem. **12 October:** UN

Security Council condemns Israel and sends a fact-finding mission to Jerusalem; Israel refuses to cooperate.

1991 **17 January:** United States launches a preemptive strike against Iraq. **17 January:** Abu Nidal group assassinates Abu Iyad (Salah Khalaf) in Tunis. **18 January:** Iraq fires eight Scuds against Israel; by the time the Kuwait War ends, 39 Scuds have been fired at Israel. **28 February:** Kuwait War ends; Iraq agrees to unconditionally withdraw its forces from Kuwait. **18 October:** USSR reestablishes diplomatic ties with Israel; U.S. secretary of state Baker and Soviet foreign minister Aleksandr Bessmertnykh invite Israel and several Arab parties to the Madrid peace conference. **30–31 October:** Middle East peace conference commences in Madrid, with Israel represented by Prime Minister Yitzhak Shamir and the Arab states represented by their foreign ministers; the Palestinians form a part of a joint Jordanian–Palestinian delegation. **16 December:** UN General Assembly repeals its 1975 resolution on Zionism.

1992 **3 January:** Israel deports 12 Palestinians to southern Lebanon. **28–29 January:** Multilateral Middle East peace talks begin in Moscow. **17 March:** Israeli embassy in Buenos Aires is bombed; five people are killed and more than 100 wounded in the attack. **16 July:** Israel announces partial freezing of its settlement activities in the occupied territories. **20 July:** Israel makes a formal request for $10 billion in loan guarantees from the United States. **11 August:** Prime Minister Rabin meets U.S. president George H. W. Bush in Kennebunkport, Maine, and reaches an understanding regarding the loan guarantees. **10 September:** Rabin announces Israeli readiness to accept territorial compromise on the Golan Heights. **13 December:** An Israeli border policeman is kidnapped and killed by Hamas militants. **18 December:** In response to the kidnapping, Israel deports 415 suspected Hamas activists to the Lebanese border; because of Lebanon's refusal to admit them, they are left in the no-man's land near the Israel-held security zone.

1993 **19 January:** Knesset repeals a 1986 law banning meetings between Israelis and members of terrorist organizations, including the Palestine Liberation Organization (PLO). **25–31 July:** Responding to Katyusha rocket attacks, Israel conducts Operation Accountability, with air strikes on Hezbollah and Popular Front for the Liberation of Palestine (PFLP) bases in southern Lebanon. **20 August:** Israel and the PLO secretly initial the Declaration of Principles (DoP) in Oslo. **9 September:** Israel and the PLO formally recognize one another. **11 September:** United States resumes ties with the PLO, suspended since 1990. **13 September:** Israel and the PLO sign the DoP in a White House ceremony. **14 September:** Israel and Jordan sign a "Common Agenda" for negotiations in Washington. **13 October:** Israeli and PLO officials meet in Taba to discuss the implementation of the DoP.

1994 **4 February:** Israel and the Palestine Liberation Organization (PLO) in Cairo sign the Agreement on Security in Gaza and Jericho. **25 February:** An Israeli settler from Kiryat Arba, Baruch Goldstein, opens fire at the Tomb of the Patriarchs/Ibrahimi Mosque in Hebron, killing 29 Muslim worshippers and wounding scores of others before being killed by those present. **27 February:** Israeli government appoints a commission of inquiry into the Hebron Massacre. **13 March:** Israel outlaws Kach and Kahane Chai. **29 April:** Israel and the PLO sign an economic agreement in Paris. **4 May:** Israel and the PLO sign an agreement on Gaza and Jericho in Cairo. **13 May:** Israel hands over the Jericho area to Palestinian police. **20 May:** Israel kidnaps Hezbollah leader Mustafa Dirani from southern Lebanon. **1 July:** Arafat enters Gaza. **5 July:** Arafat visits Jericho and is sworn in by the Palestinian Council. **18 July:** A car bomb destroys the Jewish Community Center in Buenos Aires, killing 102 and wounding scores. **25–26 July:** Rabin and King Hussein sign the Washington Declaration, ending the state of war between Israel and Jordan. **30 September:** Saudi Arabia and other Gulf Cooperation Council (GCC) countries announce the lifting of secondary and tertiary economic boycotts against Israel. **26 October:** Israel–Jordan Peace Treaty signed in the Arava. **30 October:** Middle East and North Africa Economic Summit opens in Casablanca.

1995 **15 January:** Rabin orders construction of bypass roads in the West Bank. **27 April:** Israel confirms its intention to confiscate 130 acres of land in East Jerusalem. **22 May:** Following severe protests and criticisms, Israel suspends the plan to seize East Jerusalem land. **11 August:** Israel and the Palestine Liberation Organization (PLO) reach an agreement on the redeployment of forces in the West Bank. **24 September:** Israel and the PLO in Taba initial an interim agreement on self-rule for Palestinians. **28 September:** Rabin and Arafat sign the "Israel-Palestinian Interim Agreement" at the White House. **24 October:** U.S.

Congress approves a bill calling for the transfer of the U.S. embassy in Israel to Jerusalem no later than 1999. **29–30 October:** Amman hosts the second Middle East and North Africa Economic Summit. **31 October:** Beilin-Abu-Mazen Plan. **4 November:** Prime Minister Rabin assassinated in Tel Aviv by a Jewish extremist. **20 November:** Israel completes its pullout from six West Bank towns. **27 December:** Israeli and Syrian negotiators meet at Wye Plantation near Washington.

1996   5 January: Israel assassinates Yahya Ayyash (popularly known as "The Engineer"), a militant leader belonging to Hamas in the Gaza Strip who was accused of masterminding the killing of 60–70 Israeli civilians. **25 February:** A suicide bomber blows up a bus in Jerusalem, killing 12 and injuring 20; another explosion near Ashkelon kills 13 Israelis. **2 March:** Another suicide explosion kills 20 Israelis in Jerusalem. **4 March:** 14 more are killed in Tel Aviv in another suicide bombing; Hamas claims responsibility for all four recent attacks. **13 March:** Egyptian president Hosni Mubarak hosts an antiterrorist summit conference, called the Summit of the Peace Makers, in Sharm al-Sheikh, attended by 25 world leaders. **11 April:** Israel launches Operation Grapes of Wrath against Hezbollah in southern Lebanon. **18 April:** Kfar Kana Massacre. **28 April:** A cease-fire in Lebanon is arranged by the United States. **4 May:** The Palestine Liberation Organization (PLO) announces that it has amended its National Covenant by removing anti-Israel sections. **21 August:** Citing Oslo Accords, Israel shuts down two offices of Force 17 in El-Izariyah near Jerusalem. **25 August:** Palestinian National Authority (PNA) claims that it closed down three Force 17 offices affiliated with the PNA in East Jerusalem. **4 September:** Prime Minister Benjamin Netanyahu and Chairman Arafat meet for the first time at Erez Checkpoint. **5 September:** Speaking to the Likud Central Committee, Netanyahu vows to oppose the creation of a Palestinian state. **15 September:** Meeting in Cairo, Arab foreign ministers warn Israel that they would freeze ties with Israel if there is no progress in the peace process and also call on Qatar, Oman, Tunisia, and Morocco to reexamine their ties with and their low-level missions in Israel. **23 September:** Israel opens a new exit to the Western Wall tunnel, resulting in large-scale violence in the occupied territories in which 14 Israelis and 56 Palestinians are killed in clashes. **8 October:** Israeli president Ezer Weizmann hosts Arafat in his Caesarea home. **25 October:** Israeli cabinet lists 10 major Palestinian violations of the Oslo Accords. **6 November:** Azzam Azzam, an Israeli

Druze working in an Israeli–Egyptian plant in Cairo, is arrested and charged with spying for Israel. **12–14 November:** Cairo hosts the Third Middle East and North Africa Economic Summit. **13 December:** Israel reinstates financial subsidies to all settlements in the territories.

1997 15 January: Netanyahu and Arafat meet in Erez and agree on the Hebron Protocol. **16 January:** Knesset approves the Hebron agreement. **26 February:** Israel's Ministerial Committee on Jerusalem approves construction of new houses in Har Homa. **13 March:** Seven Israeli schoolgirls are killed in Naharayim by a Jordanian soldier. **16 March:** King Hussein pays a condolence call on the families of the slain Israeli girls. **1 April:** Arab League calls on the Arab states to freeze ties with Israel. **27 July:** Israel postpones construction and settlement in Ras al-Amud in East Jerusalem. **August:** Azzam is convicted of spying for Israel and given 15 years' imprisonment. **4 September:** A seaborne Israeli operation against Hezbollah in Lebanon fails and 11 Israeli soldiers are killed. **24 September:** Israeli agents make an unsuccessful attempt on Khalid Masha'al, the Hamas political bureau chief in Amman; the assassins are caught and, following political and diplomatic pressures from Jordan, Israel releases Hamas spiritual leader Sheikh Ahmed Yassin in return for its agents.

1998 2 January: Israeli defense minister Yitzhak Mordechai declares that Israel accepts the UN resolution on withdrawal from Lebanon but would insist on security guarantees. **13 January:** Israel issues a list of conditions for its agreeing to further redeployment in the West Bank. **20 January:** Prime Minister Netanyahu meets U.S. president Bill Clinton in the White House; the United States presents a plan for a three-stage further redeployment of at least 10 percent of the West Bank. **22 January:** Arafat informs Clinton that the anti-Israeli clauses in the Palestine Liberation Organization (PLO) Covenant (also known as the Palestine Liberation Organization Charter) were annulled in May 1996. **31 January:** PLO Executive Committee approves by voice vote the annulment of offensive PLO Covenant (also known as the Palestine Liberation Organization Charter). **8 February:** King Hussein sends President Weizmann a check for $1 million as compensation to the families of the seven girls slain by a Jordanian soldier in Naharayim in March 1997. **12 February:** Arafat threatens to unilaterally declare a Palestinian state in 1999 if no progress is achieved through negotiations. **1 March:**

Netanyahu offers an Israeli withdrawal from southern Lebanon in return for adequate Lebanese security guarantees; Lebanon rejects the proposal. **22 March:** Israeli cabinet unanimously agrees that 13.1 percent further redeployment in the West Bank is unacceptable. **1 April:** Israel's inner cabinet accepts UN Security Council Resolution 425 of 1978. **21 June:** Israeli cabinet approves a plan for new Jerusalem boundaries. **7 July:** UN General Assembly votes to upgrade the PLO's observer status to that of nonvoting member. **15–23 October:** Israel and the Palestine National Authority (PNA) negotiate an agreement at the Wye River Plantation. **23 October:** Netanyahu and Arafat sign the Wye Memorandum in the White House in the presence of President Clinton and King Hussein. **11 November:** Israeli cabinet ratifies the Wye Memorandum but adds new conditions. **14 November:** Speaking in Nablus, Arafat calls for the establishment of a Palestinian state with East Jerusalem as its capital by 4 May 1999. **19 November:** Israeli cabinet authorizes the first phase withdrawal. **20 November:** Israel carries out the first of the three further redeployments outlined in the Wye agreement. **24 November:** Israel allows the opening of Gaza International Airport. **14 December:** Meeting in Gaza, the Palestinian National Council reaffirms the annulment of the anti-Israel provisions of the PLO Covenant (also known as the Palestine Liberation Organization Charter), with Clinton present during the vote.

1999   26 January: Knesset adopts a bill requiring an absolute majority of Knesset members and a majority in a referendum before any territorial concessions are made on the Golan Heights. **28 May:** Israeli defense minister Moshe Arens approves plans to extend Ma'aleh Adumim boundaries. **31 May:** South Lebanese Army (SLA) troops begin withdrawal from the Jezzin area in the security zone in southern Lebanon. **29 June:** Accusing Hezbollah of violations, Israel pulls out of April 1996 arrangements concerning Israel's participation in the Israel–Lebanon monitoring group; on 8 July Prime Minister Ehud Barak reverses this decision. **27 July:** Barak and Arafat meet at Erez to discuss the implementation of the Wye agreement. **8 August:** Israel decides to implement the Wye agreement from 1 September. **9 August:** Chief Palestinian negotiator Mahmoud Abbas declares that the Palestine National Authority (PNA) agrees to delay the second stage of the further redeployment to 1 October. **4 September:** Barak and Arafat sign the second Wye Accord in Sharm al-Sheikh. **10 September:** Israel transfers

7 percent of the West Bank land from Area C to Area B. **5 October:** Israel and the PNA sign the Gaza–West Bank Safe Passage Protocol. **10 October:** Israeli cabinet approves removal of 42 settlements built since the October 1998 Wye accord. **12 October:** Barak orders the dismantling of 15 settlements built since October 1998; 11 are to remain, while, in the remaining 16, no new buildings are to be allowed. **25 October:** Israel opens the safe passage road from Gaza to the West Bank. **8 November:** Israel and the PNA start talks on Framework Agreement on Final Status. **14 November:** Israel decides to delay the second stage of the Wye II further redeployment. **15–16 December:** Israel and Syria hold talks in Washington, D.C., following an opening ceremony at the White House attended by Barak, Clinton, and Syrian foreign minister Farouq al-Shara.

2000   **3–10 January:** Israel and Syria hold negotiations in Shepherdstown, West Virginia, near Washington, D.C., with the active participation of President Clinton. **5 January:** Israel transfers to the Palestinian National Authority (PNA) 3 percent of the land from Area C to Area B and 2 percent from Area B to Area A. **17 January:** United States announces freezing of the Israel–Syria talks due to fundamental differences. **19 January:** Syria declares that it will not resume talks with Israel unless Israel agrees to withdraw to the 4 June 1967 lines. **8–11 February:** Israel leaves the Israel–Lebanon Monitoring Group meeting. **5 March:** Israeli cabinet approves unilateral Israel Defense Forces (IDF) withdrawal from Lebanon to be completed no later than July 2000. **21 March:** Israel hands over 6.1 percent of Area B to Area A. The PNA now controls 18.2 percent (Area A) and partially controls 21.8 percent (Area B) of the West Bank. **26 March:** Following his meeting with Syrian president Hafez al-Assad in Geneva, President Clinton admits that the Israel–Syrian differences could not be bridged. **24 April:** Israel gains full membership in the UN regional group of Western European and Others. **14 May:** Back-channel talks between Israel and the PNA in Stockholm become public knowledge. **15 May:** Israel's cabinet approves the transfer of Abu Dis, Izariyah, and Sawarah al-Sharquiya in the Jerusalem neighborhood to Area A. **21 May:** Following attacks on Israeli civilians near Jericho, Israel suspends the Stockholm talks and postpones transfer of the three villages near Jerusalem to the PNA. **21–23 May:** Israeli troops withdraw from southern Lebanon. **11–25 July:** Clinton, Barak, and Arafat hold a summit meeting at Camp

David; the summit ends in failure. **5 August:** The United Nations Interim Force in Lebanon (UNIFIL) completes its deployment along the Israel–Lebanese border. **10 September:** The Palestine Liberation Organization (PLO) Central Committee votes to postpone plans to declare Palestinian statehood. **26 September:** Israeli and PNA peace teams start talks in Washington. **28 September:** Likud leader Ariel Sharon visits the Temple Mount under heavy security; this sparks violence in Jerusalem, which soon spreads to the occupied territories and transforms into Al-Aqsa Intifada. **4 October:** Barak and Arafat meet in Paris with U.S. secretary of state Madeleine Albright, with French president Jacques Chirac and UN secretary-general Kofi Annan also involved in the intense talks; demanding an international inquiry, Arafat refuses to sign a document. **12 October:** Two Israeli reservist soldiers who strayed into Ramallah are captured and lynched by a Palestinian mob. **13 October:** Oman closes its trade office in Tel Aviv, and Morocco recalls its envoy from Israel. **16 October:** Sharm al-Sheikh summit is attended by Barak, Arafat, Clinton, Mubarak, King Abdullah II of Jordan, and representatives of the European Union, with Israeli and Palestinian leaders reaching a verbal understanding on ending the Intifada; Clinton decides to appoint an international inquiry commission and later names Sen. George Mitchell to head the commission. **22 October:** Citing continued Palestinian violence, Barak suspends the peace process; Tunisia demands the closure of Israeli trade mission in Tunis. **30 October:** Israel fires missiles at Force 17 and Fatah offices in Nablus, Khan Yunis, and El-Bireh. **7 November:** United States names members of the Mitchell Commission. **9 November:** Qatar orders the closure of the Israel trade mission in Doha. **21 November:** Egypt recalls its ambassador from Israel. **19 December:** Clinton presents his peace plans to Israel and the PNA.

2001 **16 January:** Israel–Palestine National Authority (PNA) talks resume at Erez. **20 January:** Israel accepts Arafat's offer to embark on intensive talks in Taba starting 21 January. **21–27 January:** Israeli and PNA negotiators meet in Taba to try to reach a comprehensive final status agreement; both sides agree that no progress is possible before the Knesset election in Israel slated for 6 February. **20 May:** Mitchell Committee Report is made public. **9 August:** Israeli forces seize and seal the Orient House in East Jerusalem. **27 August:** Israel assassinates Popular Front for the Liberation of Palestine (PFLP) leader Abu Ali Mustafa. **17 October:** PFLP militants assassinate right-wing Israeli minister

Rehavam Ze'evi in a Jerusalem hotel. **4 December:** Israeli tanks encircle and seize Arafat's headquarters in Ramallah.

2002   3 January: Israel seizes the Lebanese-registered ship *Karine A* in international waters in the Red Sea carrying an arms shipment from Iran to the Palestine National Authority (PNA). **22 January:** Israel Defense Forces (IDF) raids an explosives lab in Nablus, West Bank. **2 March:** Ten people are killed and about 50 injured in a suicide bombing in Beit Yisrael neighborhood of Jerusalem. **9 March:** Suicide bombing at Café Moment in Jerusalem kills 11 people and injures more than 50 others; Hamas claims responsibility. **27 March:** Suicide bombing at Park Hotel in Netanya in the midst of the Passover Seder kills 30 people and injures 140; Hamas claims responsibility. **29 March:** Arab Summit in Beirut endorses Abdullah peace plan. **29 March:** Israel launches Operation Defensive Shield against the PNA; the operation lasts until 21 April. **30 March:** Security Council Resolution 1402, calling on both Israelis and Palestinians to accept a cease-fire, passes by a vote of 14–0, with Syria abstaining. **5 June:** Suicide bombing at a bus at Megiddo Junction kills 17 people; Islamic Jihad claims responsibility. **18 June:** In another suicide bombing in Jerusalem, 19 people are killed and 74 injured; Hamas claims responsibility. **24 June:** U.S. president George W. Bush outlines his vision for Middle East peace. **16 July:** An attack on a bus at Emmanuel in the West Bank kills nine and injures about 20. **23 July:** Israel assassinates Saleh Shehadeh, head of Hamas's Izzedin-al-Qassem armed brigades, who was held responsible for several terror attacks. **31 July:** Nine people are killed and 85 injured in an explosion at Hebrew University cafeteria; Hamas claims responsibility. **4 August:** Thirteen people are killed in simultaneous terror attacks in Israel. **19 August:** Palestinian militant Abu Nidal is found dead in Baghdad. **21 October:** In a suicide bombing on a bus at Karkur Junction, 14 people are killed and 50 wounded; the Al-Quds Brigade, military wing of Islamic Jihad, claims responsibility.

2003   28 January: Knesset elections held in Israel. **28 February:** Ariel Sharon sworn in as prime minister. **29 April:** Mahmoud Abbas nominated as the prime minister of the Palestine National Authority (PNA). **4 June:** At the Aqaba Summit in Jordan, Sharon and Abbas endorse the Middle East Road Map in the presence of President Bush and King Abdullah. **11 June:** Another suicide bombing on a bus in

Jerusalem kills 17 people and wounds more than 100; Hamas claims responsibility. **29 June:** Militant Islamic organizations agree to a *hudna*—temporary cease-fire—vis-à-vis Israel. **1 July:** Prime Ministers Abbas and Sharon meet in Jerusalem. **19 August:** Suicide attack on a bus in Jerusalem kills 23 and wounds more than 130; Hamas claims responsibility. **6 September:** Owing to differences with Chairman Arafat, Abbas resigns as prime minister. **8 September:** Ahmed Qurei replaces Abbas as PNA prime minister. **9 September:** Sixteen people are killed and more than 80 wounded in two separate suicide bombings in Israel; Hamas claims responsibility. **19 November:** UN Security Council passes Resolution 1515 in support of the Road Map for Peace. **1 December:** Geneva Initiative is launched by Yossi Beilin and Yasser Abed Rabbo.

2004 22 February: In another suicide attack on a bus in Jerusalem, eight people are killed and more than 80 wounded; the Al-Aqsa Martyrs Brigade claims responsibility. **8 March:** Palestine Liberation Front (PLF) leader Abu Abbas dies in Iraq in U.S. custody. **14 March:** In a double suicide bombing at the Ashdod Port, 10 people are killed and 16 wounded; Hamas and Fatah claim responsibility. **22 March:** Israel Defense Forces (IDF) assassinates Hamas spiritual leader Sheikh Ahmed Yassin in Gaza City. **17 April:** IDF assassinates Hamas leader Abdel Aziz Rantisi. **17 May:** IDF launches Operation Rainbow to stop transfer of arms from the Sinai Peninsula to the Gaza Strip. **9 July:** International Court of Justice rules that the Israeli security fence violates international law and must be torn down. **7 October:** In terror attacks on two holiday resorts in Sinai (Taba Hilton and Ras-e-Satan), 32 people are killed and more than 120 wounded. **25 October:** Israeli parliament approves the Gaza Disengagement Plan. **11 November:** Palestinian National Authority (PNA) president Yasser Arafat dies in a military hospital in Paris and is buried in Ramallah the following day. **5 December:** As part of a prisoner exchange deal, Druze Israeli Azzam Azzam is released from Egypt.

2005 9 January: Mahmoud Abbas is elected president of the Palestinian National Authority (PNA). **10 January:** Ariel Sharon forms a unity government with the Labor Party and United Torah Judaism. **8 February:** Sharon, Abbas, Egyptian president Mubarak, and King Abdullah of Jordan participate in the Sharm al-Sheikh summit. **25 February:** In a suicide bombing carried out by Islamic Jihad in Tel Aviv, five people are killed; in retaliation, Israel freezes the planned handover of Palestinian towns. **1 March:** Great Britain hosts the London Conference aimed at reorganizing Palestinian security forces and getting financial backing for the PNA. **16 March:** In Cairo, Palestinian militant groups agree to a *tahediyeh*—a lull in the fighting—vis-à-vis Israel. **16 March:** Israel withdraws from the West Bank town of Jericho. **5 May:** Palestinians from 82 districts in the West Bank and Gaza Strip take part in local elections to choose their village council members. **26 May:** President Bush hosts President Abbas at the White House and vows to stand by the Palestinian leader "as you combat corruption, reform the Palestinian security service and your justice system and revive your economy," reiterates his support for a two-state solution, called for territorial "continuity of the West Bank [because] a state of scattered territories will not work," and in a significant move, also declares that "any final status agreement must be reached between the two parties and changes to the 1949 armistice lines must be mutually agreed to"; for his part, Abbas promises to promote Israeli–Palestinian settlement on "an accelerated phase." **4 June:** Citing additional time needed "to resolve a dispute over proposed reforms to the voting law," Abbas postpones the elections to the Palestinian Legislative Assembly slated for 17 July; the move is attributed to growing popularity of Hamas over the ruling Fatah-led coalition. **9 June:** Israeli Supreme Court rejects a petition by a group of settlers against the Evacuation Compensation Law and the Disengagement Plan and also rules that the occupied territories are "lands seized during warfare and are not part of Israel." **16 June:** Hamas discloses that the European Union is holding low-level contacts with the organization, established with Hamas members who were recently elected in the May municipal elections; this disclosure evokes strong protests from the Israeli government. **18 June:** Palestinian Legislative Assembly approves new electoral laws that increase the size of the parliament from 88 to 132 seats, with 66 seats to be filled by constituency-based elections and the other half by a proportional representation system. **21 June:** Prime Minister Sharon and President Abbas meet for the first time in Jerusalem, and during the meeting, Israel makes a conditional offer to withdraw from the West Bank towns of Bethlehem and Qalqilya; however, on the substantial issues such as reopening of the Gaza airport, further release of Palestinian prisoners in Israeli jails, and the expansion of Jewish settlements in the West Bank, there is no progress; moreover, before the meeting, Israel had arrested more than 50 suspected militants belonging to the Islamic Jihad in the West Bank, while senior defense officials tell *Ha'aretz* that Israel will resume its policy of targeted killing of militants. **25 June:** An Israeli settler is killed and four others injured in a drive-by shooting incident near Hebron; both Hamas and Fatah claim responsibility. **26 June:** As the first step toward the impending Gaza withdrawal plan, Israel destroys a row of abandoned cottages in the Gaza Strip settlement of Shirat Hayam along the seashore. **27 June:** Israel's housing minister, Isaac Herzog, tells the ministerial committee on settlements that the construction work in 50 West Bank settlements has been suspended; Israeli settlers opposed to the Gaza withdrawal plan to stage massive protests in different parts of the country. **28 June:** Sharon warns that use of force by settlers against the security forces threatens Israeli democracy and criticizes calls for soldiers to refuse orders to evacuate settlers during the planned Gaza withdrawal plan. **29 June:** Israelis opposed to the planned disengagement block busy roads in many parts of the country. **30 June:** Sharon describes the right-wing extremists who were using violence in their campaign against the Gaza Withdrawal Plan as "radical gangs" and vows to handle them "with an iron fist"; declaring the Gaza Strip a "closed military zone," the Israel Defense Forces (IDF) evacuates a group of extremists. **30 June:** The Fatah Central Committee holds its first meeting in Amman since the death of its founder, Yasser Arafat; besides Palestinian president Abbas, it is also attended by Faruq Qaddumi, who has taken over the Fatah leadership after Arafat's death. **3 July:** Israeli Cabinet rejects a proposal to delay the Gaza Disengagement by three months by a vote of 18–3. **5 July:** Knesset holds a special session on the planned deployment of Egyptian forces along the Philadelphi route between the Gaza Strip and Egypt, an area demilitarized under the Israel–Egypt peace treaty. **7 July:** Israeli forces and police hold their first comprehensive evacuation simulation exercises in preparation for the Gaza Disengagement Plan. **11 July:** Hamas denies reports that its leaders abroad, mainly in Syria, would return to the Gaza Strip after the Israeli pullout. **13 July:** Gaza is closed to Israelis who are not residents of the strip to prevent them from protesting against the planned disengagement. **14 July:** PNA declares a state of emergency in the Gaza Strip after an Israeli woman is killed when a Qassem rocket slams into her house in Moshav Netiv Ha'asara, north of the Strip;

Hamas claims responsibility. **15 July:** IDF kills seven Hamas activists in operations in Gaza and in Salfit, in the West Bank. **23 July:** U.S. secretary of state Condoleezza Rice makes a brief visit to Ramallah. **24 July:** Israeli defense minister Shaul Mofaz meets with PNA interior minister Nasser Yousef to discuss measures to coordinate the Disengagement Plan and the question of allowing PNA security forces to carry weapons. **25 July:** The president of the United Arab Emirates proposes to give $100 million to build a city that can accommodate 30,000 Palestinians on the remains of Israeli settlements in Gaza Strip, which will soon be evacuated. Palestinian leader Abbas relocates himself to the Gaza Strip in preparation for the Israeli Disengagement Plan. **3 August:** King Abdullah of Jordan and Abbas hold talks in Amman on the Gaza Disengagement Plan. **4 August:** Security forces prevent thousands of Israeli protesters from marching into Gaza settlements; a Jewish soldier who had gone AWOL several weeks earlier in protest over the Disengagement Plan opens fire in a bus in the Arab town of Shfaram, killing four people; he is beaten to death by an angry mob that storms the bus. **5 August:** The Higher Arab Monitoring Committee declares a general strike in protest against the previous day's killings. **6 August:** PNA judges protest against inadequate security arrangements, while the chief justice resigns over the prevailing lawlessness. **7 August:** Israeli cabinet approves the evacuation of first batch of settlers from the Gaza Strip; following the cabinet decision, Finance Minister Benjamin Netanyahu resigns from the government. **8 August:** Gunmen from the Al-Aqsa Martyrs Brigade storm a building in the Gaza Strip owned by the Palestinian Red Crescent Society and take away a top Fatah official; protesting against the deteriorating security situation, the International Committee of the Red Cross suspends its field operations in the Gaza Strip and also closes its offices in Khan Yunis after masked gunmen fire at them. **9 August:** Senior Palestinian cleric and Hamas leader Sheikh Hamed al-Bitawi is arrested by Israeli police in Jerusalem's Old City. **14 August:** The Kissufim crossing is shut down, and the Gaza Strip becomes officially closed for entrance by Israelis; a senior Palestinian official announces that leaders of Hamas and Islamic Jihad will attend a forthcoming meeting of the Palestine Liberation Organization (PLO), and Palestinian leader Abbas approves the Palestinian basic law that was passed by the Palestinian Legislative Council (PLC) the previous week. **15 August:** The Israeli government formally notifies the Jewish settlers in the Gaza Strip that they have 48 hours to leave their homes or they will be forcibly removed; thousands of soldiers deliver eviction orders, but most settlers refuse to leave. **17 August:** The first forced evacuation of settlers in the Gaza Strip starts with about 14,000 Israeli soldiers and police prepared to forcibly evacuate settlers and *mistanenim* (infiltrators). There are scenes of troops dragging screaming settlers from houses and synagogues but no outbreak of violence as feared earlier. **20 August:** Abbas signs a decree appropriating lands belonging to the Jewish settlements for public use once Israel's evacuation of Gaza is complete; he also announces that Palestinian legislative elections will be held on 25 January 2006. **22 August:** The settlement of Netzarim is peacefully evacuated, marking the end of a 38-year-long Israeli presence on the Gaza Strip; the demolition crews continue to work as Israeli soldiers remove the last Jewish settlers and protesters from the Gaza Strip and move on to the final stages of the Disengagement Plan, namely, the withdrawal of four small settlements in the West Bank. **23 August:** The evacuation of the four West Bank settlements is accomplished; while the residents of Ganim and Kadim have long left their homes, several families and about 2,000 outsiders try to prevent the evacuation of Sa-Nur and Homesh, but following negotiations, the evacuation is completed relatively peacefully—ending, according to IDF commander-in-chief Dan Halutz, the first of four stages of disengagement, namely, evacuation of residents, evacuation of civilian property, demolition of houses, and finally relocation of IDF installations. **1 September:** Hamas rejects any Israeli presence at the Rafah crossing on the Gaza–Egypt border after the planned Israeli pullout. **3 September:** Israeli military says it will complete its withdrawal from the Gaza Strip by 15 September but threatens to strike back if Israel comes under threat. **7 September:** IDF announces that it plans to advance its full withdrawal from the Gaza Strip to 12 September, pending Israeli cabinet approval; it is also announced that in the area evacuated in the West Bank, the IDF plans to transfer all control (excluding building permits and antiterrorism) to the PNA—the area will remain Area C (full Israeli control) de jure, but Area A (full PNA control) de facto. PNA interior minister Nasr Yussef puts security forces on alert after gunmen kill President Abbas's military adviser Moussa Arafat in the Gaza Strip; the armed wing of the Palestinian group the Popular Resistance Committees claims responsibility for the killing and for kidnapping Moussa Arafat's eldest son Manhal. **10 September:** Saudi Arabia agrees to lift certain aspects of its boycott against Israel in an attempt to satisfy U.S. demands regarding the Saudi application for World Trade Organization membership. **12 September:** General-officer-in-command Southern Command head Maj. Gen. Dan Harel signs a proclamation bringing to an end the 38-year military rule of the Gaza Strip and transferring responsibility for the area to the PNA. **13 September:** Egyptian and PNA security officials decide to close the Gaza–Egypt border, which had been overrun by thousands of people since Israeli troops withdrew. **15 September:** Israel's Supreme Court orders the government to reroute part of its security fence in the West Bank to reduce Palestinian hardship. The foreign ministers of Israel and Qatar meet on the sidelines of the UN summit. Sixteen Palestinian members of parliament file a motion of no confidence against Prime Minister Qurei, holding his government responsible for the increasing anarchy in the West Bank and Gaza Strip. **20 September:** Hamas leader Mahmoud Zahar warns of ending a truce with Israel if the Jewish state is to disrupt the upcoming Palestinian parliamentary elections. Palestinian security sources say that the Israeli army has withdrawn from the northern West Bank settlement of Sa-Nur. **22 September:** IDF withdraws from the settlement of Mevo Dotan and completes its planned withdrawal in the northern West Bank. **23 September:** An explosion at a Hamas rally in a Gaza refugee camp kills 10 people and injures at least 85, some of them seriously; the blast in a pickup truck carrying Hamas fighters in the Jabaliya refugee camp happens hours after Palestinians fire rockets into Israel. **26 September:** Israel assassinates top Islamic Jihad commander Mohammed Khalil in a missile attack in Southern Gaza; Khalil's bodyguard is also killed in the attack and four bystanders are wounded. **29 September:** Israel shuts down charities with ties to Hamas across the West Bank and fires artillery into the Gaza Strip for the first time, as it widens a five-day offensive against Palestinian fighters, despite their pledges to stop firing rockets at Israel. **1 October:** In the third phase of the local Palestinian elections, Fatah wins 51 councils in Palestinian local elections with Hamas gaining control of 13; the remaining 40 councils go to other factions. **8 October:** Rival Palestinian militant groups, including Hamas, Islamic Jihad, and the Al-Aqsa Martyrs Brigades, put up a united front to denounce interfactional kidnappings and violence. Abbas lays the cornerstone for a new housing project set to rise from the rubble of a former settlement, the first major construction project in the Gaza Strip since Israel completed its withdrawal, located at the site of the bulldozed Morag settlement in the south of the coastal strip. **10 October:** IDF soldiers shoot dead three Palestinians near the Israel–Gaza frontier, while internal violence in Gaza intensifies as militants and police engage in a gunfight. **15 October:** Israeli security guards find an unexploded Palestinian Qassem rocket on the property of Prime Minister Sharon's ranch in Negev. **16 October:** Three Israeli civilians are killed and three others are wounded in a drive-by shooting in the West Bank, while a fourth Israeli is moderately wounded in a separate attack a short while later; the Al-Aqsa Martyrs Brigades claim responsibility. A Border Police undercover unit kills a senior regional Islamic Jihad activist near Jenin. **18 October:** For the first time in several months, the IDF begins restricting Palestinian traffic on the road linking Nablus and Hebron with Jerusalem (Road 60), in response to shooting attacks that occurr on 16 October that leave three Israelis dead and seven wounded. **23 October:** The main border crossing between the Gaza Strip and Egypt reopens for 48 hours to allow humanitarian crossings; Israel closes the Rafah terminal shortly before withdrawing from the Gaza Strip on security grounds. **24 October:** IDF troops kill Luay Sa'adi, 26, the leader of Islamic Jihad's military wing in the West Bank; a few hours later, Islamic Jihad militants launch five Qassem rockets into Israel from the Gaza Strip. **26 October:** Iran's new ultraconservative president, Mahmoud Ahmadinejad, declares that the Jewish state is a "disgraceful blot" that should be "wiped off the map," evoking strong reactions in the Middle East and elsewhere. **27 October:** More than a million Iranians stage anti-Israel protests across the country; Ahmadinejad repeats his earlier call for Israel's destruction. **8 November:** IDF shoots and kills a wanted Islamic Jihad militant and wounds another in south of Jenin. **9 November:** Bombs rock three hotels in Amman, one of them popular with Israeli tourists, killing at least 57 people and wounding more than 115 in apparent suicide attacks; Al-Qaeda in Iraq, led by Jordanian militant Abu Musab al-Zarqawi, claims responsibility. **10 November:** In a close race, Amir Peretz defeats Shimon Peres in the election for the chairmanship of the Labor Party. **16 November:** Israeli and Palestinian officials clinch a long-awaited deal on the manning of the Gaza–Egypt and Gaza–Israel border crossings; under the deal, the Rafah border will open on November 25, when the

European Union monitors arrive, and the terminal will be under the control of the Palestinian Authority and Egypt, with each party patrolling its own side of the border. **17 November:** Two members of the military wing of Fatah are killed during an IDF operation near the West Bank city of Jenin. **21 November:** At least four Hezbollah gunmen are killed when they tried to kidnap soldiers from IDF outposts on the Lebanese border; seven soldiers and four civilians are wounded in the series of clashes. Prime Minister Sharon announces his resignation from the Likud and the establishment of a new political party, Kadima (Forward), which he will lead in the upcoming elections; 13 Likud members of the Knesset (MKs), including some ministers, join the new party. **22 November:** Under an agreement worked out between various political parties, 28 March 2006 is agreed upon as the date for the Knesset elections; the agreement, which is approved by 84 MKs with no dissenters, authorizes the Knesset to continue legislating a bill to dissolve the house. **23 November:** A Palestinian man is shot dead and 12 more wounded in gunfights after IDF troops enter the West Bank town of Jenin in pursuit of suspected militants. **30 November:** Former Labor Party chairman Peres announces that he is leaving the party and expresses his support for Sharon's Kadima Party.

Introduction

Everything the same; everything distinct.

—Zen proverb

Competing Jewish and Arab national claims over the Holy Land form the core of the Arab–Israeli conflict, thereby transforming it into the most intensely fought struggle in the history of humanity. It evokes unparalleled passion and hostility not only among its immediate participants and neighbors but also in the wider international community. Moreover, it often contributes to frequent bouts of violence and turmoil in the Middle East and elsewhere.

Traditionally, the Arab–Israeli conflict is traced either to the beginning of the first wave of Jewish immigration—the first *Aliya*—to Palestine in 1882 or, more often, to the issuance of the Balfour Declaration in 1917 whereby Great Britain expressed support for the establishment of a Jewish national home in Palestine. Important as it is, the Arab–Israeli conflict, especially the historic Jewish longing for statehood, could not be understood with such a narrow frame of reference. Even if one were to question, challenge, and even dismiss the Judeo-Christian tradition that God had promised the Holy Land to Moses, it would still be imperative to understand the historic links and emotional attachment of Jews to the land of their forefathers.

Meaningful appreciation of the Arab–Israeli conflict, therefore, would have to begin with the destruction of the Second Temple by the Romans in A.D. 70 and the subsequent dispersal of the Jews into the Diaspora. For nearly two millennia, the Jewish people lived a life filled with suffering, subjugation, destruction, and death. Both religious beliefs and cultural heritage differentiated them from the Christian and Muslim majorities among whom they lived during this period. Living as strangers everywhere, they by turns enjoyed benevolence and toleration and suffered persecution. Despite living in a particular place for generations, for example, they remained strangers to a large extent.

The Jews' stay often has been temporary and transient without any hope of permanency. The sense of Jewish alienation from the majority population was often mutual. Neither could they integrate themselves with the majority nor could the latter accept them as different but equal subjects.

The Jewish life in the Islamic world was generally peaceful. As a People of the Book, Islam recognizes them as the possessors of a revealed and sacred (though not final) text and hence their lives and properties were to be guaranteed and safeguarded. Of course, this protection and toleration of Jews who accepted and lived under Islamic rule should not be confused with equal status vis-à-vis the majority population.

The Jewish life in Christian Europe was much more complicated. At one level, the Jewish communities suffered from periodic anti-Semitic activities such as organized violence, forced conversion, forceful expulsions, persecution, ghettos, and pogroms. Seen in this larger context, the Nazi holocaust was the ultimate cruelty that visited the community under Christianity.

At the same time, it is essential to recognize the positive contributions of the Renaissance and the French Revolution, which brought about an overall improvement in their condition. Religion ceased to be a stigma in public domain and avenues that were hitherto closed to the Jews such as educational opportunities, political participation, and commercial activities were opened up, thereby enabling the Jews to play a constructive role in the building of the industrializing Europe.

Correspondingly, the rising fervor of nationalism in Europe brought about two conflicting trends. At one level, it rekindled anti-Semitism, as witnessed during the Dreyfus trial in 1894. However, it also generated similar nationalist aspirations among the Jewish people. Despite the absence of a clearly defined territorial dimension, the Jews living in Europe began perceiving themselves as a nation—and if the Jews perceived themselves as a nation different from the rest, then their nationalist aspirations could be fully realized only through achieving a national home. It is in this European context that Zionism emerged as a rallying point for Jewish nationalism. It was not only a reaction to the prevailing anti-Semitism in Europe but also a response to the prolonged Jewish suffering and longing. The establishment of a national home was seen as the answer to the Jewish question. By aspiring for a "normal national life" in a Jewish environment, the pioneering Zionists sought to remedy the problem of statelessness.

Austrian journalist Theodore Herzl (1860–1904), who covered the Dreyfus trial, is often seen as the founder and architect of modern political Zionism. Synthesizing the prevailing nationalist sentiments in Europe and the prolonged Jewish statelessness, he visualized the formation of a homeland as the answer to the Jewish problem. Through the convening of the World Zionist Congress in Basel, Switzerland, in 1898, he sowed seeds for the Jewish homeland project.

Zionism, however, was not an ordinary national movement. Unlike other similar movements that emerged in different parts of the world against European colonialism and imperialism, Zionism suffered from a number of drawbacks and handicaps. While other national liberation movements sought to liberate both people and land from colonialism, Zionism was different. It primarily sought to free the Jews not from their immediate rulers in Europe but to liberate their historic suffering. The diasporic life rather than any specific oppressor was its adversary.

Moreover, unlike other liberation movements, Zionism did not aspire to liberate the land where the Jews were living. On the contrary, it sought to liberate a land where Jews did not live in a substantial number but to where the Jews would go for their own liberation. Since most of them were living outside their proposed "homeland," the Jews living in the Diaspora would have to immigrate to that land and "liberate" it. This migration or Aliya became the central plank upon which the liberation of the Jewish people would take place.

Aliya, therefore, became the cornerstone of Zionism and differs from other forms of migration. Economic incentives, religious compulsions, or social violence have often resulted in mass human migration. But by organizing a massive migration from the Diaspora to their ancient land, Zionism sought to create—or re-create after a two-millennium absence—a Jewish home in Palestine. It was not a home to which a group of people would return but a place where the people would go so that a home could be established. Its supporters believed that not only was a people in search of a home but also a home was in search of its people. In this sense, Zionism is unique in the annals of history.

The first wave of organized Jewish immigration began in 1882. Since the first *Aliya*, thousands of Jews have immigrated to Palestine. Between

1882 and 1947, 512,000 Jews came to Palestine for the purpose of constructing their homeland. Following the establishment of Israel in 1948, around 685,000 more Jews immigrated to the new state. Thus, more than a million Jews from the Diaspora came to the land of their forefathers in a bid to transform it into their national home. The immigration movement not only proved to be a refuge for the Jews in the Diaspora but also contributed to massive population shifts that took place in Palestine and, later, Israel.

To ensure a massive and organized migration of the Jewish people to their homeland, Zionism recognized the importance of securing the support and backing of the Great Powers. If *Aliya* was central to the creation of a homeland for the Jews, support of the Great Powers became its midwife. Therefore, since the days of Herzl, Zionist leadership had recognized the importance of and the need to cultivate major powers that had a stake in the Middle East, especially Palestine. Of the numerous efforts and contacts, Great Britain proved extremely useful to the Zionist cause when Lord Arthur Balfour, on 2 November 1917, pledged the British government's support for a Jewish national home in Palestine (the Balfour Declaration). This changed the destiny of the Middle East beyond recognition.

The two key components—*Aliya* and imperial politics—placed Zionism in conflict with other nationalist movements, especially the nascent Arab nationalism in the Middle East. As the rest were fighting the British, French, and other European imperial powers, Zionism was actively engaged with and benefiting from the colonial powers and their designs in the Middle East. Any realistic achievement of a Jewish national home in Palestine necessitated the support of a Great Power. Correspondingly however, the pro-British policies of the mainstream Zionist leadership undermined its equation with their contemporaries in other parts of the world. While the Arab nationalists were forging fraternal ties with other nationalist movements, Zionism was perceived to be a collaborator of imperialism. This perception of Zionism took a different turn following the establishment of Israel and decolonization. Instead of viewing Israel as part of the newly independent world, the former colonies began to perceive the Jewish state as an ally of the imperial powers. Such a perception, though partly promoted by Israel joining hands with Britain and France during the Suez War, largely contributed to the prolonged isolation of Israel in the developing world.

Seen in its historic context, the Jewish aspiration for a homeland was both logical and inevitable. There was, however, one major problem. Palestine—the Zionist destination for the Jewish national home—was not an empty land but had been inhabited by Arabs for centuries. Except for a brief period during the Crusades (1099–1291), it had remained under Islamic rule since the late seventh century. The realization of Jewish aspirations for a homeland, inevitably, put them in confrontation with the rights of a well-established native population.

This denial of the "other" in Palestine by the Zionist leadership was manifested through the absence of substantial and meaningful political dialogue with the Arabs of Palestine. Zionism, which otherwise exhibited foresight and vision, did not pursue negotiations with the Arabs toward realizing its nationalist aspirations. The Arab opposition to the primary Zionist activities—*Aliya* and land purchases in Palestine—were dismissed in favor of the "economic absorptive capacity" of Palestine and the economic benefits brought about by the immigration of Jews from Europe.

Thus, the exercise of the Jewish national home came into conflict with the rights of the Arab inhabitants of Palestine. The realization of the national aspirations of the Jews in the Diaspora came into inevitable and even irreconcilable conflict with the rights of the native inhabitants. If the rise of nationalism in Europe spurred the emergence of Jewish nationalism, the birth of Zionism paved the way for the emergence of Palestinian nationalism.

Palestine, therefore, became the battleground for two intense nationalist movements seeking to realize their respective politico-national aspirations. In other words, two rival nationalisms began fighting over the same piece of territory. Since then the conflict has remained intense, intransigent, and acrimonious, naturally evoking enormous and unparalleled passion among the participants as well as outside observers.

For a long time, this intense confrontation between two nationalist movements was manifested in their attempts to negate one another. Writing in the early 20th century, British author Israel Zangwell observed that Zionism was about "people without land going to land without people." This statement summed up the attitude of the pioneering Zionist leadership toward the Arab inhabitants of Palestine and their political rights. Even the Balfour Declaration only talked about "civil and religious rights of existing non-Jewish communities in Palestine"—which constituted more than 90 percent of the population of Palestine in 1917.

Similarly, the nascent Palestinian nationalism found it difficult to recognize, let alone accept, the historic links of the Jews to the land of their forefathers. Driven by a desire to repudiate any Jewish claims to Palestine, the leadership refused to consider even a federal option whereby the Jewish community would be given limited internal autonomy within a largely Arab state of Palestine. In 1947, while some Zionist leaders were advocating a binational Palestine as the solution, the Arab leadership was uncompromising on the possibility.

The formation of Israel merely intensified Palestinian hostility, and reflecting the prevailing sentiments, the Palestine Liberation Organization (PLO), founded in 1964, explicitly called for the annulment of the Partition Plan and destruction of the Jewish state. In its view, the Balfour Declaration and the immigration of Jews from the Diaspora were morally wrong and hence had to be reversed. This view prevailed until 1988, when the Algiers meeting of the Palestinian parliament-in-exile accepted the partition resolution of 1947 and declared a Palestinian state that would coexist with Israel. This sentiment of coexistence was manifested in September 1993, when Israel and the PLO granted mutual recognition to each other, thereby ushering in the peace process in Oslo.

PARTITION OF PALESTINE

During World War I, through a series of letters, known as the Hussein-McMahon Correspondence (July 1915–March 1916), Britain pledged to create an independent Arab kingdom under the leadership of Sharif Hussein of Mecca, in return for the latter joining hands with the British against the Ottoman Empire. Then, through the Balfour Declaration of 1917, it promised support to the creation of a Jewish national home in Palestine. This meant that Palestine would be kept out of the Arab kingdom promised to Hussein. To complicate the matter further, under the Sykes–Picot Agreement of May 1916, Britain and France agreed to divide the spoils of the Ottoman Empire after the war.

Upon taking over the mandate of Palestine in 1922, Great Britain tried to reconcile its conflicting commitments to the Arabs and the Jews. In the early years, while living up to its commitments under the Balfour

Declaration, it hoped to secure Arab consent for the waves of Jewish immigrants to Palestine. *Aliya* and Zionist land purchase caused social tension in Palestine and evoked strong opposition from the Arab inhabitants, which was often manifested in protests, intercommunal tension, and organized or unorganized violence. Eventually, this culminated in the protracted fighting in Palestine known as the Arab Revolt (1936–1939) and brought into focus the irreconcilable nature of the contradictory British promises to the Jews and Arabs.

In 1939 Arab opposition forced the British to abandon their commitment to the Balfour Declaration and to impose a ceiling on Jewish immigration to and land purchases in Palestine. The outbreak of World War II soon posed new challenges to all parties. While supporting the British war efforts in Europe, the Zionists opted to oppose the mandate policies in Palestine and to smuggle illegal immigrants into the region.

The end of the war exposed British vulnerabilities and forced the British government to reconsider its overseas interests and possessions. Its decision in 1946 to withdraw from the Indian subcontinent considerably weakened British interests in Palestine. The onset of anti-British violence from the Revisionist Zionists stretched the British military. After a quarter of a century of efforts, Britain was forced to recognize the irreconcilable nature of its promises to the conflicting parties and the failure of the mandate to prepare Palestine for self-governance. Eventually in April 1947, Great Britain formally handed over the problem of Palestine to the newly formed United Nations and requested the world body to suggest ways of determining the future of Palestine.

After weeks of deliberations, on 15 May 1947 the UN appointed an 11-member United Nations Special Committee on Palestine (UNSCOP) to determine the future of Palestine. The committee held its deliberations in New York, Palestine, Beirut, and Geneva and on 1 September 1947 submitted its report. There was widespread unanimity on a host of issues such as ending the mandate, economic cooperation, and protection of holy places, but the committee was divided on the central issue of the future of Palestine. A seven-member majority advocated a Partition Plan, whereby Palestine would be partitioned into independent Arab and Jewish states, with Jerusalem and its environs being declared an international city. A three-member minority led by India advocated a federal plan that would grant greater internal autonomy to the Jews within a federal Palestine. Australia abstained from endorsing either of the plans.

Both the Zionist leadership and the Arabs rejected the federal plan. It offered Jews religious and civil rights whereas they were demanding political rights and sovereignty. For their part, the Arabs felt the plan offered too many concessions to the Jews who had immigrated to Palestine.

The Partition Plan, on the contrary, at least enjoyed the support of one of the parties to the conflict—the Zionists. Despite reservations over its size and territorial limits, the proposed Jewish state was an attractive option and provided a hope for ending two millennia of Jewish statelessness. For the first time, it offered Jewish sovereignty over the land of their forefathers. Hence, the *Yishuv*, the Jewish community in Palestine, overwhelmingly endorsed the Partition Plan. After hectic diplomatic activities, political parleys, and pressure tactics from the United States, the UN General Assembly approved the Partition Plan on 29 November 1947. Thirty-three countries voted in favor and 13 voted against, while 10 members abstained.

The UN vote and the British decision to pull out of Palestine by 15 May 1948 intensified Arab–Jewish tension and violence in Palestine. As both sides were preparing for an eventual military confrontation, the neighboring Arab states committed themselves to prevent the implementation of the partition resolution. The British presence in Palestine kept them from directly intervening militarily. The violence forced the United Nations to convene a second special session of the General Assembly, where plans to "freeze" the partition resolution were actively pursued.

On 14 May 1948, hours before the impending British departure from Palestine and onset of Shabbat, the Jewish Sabbath, Zionist leaders met in Tel Aviv and declared the establishment of the State of Israel. Within minutes, the United States recognized the Jewish state, and it was followed by other countries around the world. The following day, the regular armies of the neighboring Arab states, along with Palestinian fighters and Iraqi troops, invaded the territories of the Palestine Mandate to prevent the emergence of Israel. Thus began the Arab–Israeli military confrontation and hostilities.

ARAB–ISRAELI CONFLICT

While formal hostilities between Israel and its Arab neighbors began on 15 May 1948, the Partition Plan had already unleashed large-scale violence in the mandate and sowed the seeds of the 1948 war. The Jewish–Arab fighting intensified as the British withdrawal approached and at times led to the brutal and wanton killing of civilian populations, as in the Deir Yassin massacre of April 1948 and the killing of scores of Jewish doctors a few days later. The establishment of Israel and the subsequent declaration of war by the Arab states transformed the Arab–Jewish conflict in Palestine into an interstate Arab–Israeli conflict.

In the early years of the mandate, Arab–Jewish confrontation and violent incidents such as the Western Wall riots and the Hebron Massacre (both in 1929) resulted in the socialist-Zionist dominated *Yishuv* organizing into self-defense groups and forming organizations such as Hashomer and Haganah. Not to be left behind, Revisionist Zionists formed their own militant groups, such as Irgun and the Stern Gang. Upon the establishment of Israel, these groups were combined and a unified Israel Defense Forces (IDF) was formed on 27 June 1948.

The Arab side was more divided. By the summer of 1948, the official Palestinian leadership, including Hajj Amin al-Husseini (1893?–1974), the grand mufti of Jerusalem, was residing outside the Palestine Mandate, and hence the Arab states took over the task of "liberating" Palestine and preventing the birth of the Jewish State. The Arab forces comprising of the armies of Egypt, Syria, Lebanon, the erstwhile Transjordan, and Iraq were numerically larger than the fighters commanded by the embryonic Israeli state.

Transjordan, which commanded the Arab Legion, the strongest and best-organized army in the Middle East, had strong territorial ambitions. Its ruler, King Abdullah, was secretly coveting those territories that were to become part of the independent Arab state envisaged under the Partition Plan. In the end, however, internal divisions, lack of coordination, conflicting political ambitions, and above all poor military planning proved to be too costly for the Arab states in their resolve to destroy Israel.

By the time the second UN-mediated cease-fire came into force on 18 July 1948, Israel had managed to preserve its independence, retaining most of the territories allotted to it under the UN plan and even making additional territorial gains. Palestinian territories west of the River Jordan, that is, the West Bank, including East Jerusalem, had come under the Jordanian control while Egypt controlled the Gaza Strip. Jordan formally annexed the West Bank in April 1950, further aggravating internal tensions with the Arab ranks.

In early 1949, under the UN-mediated talks on the Greek island of Rhodes, Israel and its Arab neighbors signed a series of separate armistice agreements. They signaled a temporary cessation of hostilities, but the much awaited formal peace between Israel and its neighbors did not materialize. For the next several years, the region witnessed a series of cross-border infiltrations from Jordan and the Gaza Strip into Israel that resulted in Israeli reprisal attacks against Jordan and Egypt.

The emergence of Gamal Abdel Nasser in Egypt and his growing popularity in the Arab world aroused concerns in Israel. The much-publicized Czech arms deal of 1955 added a security dimension to Israeli apprehensions over Nasser's designs. The Anglo-Egyptian agreement over British withdrawal from the Suez Canal area also contributed to Israeli fears. Against this background, Nasser's decision in July 1956 to nationalize the Suez Canal precipitated the Suez War. Joining hands with Great Britain and France, who owned the company that operated the Suez Canal, Israel launched a war against Egypt that resulted in Israel capturing the Sinai Peninsula and the Gaza Strip. Under strong pressure from U.S. president Dwight D. Eisenhower, however, in early 1957 Israel was forced to vacate these territories. The end of hostilities also witnessed the formation of the first United Nations Emergency Force (UNEF I).

A decade of relative quiet came to a sudden halt in June 1967. In the previous month, media reports had suggested a concentration of Israeli forces along its border with Syria, which prompted Nasser to demand the withdrawal of the UNEF deployed on the Egyptian side of its border with Israel. This was followed by the closure of the Gulf of Tiran to Israeli shipping, thereby creating domestic apprehensions and security concerns in Israel. The inability of the international community, including the United Nations, to lift the closure of the gulf—along with the formation of a military alliance among Egypt, Syria, and Jordan—compelled Israel to respond unilaterally.

In a well-planned military campaign on 5 June, the Israeli air force launched a preemptive air strike against bases in Egypt, Syria, and Iraq and destroyed the bulk of the Arab air force, facilities, and runways. The complete air superiority enabled Israel to take full control of the military campaign. The Jordanian decision to join the war led to Israel capturing the West Bank, including East Jerusalem. By the time the war ended on 10 June, Israel had captured the whole of the Sinai Peninsula, the Gaza Strip, and the Golan Heights as well.

The June War, also known as the Six-Day War, introduced a host of new terminologies to the Arab–Israeli conflict, such as Green Line, Occupied Territories, and settlements. On 22 November 1967, the UN Security Council adopted Resolution 242, which not only called for an Israeli withdrawal from the Occupied Territories but also demanded the right of all states in the Middle East, including Israel, to live within "secured and recognized" borders.

Israel and its Arab opponents responded differently to the war and its aftermath. The former sought to keep the newly captured territories as leverage in securing its recognition and regional acceptance. This, however, did not prevent Israel from initiating a process of building Jewish settlements in the Occupied Territories, as well as from articulating a desire to retain parts of the West Bank, especially the areas along the Jordan River Valley in any future settlement with the Arabs. For their part, the Arab states reiterated their opposition to Israel. Meeting in Khartoum in August–September 1967, the members of the Arab League vowed not to recognize, negotiate with, or make peace with Israel. At the regional level, the military defeat also brought about the political demise of the secular Arab nationalism represented by Nasser and a corresponding resurgence of conservative religious forces spearheaded by Saudi Arabia.

Even while refusing to recognize or negotiate with Israel, Egypt was not prepared to leave the Sinai Peninsula under Israeli occupation. This resulted in the low-intensity conflict along the Suez Canal commonly known as the War of Attrition (1969–1970). The death of Nasser in September 1970 and the emergence of Anwar Sadat as his successor brought about a new Egyptian calculation vis-à-vis Israel. Egypt lacked the military means to inflict a defeat on Israel and regain the Sinai, but at the same time Sadat was keen to initiate limited hostilities and establish a presence on the eastern bank of the Suez Canal.

On 6 October 1973, Egypt, in collaboration with Syria, launched a preemptive strike against Israel. Within hours, Egyptian forces broke the Israeli defenses and established a foothold on the eastern bank of the Suez Canal. The war, which began on the Jewish day of Yom Kippur, dispelled the aura of Israeli invincibility, inflicted an element of surprise, and exposed Israeli dependence on the United States for urgent military supplies. In a bid to support the Egyptian-Syrian war efforts, the oil-exporting Arab countries introduced an oil embargo on those

Western countries that supported Israel. This resulted in steep increase in oil prices and the disruption of oil supplies. The oil crisis in turn brought about swift changes in the Middle East policies of Europe and Japan. The war also raised apprehensions over the possible use of undeclared nuclear weapons by Israel.

By the time a cease-fire came into force on 22 October, a small Israeli contingent led by Maj. Gen. Ariel Sharon had established a foothold on the western bank of the canal, resulting in the encirclement of the Egyptian Third Army. Israel also managed to repel Syrian advances in the Golan Heights. But the war continues to be remembered for the strategic surprises inflicted by Egypt upon Israel.

While earlier Arab–Israeli conflicts sowed the seeds for the next round of hostilities, the October War resulted in the first peace between Israel and an Arab state. His psychological victory over Israel enabled President Sadat to initiate a policy of accommodation with Israel. The defeat of the Labor Party in the 1977 Knesset elections and appointment of Menachem Begin as the first right-wing prime minister of Israel proved to be favorable. On 20 November 1977, Sadat became the first Arab leader to address the Knesset. The following September, U.S. president Jimmy Carter hosted both leaders at a retreat outside of Washington, D.C., and facilitated the Camp David accords. In March 1979 the Egypt–Israel Peace Treaty was signed, paving the way for Israeli withdrawal from the Sinai Peninsula, a measure that was completed on 25 April 1982.

The Egypt–Israeli peace agreement led to the establishment of formal diplomatic relations between the two countries, and Egypt became the first Arab state and the second Islamic country after Turkey to establish formal relations with the Jewish state. Around the same time, the prolonged but clandestine relations between Israel and Iran came to an end following the Islamic revolution in Iran.

Sadat's decision to break ranks with other Arab countries and conclude a separate peace agreement with Israel, however, did not enjoy regional support. Countries such Iraq and Syria, as well as the PLO, were strongly opposed to such a measure. While Egypt was on the way to regaining full control over the Sinai Peninsula, its regional influence diminished considerably. Egypt was also expelled from the Arab League and the Organization of the Islamic Conference, and this in turn brought Egypt closer to the United States.

Meanwhile the Palestinian forces were gaining regional influence and attention following the formation of their umbrella organization, the Palestine Liberation Organization, in 1964. In the initial years, the PLO was largely seen as an Egyptian outfit. But the Arab defeat in the June 1967 war and the entry of Fatah into its fold considerably changed the status and influence of the PLO. Under the leadership of Yasser Arafat, who took over as chairman in 1969, the organization slowly evolved into being the most prominent Palestinian force. In 1974, the Arab summit in Rabat recognized the PLO as the "sole and legitimate representative" of the Palestinians and paved the way for its entry into the UN General Assembly as an observer.

The 1970s also witnessed the radicalization of Palestinian movements and intensification of guerrilla attacks against Israel. This period saw the beginning of international terrorism and air piracy. Palestinian Fedayeen guerrillas frequently infiltrated into Israel and carried out militant attacks, often aimed at the civilian population. Such terrorist attacks popularized the Palestinian cause and brought their plight to the attention of the international community. They also resulted in numerous counterterrorism measures from Israel (one of the most successful being the Entebbe Operation of June 1976) and the West.

Since late 1970, Lebanon had become the focus of Palestinian guerrilla operations against Israel. The near–civil war in Jordan in September that year had resulted in the Hashemite Kingdom's crackdown against Palestinian militants and the expulsion of the PLO from Amman. Operating from the immunity granted by the Lebanese government, the Palestinians often carried out military attacks against northern Israel.

Partly as a response to such attacks and partly to pacify critics within his ruling coalition over the Sinai withdrawal, Prime Minister Begin adopted a tougher stand against the PLO. In June 1982, Israel launched an invasion of Lebanon, commonly known as Operation Peace for Galilee. Even though it managed to remove the PLO and Chairman Arafat from Beirut, Israel was unable to extricate itself from the Lebanese quagmire. Its occupation of the Lebanese capital proved to be a disaster. Responding angrily to the killing of President-Elect Bashir Gemayel on 16 September 1982, Christian Phalangist militants entered Palestinian refugee camps in Sabra and Shatila on the outskirts of Beirut and massacred scores of civilians. The camps had been under the control of the IDF, and in spite of the rising tensions over Gamayel's assassination, Israel had allowed the gunmen to enter the refugee camps. This brought renewed criticism both within Israel and from the international community over the Lebanese invasion.

By 1983, Israel had withdrawn from much of Lebanon but retained control over a narrow strip of territory in southern Lebanon. Known as the "security zone," this area remained under the nominal control of the pro-Israeli South Lebanese Army, which was trained, armed, paid, and maintained by Israel. The Israeli invasion resulted in the birth of Hezbollah, a Shia militant group active in conducting raids both within the security zone and also against northern Israel. The mounting Israeli casualties in southern Lebanon generated widespread opposition within Israel over its continued presence in southern Lebanon and the military rationale behind the security zone. After protracted public pressure and increasing casualties, in the summer of 2000, Israel unilaterally pulled out of the security zone and returned to the 1923 lines that marked the borders between Lebanon and Mandate Palestine.

In December 1987, the Arab–Israeli conflict took a turn for the worse with the onset of the *Intifada* in the Occupied Territories. What began as a protest over the death of a few Palestinian workers in a road accident in Gaza City soon spread to other parts of the area and then engulfed the whole of the Occupied Territories. The popular uprising not only reinforced the impossibility of the status quo of occupation but also reintroduced the Palestinian issue as the principal problem facing the Middle East. It shifted the regional focus back from the ongoing Iran–Iraq War and reminded the international community that the Palestinian question was the core of the Arab–Israeli conflict. Not only was Israel's regional isolation increased but the Intifada also contributed to significant erosion in its support base in the West, especially among liberal elements in the United States.

The Iraqi invasion, occupation, and annexation of Kuwait in August 1990 temporarily shifted the international focus from the Palestinians to the Persian Gulf region. Iraqi president Saddam Hussein's efforts to link his occupation of Kuwait to the Israeli occupation of Arab territories evoked strong support among the Palestinians and the PLO leadership. This was short lived, however, and the U.S.-led international campaign resulted in the defeat of Iraq and its withdrawal from Kuwait in February 1991.

Capitalizing on the new international climate and the end of the Cold War, the United States initiated a Middle East peace initiative. Cosponsored by the United States and the USSR, the Madrid Conference was inaugurated on 31 October 1991, whereby Israel and its Arab neighbors, including the Palestinians, agreed to seek a political and negotiated settlement to the Arab–Israeli conflict. The formal exclusion of the PLO proved to be a major handicap to the peace efforts, though. The reelection of Yitzhak Rabin as prime minister in June 1992 brought a new momentum to the peace talks. He agreed to forgo the erstwhile taboo over the participation of the PLO and to seek a direct peace agreement with the official and recognized Palestinian leadership. This process, which came to be known as the Oslo process, culminated in the signing of the Declaration of Principles on the White House lawn on 13 September 1993. Under the Gaza-Jericho agreement, signed on 4 May 1994, Israel agreed to hand over control of the two areas to the newly established Palestinian National Authority (PNA). On 1 July 1994 Arafat returned to the Gaza Strip and took control of the PNA. By late 1995, Israel had pulled out of most of the Arab towns except Hebron.

The Oslo process, however, was anything but smooth. Opponents of the efforts, especially Hamas and Islamic Jihad, sought to sabotage the process, initiating a wave of suicide attacks against Israel. This campaign reached its peak in early 1996, when nearly a hundred Israeli civilians were killed in a spate of suicide attacks. This resulted in the defeat of the Labor Party and the victory of Likud, now headed by Benjamin Netanyahu. He considerably reversed the progress made since 1993 and not only slowed down the process but also impeded further Israeli withdrawal from the West Bank and the Gaza Strip.

In an effort to jump-start the process, Ehud Barak, who became prime minister in 1999, decided to conclude a comprehensive agreement with the Palestinians. In the summer of 2000, U.S. president Bill Clinton hosted Barak and Arafat and hoped for the conclusion of a peace accord. However, not only did the well-intentioned talks fail but they also contributed to growing Palestinian disillusion over the peace process. The controversial visit of the leader of the opposition, Ariel Sharon, to the Temple Mount/*Haram al-Sharif* area on 27 September 2000 proved to be fatal. The visit sparked widespread protests and soon led to the Al-Aqsa Intifada.

Unlike the earlier Intifada, popular participation was absent from the Al-Aqsa Intifada, which was largely confined to suicide attacks against

Israeli civilians within the Green Line. This rekindled the Israeli sense of insecurity witnessed in the early years of the state. For its part, Israel resorted to a host of brutal measures, including a policy of assassinating known military as well as political leaders belonging to various militant organizations. In March 2004, Sheikh Ahmed Yassin, the spiritual head of Hamas, was assassinated, and so was his successor Abdul Aziz Rantisi the following month. At the height of its campaign, Israel even threatened to assassinate PNA Chairman Arafat. In addition, Israel resorted to the reoccupation of Palestinian towns it had vacated in late 1995 and introduced an array of measures such as detention, land confiscation, general curfew, travel restrictions between Palestinian areas, and refusal to allow Palestinians to work inside Israel.

The onset of the Al-Aqsa Intifada resulted in the marginalization of Arafat and his exclusion from the negotiating process. From the time he came to power in February 2001, Prime Minister Sharon not only refused to negotiate with Arafat but also confined him to his headquarters in Ramallah. On a few occasions he even threatened to order the assassination of the Palestinian leader. Arafat died after a brief illness on 11 November 2004 in a military hospital in Paris. His successor, Mahmoud Abbas, managed to secure a temporary truce among various Palestinian groups vis-à-vis Israel.

The Arab–Israeli conflict at times turned outward and adversely affected other Arab states as well. The civil strife in Jordan and the resultant Black September Massacre (1970) was largely linked to the conflict. Similarly, the expulsion of the PLO to Lebanon in 1970 eventually contributed to the Lebanese civil war (1975–1989). Attempts by regional leaders to seek a political settlement to the Arab–Israeli conflict were often confronted brutally. The assassinations of King Abdullah of Jordan (July 1951), Anwar Sadat of Egypt (October 1981), and Yitzhak Rabin (November 1995) of Israel grew primarily out of complaints over their "concessions" to the enemy.

CONCENTRIC CIRCLES

The Arab–Israeli conflict operates within three concentric circles: the Palestinian, Arab, and Islamic. With considerable overlapping, these three circles are the most prominent dimensions of the problem. The

Jewish–Palestinian and Israeli–Palestinian aspect forms the core of the Arab–Israeli conflict. But its importance is neither uniform nor consistent. This was evident during the *Yishuv* years when the Palestinians under the leadership of the grand mufti of Jerusalem resisted the Zionist policy of immigration and land purchase. The widespread Arab Revolt that began in 1936 was the high point of this confrontation that eventually compelled Great Britain to abandon its support for the Balfour Declaration.

At the same time, it is essential to recognize that despite its long historic presence and affiliation to the land, modern Palestinian nationalism is of recent origin. Indeed, it emanated as a response and reaction to Jewish nationalism and the Zionist policy of *Aliya* and land purchase. Like most other "nations" in the Middle East, the Palestinian nation has largely been newly created. The dependence of the Palestinian leaders on the Arab states during the 1948 Arab–Israeli war underscored the limitations of the Palestinian nation. Despite enjoying the support and backing of the British, the *Yishuv* leaders were able and willing to provide an effective leadership. This proved critical during the war when the Jewish forces led by David Ben-Gurion succeeded in consolidating and even expanding the newly formed state.

This, however, was not the case for the Palestinians. On 14 May 1948, when the State of Israel was proclaimed, the top leadership of the Arab Executive was outside of Palestine. Critical decisions were made by the Arab League, while there were serious conflicts of interest between Transjordan and other Arab states. These differences proved to be fatal for the Palestinians when Amman overruled the Arab consensus and annexed the West Bank in April 1950. Indeed, between 1948 and 1967, Jordan's claims to these areas rested on "acquisition of territories by war," something that was declared inadmissible by UN Resolution 242 after the June War. The Jordanian occupation of the West Bank was the most critical factor in the collapse of the All Palestine Government that was proclaimed in September 1948. Even though Israel is normally blamed for the absence of Palestinian statehood, at least until 1967 the Arab states were equally responsible for that failure. Until then, they occupied most of the territory that was given to Palestine under the UN partition, and their failure to create a state in these territories not only weakened the Palestinian cause but, more importantly, created doubts about their commitment to Arab unity.

Following the 1948 Arab–Israeli war, the Palestinian dimension took a back seat and Israel's confrontation with the neighboring Arab states became the prime focus. Palestinians who had largely become refugees following the war were completely marginalized, and the problem was widely regarded as an Arab–Israeli conflict. The Arab states, led by Egyptian President Gamal Abdul Nasser of Egypt, were at the forefront of that anti-Israeli war. Even the formation of the PLO in 1964 did not take away the primacy of the Arab component.

The wording of UN Security Council Resolution 242, adopted in November 1967, illustrates this dilemma. It called for

termination of all claims or states of belligerency and respect for and acknowledgement of the sovereignty, territorial integrity, and political independence of every state in the area and their right to live in peace within secure and recognized boundaries free from threats or acts of force.

It made no direct references to the Palestinians but merely talked about "a just settlement of the refugee problem."

Ironically it was the defeat of the Arab states in June 1967 and the rise in the popularity of the Fedayeen that began to shift the focus back to the Palestinians. Though partly unpopular, the spate of airplane hijackings and other militant acts gradually brought the Palestinians back to the center. The October War temporarily halted, but did not reverse, this process. The recognition granted to the PLO by the Arab summit in Rabat in 1974 firmly put the focus on the Palestinians.

Israel's confrontation with the Arab states dominated the discourse. President Sadat's decision "to abandon" the larger Arab cause and to pursue the national interest of Egypt meant the abandonment of the Palestinian cause by the most populous Arab state. For countries such as Iraq and Syria, the Palestinian cause therefore proved to be a rallying point. The Israeli invasion of Lebanon in 1982 and the subsequent dispersal of the PLO leadership to various Arab countries formed another milestone in the fluctuating fortunes of the centrality of the Palestinian question. The Intifada that broke out in December 1987 and the Oslo Accords once again brought the Palestinian dimension to the center stage.

For its part, Israel has been comfortable to present the whole question as an Arab–Israeli, rather than Israeli–Palestinian, conflict. It is obvious

that a successful conclusion of any peace agreement with neighboring
Arab states would entail an Israeli withdrawal from the territories it had
conquered in 1967. For a long time, Israeli leaders, especially from the
Labor Party, hoped to resolve the status of the West Bank through the
Jordanian option. This, they hoped, would circumvent the formation of
a Palestinian state. By the late 1970s and early 1980s, there was a growing international consensus in favor of the Palestinian right to statehood, and under such circumstances any Israeli settlement with the
Palestinians would result in the formation of a separate Palestinian entity. Given this stark reality, Israel long resisted negotiating with the
PLO and at times even looked for a "moderate" alternative leadership
that would be willing to settle for autonomy rather than statehood. It
banned all contacts between its citizens and members of the PLO.

The Oslo process once again brought the focus back to the Palestinians. It was the signing of the Israel–PLO Declaration of Principles that
enabled Jordan to conclude a peace treaty with Israel. The ongoing
peace negotiations with the Palestinians also encouraged a number of
Arab and non-Arab countries to reexamine their erstwhile hostility toward Israel and normalize diplomatic ties with the Jewish state. However, even after Oslo, Israel often shifted the focus to the Jordanian,
Syrian, and Lebanese tracks whenever its negotiations with the Palestinians reached an impasse. It has been relatively easier for Israel to be
flexible in dealing with Arab states than with the nonstate Palestinian
leadership. But the outbreak of the Al-Aqsa Intifada in September 2000
once again brought back the centrality of the Palestinian question to the
Arab–Israeli conflict. As the hostilities intensified, it compelled a number of states, including Egypt and Jordan, which have diplomatic ties,
to reevaluate their policy toward Israel.

The Arab world forms the second ring of the Arab–Israeli conflict,
and until the late 1970s the conflict was largely dominated by the Arab
states neighboring Israel. Since the late 19th century, the Palestinians
were the principal and immediate victims of the *Aliya* and land purchase. But internal rivalries among various factions paved the way for
a greater role for the external powers. Following the formation of the
Arab League in 1945, the Palestinian question was transformed not only
as an Arab agenda but also as the primary political platform that could
unite rival Arab states. As a result, not only was the Palestinian leadership marginalized but also the Palestinian cause became subservient to

the national-interest calculations of principal Arab states. Since the mid-1940s, therefore, the Palestinian struggle was largely led by the non-Palestinian Arab leadership.

The formation of the PLO was primarily a gesture by Egypt and others to exhibit their commitment to the Palestinians. While the emergence of Yasser Arafat in 1969 ushered in a new era and an independent role for the Palestinians, it was only in 1974 that the Arab states recognized the PLO as the sole and legitimate representative of the Palestinian people.

Moreover, Palestinian and Arab interests were not always coterminous. The desire of President Sadat to pursue a separate peace with Israel and the prolonged but clandestine relations maintained by Jordan underscored the inbuilt differences between these countries and the Palestinians. The prolonged tension between the PLO and some of the Arab states should be read within the context of this dichotomous relationship. The Palestinian desire to upstage the Hashemite monarchy resulted in the civil war and the Black September Massacre of 1970. Similar conflicting interests and actions vitiated the Palestinian relations with countries such as Kuwait, Lebanon, and Syria.

Despite the periodic tensions with the Palestinians, the Arab world had not abandoned its hostility toward Israel. Egypt became the first Arab state to recognize Israel when it signed the Camp David accords in 1978, but contrary to the hopes of Israel and the United States, other Arab states did not follow Egypt's example. It was only after the signing of the Declaration of Principles between Israel and the PLO in September 1993 that Jordan was prepared to negotiate with Israel formally and openly. While the heyday of the Oslo process enabled a number of countries such as Qatar, Morocco, Tunisia, and Oman to open low-level consular relations with Israel, the Arab world in general has been extremely reluctant to normalize political ties with Israel. Moreover, whenever there was a significant deterioration in the peace process, countries such as Egypt and Jordan have not hesitated to recall their ambassadors from Israel. Indeed, more than half a century after the formation of Israel, Mauritania remains the only other Arab state that maintained normal ties with the Jewish state.

Even in the absence of any bilateral dispute with Israel, the Arab countries as a whole espouse the Palestinian cause to such an extent that their policy enjoys overwhelming domestic support. Their periodic differences with the Palestinian leadership have not mitigated the Arab states adopting a hostile posture vis-à-vis Israel. The resolution of the Palestinian question has become a *sine qua non* condition for Israel's normalization of relations with the Arab world.

The Arab circle of the conflict could also be seen through the prolonged policy of the economic boycott of Israel. In the early 1940s, the Arab states introduced a policy of imposing economic sanctions against national and international companies that were engaged in business activities with or in Israel. The formation of the Damascus-based Arab Boycott Office provided an institutional framework to this policy. Under this policy, a number of European and other non-Arab companies were threatened with economic sanctions if they pursued business ties with Israel. Fearing such measures, a number of companies avoided trading with Israel. During the October War of 1973, Arab oil-exporting countries instituted an oil embargo that brought about swift changes in the Middle East policies of Western Europe as well as Japan. This policy, however, was somewhat diluted following the Oslo process when the Arab states decided to abandon tertiary boycotts.

At times, the Arab boycott policies also permeated the political arena, and Israel was prevented from joining various regional organizations and forums. Its exclusion from the Afro-Asian Conference in Bandung in April 1955, the forerunner of the Non-Aligned Movement and Group of 77, could be directly traced to the Arab threat of boycott if Israel were to be invited. This solidarity between Arab states and other members of the Third World largely explains the innumerable anti-Israeli resolutions adopted by the United Nations and other international forums. Primarily due to the Arab factor, anti-Israeli rhetoric often became a common platform for most of these gatherings.

The Islamic dimension forms the third concentric circle confronting Israel. As with the Jewish nationalism, the Palestinian struggle against Israel also manifests itself through religion and the Islamization of the problem can be traced to the early 1920s. Embattled by the growing number of Jewish immigrants to Palestine and the perceived pro-Zionist policies of the mandate authorities, the mufti of Jerusalem sought to expand his power base by enlisting the support of the influential Islamic regions in the Middle East and elsewhere. Islamization of the problem was seen as essential to confront the threat posed by Zionism. In an attempt to transform the problem faced by the Palestinians into a wider Islamic agenda, the mufti undertook foreign trips and organized meetings with Islamic scholars from various countries. By organizing a fund-raising campaign to renovate the Al-Aqsa Mosque, the third holiest shrine in Islam, he forged personal ties with leaders of other Muslim communities. Since then, Islam has assumed an important role in Palestinian nationalism as well as in the Arab–Israeli conflict.

For a while, this Islamic undercurrent was gradually replaced by secular Palestinian nationalism represented by Fatah and the PLO. The Arab defeat in the June War and subsequent erosion of secular Arab nationalism witnessed sweeping Islamic trends in the entire region. The formation of the Organization of the Islamic Conference in 1969 marked a new beginning and signaled the ascendance of Islamic forces in Middle Eastern politics.

In the early years, the Palestinian leadership remained immune to this shift and continued to be dominated by the secular Fatah/PLO combine. The outbreak of the Intifada and the emergence of Hamas in the late 1980s brought the secular–Islamist rivalry to Palestinian turf. Since then, there has been an intense internal rivalry between the secular forces, represented by Fatah, and the religious radicalism championed by Hamas and Islamic Jihad. Through its persistent and uncompromising stand against Israel, the latter has successfully ended the monopoly of secular nationalism in Palestinian politics. It is therefore no longer possible to visualize any settlement to the Israeli–Palestinian conflict without an accommodation with Hamas and its allies. While it might be too early to foresee Islamic radicalism as the public face of the official Palestinian leadership, it is essential to recognize that the ideology represented by Hamas is here to stay. This trend would not only influence any settlement with Israel but also will shape the nature of the future Palestinian state.

Even when secular Arab nationalism was the preeminent force in the region, the Palestinian issue—especially the Jerusalem question—remained high on the Islamic agenda. The prolonged Arab opposition to the idea of Jewish sovereignty in Palestine flows from the traditional Islamic views toward the Jews. As a People of the Book, the Jews were given a certain degree of conditional protection under Islam. Conservative interpretations view historic Palestine as an Islamic *waqf*—property that could not be ceded, partitioned, or handed over to any non-Islamic rule. They see Israel's existence as the granting of sovereign rights over an area that has been continuously (except briefly during the Crusades) a part of the Islamic empire since the seventh century. Recognition of Israel has, therefore, been problematic for the radical elements.

This line of argument became vociferous following the defeat of Nasser in the June War and resurgence of religious conservatism. Moreover, as a consequence of the war, Al-Aqsa Mosque, the third holiest shrine in Islam, came under Jewish control and this in turn galvanized the support of Islamic countries in favor of the Palestinians. The refusal of militant groups such as Hamas to recognize Israel within the June 1967 boundaries is a reflection of the Islamic dimension of the problem.

The refusal of the international community to recognize Jerusalem as the capital of Israel was also due to the Islamic dimension of the conflict. As a result, a number of non-Arab Islamic countries have remained wary of establishing political ties with Israel. Even Muslim states such as Iran and Turkey that share an anti-Arab sentiment were not prepared to adopt anti-Palestinian positions. Moreover, perceived opposition from powerful Islamic countries inhibited Chairman Arafat from reaching any agreement on the Jerusalem question during the Camp David talks in July 2000.

The reluctance and refusal of countries such Indonesia and Pakistan, which are far removed from the Middle East, to establish normal ties with Israel could be attributed to the Islamic dimension. Therefore, most Islamic countries do not have any formal ties with Israel and are often in the forefront of anti-Israeli postures. This became more palpable in powerful forums such as the Organization of the Islamic Conference. Above all, the Islamic dimension takes strange twists. Until the late 1970s, for example, Saudi Arabia kept Israeli Muslims from performing the *Hajj*, one of the five pillars of Islam.

This religious angle also has a Jewish dimension. The Israeli military conquest during the June War, especially the capture of the West Bank and East Jerusalem, ushered in what is commonly understood as Messianic Zionism and the emergence of a right–religious combination. Religion-based claims to the Occupied Territories intensified following the inauguration of the Oslo process, wherein Israel was expected to cede a substantial portion of the West Bank and Gaza Strip to the Palestinians. Right-wing elements opposed to the peace process were strengthened when religious leaders joined the fray. They argued that since these territories were promised by God to Moses, they could not be handed over to non-Jewish control. Extremist elements within the religious circles even suggested that anyone who "abandons" these territories could be killed for violating God's commandments. The concept of *din rodef*, offering religious sanction to kill a fellow Jew, was used by former yeshiva student Yigal Amir to justify his assassination of Prime Minister Rabin in November 1995. Even though popular support for such a line of thinking has been minuscule, it still remains a powerful force among the religious extremists in Israel.

The bull's-eye of the concentric circles is Israel itself, and the Arab–Israeli conflict also has an internal Israeli dimension that is reflected in the growing debates within its Jewish as well as Arab populations over the country's identity. The prevailing hostility highlighted the need for internal cohesion inside the *Yishuv* and later in Israel. Surrounded by hostilities, isolation, periodic violence, and routine condemnation from the outside world, the ability of an Israeli government to ensure the welfare and security of its people depended entirely upon it enjoying the unquestionable support of its citizens. In the first two decades of statehood, this was not a problem, and the Labor Zionist Mapai/Labor Party enjoyed a virtual monopoly over the foreign and security policies of the state. Even the internal dissent from people like Moshe Sharett did not undermine Prime Minister David Ben-Gurion's determination to initiate and pursue the Suez War.

The strategic surprise inflicted by President Sadat during the October War dented this internal cohesion vis-à-vis the military establishment. While Golda Meir and the Labor Party managed to retain their position in the elections held within weeks after hostilities ended, the general Israeli consensus in favor of the war came to an end. The Israeli invasion of Lebanon, described by Prime Minister Begin as "a war of choice," was a watershed. As the Israeli army was embattled in the Palestinian refugee camps in Lebanon, the domestic support for the war began to erode. The massacre of Palestinian refugees by the Lebanese Christian Phalangist militia in Sabra and Shatila camps in September 1982 led to widespread public protest in Israel. The coastal city of Tel Aviv witnessed the largest antiwar demonstrations in the entire Middle East and culminated in the formation of Peace Now, a mass movement that eventually blossomed into an antioccupation forum.

These protests exhibited a lack of national consensus toward the war and underlined deep internal divisions within Israel with regard to its conflicts with the Arabs. While Begin and Likud took most of the blame for the unpopular war, it practically ended internal unanimity toward military confrontation. The erosion of public support was palpable during the two intifadas in the Occupied Territories. Even if the opposition was not decisive and overwhelming, domestic support for war and other forms of military operations against the Arabs could no longer be taken for granted.

Indeed, the onset of the Intifada in December 1987 led to the formation of the B'tselem, a human rights organization devoted exclusively to Israel's policies in the Occupied Territories. There are scores of movements leading a domestic campaign in Israel against occupation. The mounting Israeli casualties in the self-declared "security zone" in southern Lebanon witnessed the formation of another activist group, the Four Mothers Movement. Members of this voluntary movement played a significant role in generating public opinion against continued Israeli presence that ended in the summer of 2000 when the IDF unilaterally pulled out of Lebanon.

The Arab–Israeli conflict also influences and shapes the internal debate over Israel's identity. Though not directly related, the conflict has a bearing on Jewish–Arab relations within the country's borders. Internal tension and contradictions between Israel's Jewish and democratic identities are as old as the state itself. So long as Israel faced an existential threat but no genuine peace partner, they remained dormant or less visible. But with the gradual Israeli recognition of the Palestinians in the Occupied Territories as a nation that is entitled to political rights, pressure has mounted on Israel's dual identities. The overwhelming support among the Israeli Arabs for the political rights of the Palestinians in the Occupied Territories added a new dimension. Those segments of the Israeli public that are opposed to any territorial compromise with the Palestinians have tended to view the support of Israeli Arabs for the PLO with suspicion. The political motives of the Arab citizens came under greater scrutiny, and their demands for equal rights were viewed as a euphemism for the destruction of Israel as a Jewish state.

There is also a dichotomy on the part of the Israeli Arabs. They have the potential to function as a bridge between Israel and its neighboring Arab states, but their unqualified support for the groups committed to the defeat and even destruction of Israel jeopardizes their position. This dichotomous position of the Israeli Arabs was the result of the conflict between nation and state; they are citizens of the Israeli state but part of the wider Arab–Palestinian nation. Therefore, the Arab–Israeli conflict also affects Israel's ability to adopt an inclusive modus vivendi vis-à-vis its Arab population.

Above all, the Cold War that dominated international relations for more than four decades has also adversely affected the Arab–Israeli conflict. Since the days of the UN deliberations over the Partition Plan, the United States has been the principal supporter of the Jewish state, and in the mid-1960s this transformed itself into a strategic partnership. The political and economic support provided by Washington not only largely contributed to Israel's strength but also provided a sense of confidence. U.S.–Israeli relations were largely instrumental in Israel emerging as a regional power in the Middle East. At the same time its political proximity to the United States prevented Israel from pursuing the Arab neighbors more vigorously.

The situation was not different in the Arab world. Due to political and ideological considerations, the erstwhile Soviet Union found common cause with the Arab nationalists. This in turn enabled Arab countries neighboring Israel, especially Egypt and Syria, to reduce the security imbalance of power that favored Israel. Correspondingly, however, the support from Moscow strengthened their determination not to recognize Israel and instead to pursue a military option opposing the Jewish state. With the end of the Cold War and disintegration of the USSR, both parties were compelled to reexamine their erstwhile positions and look for a negotiated solution to the problem. It is in this context that one should view the Madrid Middle East Peace Conference that began on 31 October 1991.

CONFLICTING ISSUES

The problem has been made intractable by a host of issues and contentions that are intertwined in the Arab–Israeli conflict. Of the many issues, Israel's right to exist, the problem of borders, issue of refugees, construction of settlements, and status of Jerusalem need special attention. While recognition is a normal aspiration for any individual, community, or state, it assumes special importance to Israel. The establishment of the state in 1948 has been seen as an end as well as an answer to centuries of suffering and statelessness of the Jewish people. Securing recognition from the outside world, including from the immediate Arab neighbors, has been a major goal of Israeli foreign policy. At the same time, recognition of Israel also meant accepting its consequences for the Palestinians and their statelessness.

Compared to other countries that have unresolved territorial disputes with their neighbors, the Israeli case is unique. The issue is not where the boundary is to be demarcated but rather Israel's very existence itself. For many years, the Arab world was vehemently opposed to Israel's existence. Weeks after the June War, the Arab League pledged not to recognize, negotiate with, or make peace with Israel. The war and its aftermath, especially the October War, brought about a greater sense of realism, ushering in recognition and resignation among the Arabs of Israel's existence. Arab peace initiatives such as the Fahd Plan of 1981 clearly indicated the willingness of principal Arab states to come to terms with Israel as a part of the Middle East. Their lack of unity resulted in military weakness and Israel's widely believed nuclear threat imposed a kind of inaction.

This realism slowly permeated to mainstream Palestinian leaders and enabled them to come to terms with Israel's existence in the land of their forefathers. The Algiers declaration of November 1988, which proclaimed the State of Palestine, also signaled Palestinian acceptance of UN Resolution 181, which called for the partition of Palestine. However, until 9 September 1993, when Israel and the PLO granted mutual recognition as a prelude to the signing of the Declaration of Principles, neither side was prepared to formally recognize and accept the other as a distinct nation.

This does not mean that the mutual recognition is complete, wholehearted, and universal. On both sides there is considerable opinion that has sought to negate the political and national rights of the other. Hamas and other militant groups have consistently challenged Israel's legitimacy as a state, while right-wing elements inside Israel have argued against the portrayal of Palestinians as a distinct national group.

The question of borders forms the second complex dimension of the Arab–Israeli conflict. Israel is perhaps the only country that lacks well recognized borders, and debates on this issue introduce nomenclature such as international borders, natural borders, Green Line, armistice line, recognized borders, defendable borders, security fence, historic border, and biblical frontiers. It has never been a simple issue of Israel's boundaries.

This peculiar situation is partly the result of the historic process through which the Jewish state evolved. In spite of its historic foresight, from the beginning the Zionist leadership consistently avoided defining the territorial limits of the proposed Jewish national home or, later on, the State of Israel. The question of the size of the homeland/state remained vague and imprecise. While accepting the Partition Plan of the United Nations, the Zionist leadership avoided committing itself to the actual size proposed by the plan. This becomes essential if one looks at the reservations the Zionists had over the allotment of the Negev to the Arabs. In tune with this position, the Declaration of Independence was silent on the territorial jurisdictions.

By the time Israel had signed the armistice agreements in 1949, it had acquired more territories than envisaged by the UN plan. Because the armistice agreements did not lead to formal peace between Israel and its Arab neighbors, however, the boundary issue remained unresolved. This frontier that separated Israel and the Arab states on the eve of the June War of 1967 gradually emerged as the de facto border, commonly known as the Green Line.

The signing of peace treaties with Egypt (1979) and Jordan (1994) and Israel's unilateral withdrawal from Lebanon (2000) partly mitigated the situation and formalized Israel's borders with these countries. The absence of formal peace agreement has precluded the settlement of the border issue with the two other players, Syria and the Palestinians.

The resolution of the border issue vis-à-vis the Palestinians would imply that Zionism has finally defined its territorial limits. In the early part of the 20th century, it aspired for a Jewish national home on both sides of the Jordan River. Therefore, the Revisionist Zionists were appalled when Great Britain decided to partition Palestine in 1921 and create the emirate of Transjordan. Indeed, until 1990 the party anthem of the Likud contained references to the East Bank of the Jordan River.

The capture of the West Bank in 1967 ushered in a messianic spirit in Israel, which spoke of the redemption and return of the biblical land of Judea and Samaria—including Hebron, where the Cave of the Patriarch/Ibrahimi Mosque is located—to Jewish control. Since then,

Eretz Yisrael (Greater Israel) has become a potent concept among the religious-Zionist circles. The annexation of East Jerusalem and the Golan Heights and the uninterrupted construction of Jewish settlements in the occupied Arab territories placed Zionism as an ideology that seeks territorial expansion. In short, for over a century not only did Zionism not define the territorial dimensions of its aspirations but it also expanded the scope and extent of territories under its actual control.

The third dimension of the conflict revolves around the capital city. Israel is the only country in the world that does not have a recognized capital. This is partly because of the peculiar nature of the Partition Plan, which declared Jerusalem to be a *corpus separatum*. Given the importance of the city to all three Semitic religions, the United Nations preferred to declare Jerusalem to be an international city. At the same time, none could ignore the centrality of Jerusalem (or Zion) to the Jewish people and their struggle for a homeland.

Therefore, as they prepared to declare the statehood, the Zionist leaders were conscious of the international position regarding Jerusalem. While Zionism could not be expected to flourish without Zion, any explicit reference to Jerusalem would result in international opposition to the newly born state. Given the anticipated opposition from the Arab neighbors, Israel could ill afford to make new enemies. Therefore, the Declaration of Independence issued in Tel Aviv eloquently dealt with the historic rights of the Jews to the land of their forefathers but was silent on the question of the capital city.

In the ensuing war, the city was divided, with Israel taking control over the western part while Jordan captured East Jerusalem, including the sites most holy to Judaism, Christianity, and Islam. This division was formalized in the armistice agreement signed on 3 April 1949. In December of that year, a few months after its admission to the United Nations, Israel proclaimed Jerusalem its capital. During the June War of 1967, Israel captured the West Bank—including East Jerusalem, which it subsequently annexed.

The international community, however, does not recognize even West Jerusalem, let alone the post-1967 unified city, as Israel's capital. The United Nations and various other international forums and organizations have adopted innumerable resolutions condemning Israel's policy on Jerusalem. With the exception of a few Latin American countries, most states that have diplomatic ties with Israel consider Tel Aviv to be its capital. There is, however, an anomaly. All state institutions such as the seat of the presidency, the Supreme Court, the Knesset, and most ministries and government offices are located in Jerusalem; for logistical reasons, the defense ministry still remains in Tel Aviv. All official meetings and transactions take place in Jerusalem. Even though foreign embassies are located in Tel Aviv, all ambassadors, including Arab ambassadors accredited to Israel, present their credentials in Jerusalem.

The Jerusalem issue also has another dimension. If the international community led by the United Nations does not recognize Jerusalem as the capital of Israel, it also does not recognize the city to be the capital of a future Palestinian state. Since both parties stake exclusive claims to Jerusalem, especially the Old City, an imaginative compromise acceptable to both becomes a precondition. By placing Jerusalem in the Oslo Accords as an issue to be decided during the final status negotiations, Israel conceded that its claim to Jerusalem as the united, undivided, and eternal capital was not final.

It ought to be recognized that because Jerusalem has also been on the Islamic agenda, any compromise worked out between Israeli and Palestinian leaders would have to be acceptable to the larger *ummah*. Indeed, Jerusalem is the issue where the wider non-Palestinian Islamic world wields a veto. This issue in turn makes the Jerusalem question the most intractable aspect of the Arab–Israeli conflict.

The status of the Occupied Territories constitutes the fourth dimension of the conflict. This phrase has been used to denote those lands that Israel captured during the June War of 1967, namely, the Sinai Peninsula, the Gaza Strip, the Golan Heights, and the West Bank, including East Jerusalem. However, if one defines "occupied territories" as those nonsovereign territories captured during armed conflict, then the Jordanian claims to the West Bank are questionable as well. King Abdullah I captured these areas during the Arab–Israeli War of 1947–1948 and subsequently annexed them, contrary to the prevailing sentiment in other Arab states. On the other hand, Egypt, which took control of the Gaza Strip, retained it as a custodian rather than its owner. Therefore, the West Bank was an occupied territory from 1948 to 1967 as part of Jordan. Following the June War, the areas remained occupied territories, but now under a new occupying power, Israel.

Israel's policy toward the Occupied Territories reveals another dilemma. At one level, especially the right wing stakes a claim to the territories, which they sometimes even referred to as "liberated" or "administered" territories. Commonly known by the biblical names Judea and Samaria, the West Bank is considered by some to be an integral part of the *Eretz Yisrael*. The settlement policy in the Occupied Territories has reflected that claim. If it is considered part of the state, Israel has full rights to pursue activities that promote the settling of its citizens in these areas.

Even those not swayed by religious sentiments have advocated some form of Israeli control over the portions of the West Bank. There is a general view in the country that Israel strategically cannot afford to withdraw to the positions it held prior to the outbreak of the June War. Indeed within weeks after that war, but before the Khartoum Arab summit resolution of "three *no*'s," Yigal Allon argued that Israel would have to retain portions of Jordan Valley in any peace deal over the West Bank. Domestic opposition to the Green Line becoming the final boundary between Israel and a future Palestinian state remains one of the few issues that enjoy widespread support in Israel.

Despite such claims, Israel has been unable to translate its claims over the Occupied Territories. With the notable exception of East Jerusalem and the Golan Heights, it refrained from annexing any other portions of territory. Even these two measures were linked to the Camp David accords and the domestic opposition that Prime Minister Begin faced in agreeing to completely withdraw from the Sinai Peninsula. The deterrence came in the form of demographic compulsions.

Formal annexation of the Occupied Territories would require Israel to follow the example set by Jordan earlier when it annexed the West Bank—granting full citizenship to all Palestinian residents. Such a move would immediately transform Israel into a binational state, and it would cease to be a Jewish state. The alternative would be to opt for the apartheid model, annexing the territories without granting citizenship rights to the Palestinian residents or engineering their expulsion from the Occupied Territories. Such a move would not only be unfeasible but would plunge Israel into an irreversible cycle of violence, international uproar, and complete isolation. Above all it, would deprive Israel of its democratic and moral credentials. It was largely due to this demographic nightmare that Israel opted for the unilateral withdrawal from the Gaza Strip that was completed in August 2005.

Closely related to its policy toward the Occupied Territories is the settlement policy that constitutes the fifth dimension of the conflict.

Since 1967 both the left-wing and right-wing governments in Israel have been aggressively pursuing settlement construction in the Occupied Territories. Though such activities were pursued in the Sinai Peninsula and on the Golan Heights, the primary focus has been on the Palestinian areas. Under the Labor Party, Israel built settlements in areas that were considered vital for security, such as the Jordan Valley. The Likud, on the contrary, perceived Jewish settlements as an instrument for preventing the territorial continuity of the West Bank and thereby precluding the formation of a Palestinian state. As a result, while in power, the Likud encouraged settlement activities in areas closer to the Palestinian population centers. Even though the Labor Party was opposed to such a strategy, it was unable to escape from its consequences.

The fallout of the settlement policy became apparent following the Israeli withdrawal in 1995 from Palestinian towns. The presence of Jewish settlements scattered all over the region meant that Palestinians could not move from one nominally free town to another without passing through barriers and checkpoints at both ends. This was also true for the Gaza Strip, where the presence of settlement blocs meant Israeli control over vast areas of Palestinian lands until the unilateral withdrawal.

IS THERE A SOLUTION ON THE HORIZON?

For decades, numerous attempts at Arab–Israeli reconciliation have collapsed because neither side was prepared to recognize the claims and demands of the other. The Arab leaders were looking for a non-Israeli partner to resolve their problem with Israel, while the Jewish state was looking for non-Palestinian leaders to solve the Palestinian problem.

Ideally, the mutual recognition of Israel and the PLO that led to the historic Rabin-Arafat-Clinton handshake on the White House lawn should have resulted in an irreversible process of reconciliation. Despite their earlier grievances, reservations, and sense of injustice, both sides were prepared to leave the past behind and seek reconciliation. The mainstream Palestinian leadership was prepared to recognize the success of the Zionist enterprise in the Palestine Mandate, while the Israeli government was prepared to recognize the political rights of the Palestinians who were living under its occupation. In spite of delays, hiccups, and near-crisis situations, both were determined to pursue a peaceful settlement to the problem. Increasing domestic unpopularity did not prevent Rabin or Arafat from deviating from their goals.

Unfortunately, the assassination of Rabin in 1995 and the spate of suicide attacks in early 1996 brought the whole process to a grinding halt. Even though the Camp David summit negotiations in the summer of 2000 were aimed at resolving some of the core issues, erstwhile trust was absent. Despite their best efforts, Prime Minister Barak and Chairman Arafat could not resolve sensitive issues such as borders, refugees, and the Jerusalem question. And the outbreak of the Al-Aqsa Intifada more or less formalized the demise of the Oslo process.

The spirit of compromise and reconciliation embedded in the Oslo process still remains the essence of any resolution of the Arab–Israeli conflict. Devoid of all other issues, it is primarily a conflict between two intense and rival nationalist movements over the same piece of territory. Compromise and accommodation is, therefore, the only way of resolving this enduring Arab–Israeli conflict. External players may facilitate a solution but cannot impose any settlement on the parties.

THE DICTIONARY

– A –

ABBAS, MAHMOUD (1935–). Known widely as Abu Mazen, Mahmoud Abbas is a veteran Palestinian leader who briefly served as prime minister of the **Palestinian National Authority** (PNA). Born in Safed in the Palestine **Mandate**, Abbas and his family left their hometown for **Syria** during the **Arab–Israeli War of 1947–1948**. After pursuing initial studies in Syria and **Jordan**, he obtained a Ph.D. in history from the Oriental College in Moscow. In 1959, along with **Yasser Arafat** and Farouq Qaddoumi (1934–), Abbas founded **Fatah**, which joined the **Palestine Liberation Organization** (PLO) in 1969. In 1980, Abbas was elected to the PLO Executive Committee and, following the **assassination** of Issam Sartawi (1935–1983), he supervised Fatah's relations with the Israeli left. During the 1980s, he also handled the PLO's negotiations with King **Hussein** of Jordan.

In early 1993, Abbas coordinated the secret Israeli–Palestinian negotiations in Norway that culminated in the **Oslo Accords**. On 13 September 1993, he signed the **Declaration of Principles** on behalf of the PLO. After the establishment of the PNA, Abbas returned to Palestinian territory in July 1995 and played an important role in the conclusion of the **Taba Agreement** that outlined the phased Israeli **redeployment** from Palestinian towns in the **West Bank**.

Simultaneously, Abbas engaged in secret talks with Israeli officials that culminated in the **Beilin–Abu Mazen Plan**, a draft proposal concerning the permanent status agreement between the two sides. In July 2000, he took part in the **Camp David Talks** that discussed the final status of the **Occupied Territories**. Abbas was critical of the **Al-Aqsa Intifada**, which broke out in September 2000. Publicly criticizing **suicide attacks**, he called for the cessation of the "militant

Intifada." To this end, in January 2003, he took part in the **Cairo Dialogue** with **Hamas** and other Palestinian factions mediated by **Egypt**. Repeated U.S. and Western demands for Palestinian reform resulted in Arafat creating the post of prime minister of the PNA and, in March 2003, Abbas became the first person to hold that office. Increased violence in the PNA-controlled areas, the Israeli policy of **targeted killing** and reprisal attacks, and Arafat's refusal to relinquish substantive powers to the prime minister severely undermined Abbas's position. On 6 September 2003, Abbas resigned his position, and he was replaced by **Ahmed Qurei**. After the death of Arafat on 11 November 2004, Abbas took over as leader of the PNA as well as the PLO.

In the direct presidential election held on 9 January 2005, Mahmoud Abbas contested as the Fatah candidate and won the election, securing 62 percent of the popular votes. Soon after his swearing in on 15 January, he secured a cease-fire agreement with Hamas and, threatening to act against security chiefs, he managed to stop rocket attacks from the **Gaza Strip** into Israel. In pursuance of the reform process, he attended the diminutive **London Conference** in January 2005. *See also* AQABA SUMMIT; BUSH, GEORGE W.; SHARM AL-SHEIKH SUMMIT (2005).

ABDULLAH I, KING (1882–1951). The second son of Sharif Hussein ibn Ali of Mecca (1852–1931), Abdullah ibn Hussein ruled **Transjordan** and **Jordan** until his **assassination** in July 1951. Born in Mecca in 1882, Abdullah traced his lineage to the scion of the Prophet Mohammed's Hashemite clan of the Quraishi tribe. The **Hussein–McMahon Correspondence** resulted in Sharif Hussein launching the **Arab Revolt** (1916–1918) against Ottoman rule, and Abdullah played a leading role in the Arab drive for independence. He subsequently became foreign minister when his father assumed the title of King of Hijaz (presently in **Saudi Arabia**).

In March 1921, following the defeat of his father by the House of Saud, Abdullah arrived in Amman with the intention of establishing Arab-Hashemite rule over an area that would include **Syria**. Determined to avoid a confrontation with **France**, which had interests in Syria, in April 1921 **Great Britain** partitioned Palestine, created a new emirate called Transjordan, and made Abdullah its emir. In return, Abdullah renounced his ambitions regarding Syria and

Mesopotamia (**Iraq**). In May 1923, Britain recognized Transjordan as an autonomous emirate, began offering support in the form of political patronage and financial assistance, and helped in the formation and maintenance of the **Arab Legion**. In May 1946, Britain granted independence to Transjordan, upon which Abdullah became king; in 1948, Transjordan was renamed the Hashemite Kingdom of Jordan.

In 1947, as the future political status of the Palestine **Mandate** was being debated by the **United Nations Special Committee on Palestine** (UNSCOP), Emir Abdullah developed an interest in acquiring parts of the territory inhabited by Palestinian Arabs. After the **United Nations** approved the **Partition Plan**, he conducted a substantive political dialogue with the *Yishuv* leadership, meeting with **Golda Meir** days before the British mandate ended. During the **Arab–Israeli War of 1947–1948**, the Arab Legion took over the Arab-inhabited parts of the central areas subsequently known as the **West Bank**. The Legion fought bitterly and captured **East Jerusalem**, including the Old City, which contains many sites holy for Christians, Jews, and Muslims.

In December 1948, prior to the conclusion of the **armistice agreement** with Israel, King Abdullah orchestrated the **Jericho Conference**, which asked the Hashemite ruler to "take over" the West Bank. As a result, in April 1950 Abdullah formally annexed the West Bank and granted Jordanian citizenship to all its residents, including the Palestinian **refugees** who were forced to flee from areas that became the State of Israel. On 3 April 1949, Jordan signed an armistice agreement with Israel. The Palestinians vehemently resented Abdullah's refusal to recognize the **All Palestine Government** proclaimed by the grand mufti of Jerusalem in September 1948 and his collaboration with Israel both during and after the 1948 war. On 20 July 1951, as he was entering the Al-Aqsa Mosque in **Jerusalem** for Friday prayers, King Abdullah was assassinated by a Palestinian. He was briefly succeeded by his son, and in May 1953 Abdullah's grandson, **Hussein**, became the king of Jordan.

ABDULLAH II, KING (1962–). Eldest son of King **Hussein**, Abdullah bin al-Hussein was enthroned as king of **Jordan** following the death of his father. Named after his great-grandfather, the founder of the Hashemite dynasty, he took the title Abdullah II after he assumed the throne on 7 February 1999. Prior to his enthronement, Abdullah had served in an elite unit of the Jordanian army and was rarely seen in public. He became king after Hussein changed his earlier succession decree and removed his younger brother, Crown Prince Hassan (1947–), from the line of succession.

Since assuming power, Abdullah has adopted a tougher stand toward **Hamas** and declared it a non-Jordanian organization in September 1999. Fearing an exodus of Palestinians from the **Occupied Territories** due to Israeli policies, in June 2001 he imposed travel restrictions upon Palestinian residents of the **West Bank**. To express his displeasure at Israel's handling of the **Al-Aqsa Intifada**, after October 2000 he postponed appointing an envoy to Israel. At the same time, reflecting the prevailing criticisms by the **United States**, he had indirectly called upon the Palestinians to elect new leaders who were prepared to shoulder responsibilities and introduce internal reforms.

In June 2003, King Abdullah hosted the **Aqaba Summit** attended by U.S. president **George W. Bush**, Israeli prime minister **Ariel Sharon**, and Palestinian prime minister **Mahmoud Abbas**. The leaders endorsed the **Middle East Road Map**, but the exclusion of Palestinian leader **Yasser Arafat** resulted in the summit not making any progress in containing violence. In February 2005, during the **Sharm al-Sheikh Summit**, King Abdullah agreed to name an ambassador to Israel and, on 21 March 2005, Marouf Suleiman Bakhit presented his credentials to Israeli president Moshe Katsav (1945–). His attempts to initiate a fresh peace initiative during the Algiers **Arab League** summit in March 2005 came under severe criticisms for its pro-Israeli bias.

ABDULLAH PLAN. In early 2002, Crown Prince Abdullah ibn Abdel Aziz (1923–) of **Saudi Arabia** (who became king in August 2005) unveiled a Middle East peace initiative that called on Israel to withdraw completely from all the Arab territories it had occupied during the **June War of 1967** and suggested the establishment of a **Palestinian state** with **Jerusalem** as its capital. In return, it offered collective Arab normalization of relations with Israel. A slightly diluted proposal with a rider on the **refugee** question was adopted unanimously by the Beirut **Arab League** summit in March 2002. **Palestine Liberation Organization** chairman **Yasser Arafat**, whose Ramallah compound was surrounded by Israeli forces, was prevented from attending the meeting. As a result, President **Hosni Mubarak** of **Egypt** and King **Abdullah II** of **Jordan** opted to stay away from the Arab summit, thereby underscoring the internal divisions within the Arab League. The Abdullah Plan was introduced against the background of the **Al-Aqsa Intifada**, an increase in Israeli–Palestinian violence, and mounting U.S.–Saudi tensions following the 11 September 2001 attacks in the **United States**. *See also* ARMISTICE AGREEMENT/S; FAHD PLAN; FEZ PLAN.

ABSENTEE PROPERTY LAW. In March 1950, Israel adopted a law that declared anyone who was a citizen or resident of one of the Arab states or a Palestinian citizen on 29 November 1949, but who had left his or her place of residence—even as a **refugee** within Palestine—to be an "absentee." The Israeli "custodian of absentee property" was empowered by the Knesset to sell absentee-owned properties to the Development Authority. This legalized the possession and distribution of movable and immovable properties abandoned by the fleeing Arab population to the Jewish citizens of Israel. The custodian was thereby able to appropriate lands, households, and farms for the new wave of Jews who immigrated to Israel after 1948. As most of the owners had fled the Palestine **Mandate** following the outbreak of hostilities in 1948, compensation was dispensed with. *See also* ISRAELI ARABS; NAQBA, AL-.

ABU DIS. The Arab neighborhood of **East Jerusalem** that often is presented as the capital of the future **Palestinian state**. As part of the **redeployment** plan, on 15 May 2000 the Israeli cabinet approved a plan to transfer Abu Dis to Palestinian control, which was endorsed by the Knesset by a simple majority (56–48). This area, comprising the Arab villages of Azariya, Abu Dis, and Sawahara al-Sharqiyah, was to have constituted the next stage of the three-phase withdrawal agreed under the **Sharm al-Sheikh Memorandum**. However, the implementation of this cabinet decision was postponed due to rioting in **Jerusalem** connected to **Al-Naqba** Day. *See also* BEILIN–ABU MAZEN PLAN.

ABU NIDAL ORGANIZATION. *See* FATAH REVOLUTIONARY COUNCIL.

ABU SHARIF DOCUMENT. During the Algiers summit meeting of the **Arab League** in June 1988, Bassam Abu-Sharif (1946–), a close adviser of **Yasser Arafat**, distributed a paper entitled "The PLO Views

Prospects of a Palestinian–Israeli Settlement," which came to be known popularly as the Abu Sharif Document. This maintained that the **Palestine Liberation Organization** sought peace with Israel through direct negotiations based on all the relevant **United Nations** resolutions, including **Resolution 242** and **Resolution 338**. The proposal was made during the ongoing Palestinian **Intifada**, and although Arafat did not endorse the document publicly, it generated a serious debate among Palestinians and eventually paved the way for the **Algiers Declaration** on 15 November 1988, which proclaimed the **Palestinian state**.

ACCOUNTABILITY OPERATION. In July 1993, tension along Israel's borders with **Lebanon** increased, as **Hezbollah** and radical Palestinian groups in southern Lebanon fired a number of Katyusha rockets against Israel's **security zone** as well as northern Israel itself. When U.S. intervention proved futile, on 25 July Israel launched a military campaign named Accountability. Primarily composed of artillery, air force, and naval units, it was aimed at putting pressure on the Lebanese government to act against the militants north of the security zone. This led to a massive civilian exodus from southern Lebanon toward Beirut in the north. On 31 July, the military campaign ended when the **United States** managed to secure an informal understanding with **Syria** and Hezbollah, under which the latter agreed not to attack Israeli settlements in the north. This arrangement brought about a temporary truce in northern Israel, but attacks inside the security zone increased.

ACHILLE LAURO **AFFAIR.** On 8 October 1985, four members of the **Palestine Liberation Front** (PLF) hijacked the Italian cruise ship *Achille Lauro*, which had 400 passengers on board. The hijackers threatened to blow up the ship if 50 Palestinian prisoners were not released from Israeli jails. To intensify the pressures, the hijackers threw Jewish-American passenger Leon Klinghoffer, who was confined to a wheelchair, overboard, killing him. This generated worldwide criticism, and the hijackers eventually surrendered following Egyptian mediation. Though the hijacking was carried out by a faction opposed to **Yasser Arafat**, the membership of the PLF in the **Palestine Liberation Organization** (PLO) Executive Committee complicated matters for the PLO. Following the **Oslo Process**, on 19 January 1996 the PLO agreed to finance a Peace Studies Center in the **United States** in return for Klinghoffer's family dropping a lawsuit.

In April 2003, during the U.S.-led military campaign against **Iraq**, Abu Abbas (1948–2004), the leader of the PLF, was captured by the Allied forces, and Klinghoffer's family demanded his trial for the murder. On 8 March 2004 he died while in allied custody.

ACTIVE ORGANIZATION FOR THE LIBERATION OF PALESTINE (AOLP). In 1967, Issam Sartawi (1935–1983) established the AOLP, a noncombatant medical aid organization. It temporarily merged with **Fatah** in February 1968 and rejoined the organization in July 1971. After dissolving the organization, Sartawi became a close adviser to **Yasser Arafat** and functioned as the unofficial ambassador of the **Palestine Liberation Organization** (PLO) in Western Europe. Together with Israeli peace activist Arie Lova Eliav (1921–), he encouraged and initiated an Israeli–Arab dialogue. On 12 April 1983, Sartawi was assassinated during the Socialists International Conference in Lisbon by members of the Abu Nidal Organization.

ADMINISTRATIVE DETENTION. Since its occupation of the **West Bank** and the **Gaza Strip** in June 1967, Israel has placed thousands of Palestinians under what is termed "administrative detention." Even though such practices are common in a number of states, Israeli practice in the **Occupied Territories** adds further complications and criticisms, since this procedure enables the authorities to detain Palestinian individuals without charges and without judicial trial. Israel has used this as a collective punishment as well as deterrence. The outbreak of the **Intifada** in 1987 saw a rapid increase of administrative detainees, and more than 14,000 Palestinians were kept under administrative detention. Israel also used this measure against Lebanese citizens it had captured in southern **Lebanon**. Some Lebanese citizens were imprisoned for more than 12 years before being brought to trial. The outbreak of the **Al-Aqsa Intifada**, especially the **Defensive Shield Operation**, resulted in the capture of a large number of Palestinians who were held without trial. To accommodate 4,000 new prisoners, Israel reopened the dreaded Ketziot prison in the Negev, where most of the Palestinian prisoners were held during the 1987–1993 Intifada.

AGRANAT COMMISSION. On 21 November 1973, the Israeli government of Prime Minister **Golda Meir** appointed a commission of inquiry, headed by Chief Justice of the Supreme Court Shimon

Agranat (1906–1992), to investigate the events leading up to the **October War of 1973**. Other members of the commission were Justice Moshe Landau of the Supreme Court, State Comptroller Yitzhak Nebenzahl, and two former chiefs of the **Israel Defense Forces** (IDF), Yigal Yadin and Chaim Laskov. The Commission published an interim report on 1 April 1974, a second report on 10 July 1974, and its final report on 30 January 1975. The interim report dealt with the immediate events prior to the outbreak of hostilities and the conduct of the war during the initial stages. It absolved Meir and Defense Minister **Moshe Dayan** of any direct responsibility for the lack of military preparedness. It also attributed the element of surprise to Israel's "conception" that **Egypt** would not initiate an attack without superior airpower. It recommended, inter alia, the establishment of a ministerial committee on security, the reevaluation of the intelligence establishment, and the replacement of Maj. Gen. Eliahu Zaira (1928–) as chief of military intelligence and removal of Lt. Gen. David Elazar (1925–1976) as chief of staff.

The political consequences of the war took their toll. Despite victories in the Knesset elections held in December 1973, the political leadership came under pressure and gradually all the senior leaders involved in the war, including Meir, Dayan, and Elazar, resigned from their positions. Meir was replaced as prime minister by **Yitzhak Rabin**, who at the time of the war was outside the government. On 25 January 2005, the Knesset approved a law aimed at preventing the publication of the full report of the Agranat Commission as required by the 30-year principle governing official documents. The amendment to the Commissions of Inquiry Law would enable the prime minister to establish a public commission to consider whether the publication of a report would be in the national security interest.

AL-AQSA FIRE. On 21 August 1969, a disastrous fire broke out in the Al-Aqsa Mosque in the Old City of **Jerusalem**, enraging Muslims all over the world. An official Israeli inquiry attributed the arson to a deranged Australian Christian tourist, Denis Michael Rohan. While the physical damage to the mosque was limited and subsequently repaired, the incident raised widespread concerns for the safety of Islamic and Christian shrines in the Israeli-occupied Old City. These concerns were manifested in the form of the Rabat Summit of Islamic countries in September 1969, which paved the way for the formation of the Organization of the Islamic Conference and the Jerusalem Committee, headed by King Hassan II (1929–1999) of Morocco.

AL-AQSA INTIFADA (2000–). Trouble began when Israel's opposition **Likud** leader, **Ariel Sharon**, visited the Al-Aqsa compound at the Temple Mount/*Haram al-Sharif* area of the Old City in **Jerusalem** on 28 September 2000, accompanied by a large contingent of bodyguards and security personnel. Coming in the midst of growing Palestinian disappointment with U.S. president **Bill Clinton** (1946–) and Israeli leaders for blaming the **Palestine Liberation Organization** chairman **Yasser Arafat** for the failure of the **Camp David Talks**, the visit was seen by the Palestinians as provocative and an attempt by the Israeli leader to reassert Israeli sovereignty over Islamic holy sites. The following day, Palestinians at the compound staged a demonstration after Friday midday prayers, and it soon turned violent. Israeli security forces responded with rubber bullets and live ammunition that resulted in the death of seven Palestinians and injuries to more than 200. The unrest quickly spread to other parts of the **Occupied Territories** and transformed into a large-scale violence.

The Al-Aqsa Intifada differed from the earlier **Intifada** of 1987. Popular participation remained marginal, and violent actions by individuals and select groups dominated the unrest. Hence—despite widespread usage within the Middle East and elsewhere—many, including leading Palestinians, have questioned the usage of the term *Intifada* with respect to this period of violence. The availability of weapons provided to various Palestinian security agencies under the **Oslo Accords** enabled Palestinian security personnel to participate in militant campaigns against Israel.

Unlike 1987, much of the anti-Israeli violence has taken the form of **suicide attacks** conducted inside the **Green Line**. **Hamas** has emerged as the key player in this suicide campaign. This exposed the inability of the **Palestinian National Authority** (PNA) to rein in militants and, on the other hand, it encouraged even secular elements such as **Fatah** to emulate Hamas in organizing militant attacks and even suicide attacks against Israel. Through May 2005, in the Intifada-related violence, 657 Israeli civilians had been killed by Palestinians and 3,235 Palestinians by Israeli security forces. Palestinians also killed 33 foreign citizens and

303 members of the Israeli security forces. For its part, Israel has extensively used its military power to systematically destroy and dismantle the Palestinian economy and infrastructure and has resorted to **targeted killing** of suspected militants and even political leaders.

At an emergency **Arab League** summit held in Cairo on 21–22 October 2000, the member states refused Libya's call to use the oil weapon to counterbalance Israel and the **United States**, but agreed to "halt" the establishment of new diplomatic ties with Israel. **Saudi Arabia** proposed setting up two funds, one of $800 million to preserve the Arab identity of Jerusalem and another of $200 million to support the families of those killed in the uprising. Various Arab countries organized live fund-raising television shows.

The ongoing cycle of violence has brought the peace process to a grinding halt. In a bid to revive the process, a host of bilateral and multilateral measures has been initiated. These include the **Sharm al-Sheikh Summit** (October 2000), **Clinton Plan** (December 2000), **Mitchell Committee Report** (May 2001), **Tenet Plan** (June 2001), **Abdullah Plan** (February 2002), **Bush Plan** (June 2002), **Middle East Road Map** (April 2003), **Ayalon-Nusseibeh Proposal** (September 2003), and **Geneva Initiative** (December 2003). However, none of the ideas has succeeded in diminishing the level of violence or compelled the parties to the negotiating table, although with the proposed **Gaza Withdrawal Plan** and the election of **Mahmoud Abbas** as leader of the PNA there has been some improvement.

Meanwhile, the uprising has increased Israel's political and diplomatic isolation in the Middle East. The surging popular support for the Palestinians in the region obliged various countries to reevaluate their policies vis-à-vis Israel. Oman, Tunisia, and Morocco closed down their trade offices in Tel Aviv, and succumbing to pressure, Qatar briefly shut down the Israeli mission in Doha. In October 2000, **Jordan** postponed the departure of its new ambassador. Responding to the Israeli missile attack in Gaza on 21 November 2000 (itself a response to a mortar attack on an Israeli school bus in a Gaza settlement), **Egypt** recalled its ambassador from Israel. At the **Sharm al-Sheikh Summit** (2005), both Egypt and Jordan agreed to return their ambassadors to Israel. *See also* DEFENSIVE SHIELD OPERATION; DETERMINED PATH OPERATION; JENIN CONTROVERSY; RAINBOW OPERATION; SECURITY FENCE; YASSIN, SHEIKH AHMED.

AL-AQSA MARTYRS BRIGADE. Following the outbreak of the **Al-Aqsa Intifada** in September 2000, a group of Palestinians belonging to the **Fatah** militant outfit known as **Tanzim** broke out and formed the Al-Aqsa Martyrs Brigade, which has conducted periodic military attacks against Israeli citizens and Jewish settlers in the **Occupied Territories**. Largely composed of residents of the Balata **refugee** camps near Nablus, its members initially confined their campaign to shooting attacks against Israeli soldiers at roadblocks in the **West Bank**. This gradually escalated into **suicide attacks** inside Israel as well as the employment of female suicide bombers, both of which were not the hallmark of traditional Fatah strategy. *See* also HAMAS; ISLAMIC JIHAD.

AL-AQSA MOSQUE ATTACK. On 11 April 1982, Allan Goodman, a new Israeli immigrant from the **United States** doing his compulsory military service, went on a rampage at the Temple Mount/ *Haram al-Sharif* area, near the Al-Aqsa Mosque in **Jerusalem**. Before he was overpowered by Israeli troops, he had killed 12 Arabs and wounded 12 others.

AL-ARD. *See* ARD, AL-.

ALGIERS DECLARATION. Responding to the **Intifada** (1987–1993), the 19th extraordinary Session of the **Palestine National Congress** met in Algiers in November 1988. After days of deliberations, on 15 November it adopted the Algiers Declaration, which proclaimed the **Palestinian state**. Out of 447 Congress members, 338 attended the session; Israel, **Jordan**, and **Syria** had prevented most of the others from going to Algiers. Among other things, the declaration recognized the 1947 **Partition Plan** of the **United Nations**, demanded complete Israeli withdrawal from the territories occupied during the **June War of 1967**, and called for a Palestinian state in the **Occupied Territories**, with **Jerusalem** as its capital. A number of the groups belonging to the **Palestine Liberation Organization** (PLO), as well as non-PLO groups such as **Hamas** and **Islamic Jihad**, opposed the decision. *See also* MUTUAL RECOGNITION.

ALI MUSTAFA, ABU (1938–2001). On 27 August 2001, Israeli troops assassinated Abu Ali Mustafa, who had succeeded **George Habash** as leader of the **Popular Front for the Liberation of Palestine** (PFLP). Adopting an uncompromising opposition to the **Oslo Process**, he had returned to the **Occupied Territories** in 1999, after a gap of 30 years, following an understanding with Israel. Though he led the organization, Ali Mustafa was a political figure and was not known to be involved with the military wing. By explicitly targeting a political leader rather than militants, Israel had escalated the situation. On 17 October 2001, the PFLP retaliated through the assassination of right-wing Israeli minister Rehavam Ze'evi (1926–2001), a strong advocate of the transfer doctrine, in a hotel in **East Jerusalem**. This in turn provoked Israeli demands for the surrender of those responsible for the murder, including Ali Mustafa's successor, Ahmad Sadaat. Under pressure from Israel and the **United States**, in April 2002, during the **Siege of Bethlehem**, a hastily arranged military court convicted Sadaat and three others for their involvement in Ze'evi's murder and gave them prison terms ranging from 1 to 18 years. On 3 June 2002, the Gaza High Court ordered the release of Sadaat, but **Yasser Arafat** overruled it. *See also* TARGETED KILLING.

ALIYA. This expression, meaning "to ascend," refers to the migration of Diaspora Jews to the historical Land of Israel (***Eretz Yisrael***). It is used to refer to the large-scale *Aliya*, which began in 1882. Unlike earlier immigration, the new wave sought *Aliya* as a means of "returning" to the land of their ancestors and ending their exile in the Diaspora. The immigration of Jews to and settlement in *Eretz Yisrael* is the core of **Zionism** and an "ingathering of the exile" was the primary objective of the movement. Unlike the religion-induced immigrations in the past, the new group of Jews either sought refuge from prolonged persecution or aspired to create a homeland for the Jews.

From the 1880s until the end of World War II, Palestine experienced five major phases or waves of *Aliya*. During the First *Aliya* (1882–1903), around 20,000–30,000 Jews came to Palestine from Russia, Romania, and Galicia. The Second *Aliya* (1904–1914) consisted of 35,000–40,000 pioneering youth who largely came from Russia. Another 35,000 young pioneers who made *Aliya* to Palestine from Russia, Poland, and Romania constituted the Third *Aliya* (1919–1923); many of the future leaders of Israel belonged to this *Aliya*. The Fourth *Aliya* (1924–1931) included about 88,000 Jews who emigrated from Poland. The rise of Nazism in Europe then caused a large number of Jews to emigrate from Central Europe to Palestine. During this Fifth *Aliya* (1932–1938), about 215,000 Jews fled to Palestine. Later, during World War II, about 82,000 Jews arrived in Palestine and another 57,000 made *Aliya* between the end of the war and the end of the **mandate** of **Great Britain** in Palestine.

Since the establishment of the State of Israel, encouragement of *Aliya* has become official policy, with near-unanimous consensus in Israel. The policy of granting Israeli citizenship to Jewish immigrants under the **Law of Return** encouraged large-scale *Aliya*. Determined and organized efforts to bring Jews from Diaspora, especially from "crisis areas," resulted in massive immigration to Israel.

Between May 1948 and 1951, about 685,000 immigrants arrived in Israel and contributed to a fundamental shift in the demography in favor of the Jews. Most of these immigrants came from Islamic countries in the Middle East. According to another estimate, between 1948 and 1986 as many as 1,800,000 Jews immigrated to Israel. Following a thaw in relations with Israel, in 1987 the **Soviet Union** relaxed its emigration rules and facilitated a new wave of *Aliya*, which saw about 750,000 Jews reach Israel. *See also* JEWISH AGENCY; REFUGEE/S; WORLD ZIONIST ORGANIZATION; YISHUV.

ALLON PLAN. In July 1967, Yigal Allon (1918–1980), minister of labor and former commander of the Israeli army (later foreign minister and deputy prime minister), proposed a plan that envisaged Israel's position toward the territories captured during the war, especially the **West Bank**. This plan was formulated prior to the **Khartoum Arab Summit** in August that rejected the recognition of, negotiations with, or peace with Israel. Allon's plan called for the return of densely populated areas in the West Bank and the **Gaza Strip** to Arab control and the return of most of the **Sinai Peninsula** to **Egypt**. At the same time, it advocated Israeli control of the Jordan River Valley and mountain ridges and the establishment of Jewish **settlements** and early warning systems against possible attacks from the east. The 1949 armistice lines would be adjusted in favor of Israel, with the annexation of strategically important and sparsely populated areas. Israel would also retain the whole of **Jerusalem** and Etzion Bloc of settlements south of the city.

There was no single version of the Allon Plan, which was modified and amended in June 1968, December 1968, January 1969, and September 1970. Subsequently it served as the Alignment/**Labor party** platform for the 1974, 1977, 1981, 1984, and 1988 Israeli elections. Though never officially approved, until 1977 it served as a guideline for the settlement policies of the Alignment/Labor governments. The authorized version of the plan was never published, but in an article published in *Foreign Affairs* in 1976, Allon outlined his ideas. However, he quickly renounced the accompanying map in the journal.

The plan broadly advocated the return of Sinai to Egypt except Sharm al-Sheikh and a connecting land corridor from Eilat, the Rafah area in the Gaza Strip, and a narrow strip along the Negev-Sinai border. On the Jordanian front, it suggested the return of most of the **Occupied Territories** but advocated Israel retaining most of the Jordan Valley, the eastern slopes of the Judean deserts toward the Dead Sea, the Etzion Bloc south of Bethlehem (owned and settled by Jews before 1948), and certain border areas. It primarily sought to annex areas that were uninhabited or sparsely inhabited by Palestinians. Through a limited territorial expansion, it sought to keep Israel a demographically Jewish and politically democratic state by minimizing the number of non-Jews living inside Israel. This gradually became the Labor party's platform for "territorial compromise" with the Arabs, but it was never accepted by Israel's interlocutors as a basis for negotiations.

The Allon Plan resurfaced in 1996, when a new Israeli political party, Third Way, remodeled it for the future status of the West Bank. In late 1996 and in June 1997, **Likud** prime minister **Benjamin Netanyahu** proposed the "Allon Plus" Plan, whereby Israel would keep "**Greater Jerusalem**" including the **Ma'aleh Adumim** and the Gush Etzion bloc settlements under Israeli sovereignty. It visualized the construction of a security belt parallel to but east of the **Green Line** incorporating all Jewish settlements in the Occupied Territories. *See also* ARMISTICE AGREEMENT/S; GALILI DOCUMENT.

ALL PALESTINE GOVERNMENT (APG). Responding to the Israeli declaration of independence, the Palestine National Conference met in Gaza on 1 September 1948 and proposed the formation of a Palestinian government. On 22 September, the **Arab Higher Committee** met in Gaza and announced the formation of the All Palestine Government, which assumed the responsibilities of the Administrative Council for Palestine established by the **Arab League** in July 1948. A national council met on 30 September and elected Mufti Hajj Amin al-Husseini (c. 1895–1974) as president. The following day, Palestinian independence was proclaimed, a cabinet headed by Jamal al-Husseini (1892–1982) was named, and an 86-member General Assembly was elected. While **Egypt, Syria,** and **Saudi Arabia** recognized this move, King **Abdullah I** of **Transjordan,** who controlled the **West Bank,** vehemently opposed it. The **Jericho Conference** of 1 December 1948 and the subsequent annexation of the West Bank into Transjordan eroded the raison d'être of the APG. In 1952, the Arab League announced its demise and placed the Palestinians under the aegis of individual Arab states—Egypt for the **Gaza Strip** and **Jordan** for the West Bank. *See also* PARTITION PLAN.

AL-NAQBA. *See* NAQBA, AL-.

ALPHA PLAN. In October 1954, **Great Britain** and the **United States** conceived an ambitious plan that sought a comprehensive peace settlement between Israel and its Arab neighbors, with Egyptian–Israeli rapprochement as the initial move. They sought to resolve issues such as **refugees,** resettlement, territorial adjustments between Israel and its neighbors, problems over the status of **Jerusalem,** sharing the waters of the Jordan River, and an end to the **Arab boycott of Israel.** These efforts arose against the background of the Anglo-Egyptian negotiations over the presence and evacuation of British forces from the **Suez Canal** base. Code-named Alpha Plan, this coercive diplomacy remained secret until it was disclosed on 15 April 1955. The efforts ended in failure, as none of the principal players was ready to make the kind of concessions necessary for a peace agreement. This eventually paved the way for another Anglo-American plan named **Omega Operation,** which sought to contain President **Gamal Abdul Nasser** of **Egypt.** *See also* CHAMELEON OPERATION; NATIONALIZATION OF THE SUEZ CANAL; SÈVRES CONFERENCE; SUEZ WAR.

ALTALENA **AFFAIR.** In June 1948, the *Altalena,* a French ship with immigrants on board, sailed to Israel and anchored off the coast of Tel Aviv. This ship also carried arms and ammunition for the

Irgun, the prestate Jewish underground militia led by **Menachem Begin**. Unwilling to accept the presence of armed militia following the establishment of the state and its unified **Israel Defense Force** (IDF), Israeli prime minister **David Ben-Gurion** demanded that the weapons carried by the *Altalena* be handed over to the IDF. When the Irgun refused to comply, on 22 June an IDF unit led by deputy unit commander (and future prime minister) **Yitzhak Rabin** fired at and sank the ship. The determination of the government led to the disbanding of the Irgun and the absorption of its members into the IDF. The incident shaped, influenced, and even poisoned the relationship between Ben-Gurion and Begin and characterized the prolonged animosity between the two political parties that they led, respectively, Mapai (later the **Labor Party**) and Herut (later **Likud**). The details of the sinking and the rationale behind it remain a controversial issue between the Left and the Right in Israel.

AMAL. Amal (Hope), the acronym for *Afwaj al-Muqawama al-Lubnaniya* (Lebanese Resistance Detachment), is a militant organization representing the Shia population of **Lebanon**. Though indigenous, it was founded in 1975 by Musa Sadr (1928–1978), a cleric from **Iran**, who came to Lebanon in 1957. Coming just before the outbreak of the civil war (1975–1989), Amal sought to reassert the Lebanese Shia population, especially in the wake of the demographic shift in favor of the Sunnis following the arrival of Palestinians from **Jordan** in the aftermath of the **Black September Massacre**.

The Israeli invasion of Lebanon in 1978 and the expanding Israeli–Palestinian clashes in Shia-dominated southern Lebanon helped the growth of Amal. The Islamic revolution in Iran boosted its fortunes in the initial years as it was seen as an ally in the ayatollah's aspirations for exporting Islamic revolution. In August 1978, Musa Sadr disappeared while visiting Libya and less charismatic but more secular leaders succeeded him. At the same time, Amal actively pursued a militant-terrorist campaign against Western interests in Lebanon and against Israeli forces in southern Lebanon. Operating in southern Lebanon, the Shia militia emerged in the mid-1970s as a response to the militia groups operating on behalf of other sectarian groups, especially the **Phalanges** linked to Maronite Christians. In the initial years following the outbreak of the 1975 civil war, the activities of Amal were confined to protecting Shia villages, but it was gradually sucked into the conflict and began siding with the forces of **Syria**. The Israeli invasion of Lebanon in 1982 and the emergence of the more militant **Hezbollah** significantly eroded the influence of Amal. *See also* LEBANESE WITHDRAWAL; LITANI OPERATION; OPERATION PEACE FOR GALILEE.

AMANA. A **settlement** movement identified with the Israeli right wing, which sought to promote Jewish settlements in the whole of *Eretz Yisrael*, especially in the **Occupied Territories**. During 1977–1984, when the **Likud** party was in power, Amana received financial support from the government as well as from the Settlement Department of the **World Zionist Organization**. *See also* GUSH EMUNIM.

ANGLO-AMERICAN COMMITTEE. In November 1945, the governments of **Great Britain** and the **United States** appointed a 12-member committee of representatives to study the question of *Aliya* to Palestine and the future of the British **mandate**. Following numerous meetings and hearings, including a visit to Palestine in March 1946, it submitted its report on 30 April 1946. The committee recommended, inter alia, the immediate admission of 100,000 Jewish immigrants from the Displaced Persons (DP) camps in Europe. President Harry S. Truman (1884–1972) accepted the report, especially its recommendation concerning *Aliya*. Though opposition from the region including protest actions in Palestine precluded the British from accepting the report, this led to the formulation of the **Morrison–Grady Plan** of 1946.

ANNULMENT. In letters exchanged with Israel prior to the **Declaration of Principles** (DoP), **Palestine Liberation Organization** (PLO) Chairman **Yasser Arafat** affirmed:

> Those articles of the Palestinian Covenant which deny Israel's right to exist, and the provisions of the Covenant which are inconsistent with the commitments of this letter are not operative and no longer valid. Consequently, the PLO undertakes to submit to the Palestinian National Council [PNC] for formal approval of the necessary changes in regard to the Palestinian Covenant.

This commitment and **mutual recognition** enshrined in the letters exchanged on 9 September 1993 paved the way for the signing of the DoP four days later.

Palestinian compliance with this commitment has remained a main cause of disagreement between the two sides. Following the election of the **Palestinian National Authority** in January 1996, the PNC met in Gaza 22–25 April for an extraordinary session and decided to "cancel" the conflicting provisions of the **PLO Charter**. On the eve of the Israeli elections, on 4 May 1996, Arafat formally communicated this decision to Prime Minister **Shimon Peres**. Many in the Israeli opposition dismissed the move as vague, imprecise, illegal, and even unconstitutional under the PLO Charter. The controversy over the annulment continued, and on 10 December 1998, a full session of the Palestine Central Committee was held in Gaza. By a vote of 81–7 (with seven abstentions), the PNC voted to revoke the clauses, and this was ratified by a meeting of the PNC on 14 December, which was attended by U.S. president **Bill Clinton** (1946–).

AQABA SUMMIT. Against the background of the **Al-Aqsa Intifada** and the partial reforms introduced by **Palestine Liberation Organization** chairman **Yasser Arafat**, the **United States** organized a summit meeting in the port city of Aqaba on 4 June 2003. Hosted by King **Abdullah II** of **Jordan**, it was attended by U.S. president **George W. Bush**, Israeli prime minister **Ariel Sharon**, and the newly appointed Palestinian prime minister **Mahmoud Abbas**. This was preceded by a meeting in Sharm al-Sheikh a day earlier, where Bush met Abdullah, President **Hosni Mubarak** of **Egypt**, Crown Prince Abdullah of **Saudi Arabia**, and King Hamad al-Khalifa of Bahrain. In a statement issued after the Aqaba Summit, Sharon referred to the possibility of establishing a demilitarized **Palestinian state** within temporary borders, if certain conditions were met. The leaders also endorsed a peace plan sponsored by the United States, the **United Nations**, the European Union, and **Russia** that called for reciprocal steps to be taken by Israel and the **Palestinian National Authority** toward creating an independent Palestinian state by 2005.

ARAB BOYCOTT OF ISRAEL. Since the 1920s, as *Aliya* continued, the Arabs of Palestine had campaigned for boycotting products and services offered by the *Yishuv* (the Jewish community of the Palestine **Mandate**). This complemented the determination of the latter to rely exclusively upon "Hebrew labor." In December 1945, months after its formation, the **Arab League** called for the complete economic boycott of the Jews of Palestine, which was extended to the State of Israel after its formation in May 1948. Later on, the office of Arab Boycott of Israel was established in Damascus with regional branches in various Arab countries.

Initially, the boycott covered only the economic activities of Israel, but it was gradually extended to other countries when secondary and third-party boycotts were introduced. A number of firms and corporations doing business with Israel were put on an Arab blacklist and were prohibited from doing business in member states of the Arab League. Any commercial activity beyond normal trade was brought under its ambit, and the boycott was aimed at preventing foreign enterprises from investing in Israel, establishing plants, or granting franchises to Israeli companies. Over the years, a number of Western airlines were prevented from using Arab airspace for any flights to and from Israel, and a **naval blockade** was imposed on ships calling at Israeli ports.

In the early 1950s, the Arab League decided not to participate in any regional conferences, gatherings, or organizations if Israel was to be a participant, and this led to Israel's exclusion from the first Afro-Asian Conference at Bandung in April 1955. Since then, Israel has been excluded from all the Third World groupings, including the Nonaligned Movement.

A number of Western countries, especially the **United States**, sought to introduce domestic legislation to prevent national companies from complying with the demands of the Arab boycott. The enforcement of the boycott, however, has not been uniform, and Israel has managed to attract significant foreign investment. At the same time, the economic boycott significantly affected Israel's progress, while the Arab-linked political boycott contributed to Israel's prolonged isolation from the outside world and its growing condemnation by the **United Nations** and other international bodies.

The signing of the **Camp David Accords** removed **Egypt** from the boycott of Israel, but the real progress was made following the **Madrid Conference** of 1991. In the wake of the **Oslo Accords** and the **Israel–Jordan Peace Treaty** in September 1994, the six-member Gulf Coop-eration Council (GCC) announced the termination of the secondary boycott of Israel, and some Arab states established low-level trade missions in Israel. The annual **Middle East and North**

Africa Economic Summit, inaugurated in November 1994, further dented the Arab boycott.

The deterioration of the peace process and the onset of the **Al-Aqsa Intifada** rekindled the call for an Arab boycott of Israel. The Arab League renewed its call for the political isolation of Israel, and at its meeting in Cairo on 21 October 2000, the League urged its member states to suspend normalization of relations with Israel. The Intifada has significantly reversed the normalization process, and Arab states have not only reintroduced the economic boycott but also frozen, suspended, or withdrawn their limited political relations with Israel. While countries such as Morocco, Tunisia, and Qatar closed down their trade offices, in November 2001 Egypt recalled its long-serving ambassador from Israel, and **Jordan** postponed the nomination of its new ambassador to Israel; at the **Sharm al-Sheikh Summit** in February 2005, both countries agreed to return ambassadors to Israel. As part of its efforts to secure the membership of the World Trade Organization, in November 2005 **Saudi Arabia** agreed to lift its economic embargo against Israel.

ARAB EXECUTIVE. The Arab Executive was set up in Haifa in December 1920 during the third **Palestine National Congress**. It was headed by Mussa al-Husseini (1850–1934) who briefly served as the mayor of **Jerusalem**. This was the first attempt to politically unify various Palestinian groups and organizations to protest against *Aliya* into Palestine. It sought formal recognition from the **Mandate** authorities, especially in the wake of the formation of the **Jewish Agency**. Husseini held numerous diplomatic parleys with **Great Britain** and unsuccessfully sought to have the **Balfour Declaration** revoked. The Executive disappeared following Husseini's death in March 1934, and its activities were taken over by the **Arab Higher Committee**, formed two years later.

ARAB HIGHER COMMITTEE (AHC). On 25 April 1936, Mufti Hajj Amin al-Husseini (c. 1895–1974) formed the Arab Higher Committee as an umbrella organization, comprising six Arab parties and groups. It sought to unify and strengthen various Palestinian political parties and organizations in the aftermath of the demise of the **Arab Executive** headed by Mussa al-Husseini (1850–1934) until his death. The committee was primarily concerned about the growing *Aliya* into

Palestine and its consequences upon the demography of the Palestine **Mandate**. Protesting against both these developments, it organized a series of strike actions, which lasted for six months. This gradually transformed into an open revolt against the mandate authorities.

Accusing the AHC of directing the **Arab Revolt** (1936–1939), the British banned the committee in October 1937 and deported some of its leaders to the Seychelles Islands. Even though the popular rebellion continued, the committee experienced internal differences, and some members left the group and formed a separate body called the Arab Higher Front. For his part, the mufti escaped from Palestine and directed the AHC from abroad. Due to changed policies of **Great Britain**, the committee headed by the Mufti was not invited to the **St. James Conference** of 1939.

In April 1947, when the **United Nations** General Assembly convened a special session to discuss the Palestine question, the AHC was invited to present the Palestinian case, but it declined. Similarly, it boycotted the proceedings of the **United Nations Special Committee on Palestine** when that body visited Palestine to deliberate and decide the future political status of the mandate. The AHC also organized a general strike when the UN team came to Palestine. It led the Arab opposition to the **Partition Plan**, and in September 1948, meeting in Gaza, the AHC declared Palestinian independence and announced the formation of an **All Palestine Government**. This was soon folded up due to the control of the **West Bank** by **Jordan** and Jordanian opposition to the mufti's leadership.

ARAB–ISRAELI WAR OF 1947–1948. The Arab–Israeli War, which was fought in the months surrounding the formation of the State of Israel, intensified the Arab–Jewish conflict in Palestine. The military events of that war began in November 1947 and were concluded by the **armistice agreements** in early 1949. They can be broadly classified into seven phases.

The *first phase* lasted from just before the adoption of the **Partition Plan** by the **United Nations** General Assembly on 29 November 1947 until 14 May 1948, the date the State of Israel was proclaimed. As **Great Britain** was planning to withdraw its forces from **Mandate** Palestine, scheduled for 15 May 1948, both Arabs and Jews sought to consolidate their respective military advantages for the future by securing military assets and strategic positions that were being vacated by the British. This facts-on-the-ground strategy was accompanied by a series of low-level violence and underground operations. This period also witnessed the Jewish forces gaining control and access to predominantly Arab areas and the beginning of a mass exodus of Arab **refugees** out of Palestine.

The *second phase* (14 May–11 June 1948) began with the declaration of Israeli independence and continued until the first United Nations–enforced truce came into force. On 15 May, the day the mandate officially ended, the regular armies of the Arab states neighboring Palestine —**Egypt**, **Jordan**, **Lebanon**, and **Syria**—as well as troops from **Iraq**, launched an invasion into mandate territory. During this period, Israel managed to survive as a state, but suffered numerous casualties and could not hold most of the areas allotted to it under the Partition Plan.

The *third phase* (11 June–6 July 1948) was the period of the UN-sponsored truce. Israel successfully exploited the truce to reorganize, reequip, and regain its positions, which proved decisive when fighting resumed. During this phase, internal divisions between various Arab countries were exposed and precluded any coordinated politico-military strategy against Israel.

The *fourth phase*, also referred to as the "ten days' offensive," lasted from 8 to 18 July 1948. During this phase, Israel consolidated its gains, repulsed Arab armies on all the fronts, and greatly expanded areas under its control. The Negev, which was allotted to the Jews by the Partition Plan, still remained outside their control and was partially occupied by the Egyptian forces. However, Israeli forces captured the Arab towns of Lydda (now Lod) and Ramleh and expelled most of the Arab residents. **George Habash**, the future leader of **Popular Front for the Liberation of Palestine**, was one such expellee.

A second UN-enforced truce came into force on 18 July 1948, marking the *fifth phase* of the Arab–Israeli war, which lasted until October. This period witnessed UN mediatory efforts toward a peace agreement between Israel and the neighboring Arab states and the **assassination** of **United Nations mediator** Count Folke Bernadotte (1895–1948) by Jewish extremists.

The *sixth phase* began on 15 October 1948 when Israel broke the truce and launched an offensive against Egypt. During this phase, the Negev was captured and incorporated into Israel. Advancing southward, Israeli forces also managed to reach the eastern shores of the Gulf of Aqaba, ousting a small Jordanian contingent and gaining an outlet to the Red Sea. A similar offensive in the north resulted in Israeli gains in the Galilee.

The *seventh phase* of the first Arab–Israeli war was marked by intense negotiations on the Greek island of Rhodes and the signing of the armistice agreements between Israel and its neighbors. However, even while negotiating and concluding the armistice agreements, Israel sought to gain additional territories. Following fighting during 5–10 March 1949 in the Negev, Israeli forces moved southward and captured Eilat.

During the war, Israel suffered substantial casualties—more than 6,000, including 1,500 civilians, were killed and another 3,000 wounded. On the Arab side, about 2,000 members of the invading armies were killed, along with an unknown number of irregulars and civilians. When the armistice agreements were signed, Israel controlled a territory of 20,255 square kilometers —more than the roughly 16,000 square kilometers it had been allotted by the UN plan. About 5,600 square kilometers of territory came under Jordanian control, while the 378-square-kilometer **Gaza Strip** came under Egyptian control. The war also resulted in the mass exodus of Arab populations from Israel and witnessed the birth of the refugee problem. *See also* BEN AMI OPERATION; BERNADOTTE PLAN; BROSH OPERATION; DALET PLAN; DEKEL OPERATION; DEIR YASSIN MASSACRE; FACT OPERATION; HAGANAH; HIRAM OPERATION; HOREV OPERATION; MACCABEE OPERATION; NACHSHON OPERATION; NAQBA, AL-; PALMAH; UVDA OPERATION; VOLCANO OPERATION; YIFTACH OPERATION; YOAV OPERATION.

ARAB LEAGUE. In late 1944, six Arab countries—**Egypt, Iraq, Lebanon, Saudi Arabia, Transjordan**, and Yemen, along with a representative from the Palestine **Mandate**—met and deliberated on the idea of a commonwealth or league of Arab states. A protocol to this effect was signed at the Egyptian resort of Alexandria on 7 October 1944 and the Charter of the Arab League came into force on 10 May 1945. Despite calls for unification and federation among Arab states, the charter opted for regional cooperation among them, an association based on the "respect for the independence and sovereignty" of Arab states. An appendix to the charter stressed the right of Palestine to be independent and pledged Arab support for the Palestinian struggle.

In January 1964, the heads of the Arab states met in Cairo for the first summit meeting to discuss and overcome inter-Arab differences. Even though the results were limited, the meeting established a precedent for a periodic summit meeting of the Arab League devoted to various intra-Arab and interregional issues. Subsequently, summit meetings have been held in September 1964 (Alexandria); September 1965 (Casablanca); August–September 1967 (Khartoum); December 1969 (Rabat); September 1970 (Cairo); November 1973 (Algiers); October–November 1974 (Rabat); October 1976 (Cairo); November 1978 (Baghdad); November 1979 (Tunis); November 1980 (Amman); November 1981 (Fez); November 1982 (Fez); August 1985 (Casablanca); November 1987 (Amman); June 1988 (Algiers); May 1989 (Casablanca); May 1990 (Baghdad); August 1990 (Cairo); June 1996 (Cairo); October 2000 (Cairo); March 2001 (Amman); March 2003 (Beirut); May 2004 (Tunis); and March 2005 (Algiers). Most of these were dominated by the Arab–Israeli conflict. Some of the summits were also overshadowed by boycotts and acrimonious disagreements. *See also* ARAB BOYCOTT OF ISRAEL; CAMP DAVID ACCORDS; EGYPT–ISRAEL PEACE TREATY; KHARTOUM ARAB SUMMIT; RABAT ARAB SUMMIT.

ARAB LEGION. At the time of the **Arab–Israeli War of 1947–1948**, the Arab Legion was the most effective and best organized Arab fighting force. Established by **Great Britain** in 1920–1921 when the Emirate of **Transjordan** was formed, the Legion was funded, trained, and commanded by British officers. Until 1939, it was led by Lt. Col. F. G. Peake; he was followed by Sir John Bagot Glubb (Pasha) (1897–1986).

When Jordan became an independent country in 1946, the Legion became a regular army but continued to receive British subsidies, supplies, and advice. During the conflict in 1948, under Glubb Pasha, it was instrumental in King **Abdullah I**'s military successes in areas that the **Partition Plan** had allotted to the Arab **Palestinian state** as well as in **East Jerusalem**. Other Arab countries and Palestinians blamed the Legion for its failure to prevent the formation of the Jewish state and for the limited and restricted Arab advances on the eastern front.

Bowing to nationalist and anticolonialist elements in the region, on 1 March 1956 King **Hussein** of **Jordan** dismissed Glubb Pasha. Thus the leadership fell into the hands of Jordanian commanders and, in 1969, the Legion was renamed the Jordanian Armed Forces.

ARAB LIBERATION ARMY (ALA). The Arab Liberation Army was an irregular force that played an important role in the **Arab–Israeli War of 1947–1948**. On the eve of the termination of the Palestine **Mandate, Syria** took over the responsibility of organizing, training, and arming the group of Arab volunteers. Recruited through centers set up in Damascus, Beirut, Baghdad, and Cairo, they were headed by Fawzi Kaukji, who had served in the Ottoman army during World War I. At the height of the 1947–1948 war, the ALA had a strength of 5,000 men and was active in northeast Palestine as well as in the **Jerusalem** area. It bore the brunt of the fighting in the Castle when the **Palmah** sought to lift the siege of Jerusalem by opening the Tel Aviv–Jerusalem road. *See also* NACHSHON OPERATION.

ARAB LIBERATION FRONT (ALF). The *Jabhat at-Tahrir al-Arabiyya*, or Arab Liberation Front, was founded by Zeid Haidar and Munif al-Razzaz as a militant, pan-Arabist, and left-leaning group within the **Palestine Liberation Organization** (PLO). Sponsored by the Ba'ath of **Iraq** and based in Baghdad, it was under the direct command of the Iraqi military and followed Iraqi positions on Middle East issues. Ideologically similar to **Al-Saiqa**, it remained loyal to **Yasser Arafat** during the 1983 coup backed by **Syria** against the Palestinian leader. Playing a key role in the **Rejectionist Front**, it is represented in the PLO Executive, but is less active.

ARAB PALESTINE CONGRESS. With the backing of Arab leaders, especially President **Gamal Abdul Nasser** of **Egypt**, Palestinian leaders met on 28 May 1964 in the Old City of **Jerusalem**, then held by **Jordan**, and announced the formation of the **Palestine Liberation Organization** (PLO) under the leadership of Ahmed Shuqeiri (1908–1980). The Congress adopted the **PLO Charter** comprising 29 articles.

ARAB REVOLT (1916–1918). Acting upon the promises of **Great Britain** expressed through the **Hussein–McMahon Correspondence**

and aimed at creating an independent Arab kingdom comprising Hijaz, **Syria**, and **Iraq**, on 10 June 1916 Sharif Hussein (1852–1931) of Mecca proclaimed Arab independence and called on his followers to rebel against Ottoman rule. Besides financial support to the tune of £200,000 pounds per month, Great Britain also provided the revolt with arms, provisions, and direct artillery support, as well as guerrilla experts, including T. E. Lawrence (Lawrence of Arabia, 1888–1935). Composed primarily of Bedouins from Hijaz, the Arab army also attracted a small number of Arab officers serving in the Ottoman army. Despite differences over its contribution to Allied war efforts, the Arab Revolt was seen as the harbinger of Arab nationalism.

ARAB REVOLT (1936). Local rioting that erupted in Jaffa on 19 April 1936 soon spread and engulfed the whole of Palestine. Young Muslim groups affiliated with the mufti of **Jerusalem**, Hajj Amin al-Husseini (c. 1895–1974) organized strikes in Nablus, Jerusalem, and Jaffa, which quickly extended to other Arab-populated areas of Palestine. Arab discontent over the increasing *Aliya* into Palestine provided the impetus for the uprising, which took the form of popular protest against the British administration and its complicity and connivance in facilitating the *Aliya*. The **Arab Higher Committee**, with the mufti of Jerusalem as its head, was formed to serve as the authoritative leadership of the Palestinian Arabs. The general strike organized by the committee made three distinct demands: self-government for Palestine, an end to *Aliya*, and the stoppage of land sales to Jews. The advocacy of a small Jewish state in Palestine by the **Peel Commission** only aggravated the Arab protests. Even though the prolonged agitation did not succeed in achieving any of these demands, it forced the Palestinian agenda upon the **mandate** authorities. A six-month general strike was followed by large-scale violence, which lasted until the outbreak of the World War II. *See also* GREAT BRITAIN.

ARAFAT, YASSER (1929–2004). The chairman of the **Palestine Liberation Organization** (PLO) from 1969 and the chairman of the **Palestinian National Authority** (PNA) from 1996 until his death. Abd al-Rahman abd al-Rauf Arafat, popularly known as Abu Ammar, was born on 4 August 1929 to a merchant from Khan Yunis; he was born in Cairo during his father's temporary residence in **Egypt**. A distant relative of the prominent **Jerusalem**-based Husseini family,

Arafat spent most of his childhood in Cairo and Jerusalem. Following the establishment of Israel, he lived as a **refugee**. In 1954, as an engineering student in Cairo, along with Khalil al-Wazir (c. 1935–1988) and Abu Iyad (1934–1991), he founded a clandestine group called **Fatah**. In 1957, during the campaign of President **Gamal Abdel Nasser** against the **Muslim Brotherhood**, Arafat was expelled from Egypt because of his membership in the organization.

During 1958–1962, Arafat was employed as a civil engineer in Kuwait, after which he moved to Beirut and Damascus. In 1954, as an engineering student in Cairo, along with Khalil al-Wazir (c. 1935–1988), he founded a Palestinian student group that later transformed into a clandestine movement called **Fatah**. Between 1956 and 1965, he was active in recruiting and organizing Palestinian refugees in the Diaspora.

In March 1968, Palestinian commandos launched a successful raid against Israel in the battle of Karameh. Against the backdrop of the **June War of 1967**, when the Arab states were routed by Israel, this operation enhanced the prestige of Fatah and its leader. In July, ending four years of boycott, Fatah attended the fifth session of the Palestine National Council. In February 1969, Arafat took over the leadership of the revamped PLO, which had transformed itself into an umbrella Palestinian organization. Thereafter, he led the Palestinian struggle for independence. The absence of a territorial base to conduct military operations against Israel and the dispersal of Palestinian refugees in the Middle East compelled Arafat to depend upon the Arab states for political support, economic largess, and military assistance. However, the relationship was often troubled.

In September 1970, Arafat helped organize a civil war in **Jordan** aimed at ousting the regime of King **Hussein** and replacing it with a PLO-dominated government. This eventually led to the expulsion of the PLO from Jordan and ushered in a tense relationship between Arafat and the king. Despite initial opposition from Jordan, at the **Rabat Arab Summit** in 1974 Arafat was able to secure Arab recognition of the PLO as the sole and legitimate representative of the Palestinian people. The PLO–Jordan tensions remained unresolved until February 1985, when Arafat and King Hussein reached an agreement on a Jordanian–Palestinian confederation. This did not go down well with the PLO, and Arafat made peace with his adversaries in April 1987 by annulling the accord.

President **Anwar Sadat**'s peace initiatives toward Israel in 1977 alienated Arafat from Egypt. The strained relations continued until Arafat's own expulsion from Beirut in December 1983, following the Israeli invasion of **Lebanon**.

After the **Black September Massacre** of 1970, Lebanon had emerged as the territorial base for Arafat's military operations against Israel. In June 1982, Israel invaded Lebanon in **Operation Peace for Galilee**, with the aim of eliminating Beirut as the base for Palestinian guerrilla operations. Consequently, in December 1983, Arafat and his forces were evacuated from Beirut under international auspices, and he and the PLO headquarters moved to Tunis.

By establishing personal contacts with the leadership of the **Soviet Union** and China, Arafat secured ideological support and military supplies from these countries. The high point of Arafat's diplomacy was his address to the **United Nations** General Assembly on 22 November 1974 and the passage of **Resolution 3236**, which secured UN observer status for the PLO. The eruption of the **Intifada** in December 1987 enhanced Arafat's position and led to the 15 November 1988 declaration of the State of Palestine at the Algiers session of the Palestinian National Council (the **Algiers Declaration**).

In 1990, Arafat's support for Iraqi president Saddam Hussein (1937–) during the **Kuwait War** led to his alienation from the oil-rich countries and the expulsion of tens of thousands of Palestinian workers from these countries. Following the end of the Iraqi occupation of Kuwait, the **United States** launched the **Madrid Conference** in October 1991. The Palestinians were represented there by a joint Jordanian–Palestinian delegation.

The absence of progress in the Madrid peace process led to secret negotiations between Israel and the PLO facilitated by Norway. On 9 September 1993, Arafat and Prime Minister **Yitzhak Rabin** exchanged letters of **mutual recognition**. This led to the signing of the **Declaration of Principles** and the start of the **Oslo Process**. Following the signing of the **Cairo Agreement** on 4 May 1994, Arafat entered the **Gaza Strip** on 1 July 1994 to establish Palestinian autonomy in the Gaza Strip and **Jericho**. In the wake of the **Taba Agreement** of September 1995, Israel withdrew from major Palestinian towns.

On numerous occasions, **assassination** attempts were made against Arafat by Israel and Arab states, as well as by rival Palestinian groups, the most prominent being the **Tunis Raid** by Israel in August 1988, in which his confidant Khalil al-Wazir was killed. In September 1992, a number of Palestinian organizations, including some affiliated with the PLO, met in Damascus and launched an opposition front against the official policy of the PLO. Similarly, following the **Oslo Accords**, **Hamas** has emerged as a major opponent of Arafat as well as his peace policies toward Israel.

In 1994, Arafat shared the Nobel Peace Prize with Rabin and **Shimon Peres**. Having remained a lifelong bachelor, at the age of 63 he married Suha al-Tawil (1963–), a journalist and the daughter of a prominent Palestinian.

On 20 January 1996, Arafat was elected chairman of the PNA and head of the 88-member **Palestinian Legislative Council** (PLC). The election of **Benjamin Netanyahu** as Israeli prime minister in 1996 marked a rapid deterioration in Arafat's relations with Israel. The signing of the **Hebron Protocol** and **Wye Memorandum** did not improve the situation.

The **Camp David Talks** initiated by U.S. president **Bill Clinton** (1946–) in July 2000 ended in failure, as Arafat and Israeli prime minister **Ehud Barak** were unable to resolve their differences. The outbreak of the **Al-Aqsa Intifada** in September virtually ended the peace process, and the electoral victory of **Ariel Sharon** in February 2001 marked the marginalization of Arafat. In December 2001, the **Israel Defense Forces** began the **siege of Yasser Arafat** in his Ramallah headquarters, which continued until October 2004 when Arafat was taken to Paris for medical treatment. Under pressure from the United States, in March 2003 Arafat created the post of PNA prime minister and appointed **Mahmoud Abbas** to the position. However, due to differences with Arafat, in September Abbas resigned and was replaced by **Ahmed Qurei**.

On 11 November 2004, Arafat passed away in a Parisian military hospital; the following day he was buried in his Ramallah compound. After his death, Speaker of the PLC Rawhi Fattouh (1949–) became interim head of the PNA, Abbas the head of the PLO, and Farouq Qaddoumi (1934–) the leader of Fatah. In December Abbas was elected president of the PNA. *See also* DEPORTATION; PLO CHARTER.

ARD, AL-. In 1959, **Israeli Arab** intellectuals such as Mansour Kardush and Sabri Jeris formed a noncommunist Arab political group called Al-Ard. Challenging the legitimacy of Israel, it was more radical than the Israel Communist Party, Maki, which accepted the legitimacy of the Jewish state. Al-Ard ran into legal problems when it sought to register as a political party. Reversing its earlier opposition, it then sought to run for the 1965 Knesset elections but was prevented by a ban imposed by the minister of defense in late 1964.

AREA OF ISRAEL. The Palestine **Mandate** originally covered an area of 90,976 square kilometers, but following the formation of **Transjordan**, the mandate area was reduced to 27,011 square kilometers. Under the 1947 **Partition Plan** of the **United Nations**, the Jewish state was awarded an area of about 16,000 square kilometers. However, by the end of the **Arab–Israeli War of 1947–1948**, Israel had gained 21 percent more territory than it had been granted under the Partition Plan, covering nearly 80 percent of the territory of the prewar Mandate. The **armistice agreements** of 1949 left Israel with an area of 20,255 square kilometers. The annexation of **East Jerusalem** in 1967 expanded Israeli territory to 20,770 square kilometers, and the annexation of the **Golan Heights** in 1981 brought the area under Israeli rule to 21,500 square kilometers. The **West Bank**, excluding East Jerusalem, covers an area of 5,878 square kilometers, while the **Gaza Strip** covers 363 square kilometers. *See also* GOLAN LAW; JERUSALEM; JERUSALEM LAW; RESOLUTION 242.

ARMISTICE AGREEMENT/S (1949). In early 1949, following the **Arab–Israeli War of 1947–1948**, Israel and its neighboring Arab states signed separate agreements that formally marked the cessation of military hostilities. Ralph J. Bunche (1904–1971), who became acting **United Nations mediator** following the **assassination** of Count Folke Bernadotte (1895–1948), played an important role in the **Egypt**–Israel armistice negotiations, which began on the Greek island of Rhodes on 12 January 1949. Israel–**Lebanon** negotiations were held in the border town of Rosh Hanikra. In March 1949, Israel–**Jordan** talks took place at Rhodes and, in the following month, Israel and **Syria** began their negotiations at Gesher B'not Yaacov on the Jordan River. The successful conclusion of the four armistice agreements led to Bunche being awarded the Nobel Peace Prize in 1950.

On 24 February 1949, Egypt became the first Arab country to sign an armistice agreement, followed by Lebanon (23 March), Jordan (3 April), and Syria (20 July). The agreements were meant to be a temporary arrangement or the first step toward the resumption of peace negotiations between Israel and its neighbors, but this did not happen and the armistice lines—later known as the **Green Line**—constituted Israel's borders with neighboring Arab states for years. The cease-fire boundaries set by the agreement between Israel and Lebanon were made redundant by frequent Israeli reprisal raids against Palestinian targets in Lebanon after the outbreak of the Lebanese civil war (1975–1989). The arrangements with the other countries collapsed during the **June War of 1967**.

On 8 February 1949, the government of **Saudi Arabia** sent a message to the **United Nations** stating that it would accept "the decisions which have already been adopted, or which may be adopted by the **Arab League**, in respect of the situation in Palestine." In response to the invitation from Bunche, on 13 February (two weeks prior to the signing of the Egypt–Israeli armistice agreement), **Iraq**'s foreign minister, A. Hafid, similarly informed the world body that "the terms of armistice which will be agreed upon by the Arab State neighbors of Palestine, namely, Egypt, Transjordan, Syria and Lebanon will be regarded as acceptable" to Iraq. The explicit Iraqi willingness to recognize and accept the armistice agreement between Israel and its Arab neighbors is often ignored in the Arab–Israeli conflict. In June 1981, Israel sought to justify its air strike on the Iraqi nuclear reactor (the **Osiraq Bombing**) by saying that a state of war still existed between Israel and Iraq because of the refusal of the latter to sign a formal armistice agreement in 1949. *See also* NAQBA, AL-.

ARMISTICE LINE. *See* GREEN LINE.

ASSAD, BASHAR AL- (1965–). The second son of **Hafez al-Assad**, who ruled **Syria** until 2000, Bashar was an ophthalmologist by training, having studied at Damascus University and in **Great Britain**. He was inducted into politics following the death of his elder brother, Basil, who had been groomed as a successor but died in a car crash in 1996. Bashar entered the military academy at Homs, north of Damascus, and became a colonel in January 1999. Following the death of his father, on 10 June 2000 Bashar al-Assad became the 16th president of Syria; soon he was also named secretary-general of the ruling Ba'ath Party and commander in chief of the armed forces. His position was reaffirmed in a popular referendum and Assad was formally inaugurated on 17 July as president. In the wake of the capture of Baghdad by the forces led by the **United States** in the summer of 2003, Assad ordered the temporary closure of the Damascus offices of the **Hamas** and other Palestinian groups that were opposed to the **Oslo Accords**.

ASSAD, HAFEZ AL- (c. 1930–2000). Born in Qardaha near Lataqia in **Syria** to an Alawi family, Hafez al-Assad as president provided political stability to Syria. In 1950, he joined the clandestine officers' cells linked to the Ba'ath Party and took part in the March 1963 coup that brought the Ba'ath officers to power, becoming commander of the air force. Following another coup in 1966, Assad became acting defense minister, the post he held during the **June War of 1967** that resulted in Syria losing the **Golan Heights** to Israel. After a series of political maneuvers, in February 1971 Assad became president, endorsed by a plebiscite in March. After that, he won seven-year terms in February 1978, February 1985, December 1991, and February 1999.

In 1973, Assad joined hands with President **Anwar Sadat** of **Egypt** and launched the **October War of 1973**. Even though military gains were marginal, the war undermined the Israeli aura of invincibility. Following the war, Assad accepted **Resolution 338** of the United Nations Security Council and this in turn formalized the Syrian acceptance of **Resolution 242**. However, his friendship with Cairo underwent a substantial change following Sadat's decision to seek a separate peace with Israel. In December 1977, Syria, together with other radical Arab states and the **Palestine Liberation Organization** (PLO), established the **Rejectionist Front** and played a central role in Egypt's expulsion from the **Arab League** and the Organization of the Islamic Conference.

In 1990–1991, Syria joined the multinational anti-**Iraq** coalition and participated in the **Kuwait War**. Deprived of the patronage of the **Soviet Union** in the post–Cold War world, Assad took Syria to the **Madrid Conference** in October 1991.

Assad's relations with the PLO were tense, and he often hosted and supported a number of Palestinian factions hostile to **Yasser Arafat**. He was highly critical of the **Oslo Accords**, as well as the **Israel–Jordan Peace Treaty**, perceiving them to be contrary to Syrian interests and Arab unity. For many years, he regarded **Hezbollah** attacks against Israel's self-declared **security zone** in southern

Lebanon as leverage for Israeli concessions with respect to the Golan Heights. Assad insisted on a complete Israeli withdrawal to the **Green Line** as a sine qua non for a peace settlement. Despite significant progress in the bilateral talks mediated by the **United States**, no agreement was reached. Israel's unilateral **Lebanese withdrawal** in the summer of 2000 significantly reduced Assad's diplomatic space.

After a prolonged but unpublicized illness, Assad died on 10 June 2000 and was succeeded by his second son **Bashar al-Assad**.

ASSASSINATION/S. The Arab–Israeli conflict had witnessed numerous politically motivated murders or assassinations. Most of these murders were carried out by individuals or groups that disapproved the policies followed by the victim. In some cases, states were also involved in assassinations or attempted assassinations. During the **Mandate** period, members of the **Stern Gang** assassinated the British minister for Middle Eastern affairs, Lord Moyne (1880–1944), in Cairo on 6 November 1944. Likewise, disapproving his pro-Arab bias, on 18 September 1948 members of the same group assassinated **United Nations mediator** Count Folke Bernadotte (1895–1948).

The policies of King **Abdullah I** of **Jordan** during the **Arab–Israeli War of 1947–1948**, especially his perceived collaboration with the Jewish leadership, were strongly resented by the Arabs. On 20 July 1951, a Palestinian gunman assassinated Abdullah at the Al-Aqsa Mosque in **Jerusalem**. In November 1971, the Black September Organization claimed responsibility for the assassination of Jordanian prime minister and defense minister Wasfi al-Tal (1919–1971), who was instrumental in the **Black September Massacre**. In October 1981, Islamic extremists who opposed his peace policies toward Israel and the **Camp David Accords** assassinated **Egypt**'s President **Anwar Sadat**.

Following the **Munich Massacre** of 1972, Israel began a policy of assassinating important Palestinian leaders it alleged were involved in **terrorism**-related violence. The most prominent result was the **Tunis Raid** on the headquarters of the **Palestine Liberation Organization** (PLO) in August 1988, in which **Yasser Arafat**'s confidant, Khalil al-Wazir (c. 1935–1988), was killed.

Internal differences among the Palestinians have also resulted in assassinations. The Abu Nidal Organization was held responsible for the murders of Issam Sartawi (1935–1983), leader of the **Active**

Organization for the Liberation of Palestine, in 1983 and **Fatah** founder Abu Iyad (Salah Khalaf; 1934–1991) in January 1991 in Tunis. An unsuccessful assassination attempt on Israel's ambassador in London, Shlomo Argov (1929–2003), by radical Palestinian groups opposed to Arafat in June 1982 resulted in the Israeli invasion of **Lebanon**. Similarly, the assassination of Lebanese president-elect Bashir Gemayel (1947–1982) on 14 September 1982 culminated in the **Sabra and Shatila Massacre**.

On 4 November 1995, Israeli prime minister **Yitzhak Rabin** was assassinated by Yigal Amir (1970–), an observant student of Bar-Ilan University at a peace rally in Tel Aviv. Amir was motivated by his strong views against Rabin's peace policies, especially his "concessions" toward the Palestinians. Citing religious arguments, he justified his action saying that by agreeing to part with *Eretz Yisrael*, Rabin had turned against his own people. On 27 March 1996, Amir was given a life sentence without parole. A section of the Israeli right has been campaigning to commute the sentence and to secure his early release. An official investigation headed by a former president of the Supreme Court, Justice Meir Shamgar (1925–), concluded that Amir acted alone. Rabin's funeral at the Mt. Herzl military cemetery in Jerusalem was attended by a number of world leaders, including President **Bill Clinton** (1946–) of the **United States**, King **Hussein** of Jordan, President **Hosni Mubarak** of **Egypt**, and ministers from Oman and Qatar.

Following the outbreak of the **Al-Aqsa Intifada**, Israel pursued an official policy of assassinating key Palestinian leaders belonging to the militant organizations such as **Hamas**, **Islamic Jihad**, and the **Al-Aqsa Martyrs Brigade**. Under this policy, officially termed "**targeted killing**," Israeli security agencies assassinated a number of key personalities, including **Abdel Aziz al-Rantisi**, **Abu Ali Mustafa**, and **Sheikh Ahmed Yassin**. This policy largely resulted in the failure of the **Cairo Dialogue** whereby the militants would offer a temporary cease-fire to Israel. *See also* MASHA'AL AFFAIR.

ASWAN DAM. To harness the waters of the Nile and for the generation of hydroelectric power, President **Gamal Abdul Nasser** of **Egypt** sought to construct a massive dam at Aswan. Alarmed by the 1955 **Czech Deal**, the **United States** and **Great Britain** tried to dissuade Nasser from joining the Eastern Bloc by offering to finance the Aswan Dam. It was hoped that through this cooperation, they could also achieve peace between Egypt and Israel. In December 1955, an agreement was reached in principle, committing the United States, Britain, and the International Bank for Reconstruction and Development (World Bank) to offer substantial funding to the project. According to this, the United States would provide $56 million and Great Britain would contribute $14 million for the first stage of construction, with a provision to consider subsequent grants of up to $200 million. Contingent upon the Anglo-American grants, the World Bank pledged to lend $200 million. Both sides were going to negotiate the terms and conditions of the funding. This became a political issue when the Western funding was linked to Nasser's acceptance of the **Alpha Plan** and peace with Israel.

By early 1956, it was clear to the Americans and British that the Alpha Plan, aimed at influencing Nasser toward an accommodative posture toward Israel, was a nonstarter. The collapse of the plan resulted from their desire to undermine Nasser and, as part of the plan, on 19 July 1956, U.S. secretary of state John Foster Dulles (1888–1959) formally conveyed the Anglo-American decision to withdraw from financing the Aswan High Dam. Angered by this about-face, Nasser nationalized the **Suez Canal** on 26 July to fund the project. This move in turn precipitated the Suez Crisis and the tripartite invasion of Egypt by British, **French**, and Israeli forces in October that year in the **Suez War**. *See also* CHAMELEON OPERATION; OMEGA OPERATION; SÈVRES CONFERENCE.

AUTONOMOUS AREAS. Those areas of the **Occupied Territories** that were transferred to the control of Palestinian authorities following the signing of the **Declaration of Principles**. Initially, the autonomous areas covered 219 square kilometers (85 square miles) of the **Gaza Strip** and 54 square kilometers (21 square miles) of the **Jericho** District. By late 1995, six **West Bank** towns—Jenin, Nablus, Tulkarm, Qalqilya, Ramallah, and Bethlehem, from where Israel carried out **redeployment**—were added to the autonomous areas. *See also* OSLO ACCORDS; OSLO PROCESS; WYE MEMORANDUM.

AUTONOMY PLAN. Officially presented by Israeli prime minister **Menachem Begin** on 13 December 1977, this plan offered limited self-administration for the Palestinian residents in the **Occupied Territories**. Among other things, it called for the cancellation of the **military government** and the creation of a **civil administration** to administer the territories. An amended version of the plan presented to the Knesset on 28 December called for a limited role for **Jordan** in its implementation. It underwent additional modifications during the negotiations with **Egypt** leading to the **Camp David Accords**, and a newer version, presented on 3 May 1979, clarified that autonomy would be personal and not territorial. Following the failure of negotiations with Egypt, Israel even contemplated unilateral implementation of the autonomy plan.

The plan was formally presented to President **Anwar Sadat** of **Egypt** on 25 December 1977 at the **Ismailia Summit** and was approved by the Knesset three days later. In May 1979, Israel appointed a Ministerial Committee on Autonomy, headed by Minister Yosef Burg (1909–1999). The first round of Egypt–Israel talks on autonomy was inaugurated in Beersheba on 25 May 1978, and the talks were held alternatively in both countries. Egypt resisted Israeli attempts to hold the talks in **Jerusalem**, and they were subsequently held in Tel Aviv or Herzilya.

On 16 January 1980, Israel presented a model for the Self-Governing Authority for the Occupied Territories, which outlined three kinds of powers to be granted to the Palestinians: full personal autonomy, "shared power, and residual powers," which would be administered by an 11-member council. Israel maintained that autonomy would not imply sovereignty or self-determination. The innumerable sessions of talks failed to make any progress, largely because of the Israeli government's refusal to envisage any role for the **Palestine Liberation Organization** (PLO) or to recognize Palestinian leadership. In an attempt to circumvent the recognized Palestinian leadership, especially the PLO, the autonomy plan offered an elected self-governing authority and as a prelude, established the **Village League** to take control of the Palestinian areas. *See also* BEGIN PLAN; PLO LAW.

AYALON-NUSSEIBEH PROPOSAL. Amidst the **Al-Aqsa Intifada**, on 3 September 2003 Sari Nusseibeh (1949–), president of Al-Quds University in **East Jerusalem**, and Ami Ayalon (1945–), former head of the Israel's internal intelligence agency Shabak (February 1996–May 2000), released a set of principles for an Israeli–Palestinian peace. Among other things, the proposal called for two states for two peoples; establishment of borders on the basis of the **Green Line**;

any border modifications to be based on equal territorial exchanges; territorial connections between the **West Bank** and **Gaza Strip**; removal of all Jewish **settlements** from the **Palestinian state**; **Jerusalem** to be an open city and the capital of both states; neither side to exercise sovereignty over the holy places; Palestinian **refugees** to return only to the State of Palestine; Israel and the Palestinian state to contribute to an international fund for refugee compensation; the Palestinian state to be demilitarized, with the international community guaranteeing its security and independence; and both sides to agree to the termination of the Israeli–Palestinian conflict. Since its unveiling, nearly 200,000 Israelis and Palestinians have signed petitions in support of this proposal. However, its unofficial nature and the ongoing violence have made the proposal a nonstarter. *See also* GENEVA INITIATIVE; SUICIDE ATTACKS.

AZZAM AFFAIR. On 6 November 1996, Azzam Azzam, an Israeli Druze working in a joint textile factory in Cairo, was arrested and charged with espionage. In August 1997, Azzam was convicted of spying for Israel and was given a sentence of 15 years' imprisonment. On 5 December 2004, under a **prisoner exchange** deal, **Egypt** released Azzam, who had served eight years in prison. In return, Israel released six Egyptian students who had sneaked into Israel in August and were charged with conspiring to kill Israeli soldiers.

– B –

BAGHDAD PACT. As part of the policy of containing the **Soviet Union**, the **United States** succeeded in encouraging **Iraq** and **Turkey** to sign a defense treaty on 24 February 1955. Gradually **Great Britain, Iran**, and Pakistan were brought into a larger ambit of the Pact of Mutual Cooperation, popularly termed the Baghdad Pact. Acting as an associate member, the United States provided the financial support for the arrangement. Even though Israel was interested in joining such a military arrangement, the United States was dissuaded because of its regional interests in the Arab world.

The Baghdad Pact drew widespread criticism from other countries of the region, especially **Egypt**, which opted for a nonaligned posture during the Cold War, and the pact became a rallying cry for President

Gamal Abdel Nasser to oppose and even discredit conservative monarchies opposed to him and his radical pan-Arabism. Serious internal strife forced King **Hussein** of **Jordan** to abandon his ideas of joining the pact.

The overthrow of the monarchy in Iraq in July 1958 in a coup led by Gen. Abdul Karim Qassem (1914–1963) reduced the fortunes of the Baghdad Pact and, in March 1959, Iraq formally withdrew from the pact. Subsequently, the alliance was renamed the Central Treaty Organization (CENTO). In a bid to promote economic cooperation among the three Middle East member states—**Iran**, Pakistan, and Turkey—the Regional Cooperation for Development (RCD) was established. In February 1979, Iran withdrew from CENTO after the Islamic revolution; Turkey and Pakistan followed suit, and CENTO ceased to exist, although the RCD remains functional.

The arrangement failed primarily because of U.S. inability to convince the Arab states that the Soviet Union was the primary threat to the Middle East and "the Northern Tier" policy was an effective barrier against such a threat. Most countries of the region, especially Egypt, considered Israel to be their primary threat.

BAKER PLAN. The deadlock between Israel and **Egypt** in 1989 over the **Mubarak Plan** led to U.S. secretary of state James A. Baker (1930–) proposing a compromise formula. Published on 1 November 1989, the Baker Plan sought to accommodate Israeli opposition to negotiating with the **Palestine Liberation Organization** (PLO) and Egyptian reluctance to substitute itself for the Palestinians. Baker suggested that Israel would participate in the dialogue only after "a satisfactory list of Palestinians has been worked out." While the dialogue would be based on the Israeli **Shamir Plan** initiative of 14 May 1989, "the Palestinians will be free to raise issues that relate to their opinion on how to make elections and negotiations succeed." On 5 November, the Israeli cabinet endorsed this proposal. The exclusion of the PLO, especially when the **United States** was conducting a substantive dialogue with the organization in Tunis, made the plan a nonstarter. Moreover, internal differences in Israel over the participation of the residents of **East Jerusalem** led to the collapse of the unity government on 15 March 1990 and the Baker Plan became defunct. *See also* JERUSALEM PALESTINIANS; PLO LAW; RABIN PLAN; SHULTZ PLAN.

BALFOUR DECLARATION • 39

BALFOUR DECLARATION. Issued by the British government on 2 November 1917, the Balfour Declaration provided a formal basis for **Zionist** claims to Palestine. Following sustained efforts by the **World Zionist Organization** and protracted internal discussions within the British government, and in recognition of the special role played by Chaim Weizmann (1874–1952) in the Allied war efforts, British foreign secretary Arthur James Balfour (1848–1930) wrote a letter to Lord Lionel Walter Rothschild (1868–1937), a prominent British Zionist leader. It stated:

> His Majesty's Government view with favor the establishment in Palestine of a national home for the Jewish people, and will use their best endeavors to facilitate the achievement of this object, it being clearly understood that nothing shall be done which may prejudice the civil and religious rights of existing non-Jewish communities in Palestine, or the rights and political status enjoyed by Jews in any other country.

Though vague, the declaration remained contentious afterward. When Balfour made those commitments endorsing and legitimizing the creation of a Jewish national home, British forces were yet to enter, let alone control, Palestine. In 1917, the "non-Jewish communities" constituted nearly 95 percent of the population in Palestine. The Arabs perceived it to be a violation of British commitments to Sharif Hussein (1852–1931) of Mecca expressed through the **Hussein–McMahon Correspondence**, in support of creating an independent Arab kingdom. However, interpreting that correspondence, the **Churchill White Paper** of 2 June 1922 excluded Palestine from the purview of British commitments to Hussein. Prominent Jews in **Great Britain**, as well as influential sections of the British bureaucracy, especially the India Office, also opposed the Balfour Declaration.

Embraced wholeheartedly by the Zionists, it suffered a setback in April 1921, when the British carved out areas east of the Jordan River and established **Transjordan** with **Abdullah I**, son of Sharif Hussein, as emir. This formally excluded the East Bank from the purview of the Jewish national home and hence was resented by influential segments of the right-wing politicians in *Yishuv*. Following prolonged Arab opposition to *Aliya*, especially the **Arab Revolt** (1936–1939), the **MacDonald White Paper** of 1939 formally disassociated the British government from the Balfour Declaration. *See also* MANDATE, PALESTINE.

BANDUNG CONFERENCE. In April 1955, 29 states from Asia and Africa met in Bandung, Indonesia, for the first Afro-Asian meeting. Five Asian powers—Burma (now Myanmar), Ceylon (now Sri Lanka), India, Indonesia, and Pakistan—were instrumental in the first official multilateral dialogue among newly independent states. Nine Arab states—**Egypt, Iraq, Jordan, Lebanon,** Libya, **Saudi Arabia,** Sudan, **Syria,** and Yemen—were represented at Bandung; two other Islamic countries, **Iran** and **Turkey,** were also present. While the grand mufti of **Jerusalem,** Hajj Amin al-Husseini (c. 1895–1974), was present as part of the Yemeni delegation, Tunisia, Morocco, and Algeria attended the sessions on North Africa as part of the Iraqi delegation.

The explicit threat of an **Arab boycott of Israel** precluded the Jewish state from being invited to the meeting, and the conference institutionalized Israel's political isolation from similar Third World gatherings in the future. The Bandung Declaration expressed support for "the right of the Arab people of Palestine" and called for the implementation of **United Nations** resolutions on Palestine and a peaceful resolution of the conflict. The conference paved the way for the first high-level contact between Arab states and the People's Republic of China and witnessed the forging of strong ties between Egypt and Communist China.

BARAK, EHUD (1942–). The most highly decorated general of the **Israel Defense Forces** (IDF), Ehud Barak served as prime minister of Israel from July 1999 to March 2001. Born in Kibbutz Mishmar Hasharon in central Israel in 1942, he joined the IDF in 1959 and served as a soldier and commander of an elite unit that carried out a number of counter**terrorism** operations including the 1985 **Tunis Raid.** After holding senior positions in the Tank Brigade and Armored Division, in April 1983 Barak was appointed head of the Intelligence Branch (Aman) of the IDF. In January 1986, he was made commander of the Central Command and, in the following year, became deputy IDF chief of staff. After the **Kuwait War,** in April 1991 he became the 14th IDF chief of staff and was promoted to the rank of lieutenant general. After the signing of the **Cairo** Agreement in May 1994, Barak oversaw the initial Israeli **redeployment** in the **Gaza Strip** and **Jericho.** He retired from the IDF on 1 January 1995.

After a brief stint in private business, Barak joined the **Labor Party** and, from July to November 1995, he served as minister of the interior in the government of **Yitzhak Rabin**. He had misgivings about the **Taba Agreement** signed in September 1995 and abstained during a crucial cabinet vote. After Rabin's **assassination** in November 1995, Barak became minister of foreign affairs under **Shimon Peres**. In the wake of Peres's defeat in the May 1996 elections, Barak was elected leader of the Labor Party and successfully led the party in the May 1999 elections. Promising to undo the damage done to the peace process by the government of **Benjamin Netanyahu**, on 4 September 1999 Barak signed the **Sharm al-Sheikh Memorandum**, which set out a phased Israeli redeployment from the **Occupied Territories**. In a bid to revive the negotiations with **Syria**, during October 1999–March 2000, Barak pursued the **Shepherdstown Talks**. Fulfilling his election promises, in May 2000 Barak completed the **Lebanese withdrawal**, pulling the IDF completely out of the **security zone** in southern **Lebanon**.

In an effort to conclude the **Permanent Status Negotiations** with the Palestinians, in July 2000 Barak accepted the invitation of U.S. president **Bill Clinton** (1946–) and intensively pursued the **Camp David Talks** with Chairman **Yasser Arafat**. Deviating from past Israeli positions, he offered substantial territorial concessions to the Palestinians and adopted an accommodating position on the issue of **Jerusalem**. But serious differences still existed between the two sides, and his attempt to end the century-old hostilities with the Palestinians was seen by many as a hasty and unrealistic move. The failure of the Camp David Talks was blamed on Arafat, and this heightened the Palestinian disappointment and anger over the peace process.

Barak's decision to allow **Ariel Sharon**, the leader of the **Likud** Party, to visit the Temple Mount/*Haram al-Sharif* on 28 September 2000 sparked off violent protests from the Palestinians and soon resulted in the **Al-Aqsa Intifada**. With dwindling support among his cabinet colleagues and the public, Barak ordered snap elections and, on 6 February 2001, was convincingly defeated by Sharon in the direct election for prime minister. Following this, Barak resigned both as the Labor leader and as a member of the Knesset and went into private business practice, but in November 2004, he returned to active politics. *See also* DEPORTATION.

BAR-LEV LINE. Responding to the **War of Attrition**, Israeli chief of staff Him Bar-Lev (1924–1994) conceived and implemented a defensive system on the eastern bank of the **Suez Canal**. The construction of the defensive line, which came to be known as the Bar-Lev Line, began in late 1968 and comprised 30 strongholds along the Suez Canal and another 11 strongholds 8–12 kilometers (5–7 miles) farther back. Only a limited number of the strongholds were fully operational when the **October War of 1973** broke out. The series of fortifications and other defensive arrangements at select points along the canal were expected to withstand any offensive on the **Sinai Peninsula** from **Egypt**. However, during the early hours of the October War, Egyptian forces not only managed to cross the canal but also easily overran the Israel defensive fortifications. Some of the heavy Israeli casualties during the war took place in those fortified bunkers and bases conceived by Bar-Lev.

BASEL PROGRAM. Less than a year after his publication of *Der Judenstaat* (*The Jewish State*), on 23 August 1897, Theodore Herzl (1860–1904) convened the first World **Zionist** Congress. Representatives of Jewish communities and organizations from around the world met in Basel, Switzerland, and established the **World Zionist Organization** (WZO). It adopted the Basel Program, which called for the establishment of "a home for the Jewish people in Palestine secured under public law." The WZO pursued this objective by organizing the *Aliya* to Palestine, while the **Balfour Declaration** provided the guarantee of the "public law" outlined at Basel.

BAT GALIM AFFAIR. On 28 September 1954, an Israel-registered ship, the *Bat Galim*, with a 10-member crew, was impounded at the southern entrance of the **Suez Canal**. It was carrying commercial cargo from the Eritrean port of Massawa to Haifa in northern Israel. The cargo, mainly meat and plywood, was expropriated by **Egypt** and the ship was confiscated and added to the Egyptian navy. The crew was imprisoned until their eventual release on 1 January 1955. *See also* ARAB BOYCOTT OF ISRAEL.

BEGIN, MENACHEM (1913–1992). Israeli politician and leader of the right-wing **Likud** Party, Menachem Begin served as prime minister from June 1977 to October 1983. Born in Poland on 16 August 1913, he was active in Betar, a youth movement affiliated with revisionist **Zionists** and, in 1932, became the head of its Organization Department in Poland. After the outbreak of World War II, Begin fled to Vilna, and in 1940 he was arrested by secret agents of the **Soviet Union** and sentenced to eight years in a labor camp in Siberia. He was freed the following year because of his Polish citizenship, however, and in May 1942, he made *Aliya* to Palestine.

Staunchly adhering to the revisionist ideology of Ze'ev Jabotinsky (1880–1940), Begin opposed the moderate policies toward **Great Britain** pursued by the *Yishuv* leadership under **David Ben-Gurion**. In December 1943, Begin took over the leadership of the **Irgun**, a Jewish militant organization affiliated to Revisionist Zionists, and actively pursued a campaign of **terrorism** against the **Mandate** authorities. Irgun and its breakaway faction, the **Stern Gang**, were held responsible for the **King David Hotel Explosion** and a number of violent actions and **assassinations** during the **Arab–Israeli War of 1947–1948**. His attempt to maintain an underground militia after the establishment of the State of Israel and the formation of the **Israel Defense Forces** (IDF) resulted in the sinking of a French ship that was carrying arms for Irgun. After this incident, known as the *Altalena* **Affair**, the Irgun was disbanded.

In August 1948, Begin formed Herut, contested the 1949 Knesset election, and emerged as the principal opposition leader of Israel. In 1965, he merged Herut with the Liberal Party and formed the Gahal faction. On the eve of the **June War of 1967**, he joined the national unity government of Prime Minister Levi Eshkol (1895–1969) and, until 1970, served as minister without portfolio. In 1977, joining hands with Ezer Weizmann (1924–2005) and **Ariel Sharon**, Begin founded the Likud. Ending a three-decade-old monopoly of the Mapai/**Labor**, Begin won the election and, in June 1977, became prime minister. He successfully led the party again in the June 1981 Knesset elections.

Taking advantage of **Anwar Sadat**'s initiative, in November 1977 Begin hosted the president of **Egypt** in **Jerusalem**. This visit eventually culminated in the **Camp David Accords** signed in September 1978, which called for a complete Israeli withdrawal from the **Sinai Peninsula** and autonomy for the Palestinians in the **Occupied Territories**. The **Egypt–Israel Peace Treaty** was signed in March 1979. In recognition of their peace efforts, in 1979 Begin and Sadat were jointly awarded the Nobel Peace Prize.

As called for by the Camp David Accords, in April 1982 Israel completed its withdrawal from the Sinai. The progress on the **Autonomy**

Plan formulated by Begin in December 1977, however, was marginal and despite numerous rounds of talks between Israeli and Egyptian leaders, the exclusion of the Palestinians precluded any progress.

Begin's decision to completely withdraw from the Sinai resulted in vehement criticism from within his Likud, which resulted in Begin intensifying **settlement** activities in the **West Bank** and **Gaza Strip**, as well as enacting the **Golan Law** whereby Israeli laws were applied to the **Golan Heights**. Determined to maintain Israel's nuclear monopoly in the Middle East, on 7 June 1981 he ordered the **Osiraq Bombing** of the nuclear reactor near Baghdad in **Iraq**.

Responding to a terrorist attack in northern Israel in March 1978, Begin launched the **Litani Operation** and sought to crush the **Palestine Liberation Organization** (PLO). After an assassination attempt on Israel's ambassador in London in June 1982, Begin ordered **Operation Peace for Galilee**, which sought to keep northern Israel safe from Palestinian Katyusha rocket attacks. This eventually resulted in a large-scale Israeli invasion of **Lebanon**. On 1 August, the IDF reached Beirut. Responding to Israeli pressure, Palestinian leader **Yasser Arafat** agreed to withdraw Palestinian militants from Lebanon and disperse them to different Arab states.

As the evacuation was under way, on 14 September, Lebanese president-elect Bashir Gemayel (1945–1982) was assassinated by Palestinian elements. Angered by this, **Phalange**, a Maronite Christian militia, entered the Palestinian refugee camps in Beirut and perpetrated the **Sabra and Shatila Massacre**. Since the area was under the control of the IDF, Begin came under strong domestic and international criticism. The anti-Begin protests in Israel resulted in the birth of **Peace Now**, and eventually, on 19 September 1983, Begin resigned as prime minister. The following month, he was succeeded by **Yitzhak Shamir**. After leaving office, Begin lived a secluded life until his death on 9 March 1992. *See also* ISRAEL–LEBANON AGREEMENT; KAHAN COMMISSION.

BEGIN PLAN. Upon his return from the **Ismailia Summit** with President **Anwar Sadat** of **Egypt** on 28 December 1977, Israeli prime minister **Menachem Begin** unveiled his peace plan, which gradually grew into the **Autonomy Plan** that was incorporated in the **Camp David Accords**. It promised limited self-rule to Palestinian residents of the

West Bank and the **Gaza Strip**, with Israel retaining security and public order. It pledged to recognize the right of the Palestinian residents of the **Occupied Territories** to apply for and be granted Israeli citizenship. At the same time, it recognized the right of Palestinians to apply for citizenship of **Jordan**. Numerous rounds of autonomy talks were held between Israeli and Egyptian delegations to implement the plan, but the exclusion of the **Palestine Liberation Organization** (PLO) precluded any progress.

BEILIN–ABU MAZEN PLAN. On 31 October 1995, just days before the **assassination** of Israeli prime minister **Yitzhak Rabin**, Israel's deputy foreign minister, Yossi Beilin, and Chairman **Yasser Arafat**'s deputy and future prime minister of the **Palestinian National Authority**, **Mahmoud Abbas**, drew up a plan for **Jerusalem**. It proposed Israeli annexation of 4–5 percent of the **West Bank** and transfer of remaining areas to the **Palestinian state**; Jerusalem would be the capital of Israel, while nearby **Abu Dis** would be the Palestinian capital. An international commission would be formed for the settlement of **refugees**. This "Framework for the Conclusion of a Final Status Agreement between Israel and the **Palestine Liberation Organization**" was made public in September 2000. *See also* EAST JERUSALEM; JERUSALEM PALESTINIANS.

BEIRUT AIRPORT BOMBINGS. On 23 October 1983, a Lebanese volunteer belonging to **Hezbollah** rammed a truck fully loaded with TNT into a building at Beirut International Airport in **Lebanon** that was being used as temporary headquarters for **United States** Marines, killing 241. This attack came against the backdrop of a similar suicide truck bombing by a member of the **Islamic Jihad** against the U.S. embassy in West Beirut on 18 April 1983, which resulted in the death of 49 people. These **suicide attacks**, especially the one against the Marine barracks, led to the reevaluation of U.S. military involvement in Lebanon and resulted in the abrupt withdrawal in early 1984 of American as well as French troops that were deployed in Lebanon to stabilize and contain growing sectarian violence. At the same time, the attacks eliminated any possibility of an early Israeli withdrawal of its military presence in southern Lebanon. *See also* OPERATION PEACE FOR GALILEE.

BEIRUT RAID. On 28 December 1968, Israel carried out an air raid against the Beirut International Airport, destroying a number of civilian aircraft belonging to Lebanese Middle East Airways. This was in response to an attack two days earlier on an El Al aircraft in Athens, Greece, carried out by commandos belonging to the **Popular Front for the Liberation of Palestine**. In the Athens attack, one passenger was killed and scores of others were injured. Through such massive retaliation, Israel hoped to pressure the government of **Lebanon** into acting against Palestinian groups operating from Lebanon. *See also* LEBANESE WITHDRAWAL.

BEIT LID BOMBING. In a **suicide attack** on 22 January 1995, two bombers struck at a bus station in the Beit Lid junction in northern Israel that was frequented by hitchhiking soldiers returning to their bases. Nineteen Israelis, most of them soldiers, were killed in the attack.

BELGIUM LAW. Legislation introduced in 1999 gave Belgian courts the authority to prosecute individuals accused of genocide, crimes against humanity, and war crimes regardless of any connection to Belgium or the presence of the accused on Belgian soil. As a result, complaints have been filed in Belgium against a number leading international personalities for their alleged human rights violations. This paved the way for possible prosecution of Israeli prime minister **Ariel Sharon** over the **Sabra and Shatila Massacre** and resulted in a major diplomatic row between Israel and Belgium. There were even suggestions that U.S. president **George W. Bush**, who had ordered the invasion of **Iraq** in March 2003, could also be brought under the ambit of the new law. The fact that Brussels is the headquarters of the North Atlantic Treaty Organization (NATO) further complicated the situation and raised the possibility that Bush and other American leaders might avoid visiting Belgium because of potential prosecution. Eventually, in August 2003, the Belgian parliament amended the 1993 law, and in September, the Belgian Supreme Court dismissed the case against Sharon. *See also* KAHAN COMMISSION.

BEN AMI OPERATION. After capturing the mixed town of Haifa in April 1948, Jewish forces sought to expand and consolidate their position in neighboring Arab strongholds. In an operation code-named Ben

Ami, they partially isolated the Arab town of Acre and then launched an attack from the seashore. The Israeli forces eventually captured the city on 17 May, three days after the formation of the State of Israel. *See also* ARAB–ISRAELI WAR OF 1947–1948; DALET PLAN; REFUGEE/S.

BEN-GURION, DAVID (1886–1973). A prominent Israeli politician, David Ben-Gurion played a significant role in the establishment of the State of Israel and served as its first prime minister. Born in Plonsk, Poland, on 16 October 1886, he joined the socialist-**Zionist** group Poalei Zion (Workers of Zion) at the age of 18. In 1906, he made *Aliya* to Palestine and worked in a kibbutz. Active in the *Yishuv*, he helped establish the Jewish self-defense group **Hashomer** (The Watchman) and the *Histadrut* labor federation. He served as *Histadrut* representative to the **World Zionist Organization** and the **Jewish Agency** and, in 1935, was elected head of both the organizations.

In the Palestine **Mandate**, Ben-Gurion provided leadership and successfully led the *Yishuv* to statehood. During the **Arab–Israeli War of 1947–1948**, he was instrumental in Israel securing and consolidating large areas beyond those allotted by the **Partition Plan** of the **United Nations**. He became the prime minister and defense minister of the provisional government of the State of Israel that was proclaimed on 14 May 1948. In that capacity, he occupied a pivotal position in the establishment of various institutions of the state such as the **Israel Defense Forces** (IDF) and successfully managed a massive *Aliya* from the neighboring Arab and Islamic countries for nation building. He was also the architect of Israel's strategic policy and its nuclear weapons program.

Ben-Gurion pursued a hard-line policy vis-à-vis the Arab states as well as the **Israeli Arabs**. Due to internal political differences in late 1953, he left the government and retired to Kibbutz Sde Boker in the Negev. After the **Lavon Affair**, he returned to the government in 1955 as defense minister and, shortly afterward, took over as prime minister. His return to power hardened Israel's policy and resulted in massive retaliations against Palestinian infiltrations from the **Gaza Strip** and in the **Gaza Raid**.

The **Czech Deal** concluded by President **Gamal Abdel Nasser** of **Egypt** made Ben-Gurion seek the removal of the Egyptian leader before he could pose a strategic threat to Israel. The July 1956

nationalization of the Suez Canal offered Ben-Gurion the opportunity to implement his plans. He sought the help of **France** and **Great Britain**, which owned and operated the **Suez Canal**. As agreed at the **Sèvres Conference**, Israel initiated the **Suez War** in October 1956. In less than 100 hours, it captured the Gaza Strip and the **Sinai Peninsula**, and on 31 October, Israeli troops reached the eastern bank of the Suez Canal. Under strong American pressure, however, Ben-Gurion agreed to completely withdraw from the Egyptian territories and the Gaza Strip. During this phase, he managed to secure an agreement with the French for the construction of the Dimona nuclear reactor in the Negev.

In June 1963, Ben-Gurion resigned from the government and was succeeded by Levi Eshkol (1895–1969) as prime minister. Two years later, differences with the ruling Mapai resulted in Ben-Gurion leaving the party and, along with his long-term associates **Moshe Dayan** and **Shimon Peres**, he started Rafi. On the eve of the **June War of 1967**, due to public pressure, Eshkol formed a unity government, with Dayan as defense minister. In 1968, Rafi joined Mapai to form the Israeli **Labor Party**. In June 1970, Ben-Gurion retired from political life and returned to Sde Boker, where he passed away on 1 December 1973.

BERNADOTTE PLAN. On 20 May 1948, the **United Nations** appointed a Swedish diplomat, Count Folke Bernadotte (1895–1948), as **United Nations mediator** for the Arab–Israeli conflict. On 27 June, shortly after the outbreak of formal hostilities in the **Arab–Israeli War of 1947–1948**, Bernadotte suggested the handing over of **Jerusalem** to the Emirate of **Transjordan**. On 26 July, he proposed the demilitarization of the city, and expanding this proposal, on 16 September he submitted a plan to the Security Council, calling for a significant territorial revision of the **Partition Plan**. Among other things, he recommended the annexation of the Arab part of Palestine and of the Negev (originally allotted to the Jewish state under the Partition Plan) by Transjordan, annexation of Western Galilee (originally allotted to the Arabs) by Israel, and the repatriation of Arab **refugees** who had fled from Palestine during the conflict. Initially, Bernadotte recommended the Arab annexation of Jerusalem, but he later modified and recommended the internationalization of the city. He further suggested that Haifa be an international port, Lydda (now Lod) be an international airport, and Haifa harbor be declared a free zone. On 26 September, the Israeli government rejected the Bernadotte Plan.

On 18 September 1948, two days after he submitted his plan, Bernadotte was assassinated in Jerusalem. Members of the militant **Stern Gang** who were opposed to his peace plan and its substantial territorial concessions from Israel, carried out the **assassination**. Despite an international outcry, the killers were never arrested and no one was prosecuted for the murder. During the debates over its **United Nations membership** application in early May 1949, Israel informed the General Assembly that the exact identification of the assassins was not available and hence it was impossible to apprehend them. Israel paid compensation to the United Nations, and a panel of the International Court of Justice held Israel to be formally responsible for the assassination. *See also* ARMISTICE AGREEMENT/S.

BILTMORE PROGRAM. Adopted by the extraordinary **Zionist** Conference in New York on 11 May 1942, the Biltmore Program laid the foundations for the future Jewish state. Named after the hotel where the meeting took place, the program was in response to the **Mac-Donald White Paper** of 1939, which imposed restrictions upon *Aliya* to purchase land in Palestine. It gave a shape to the Jewish national home enshrined in the **Balfour Declaration** and demanded that "Palestine be established as a Jewish Commonwealth." This was the first official demand from the Zionist leadership for statehood. The program also marked the shifting of Zionist political and diplomatic activities from **Great Britain** to the **United States**.

BINATIONALISM. Toward the end of the **Mandate** period, the idea of a binational Palestine enjoyed limited support among Arabs and Jews. It envisaged the resolution of the problem through the creation of a binational state of Palestine. Seeking parity between the two communities in the government, it sought internal autonomy and nondomination. The proposal was advocated by a number of leading British and **Zionist** personalities, but did not find favor among the mainstream Zionist leadership. The post-1967 Israeli reluctance to annex the **Occupied Territories** of the **West Bank** and the **Gaza Strip** partly emanated from the fear that Israel would cease to be a Jewish state but would be transformed into a binational state of Jews and Arabs. *See also* FEDERAL PLAN; ISRAELI ARABS; PARTITION PLAN.

BIOLOGICAL WEAPONS. Israel is believed to be the only country in the Middle East with biological weapons capabilities. Even though the exact nature of such capabilities is not clear, the arrest and conviction of Marcus Klingberg (1920–), a former scientist at the Ness Ziona Biological Institute, on charges of espionage, provided a strong basis for suspicions of such a capability. Klingberg was convicted of spying for the **Soviet Union** and was released in early 2003 after his 20-year prison term was commuted on health grounds.

BIOLOGICAL WEAPONS CONVENTION (BWC). Officially known as the Convention on the Prohibition of the Development, Production, and Stockpiling of the Bacteriological (Biological) and Toxin Weapons and on Their Destruction, the BWC prohibits any possession of **biological weapons** or any biological warfare agents, toxins, equipment, or delivery systems. While most of the countries of the Middle East are signatories to the Convention, which came into force on 26 March 1975, Israel is not a signatory.

BLACK LETTER. The publication in October 1930 of the **Passfield White Paper**, which recommended restrictions upon *Aliya* to the Palestine **Mandate**, evoked strong reactions from the **Zionist** leadership. Chaim Weizmann (1874–1952), who was heading the **World Zionist Organization**, spearheaded the counteroffensive whereby the government of **Great Britain** came under strong pressure. As a result, on 13 February 1931, Prime Minister Ramsay MacDonald (1866–1937) sent an official letter to Weizmann wherein he nullified the Passfield recommendations, reiterated British commitments to world Jewry, upheld a policy of the Jewish national home through further land settlement and immigration, and condoned the Zionist insistence on the employment of Jewish laborers in Jewish enterprises. This complete reversal of the recommendations of the Passfield White Paper was perceived by Arabs as the Black Letter.

BLACK SEPTEMBER MASSACRE. This refers to the September 1970 military confrontation in **Jordan** between the Jordanian army and Palestinian guerrillas. The hijacking of three international civilian aircraft and their subsequent detonation in Jordan by commandos belonging to the radical Palestinian group **Popular Front for the Liberation of Palestine** (PFLP) precipitated growing tensions between the Hashemite kingdom and the **Palestine Liberation Organization** (PLO), which grew into a civil war–like situation. The attempts by the PLO to create a "state within a state" resulted in King **Hussein** of Jordan ordering a military crackdown against the PLO in September 1970 that lasted 10 days. During this operation, scores of Palestinians (estimates range from some 2,000 to "several thousands") were killed at the hands of the army.

The confrontation began on 16 September and lasted until 25 September, ending with a decisive victory for Jordanian forces. Following mediatory efforts by President **Gamal Abdel Nasser** of **Egypt**, on 27 September both sides signed a cease-fire in Cairo. The end of the Palestinian resistance in Jordan resulted in the expulsion of the PLO leadership and militants from Jordan. Assured of tactical Israeli support, the Jordanian air force repulsed a tank column from Syria that sought to intervene in the crisis on behalf of the beleaguered Palestinians. The crisis flared up when fighting was renewed in July 1971 and this resulted in the expulsion of all Palestinian organizations from Jordan and their movement to Beirut.

Relocated in **Lebanon**, a group of **Fatah** militants established themselves as the Black September Organization (BSO). This group claimed responsibility for the **assassination** of Jordanian prime minister and defense minister Wasfi al-Tal (1919–1971), who had been instrumental in the crackdown on the Palestinians. In September 1972, the BSO was also responsible for the **Munich Massacre** that resulted in the death of 11 Israeli athletes during the Olympic Games. Supported primarily by Libya, **Syria**, and **Iraq**, it later broke into two factions led by Abu Iyad (1934–1991) and Abu Nidal (1937–2002). The PLO subsequently expelled the latter, named Black June, for "unauthorized" terror acts. *See also* CAIRO AGREEMENT (1970).

BLUDAN CONFERENCE. Against the backdrop of the ongoing **Arab Revolt** (1936–1939) in the Palestine **Mandate**, in September 1937 Arab nationalists from several countries met in Bludan, **Syria**. They expressed their support for the Palestinian struggle against **Great Britain** and the **Zionists** and their opposition to the **Peel Commission** report, which advocated the partition of

Palestine. This was the first manifestation of the pan-Arab concern and involvement in the Palestinian affairs.

BLUE-WHITE OPERATION. Acting on intelligence information from inside **Egypt**, Israel viewed an Egyptian mobilization in early 1973 as a precursor to war. While Chief of the Military Intelligence Eliahu Zaira (1928–) was skeptical about Egyptian intentions, Chief of Staff David Elazar (1925–1976) and Defense Minister **Moshe Dayan** felt differently. On 19 April, Israel implemented the Blue-White Operation, which called for a large-scale mobilization of reserve soldiers. The expected Egyptian attack did not materialize, however, and the mobilization cost Israel $45 million. This unnecessary and costly mobilization partially contributed to Israeli laxity when President **Anwar Sadat** of **Egypt** initiated a surprise attack just seven weeks later in the **October War of 1973**. *See also* KAHAN COMMISSION.

BREZHNEV PLAN. On 15 September 1982, days after the unveiling of the **Reagan Plan** and amid tension between Israel and **Syria** over the deployment of surface-to-air missile batteries in the Beka'a Valley in **Lebanon**, President Leonid Brezhnev (1906–1982) of the **Soviet Union** outlined a peace plan for the Middle East. It proclaimed the inadmissibility of territorial conquest and called for complete Israeli withdrawal to 4 June 1967 borders, exercise of the inalienable Palestinian right to self-determination and the establishment of an independent **Palestinian state**, safeguarding the security and independence of all states in the region, termination of war and the establishment of peace between Israel and its Arab neighbors, and international guarantees for a peace settlement. Reflecting the prevailing Arab positions, the Brezhnev Plan was along the lines of **Resolution 242** of the **United Nations** Security Council and was an effort by Moscow to reenter the peace-making efforts in the Middle East following President **Anwar Sadat**'s expulsion of Soviet military advisers prior to the **October War of 1973**. The plan, which called for the tacit recognition of Israel, was accepted by Arab states as well by the **Palestine Liberation Organization**, but was summarily rejected by Israel.

BROSH OPERATION. As fighting resumed in the **Arab–Israeli War of 1947–1948** after a month-long **United Nations**–arranged truce, Israel launched a counteroffensive on 9 July 1948 against the armed forces of **Syria**, which posed a threat from eastern Galilee. A seesaw battle continued for the next few days and, when a second truce came into force on 18 July, Israel was unable to dislodge the Syrian positions at the entrance to the Jordan River.

BUENOS AIRES BOMBING. On 18 July 1994, a powerful car bomb exploded at a building in the Argentinean capital that housed the office of the Jewish community in Buenos Aires. More than 90 people were killed, most of them Jews, and over 100 were injured. Due to the nature and target of the attack, it was immediately linked to the Middle East, with **Iran** being the prime suspect.

BUS 300 AFFAIR. On 12 April 1984, four Palestinians hijacked an Israeli bus on the Tel Aviv–Ashkelon route. Israel's internal intelligence agency Shabak claimed that all four Palestinians who hijacked Bus 300 were killed in the ensuing rescue operation. It was subsequently revealed, however, that two Palestinians had been taken prisoner following the operation, and their photographs appeared in Israeli media, thereby contradicting the earlier official claim. Initially, Yitzhak Mordechai (1944–), who commanded the Paratroops Corps that stormed the bus, was implicated in the cover-up.

Later investigations revealed that the Shabak chief, Avraham Shalom (1929–), had ordered the execution of the captured terrorists and had falsified evidence and suborned witnesses in two official inquiries. The demand for his removal was resisted, and efforts by Attorney General Yitzhak Zamir to secure Shalom's dismissal were quashed. On 25 June 1986, the Shabak chief and three of his senior colleagues requested and obtained a presidential pardon from Chaim Herzog (1918–1997), and Shalom subsequently resigned. In August, the president pardoned another seven Shabak agents. While most of the controversy was focused on who ordered and carried out the execution and the subsequent falsehoods surrounding it, none of the Israelis was ever prosecuted for the death of the two captured Palestinians.

In a media interview published in January 1997, Shalom admitted that he had ordered the killing of the two captured terrorists and claimed he had informed then Prime Minister **Yitzhak Shamir**; Shamir, however, denied the charge. The controversy was resurrected when Ehud Yatom (1948–), one of those pardoned for their involvement, was nominated to a senior security position in the Knesset. Yatom was elected to the Knesset in 2003 as a **Likud** member.

BUSH, GEORGE W. (1946–). The 43rd president of the **United States**, George W. Bush is the eldest son of George H. W. Bush (1924–), who served as president during 1988–1992. Born in New Haven, Connecticut, on 6 July 1946, Bush grew up in Midland and Houston, Texas. He studied at Yale University and Harvard Business School and served as an F-102 fighter pilot in the Texas Air National Guard. After graduation, he began a career in the energy business and started an oil and gas exploration company called Arbusto (Spanish for "bush"). Following the defeat of his father's reelection bid in 1992, Bush entered politics with the Republican Party, and in 1994 he was elected governor of Texas; he was reelected to the same position in 1998. Bush narrowly defeated Democratic candidate Al Gore in the 2000 presidential election and was sworn in as president on 20 January 2001. He convincingly won a second term in the 2004 election.

The terrorist attacks of 11 September 2001 in New York and Washington, D.C., by members of Al-Qaeda galvanized President Bush to launch a war on **terrorism** and pursue Al-Qaeda members in Afghanistan in 2001. Despite international unpopularity and domestic criticism, in the summer of 2003, President Bush launched Operation Iraqi Freedom, invaded **Iraq**, introduced a regime change in Iraq, and replaced the Ba'athist regime of President Saddam Hussein (1937–) by a more liberal but militancy-ridden polity. Accusing **Palestinian National Authority** chairman **Yasser Arafat** of a breach of his commitments and of collaborating with terrorism, Bush sided with Israeli prime minister **Ariel Sharon** and refused to meet with the Palestinian leader. Though less active than his predecessor **Bill Clinton**, President Bush proposed the **Bush Plan** in June 2002 and was instrumental in the **Middle East Road Map** and 2003 **Aqaba Summit**. Bush's demands for internal Palestinian reforms outlined in his plan resulted in Arafat appointing **Mahmoud Abbas** as prime minister. *See also* TENET PLAN.

BUSH PLAN. Amidst increased Israeli–Palestinian violence related to the **Al-Aqsa Intifada**, on 24 June 2002 U.S. president **George W. Bush** outlined his vision for a comprehensive peace in the Middle East. The statement was aimed partly toward pacifying the critics of his hands-off Middle East policy and partly at shoring up support for the impending military campaign against **Iraq**. Bush called for "two states, living side by side in peace and security." Supporting the idea of an independent **Palestinian state**, Bush conditioned it on the Palestinians electing a new, reformed, and accountable leadership that would fight **terrorism**. He called on Israel to withdraw its forces to the positions held on 28 September 2000, the day before the outbreak of the Al-Aqsa Intifada, and to stop building **settlements**, but at the same time he endorsed Israel's right to fight terrorism. Reflecting the views of the Israeli government of **Ariel Sharon**, Bush indirectly declared **Palestinian National Authority** (PNA) chairman **Yasser Arafat** to be irrelevant to the peace process. The statement did not refer to the **Oslo Process** or to the **Abdullah Plan** unveiled a few months earlier. The Bush Plan brought about some cosmetic changes in the PNA and the formation of the post of prime minister, filled by **Mahmoud Abbas**. *See also* MIDDLE EAST ROAD MAP; QUREI, AHMED.

BYPASS ROADS. An outcome of the **Oslo Accords** and endorsed by various **United States** administrations, bypass roads are the new roads that Israel built in the **Occupied Territories** following the peace agreement with the Palestinians. These roads link various Jewish **settlements** with one another, as well as with Israel, circumventing Palestinian population centers. Most of these roads are newly built on lands confiscated from the Palestinians. The costs incurred in theconstruction of the bypass roads were treated as "security-related" expenses in implementing the Israeli withdrawal. and as such, they were excluded from the conditions imposed by the U.S. government on the $10 billion **loan guarantees**.

– C –

CAIRO AGREEMENT (1970). This agreement governed the relationship between **Lebanon** and the **Palestine Liberation Organization** (PLO) in the aftermath of the Hashemite crackdown on the PLO in September 1970 and its subsequent expulsion from **Jordan**. The agreement was made possible through the mediatory efforts of President **Gamal Abdul Nasser** of **Egypt**, who died days before the formal agreement was signed in Cairo on 3 November 1970. It enabled the relocation of the PLO and its militia to southern Lebanon and the Lebanese concurrence and approval to the establishment of a "Fatahland" that the Palestinians could use as a base for military attacks against Israel. The arrangement enabled Palestinians to bear arms, conduct and administer their own affairs, and oversee **refugee** camps in Lebanon.

The establishment of a state-within-a-state undermined Lebanese sovereignty, and the PLO challenged any attempts by the Lebanese government to regain control in southern Lebanon. While it resolved the crisis emanating from the **Black September Massacre**, it sowed the seeds for the Lebanese civil war (1975–1989) and the country's subsequent occupation by the military forces of **Syria** and Israel. The Palestinian militant campaign against Israel from Lebanon invariably resulted in an Israeli counteroffensive against Lebanon. This spiral of activities eventually culminated in the Israeli invasion of Lebanon in 1982, forcing the expulsion of the PLO from Lebanon and its relocation to Tunis. *See also* LITANI OPERATION; OPERATION PEACE FOR GALILEE.

CAIRO AGREEMENT (1994). Also termed the Gaza-Jericho Autonomy Agreement and the Oslo Implementation Agreement, this accord was signed in Cairo on 4 May 1994 by Chairman **Yasser Arafat** and Prime Minister **Yitzhak Rabin**. It was the first of a series of agreements between Israel and the **Palestine Liberation Organization** (PLO) concerning the initial stage of Palestinian autonomy in the **Gaza Strip** and in **Jericho** in the **West Bank**. It outlined the provisions of Israeli **redeployment** from these two areas and the establishment of a Palestinian self-governing authority.

Formal negotiations had begun on 13 October 1993, a month after the signing of the **Declaration of Principles** (DoP). However, differences between the two sides over the geographical area of Jericho, the size and authority of Palestinian police, Palestinian presence on the Allenby Bridge, and the release of Palestinian prisoners held in Israeli prisons as well as security measures around Jewish **settlements** in the Gaza Strip delayed an early agreement.

Paving the way for the implementation of the DoP, the Cairo Agreement demarcated the areas of the **Occupied Territories** that would be handed over to the **Palestinian National Authority** (PNA).

Israeli forces would be redeployed from these areas to mutually agreed locations. The signing ceremony was marred by Arafat's initial refusal to sign the accompanying maps that demarcated the Jericho area. The areas under the control of the PNA would include 350 square kilometers (135 square miles) of the Gaza Strip and 62 square kilometers (24 square miles) of Jericho. Israeli troops pulled out of these areas by 18 May 1994. The Cairo Agreement set a five-year time limit for the interim period; when that deadline passes on 4 May 1999, it ignited a heated debate among the Palestinians over a **unilateral declaration of independence**. *See also* BARAK, EHUD; EGYPT; OSLO ACCORDS; OSLO PROCESS.

CAIRO CONFERENCE. Weeks after President **Anwar Sadat**'s visit to **Jerusalem**, the delegations of Israel, **Egypt**, and the **United States**, along with a representative of the secretary-general of the **United Nations**, met in Cairo on 14 December 1977 to follow up Sadat's initiative. After initial speeches by the representatives, the conference concluded without any decisions.

CAIRO DIALOGUE. Bowing to growing international pressures over **suicide attacks** against Israel, in November 2002 senior leaders of various Palestinian factions met in Cairo to negotiate a temporary cease-fire (or *hudna*). The inter-Palestinian dialogue, commonly referred to as the Cairo Dialogue, was organized and facilitated by **Egypt**. All the major Palestinian factions, including **Fatah**, **Hamas**, and **Islamic Jihad**, attended the talks. Further rounds of talks were held in January and December 2003. The dialogue sought to offer a temporary cessation of suicide attacks against Israel, but lack of reciprocal Israeli concessions complicated the Egyptian efforts. The talks have underscored the fundamental differences between Hamas and the Palestinian institutions headed by **Yasser Arafat** such as Fatah, the **Palestine Liberation Organization**, and the **Palestinian National Authority** (PNA). Issues such as a temporary suspension of suicide attacks, recognition of the PNA, and the territorial limits of a future **Palestinian state** required significant political concessions from Hamas, and this impeded any agreement between the two sides.

Mahmoud Abbas, who took over the Palestinian leadership following Arafat's death, intensely pursued the dialogue for a cease-fire. In March 2005, weeks after he was elected president, Abbas secured a *tahidiyeh* (lull in fighting) with the military groups. Though less than a full truce, militant activities have considerably reduced since then. *See also* RANTISI, ABDEL AZIZ AL-; YASSIN, SHEIKH AHMED.

CAMP DAVID ACCORDS (1978). On 17 September 1978, following 13 days of secret negotiations in the **United States** at Camp David, the presidential retreat in Maryland, Israeli prime minister **Menachem Begin** and President **Anwar Sadat** of **Egypt** concluded two agreements that provided the basis for continuing negotiations for peace: "The Framework for Peace in the Middle East" and "The Framework for Peace Treaty between Egypt and Israel." The former focused on the fate of Palestinians in the **Occupied Territories** and revolved around Israel's **Autonomy Plan** for Palestinians. The two documents were accompanied by an exchange of letters, which reiterated the positions of Egypt and Israel concerning Jerusalem and the definitional differences over expressions such as "**West Bank**" and "Palestinians." The Egyptian cabinet approved the accords on 19 September. On 28 September, the Israeli Knesset also overwhelmingly (84–19 with 17 abstentions) endorsed them, although a number of members of Begin's own **Likud** Party either voted against them (Moshe Arens) or abstained (**Yitzhak Shamir**).

The process had been set in motion on 9 November 1977, when Sadat told the Egyptian parliament that he was prepared to go to **Jerusalem** and negotiate peace with Israel directly. His offer was accepted by Israel, and on 19 November, Sadat flew to Israel for his historic **Jerusalem visit**. The following day, in an address to the Israeli Knesset, he outlined his vision for peace. The two sides began negotiations on 25 December at the Egyptian resort of Ismailia, but the Palestinian issue and Israeli **settlements** in the **Sinai Peninsula** hampered progress. Personally intervening in the process, U.S. president Jimmy Carter (1924–) invited both leaders to his Camp David retreat for intense negotiations.

On 26 March 1979, the **Egypt–Israeli Peace Treaty** was signed in Washington, D.C. The treaty called for complete Israeli withdrawal from the Sinai and guaranteed freedom of passage for Israeli shipping through the **Suez Canal** and the Strait of Tiran.

The accords and the peace treaty were warmly welcomed by the West and resulted in Sadat and Begin receiving the Nobel Peace Prize in 1979. The response in the Middle East, however, was hostile. In

November 1978, **Arab League** representatives, without Egypt, had already met in Baghdad to debate measures to isolate Sadat. Following the March 1979 signing of the peace treaty, Egypt, a founding member, was expelled from the Arab League and the league's headquarters were shifted to Tunis. Egypt was also expelled from the Organization of the Islamic Conference (OIC). Reflecting this mood, on 29 November 1979, the **United Nations** General Assembly declared, "Camp David accords and other agreements have no validity insofar as they purport to determine the future of the Palestinian people and of the Palestinian territories occupied by Israel since 1967." Sadat's peace initiatives and his willingness to negotiate and seek an independent peace with Israel were seen as a violation of Arab unity and the resolutions adopted at the **Khartoum Arab Summit** in August–September 1967. While **Jordan** and **Saudi Arabia** had strong reservations over the Camp David Accords, radical Arab states led by **Syria** joined the **Palestine Liberation Organization** in their rejections.

Despite uncertainties following the **assassination** of Sadat, Israel proceeded with the withdrawal process. During 23–25 April 1982, the town of Yamit on the northeast corner of the Sinai Peninsula was completely demolished, and on 26 April, the Rafa Salient was returned to Egypt. However, the tiny Egyptian territory of **Taba** remained a contentious issue. Following international arbitration, on 15 March 1989, nearly seven years after its pullout of the Sinai Peninsula, Israel completed its withdrawal from the 700 square meters (7,500 square feet) of the Taba enclave.

On 23 September 1984, Jordan restored diplomatic ties with Egypt. Thus, Egypt was readmitted into the Islamic forum at the Casablanca OIC summit in May 1984. In November 1987, Egypt was invited to attend the Arab summit held in Amman and was formally readmitted into the Arab League during the Casablanca summit in May 1989. On 1 November 1990, the League headquarters were moved back to Cairo.

CAMP DAVID TALKS (2000). The halting of further Israeli **redeployment** and **Palestine Liberation Organization** (PLO) chairman **Yasser Arafat**'s threat to unilaterally declare a **Palestinian state** before 13 September 2000 (the deadline for the conclusion of the **Permanent Status Negotiations** as stipulated by the **Sharm al-Sheikh Memorandum** of September 1999) led to high-level summit talks between the Israelis and the Palestinians. At the invitation of U.S.

president **Bill Clinton**, Israeli prime minister **Ehud Barak**, and Chairman Arafat came to the **United States** and held intense negotiations at Camp David from 11–24 July 2000. The talks focused on all the core issues: **Jerusalem**, the right of the **refugees** to return, borders, withdrawal, security, **settlements**, and water. The postponement of these issues to final status talks enabled both sides to agree on the **Declaration of Principles** in September 1993. The talks at Camp David, however, failed to make headway especially on Jerusalem and the refugee question. Following the talks, Clinton blamed Arafat for the failure. The Palestinian disappointment over the unsuccessful Camp David talks was an important reason for the outbreak of the **Al-Aqsa Intifada** in September 2000.

CHAMELEON OPERATION. Parallel to the **Alpha Plan** during November–December 1955, the **United States** Central Intelligence Agency launched a covert but unsuccessful mission aimed at arranging a secret meeting between Israeli prime minister **David Ben-Gurion** and President **Gamal Abdul Nasser** of **Egypt**. A special envoy of President Dwight D. Eisenhower (1890–1969) and Eric Johnston (1896–1963), who at that time was mediating negotiations over the sharing of the waters of the Jordan River, was used as the cover. At one time, the Chameleon and Alpha plans were closely intertwined. *See also* JOHNSTON PLAN; OMEGA OPERATION; SUEZ WAR.

CHEMICAL WEAPONS CONVENTION (CWC). An expanded and updated version of the 1925 Geneva Protocol on chemical warfare, this Convention prohibits not only the use of chemical weapons (banned under the 1925 Geneva Protocol) but also their development, production, acquisition, transfer, and stockpiling. All parties to the Convention undertook to disclose and destroy their chemical weapons and production facilities within a specific time frame. The Convention came into force on 29 April 1998. Israel, which refused to sign the **Nuclear Nonproliferation Treaty** and the **Biological Weapons Convention**, signed the CWC when it was opened for signature in January 1993 but has not ratified it.

CHURCHILL WHITE PAPER. In a policy statement on 1 July 1922, Winston Churchill (1874–1965), then the colonial secretary of **Great Britain**, outlined the British policy in Palestine. The Churchill White

Paper categorically declared that "the whole of Palestine West of the Jordan [River] was . . . excluded from" the pledge made by Henry McMahon (1862–1949) to Sharif Hussein (1852–1931) of Mecca in his letter dated 24 October 1915, part of the **Hussein–McMahon Correspondence**. Approved by the British House of Commons, the White Paper sought to assuage the Arabs by stating that the **Balfour Declaration** did not envisage the conversion of the whole of the Palestine **Mandate** into a Jewish national home. This policy statement reproduced a number of correspondences among the British government, Arab delegations, and the World Zionist Organization (WZO) with regard to the future of Palestine. Among other things, this official policy statement confirmed the right of *Aliya* to Palestine, but conditioned it to the economic absorptive capacity of the region. While the Zionist Executive accepted the White Paper, the fifth Arab Palestine Congress meeting in Nablus in August 1922 rejected the British policy statement. *See also* LEAGUE OF NATIONS.

CIVIL ADMINISTRATION. Since June 1967, a **military administration** has governed the **West Bank**. In a bid to change the image and as a partial concession to the autonomy talks with **Egypt**, on 8 November 1981 the Israeli cabinet decided to modify the procedure and established a separate civilian administration to handle all local concerns of the **Occupied Territories**. Military and security matters, however, remained with the army. The **Oslo Accord** and the inauguration of the **Palestinian National Authority** (PNA) superseded this arrangement. *See also* VILLAGE LEAGUE.

CLINTON, BILL (1946–). As the 42nd president of **United States** (1993–2001), William Jefferson Clinton played an active role in the Middle East peace process. Initially he facilitated bilateral negotiations between Israel and its Arab partners, but the onset of the **Oslo Process** increased his involvement. Though initially kept in the dark, on 13 September 1993 he hosted the official ceremony where the **Declaration of Principles** (DoP) was signed by Israeli foreign minister **Shimon Peres** and **Palestine Liberation Organization** (PLO) Executive Committee member **Mahmoud Abbas**. The White House ceremony was also attended by Israeli prime minister **Yitzhak Rabin** and PLO chairman **Yasser Arafat**. The following day, Clinton hosted the signing of the **Washington Declaration** by Rabin and King

Hussein of **Jordan**. On 25 July 1994, he attended a ceremony in the Arava on the Israel–Jordan border where the **Israel–Jordan Peace Treaty** was signed. He also played an active role in Israel's negotiations with **Syria**, and in January 2000 hosted the **Shepherdstown Talks**, though with limited success.

After the signing of the DoP, President Clinton played an active role in the peace process and periodically hosted Israeli and Palestinian leaders for talks. Against the backdrop of a wave of **suicide attacks** by the militant Islamic group **Hamas** in early 1996, Clinton took the initiative to organize the **Sharm al-Sheikh Summit** of 13 May 1996 in **Egypt**. He played a leading role in the signing of the **Hebron Protocol** in January 1997, which called for Israeli **redeployment** in Hebron. With a view to implementing the 1995 **Taba Agreement**, Prime Minister **Benjamin Netanyahu** and Arafat signed the **Wye Memorandum** on 23 October 1998, calling for a three-phase second redeployment.

In December 1998, Clinton became the first U.S. president to visit the areas controlled by the **Palestinian National Authority**, where he witnessed the abrogation of the clauses in the **PLO Charter** that called for the destruction of Israel or contradicted the spirit of the **OsloAccords**.

The failure of the **Permanent Status Negotiations** resulted in President Clinton organizing the **Camp David Talks**, where Prime Minister **Ehud Barak** and Chairman Arafat met during 11–24 July 2000. Despite his best efforts, the negotiations ended in failure, as both leaders were unable to resolve their key differences over **Jerusalem** and the **refugees**. Clinton publicly blamed Arafat for the failure, and Palestinian disappointment over the unsuccessful Camp David Talks was an important reason for the outbreak of the **Al-Aqsa Intifada** in September 2000.

Only a month before he left office, on 19 December 2000, Clinton outlined a peace plan, formally known as the **Clinton Plan**. It called for an Israeli withdrawal from most of the **Occupied Territories** and shared sovereignty over the Old City neighborhood of **Jerusalem**. However, little progress was made on the plan before Clinton left the White House on 20 January 2001. He was succeeded by Republican president **George W. Bush**. *See also* MITCHELL COMMITTEE REPORT.

CLINTON PLAN. In a last-minute attempt before leaving office, U.S. president **Bill Clinton** outlined a peace plan to Israel and the **Palestinian National Authority**. The plan was formally presented to the parties on 19 December 2000, on the eve of Clinton's departure and after **George W. Bush**'s victory in the November elections and against the background of the **Al-Aqsa Intifada**. With significant modifications, the plan was largely based on the **Camp David Talks** of July 2000.

The plan called for a nonmilitarized **Palestinian state** in 95 percent of the **West Bank** and the **Gaza Strip**. In return for the Israeli annexation of the three **settlement** blocs of **Ma'aleh Adumim**, Ariel, and Gush Etzion, the Palestinians would receive 3 percent of the land from within Israel's **Green Line**. The Palestinians would have sovereignty over **East Jerusalem**, and control of the holy sites in the Old City would be "shared and functional." Palestinian **refugees** would have the right to return to their Palestinian homeland, but not to their original homes in what had become Israel in 1948. Refugees who do not exercise this right would be entitled to compensation and resettlement. The demand for the refugees to forswear their right of return, recognized and guaranteed under **Resolution 194** of the **United Nations** General Assembly, was a nonstarter.

Even though both sides resumed talks in **Taba**, no agreement was possible before Clinton left the White House on 20 January 2001. The impending Israeli elections, slated for 6 February 2001, precluded any meaningful progress, and talks were formally suspended on 28 January, following **Yasser Arafat**'s criticism of **Ehud Barak** as being a "fascist." *See also* MITCHELL COMMITTEE REPORT.

COHEN, ELI (1924–1965). Eli Cohen was the most successful Israeli agent who operated from Damascus in the early 1960s. Immigrating to Israel in 1957 from **Egypt**, he was able to pass himself off as an Arab and operated under the assumed Arab name Camile Amin Thabbet, moving to **Syria** via Argentina. He befriended senior Syrian leaders, including cabinet ministers and high-ranking army officials and periodically transmitted classified information to Israel. Cohen was eventually arrested in January 1965 and was hanged in a public square in Damascus on 18 May 1965. He was buried in the Jewish cemetery in Damascus. Israel has been unsuccessfully trying to exhume his body for reburial in Israel.

COMMITTEE FOR NATIONAL GUIDANCE (CNG). Following the proscription of the **Palestine National Front** (PNF) by Israel, in October 1978 a group of Palestinians who were closely affiliated with the **Palestine Liberation Organization** (PLO) organized themselves into the CNG. The **Camp David Accords** and the **Autonomy Plan** of Israeli prime minister **Menachem Begin** provided the backdrop for its formation. Committed to the creation of a **Palestinian state** and the right of Palestinian **refugees** to return to their homes, the members of the committee were apprehensive that Israel would perpetuate its control through the Autonomy Plan. On 11 March 1982, Israeli defense minister **Ariel Sharon** declared the CNG illegal and banned it. *See also* OCCUPIED TERRITORIES.

CONSTANTINOPLE CONVENTION. On 29 October 1888, the major European powers—Austria-Hungary, **France**, Germany, **Great Britain**, Italy, the Netherlands, Russia, Spain, and the Ottoman Empire—signed the Constantinople Convention on the **Suez Canal**. Under the Convention, the canal would "always be free and open in time of war as in time of peace, to every vessel of commerce or of war, without distinction of flag." The parties to the Convention agreed not "in any way to interfere with the free use of the Canal, in time of war as in time of peace" and promised that the canal "shall never be subjected to the exercise of the right of blockade." In light of the political conditions prevailing in the latter part of the 19th century, the parties also agreed that "no right of war, no act of hostility, nor any act having for its object to obstruct the free navigating of the Canal, shall be committed in the Canal and its ports, even though the Ottoman Empire should be one of the belligerent Powers." Due to Anglo-French rivalries, the Convention did not come into force until 1904.

Even though **Egypt** was not a formal signatory to the Convention, it recognized it. This, however, did not inhibit Egypt from imposing a **naval blockade** against Israel both before and after the **nationalization of the Suez Canal**, which in turn became the pretext for initiating the **Suez War** in October 1956.

In his statement announcing the nationalization of the canal, President **Gamal Abdul Nasser** of **Egypt** reiterated his country's commitment to honor the Constantinople Convention. On 13 October 1956, shortly after the canal's nationalization, the **United Nations** Security Council adopted a resolution reiterating that any solution of the Suez question should include "free and open transit through the Canal without discrimination, overt or covert—this covers both political and technical aspects." *See also BAT GALIM AFFAIR.*

CZECH DEAL. On 27 September 1955, President **Gamal Abdul Nasser** of **Egypt** announced the conclusion of an arms deal with Czechoslovakia. This marked the formal entry of the **Soviet Union**, through its East European allies, into Middle Eastern politics and ushered in the pro-Arab Soviet foreign policy. While the estimates of the quantities of the deal vary, the Israeli intelligence assessment suggested that it involved 170 T-34 medium tanks, 60 Stalin-3 heavy tanks, 200 BTR armored personnel carriers, 100 Su-100 armored mobile antitank guns, 80 122mm Howitzers, 60 long-range field artillery pieces, 200 57-mm antitank guns, 100 30mm light antiaircraft guns, 34 85mm heavy antiaircraft guns, 90–100 MiG-15 fighter jets, 49 Il-28 bomber jets, 20 Il-14 transport planes, four radar installations, three *Skoryy*-class destroyers, four minesweepers, 12 torpedo boats, and six submarines. The deal also included a range of ammunitions, spare parts, general equipments, vehicles, small arms, and other service facilities. In the early 1950s, this was perhaps the largest single military transaction in the world and hence caused considerable anxiety and concern in Israel. The deal also sowed the seeds of an Israeli desire to topple Nasser before he could pose a military threat to Israel and resulted in the **Suez War.**

– D –

DALET PLAN. On the eve of the termination of the Palestine **Mandate** by **Great Britain**, the general staff of the Jewish forces devised a plan aimed at taking control of the areas that were allotted to the Jewish state under the **Partition Plan**. Wherever possible, it sought to capture strategic positions, with the purpose of blocking the progress of the armies from neighboring Arab states, should they decide to invade Palestine. The plan also provided for the capture of territories allotted to the Arab states and the possible expulsion of Arab residents from these areas. This aspect made the Dalet Plan a highly controversial and contentious military operation in the **Arab–Israeli War of 1947–1948**. Launched in April 1948, it outlines the plans of the prestate Israeli leadership to capture as much territory as possible before the end of the British mandate on 15 May 1948. With various subplots, the Dalet Plan guided the military operations of the *Yishuv* leadership and the capture of territories well beyond those allotted by the Partition Plan. *See also* NAQBA, AL-; REFUGEE/S.

DAYAN, MOSHE (1915–1981). Born in Nahalal agricultural settlement in the Jezreel Valley in northern Palestine on 20 May 1915, Moshe Dayan was Israel's most colorful general. As an active member of **Haganah**, he was detained for two years by **Mandate** authorities. Released in 1941, he joined the fight against the Vichy French forces in **Syria**. On 18 May 1941, he entered the newly formed **Palmah** and served under **Orde Wingate**. That June, during an Allied operation against **Lebanon**, Dayan lost his left eye and thereafter was personified by his famous eye patch. During the **Arab–Israeli War of 1947–1948**, Dayan fought in the Jordan Valley and later commanded the **Jerusalem** front. In 1949, he took part in the Rhodes talks with the Arab countries that eventually culminated in the **armistice agreements**.

After the formation of the **Israel Defense Forces** (IDF), Dayan held a number of senior positions and commanded the Southern and Northern Commands. In 1953, he became the chief of staff, and he commanded the IDF during the **Suez War**. He retired from the army in January 1958.

In November 1959, Dayan was elected to the Knesset on the Mapai party list and served as minister of agriculture during 1959–1964. Following a split in the Mapai, in 1965 he joined **David Ben-Gurion** and **Shimon Peres** in forming Rafi. Owing to public pressure, on the eve of the **June War of 1967**, Dayan was made defense minister, and he took the credit for Israel's spectacular victory over the Arab armies. He continued in this position through the **October War of 1973**, which exposed Israel's military unpreparedness. After the **Agranat Commission** submitted its preliminary reports, **Golda Meir** resigned as prime minister, and **Yitzhak Rabin**, who succeeded Meir, did not include Dayan in his cabinet.

In June 1977, Dayan joined the **Likud** government headed by **Menachem Begin** as foreign minister and played an active role in the **Camp David Accords**. Due to differences over the **Autonomy Plan** for the Palestinians in the **Occupied Territories**, Dayan resigned from the government in October 1979. He died on 16 October 1981. *See also* DALET PLAN; NACHSHON OPERATION.

DECLARATION OF INDEPENDENCE. On the eve of the British withdrawal from the Palestine **Mandate**, members of the People's Council of the *Yishuv* met in Tel Aviv on 14 May 1948 and proclaimed the creation of the State of Israel. Among other things, their declaration pledged that Israel would be a Jewish and democratic state governed by laws based on equality, and it promised nondiscriminatory treatment of its Arab minority. *See also* BEN-GURION, DAVID.

DECLARATION OF PRINCIPLES (DoP). On 13 September 1993, Israeli foreign minister **Shimon Peres** and the **Palestine Liberation Organization** (PLO) Executive Committee member **Mahmoud Abbas** signed a document concluding months of secret negotiations in Oslo, Norway, between Israeli and Palestinian leaders. U.S. president **Bill Clinton**, Israeli prime minister **Yitzhak Rabin**, PLO chairman **Yasser Arafat**, along with a host of international dignitaries, witnessed the signing of the DoP on the White House lawn. On 9 September, in separate letters addressed to Norwegian foreign minister Johan Jorgen Holst (1937–1994), Rabin and Arafat exchanged **mutual recognition**; Israel recognized the PLO as "the representative of the Palestinian people," while Arafat recognized the State of Israel.

The key provisions of the DoP included: acceptance of **Resolution 242** and **Resolution 338** of the **United Nations** Security Council as the basis for negotiations; the renunciation by the PLO of the use of **terrorism** and violence to resolve outstanding disputes with Israel; the formation of an interim Palestinian Self-Governing Authority to administer the **West Bank** and the **Gaza Strip** during a five-year transitional period leading to a permanent settlement; and an agreement to postpone contentious issues such as **Jerusalem**, **refugees**, borders, **settlements**, and security arrangements to **Permanent Status Negotiations** that would begin not later than the third year of the interim period. The DoP came into force on 13 October 1993 and subsequent negotiations led to a series of interim agreements resulting in the establishment of the **Palestinian National Authority** in Gaza and the West Bank town of **Jericho** and gradual Israeli withdrawal from Arab towns and population centers.

The unique feature of the DoP has been the commitment from both parties to a time-bound implementation. The DoP consisted of the following time line for implementation:

- 13 October 1993: formation of a joint Israel–PLO Liaison Committee to implement the DoP
- 13 December 1993: implementation of an agreed protocol on the redeployment of Israeli forces from the Gaza Strip and Jericho
- 13 April 1994: completion of Israeli redeployment from the Gaza Strip and Jericho
- 13 July 1994: election to the Palestinian Legislative Council followed by the **Siege of Bethlehem** and the transfer of its powers to an elected Palestinian National Authority
- 13 December 1995: permanent status negotiations
- 13 December 1999: permanent settlement between Israel and the Palestinians

However, with the sole exception of the DoP coming into force, none of the other deadlines outlined above were met. While most of the deadlines were deferred, often by mutual consent, the implementation of the permanent status agreement mentioned in the DoP was not adhered to even 10 years after DoP came into force. *See also* AUTONOMOUS AREAS; OSLO ACCORDS; OSLO PROCESS.

DEFENSIVE SHIELD OPERATION. This was the code name for an Israeli military response to the **Al-Aqsa Intifada** launched in March 2002 against the **Palestinian National Authority** (PNA). Israel sought "to vanquish" the Palestinian infrastructure that promoted **terrorism** and to wipe out militant networks and seize their weapons. The operation began on 29 March, primarily as a response to a series of **suicide attacks** in **Jerusalem**, Tel Aviv, and most specifically the coastal Israeli city of Netanya, where 29 Israelis celebrating the start of the Passover had been killed. The full-scale invasion of the Palestinian towns in the **West Bank** was aimed at wiping out militant networks and seizing weapons. Israeli forces surrounded PLO chairman **Yasser Arafat**'s office compound in Ramallah, while Palestinians in the West Bank were placed under prolonged internal curfews and other forms of movement restrictions inside areas nominally under the control of the PNA. The operation lasted until 21 April, when the Israeli forces pulled back from most the West Bank towns. The siege of Arafat's headquarters continued until 2 May, when he agreed to comply with the Israeli demand to arrest those responsible for the **assassination** of Israeli cabinet minister Rehavam Ze'evi in October 2001.

During this military offensive, Israel systematically destroyed various infrastructures including the security apparatus and numerous properties belonging to the PNA. The operation witnessed many Palestinian deaths, large-scale destruction of Palestinian infrastructure, capture of large quantities of weapons, and the arrest of a number of Palestinians suspected of involvement in terrorism and other forms of violence. The operations were dominated by the siege of the Church of Nativity in Bethlehem and Israeli operations in Jenin **refugee** camps. Israel claimed that it had destroyed the terrorist infrastructure and diminished the capacity of the militants to wage attacks against Israel, but a **Hamas** suicide attack in Rishon le-Zion on 7 May recalled the operational limitations of Defensive Shield. *See also* DETERMINED PATH OPERATION; JENIN CONTROVERSY.

DEIR YASSIN MASSACRE. A small Arab village overlooking the **Jerusalem**–Tel Aviv road was the scene of one of the most gruesome massacres witnessed in the Arab–Israeli conflict. On 9 April 1948, the Jewish underground groups **Irgun** and the **Stern Gang** attacked and occupied Deir Yassin, reportedly resulting in the killing of 245 Palestinian civilians, including men, women, and children (recent estimates suggest a much lower figure of 107 Arab civilian deaths, plus 12 wounded, and the death of another 13 fighters). **Haganah**, the official pre-State Jewish defense force led by future prime minister **David Ben-Gurion**, distanced itself from the activities of the underground groups led by another future prime minister, **Menachem Begin**. However, neither during the conflict nor afterward was anything done to assign responsibility and punish the guilty.

Four days after the massacre, a convoy to the Hadassah Hospital on Mount Scopus in Jerusalem was ambushed near the Arab village of Sheikh Jarrah, and 77 Jews, mostly doctors and nurses working at the hospital, were killed. This ambush was seen as an Arab retaliatory attack for Deir Yassin.

Indeed, during the **Arab–Israeli War of 1947–1948**, "Remember Deir Yassin" became an effective means of propaganda in encouraging the Arabs to flee from their homes. The village was one of hundreds of

Arab villages that politically and geographically "vanished," following the 1947–1948 war. Currently, the area of Deir Yassin constitutes the religious neighborhood of Givat Shaul of Jerusalem. *See also* DALET PLAN; ISRAELI ARABS; NAQBA, AL-; REFUGEE/S.

DEKEL OPERATION. When the fighting resumed on 8 July 1948, following the second cease-fire in the **Arab–Israeli War of 1947–1948**, Israel launched a concerted attack against Fawzi Kaukji's **Arab Liberation Army** in the center of Galilee. The Dekel ("Palm Tree") Operation ended with the Israeli capture of the lower Galilee and, on 16 July, the Arab Christian town of Nazareth, originally allotted to the Arabs under the **Partition Plan**. *See also* ISRAELI ARABS.

DEMILITARIZED ZONES. The **armistice agreement** of 1949 between Israel and **Syria** created three demilitarized zones whose sovereignty was left undetermined. Gradually, both sides resorted to what is called "creeping annexation." These zones became moot when the **June War of 1967** broke out.

DEMOCRATIC FRONT FOR THE LIBERATION OF PALESTINE (DFLP). In February 1969, Nayef Hawatmeh (1934–) broke away from **George Habash's Popular Front for the Liberation of Palestine** (PFLP) and formed a rival group. Initially called the Popular Democratic Front for the Liberation of Palestine (PDFLP), in August 1974 it became the DFLP (*Al-Jabha ad-Dimuqratiyya li-Tahrir Filastin*). Marxist in its orientation, it is more dogmatic than the PFLP and played an active role in demanding the establishment of a secular, democratic state in all of Palestine. At the same time, it was one of the first Palestinian groups to initiate a dialogue with the extreme left in Israel. Headquartered in Damascus, during the 1987 **Intifada** the DFLP was an active player in the **Unified National Leadership of the Uprising**. In December 1990, Yasser Abed-Rabbo (1945–) broke away from the DFLP and formed the Democratic Union Party.

The DFLP refused to endorse or participate in the **Madrid Conference**, was opposed to the **Oslo Process**, and did not contest the **Palestinian Legislative Council** elections in January 1996. Since then, it has accepted and recognized the **Palestinian National Authority** (PNA), and many DFLP members have returned to Palestinian areas. In August 1999, following reconciliation talks in Cairo, the DFLP made peace with **Yasser Arafat**, and it is now represented in the **Palestine Liberation Organization** Executive Committee. In October 2000, the Israeli government of **Ehud Barak** agreed to the request of Hawatmeh to return to PNA-held areas, but rescinded the permission following Hawatmeh's statement in support of the armed struggle by the Palestinians so long as Jewish **settlements** remained in the **Occupied Territories**. In August 2001, after a hiatus of a decade, the DFLP carried out an attack on an Israeli military base in Gaza.

DEPORTATION. Since its occupation of the **West Bank** and the **Gaza Strip** in 1967, Israel has deported hundreds of Palestinians from the **Occupied Territories**. Though explicitly prohibited by Article 49 of the **Fourth Geneva Convention**, Israel has applied deportation as a measure of deterrence as well as punishment. An estimated 1,700 Palestinians have been deported from their homes. The **United Nations** Security Council has periodically condemned the deportations.

On 2 June 1980, Israel deported the mayors of Hebron and Halhul and the *qadi* of Hebron for their alleged indirect responsibility for the killing of six Jewish worshippers in Hebron by the **Palestine Liberation Organization** (PLO). This policy of deportation became frequent during the **Intifada** (1987–1993), when a number of suspected leaders of the uprising were exiled. In December 1987, Israel decided to deport Palestinians it had identified as key leaders of the Intifada; on 13 January 1988, four were expelled, followed by another eight on 1 August and four more on 17 August. In January 1988 Jibril al-Rajoub (1953–), the future security chief of the **Palestinian National Authority** (PNA), was deported to **Jordan** for his role in the Intifada after he was released from prison in 1985 as part of the **prisoner exchange** with the **Popular Front for the Liberation of Palestine–General Command**.

The largest single act of deportation took place in December 1992, when Israel decided to expel a large number of suspected members of **Hamas** into southern **Lebanon**. Responding to the kidnapping and murder of border police officer Nissim Toledano, Israeli prime minister **Yitzhak Rabin** ordered the expulsion of 415 suspected Hamas activists. Following the rejection of their appeal by the Israeli Supreme Court, they were taken in a convoy and left inside Lebanon north of the **security zone**. Following international protests and condemnation, on 1 February 1993, Israel agreed to accept back 100 deportees immediately and reduce the deportation period of the rest by half. The deportees, however, refused to accept and insisted on the return of all those deported, and the last of the deportees returned by April 1993.

At the height of the **Al-Aqsa Intifada** in early 2002, Israeli leaders, including Prime Minister **Ariel Sharon**, openly advocated the deportation of Chairman **Yasser Arafat** from PNA-administered areas, but the threat was not carried out due to international pressure and explicit disapproval of the **United States**. *See also* RANTISI, ABDEL AZIZ AL-; TRANSFER.

DETERMINED PATH OPERATION. The limited success of the **Defensive Shield Operation** in March 2002 and the renewal of **suicide attacks** as part of the **Al-Aqsa Intifada** led to Israel launching a much wider operation against the **Palestinian National Authority** (PNA). On 19 June 2002, Israel launched the Determined Path Operation, which paved the way for indefinite reoccupation of any areas under the control of the PNA that Israel deemed necessary to meet its security needs. Within days, Israel had taken physical control of numerous towns of the **West Bank**. In the process, it had converted Area A, which was under full Palestinian control, into Area C, where Israel retained security control. The large-scale presence of Israeli troops in PNA-held areas reversed the Palestinian gains since the **Oslo Accords**. *See also* TABA AGREEMENT.

DISENGAGEMENT AGREEMENTS. Bilateral agreements that Israel reached with **Egypt** (18 January 1974) and **Syria** (31 May 1974) following the **October War of 1973**, governing limited troop reductions and disengagement by the belligerents. The disengagement agreements were made possible through the **shuttle diplomacy** of U.S. secretary of state Henry Kissinger (1923–). Efforts toward a similar agreement with **Jordan** were throttled by the **Rabat Arab Summit** in October 1974, which recognized the **Palestine Liberation Organization** as "the sole and legitimate representative of the Palestinian people," a move vehemently opposed by Israel and strongly resisted by Jordan. *See also* ISRAEL–SYRIA DISENGAGEMENT OF FORCES AGREEMENT; MULTINATIONAL FORCE AND OBSERVERS; SINAI I AGREEMENT; SINAI II AGREEMENT; UNITED NATIONS EMERGENCY FORCE II.

DOVECOTE OPERATION. In August 1970, Israel developed a plan to counter any possible offensive from **Egypt**. Primarily defensive in nature, the plan divided the 180-kilometer-long (110-mile) Egyptian–Israeli front into three sectors, each encompassing three lines of defense. The **Bar-Lev Line** constituted the frontal defense along the **Suez Canal**, with three battalions, and the second line of defense was placed about 5–8 kilometers (3–5 miles) behind that. Reserve soldiers constituted the third line of defense, 19–32 kilometers (12–20 miles) east of the canal. When the **October War of 1973** broke out, this plan was insufficient to hold back the massive Egyptian offensive. *See also* WAR OF ATTRITION.

– E –

EAST JERUSALEM. The Arab-dominated eastern section of the city of **Jerusalem** was annexed by **Jordan** on 24 April 1950, and the city remained divided until June 1967. Following its capture and occupation during the **June War of 1967**, Israel included the Arab parts within the municipal limits of Jerusalem on 28 June 1967. On 30 June 1980, the Israeli Knesset passed the **Jerusalem Law**, formally annexing the eastern part of the city.

Besides the Old City, East Jerusalem comprises the Arab areas of Beit Hanina, Essaweyeh, Jabal al-Mukaber, the Mount of Olives, Ras al-Amoud, Sheikh Jarah, Shu'fat, Silwan, Sur Baher, and Wadi al-Joz. Despite Israeli claims of sovereignty, the international community recognizes East Jerusalem to be beyond the **Green Line** and part of the **Occupied Territories**. The **Beilin–Abu Mazen Plan** of 1995 viewed the Arab areas around the Old City as the possible capital of a future **Palestinian state**.

On 11 October 1993, less than a month after the signing of the **Declaration of Principles**, Israeli foreign minister **Shimon Peres** wrote to his Norwegian counterpart assuring him that Israel "will not hamper . . . all the Palestinian institutions of East Jerusalem, including the economic, social, educational and cultural and holy Christian and Muslim places." This letter was disclosed in June 1994, following **Yasser Arafat**'s claim that he had Israel's commitments on East Jerusalem. On 21 March 2005, Prime Minister **Ariel Sharon** approved the construction of 3,500 new homes in a neighborhood that would link **Ma'aleh Adumim**, the largest **settlement** of in the **West Bank**, with Jerusalem. *See also* HUSSEIN, KING; ORIENT HOUSE.

EGYPT. Egypt plays a central role in the Arab–Israeli conflict as well as in Arab–Israeli peacemaking. The formation of the **Arab League**, with Cairo as its headquarters, provided an institutional framework for Egypt to play a leading role in the **Arab–Israeli War of 1947–1948**. Though not as strong as the **Arab Legion** of **Transjordan**, Egyptian forces captured the **Gaza Strip**, which had been allotted to the Palestinian Arabs under the **Partition Plan**. In the initial stages of fighting, they even held the Negev and its surrounding areas before being pushed out by Israeli forces. At the end of the hostilities, Egypt became the first Arab state to enter into negotiations with Israel, and on 24 February 1949, the two nations concluded an **armistice agreement**. This move was soon followed by other Arab countries.

Unlike Transjordan, Egypt had no territorial ambitions in Palestine, and in September 1948, it enabled the formation of a short-lived **All Palestine Government**. When that collapsed, the Gaza Strip was brought under Egyptian military rule. Egypt allowed **Fedayeen** to operate against Israel, which often resulted in massive Israeli retaliations, such as the **Gaza Raid** of February 1955 and the **Khan Yunis Raid** of August–September 1955.

Initially, the **United States** and **Great Britain** adopted a carrot-and-stick policy, hoping that President **Gamal Abdul Nasser** of **Egypt**, who came to power in 1954, could be dissuaded from joining the bloc led by the **Soviet Union** and persuaded to make peace with Israel. However, the opposition of Egypt to the U.S.-sponsored **Baghdad Pact** antagonized the West. Differences between the two sides then widened in the wake of the **Czech Deal** and the Anglo-American refusal to fund the **Aswan Dam** project. Nasser retaliated with the **nationalization of the Suez Canal**. This eventually culminated in the tripartite aggression by Britain, France, and Israel known as the **Suez War**. The military defeat at the hands of the imperial powers produced immense political gains for Nasser, who soon emerged as the unquestioned leader of the Arab world. Israel, which had captured the **Sinai Peninsula** and the Gaza Strip, was forced to withdraw completely.

Following the cease-fire, Egypt initially accepted the presence of a **United Nations Emergency Force** (UNEF) along the Israeli–Egyptian border. Responding to criticisms from his detractors, however, in May 1967 Nasser demanded the withdrawal of the UNEF and shortly afterward closed the Strait of Tiran to Israeli shipping. On 5 June, Israel retaliated with a massive preemptive air strike, followed by a full-scale ground war, the **June War of 1967**. By the time Nasser accepted another cease-fire, Israel was again in complete control of the Gaza Strip and the Sinai Peninsula. Unlike **Syria**, Egypt immediately endorsed **Resolution 242** of the UN Security Council, adopted in November 1967. After that, regaining the Sinai became a national priority for Egypt, which resulted in a prolonged but futile **War of Attrition**. Meanwhile, in 1964, Nasser facilitated the formation of the **Palestine Liberation Organization** (PLO), which soon emerged as the representative of the Palestinian people.

In a bid to change the status quo, in October 1973 Nasser's successor, President **Anwar Sadat**, launched a limited surprise attack against Israel. This **October War of 1973** exposed Israeli's military weaknesses and enabled Sadat to pursue a peace policy toward Israel. Helped by the **shuttle diplomacy** of U.S. secretary of state Henry Kissinger (1923–), Egypt concluded the **Sinai I** and **Sinai II Agreements** with Israel. Sadat's efforts soon culminated in his **Jerusalem visit** in November 1977. With the active participation of U.S. president Jimmy Carter (1924–), Egypt and Israel signed the **Camp David Accords** and the **Egypt–Israel Peace Treaty**. Normal diplomatic relations were established when Israel completed its withdrawal from the Sinai Peninsula in April 1982. Egyptian–Israeli autonomy talks, which sought to resolve the Palestinian problem without their participation, did not make any progress, however.

Its separate peace with Israel proved costly for Egypt, as most Arab countries considered it a violation of Arab unity. This eventually resulted in the formation of the **Rejectionist Front**, the **assassination** of Sadat, and the expulsion of Egypt from the Arab League and the Organization of the Islamic Conference. However, on the positive side, Egypt received substantial financial aid from the United States.

The **Kuwait War** and the **Madrid Conference** brought Egypt back to center stage. Since the signing of the **Declaration of Principles** in 1993, President **Hosni Mubarak** has been a principal trouble-shooter. Egypt facilitated a number of agreements between Israel and the **Palestinian National Authority**, including the **Taba Agreement** (1995), **Sharm al- Sheikh Memorandum** (1999), and **Sharm al-Sheikh Summit** (2000). Cairo also played a significant role in the gradual dilution of the **Arab boycott of Israel** and the organization of **Middle East and**

North Africa Economic Summits. Responding to the **Al-Aqsa Intifada**, Egypt actively pursued inter-Palestinian negotiations, popularly called the **Cairo Dialogue**, aimed at suspending **suicide attacks** against Israel. At the height of the Intifada, reacting to an Israeli missile attack in Gaza on 21 November 2000, Egypt recalled its ambassador from Israel, but at the Sharm al-Sheikh Summit in February 2005, Egypt agreed to the return of its ambassador to Israel; on 21 March 2005, its new ambassador, Mohamed Assem Ibrahim, presented his credentials to Israeli president Moshe Katsav (1945–). *See also ACHILLE LAURO* AFFAIR; ALPHA PLAN; AZZAM AFFAIR; *BAT GALIM* AFFAIR; BLUE-WHITE OPERATION; CAIRO AGREEMENT (1970); CAIRO AGREEMENT (1994); CAIRO CONFERENCE; CHAMELEON OPERATION; CONSTANTINOPLE CONVENTION; EGYPT'S PEACE PLAN; GOOD FAITH AIDE MEMOIRE; GREEN LINE; ISMAILIA SUMMIT; JARRING MISSION; KHARTOUM ARAB SUMMIT; MUBARAK PLAN (1985); MUBARAK PLAN (1989); MULTINATIONAL FORCE AND OBSERVERS; RESOLUTION 338; ROGERS PLAN; SUEZ CANAL; TABA.

EGYPT–ISRAEL PEACE TREATY. At the culmination of the **Camp David Accords**, on 26 March 1979 President **Anwar Sadat** of **Egypt** and Israeli prime minister **Menachem Begin** signed a peace treaty in Washington, D.C., in the presence of U.S. president Jimmy Carter (1924–). The treaty came into force on 25 April when the instruments of ratification were exchanged, and the borders between the two were opened on 27 May with the symbolic inauguration of an air corridor. On 26 February 1980, ambassadors were exchanged.

Following the signing of the treaty, all the Arab states, with the exception of Oman and Sudan, broke off diplomatic ties with Egypt. Egypt was suspended from the **Arab League**, and league headquarters were moved to Tunis. They also imposed sanctions against Egyptian oil and closed their airspace to Egyptian planes.

Despite the signing of a peace treaty, the relations between the two countries have witnessed periodic tensions, acrimony, and diplomatic conflict. Following the Israeli invasion of **Lebanon**, Egypt recalled its ambassador and returned him only in September 1986 when Israel partially withdrew from southern Lebanon. Similarly, reacting to an Israeli missile attack in Gaza on 21 November 2000, Egypt again recalled its ambassador. This situation continued until February 2005 when at the **Sharm al-Sheikh Summit**, Egypt agreed to return an ambassador to Israel. The following month Mohamed Assem Ibrahim took over as the new Egyptian envoy. *See also* AL-AQSA INTIFADA.

EGYPT'S PEACE PLAN. Partly in response to Israeli prime minister **Menachem Begin**'s **Autonomy Plan** and partly in an attempt to enlist the support of other countries, on 3 July 1978 the Foreign Ministry of **Egypt** released a six-point plan called "Proposal Relative to Withdrawal from the **West Bank** and Gaza and Security Arrangements." It called for:

1. "a just solution of the Palestinian question" and "legitimate security concerns of all parties"
2. an orderly transfer of authority to the Palestinians for a five-year transition period, after which "the Palestinian people will be able to determine their own future"
3. Egypt, **Jordan**, Israel, representatives of the "Palestinian people," and the **United Nations** to discuss the modalities of Israeli withdrawal and a transition regime
4. Israeli withdrawal to the June 1967 borders, including from **East Jerusalem**, and withdrawal of all **settlements**
5. the Israeli **military government** to be replaced during the transition period by a Jordanian-run authority in the West Bank and an Egyptian one in the **Gaza Strip**
6. Egypt and Jordan to guarantee "agreed upon" post-withdrawal security arrangements in the West Bank and Gaza

Israel immediately rejected the plan as "unacceptable" and a distortion of the "spirit of Jerusalem" and "spirit of Ismailia," references to the summit meetings between President **Anwar Sadat** of **Egypt** and Prime Minister Begin. Softening his position, Sadat nevertheless demanded Israeli withdrawal from El-Arish and St. Catharine before peace negotiations could be resumed. These demands, however, were rejected by the Israeli cabinet. *See also* ISMAILIA SUMMIT; PLO LAW.

EISENHOWER DOCTRINE. As part of the containment doctrine, on 5 January 1957, U.S. president Dwight D. Eisenhower (1890–1969) unveiled a policy of economic aid to the countries of the Middle East. He also sought the authorization of Congress to use American forces to protect the independence and territorial integrity of any country in the region "against overt aggression from any nation controlled by international communism." On 9 March, the Congress gave its authorization.

The following month, **Jordan** accused Communist-controlled forces—an allusion to elements sympathetic to President **Gamal Abdul Nasser** of **Eygpt**—of planning to overthrow the Hashemite monarchy. In response, the **United States** dispatched the Sixth Fleet to the eastern Mediterranean. Following the July 1958 military coup in **Iraq**, Jordan and **Lebanon** again invoked the Eisenhower Doctrine, obtaining limited military aid and assistance from the United States and **Great Britain**. The doctrine was closely embedded in the defunct Central Treaty Organization (CENTO) and has never been invoked since 1959. *See also* BAGHDAD PACT.

ENTEBBE OPERATION. On 27 June 1976, an Air France aircraft with 245 passengers and a 12-member crew flying from Tel Aviv to Paris was hijacked by members of the **Popular Front for the Liberation of Palestine** (PFLP). Initially, it was diverted to Benghazi, Libya, and after refueling, it was flown to Entebbe airport in Uganda. The hijackers demanded the release of a number of prisoners held by **France**, Israel, Kenya, Switzerland, and West Germany. On 1 July, the hijackers released all non-Israeli and non-Jewish passengers, but kept the remaining 103 passengers and crew as hostages. On 4 July, an Israeli commando team flew to Entebbe, carried out a dramatic operation, and rescued the hostages. The rescue mission remains the most daring anti-hijacking operation ever undertaken. Yoni Netanyahu, the elder brother of future Israeli prime minister **Benjamin Netanyahu**, commanded the rescue mission and was killed in the operation. *See also* TERRORISM.

ERETZ YISRAEL. The biblical expression *Eretz Yisrael*, "Land of Israel," refers to the ancient Israel that constituted a part of the Jewish kingdoms during the First and Second Temple periods. Since it covers areas to the east of the Jordan River, right-wing elements in Israel laid claims to **Transjordan** and hence opposed the partition of Palestine in 1921. The expression has acquired political meaning to refer to all of the original Palestine **Mandate**, including the Hashemite Kingdom of **Jordan**. This is a loose translation of *Eretz Yisrael Hashlemah* ("the Integral Land of Israel") and normally implies the indivisibility of the Land of Israel that includes the **West Bank**, which Israel captured in 1967. Until June 1991, the party constitution of the **Likud** referred to historic rights of the Jews on both sides of the Jordan River.

Since the **Oslo Process**, Israeli right-wing and right-leaning religious figures have used this expression to oppose any withdrawal from the **Occupied Territories**. Some have even declared the **Golan Heights** to be part of *Eretz Yisrael*, to preclude any territorial concessions to **Syria**. In 1993, leading rabbis identified with the Israeli right issued a halachic ruling that forbade religious soldiers from taking part in the eviction from or handing over of parts of *Eretz Yisrael* to non-Jewish control. This seriously impeded Israeli prime minister **Yitzhak Rabin** and his successors from making any public, explicit commitment concerning the dismantling of even isolated and sparely populated Jewish **settlements** in the **Gaza Strip**. On 9 June 2005, the Israeli Supreme Court dismissed petitions challenging the **Gaza Withdrawal Plan** and also ruled that the Occupied Territories were not legally part of Israel. *See also* GUSH EMUNIM.

EVACUATION COMPENSATION BILL. As part of the **Gaza Withdrawal Plan** announced by Prime Minister **Ariel Sharon**, on 16 February 2005 the Knesset passed the Evacuation Compensation Bill. Besides endorsing the official withdrawal from the Gush Katif **settlement** bloc in the **Gaza Strip**, it also provided the required financial support to implement the plan.

– F –

FACT OPERATION. While the Rhodes negotiations were in progress in early March 1949 toward ending the **Arab–Israeli War of 1947–1948**, Israeli forces moved toward the Gulf of Aqaba and, on 10 March, reached the port city of Eilat. This gave Israel access to the Red Sea. The following day, a new cease-fire agreement was signed between Israel and **Jordan**, which was later translated into an **armistice agreement** on 3 April 1949.

FAHD PLAN. On 7 August 1981, Crown Prince (later king) Fahd of **Saudi Arabia** (1921–2005) outlined an eight-point plan to resolve the Arab–Israeli conflict. It sought to fill the vacuum created by the failure of the **Camp David Accords** to generate similar moves on the Palestinian front, the isolation of **Egypt** in the Middle East, and the **assassination** of President **Anwar Sadat**. Among other things, it called for Israeli withdrawal from territories captured in 1967, dismantling of Jewish **settlements**, guaranteeing freedom of worship for all faiths in **Jerusalem**, recognition of the right of the Palestinians to return or be paid compensation, a **United Nations** mandate for the **Occupied Territories**, establishment of a **Palestinian state** with **East Jerusalem** as its capital, and ensuring the rights of Palestinians and the states in the region to live in peace. The last point accorded tacit recognition to Israel and made the plan controversial among some Arab states. Attempts to secure Arab endorsement at the Fez **Arab League** summit in November 1981 ended in failure. However, another attempt was made the following year, and on 6 September 1982, a version of the plan was approved as the **Fez Plan**. *See also* ABDULLAH PLAN.

FAISAL–WEIZMANN AGREEMENT. In June 1918, Zionist leader Chaim Weizmann (1874–1952) met Emir Faisal ibn Hussein (1883–1933), the leader of the **Arab Revolt** (1916–1918), at Faisal's military camp between Ma'an and Aqaba in **Transjordan**. Coming against the backdrop of the **Balfour Declaration**, the talks were aimed at establishing cooperation between Jews and Arabs toward establishing a Jewish national home in Palestine. At the conclusion of additional talks during the Paris Peace Conference on 3 January 1919, Faisal and Weizmann signed a formal agreement. Endorsing the Balfour Declaration, both leaders agreed that "all necessary measures would be taken to encourage and stimulate immigration of Jews into Palestine on a large scale." At the same time, they also declared that Arab peasants and tenant farmers would be duly "protected in their right, and . . . assisted in forwarding their economic development." Faisal made this agreement conditional upon the fulfillment of his demands for Arab independence.

The Arab Federation, in whose name Faisal spoke, was never established. Emir Faisal's brief tenure as king of **Syria**, including Palestine, and his forced exile to Baghdad, where he was installed as king in August 1921, removed any prospects of its implementation. The agreement was never accepted by the Arab nationalists and was rarely discussed by Arab commentators. *See also* MANDATE, PALESTINE.

FATAH. Fatah—meaning "conquest" and also a reverse acronym for Harakat at-Tahrir al-Filistiniya (Palestine National Liberation Movement)—was founded in 1954 by **Yasser Arafat** and his associates, including Abu Iyad (1934–1991), Khalil al-Wazir (c. 1935–1988), Mohammed Yussef An-Najjar, and Kamal Adwan. Fatah grew out of a clandestine Palestinian student organization established two years earlier. Since its inception, it was led by Arafat, and at the fifth Palestinian National Council in Cairo in 1969, it took control of the **Palestine Liberation Organization** (PLO) as the largest bloc, retaining this position ever since.

While enlisting support from the Arab world, Fatah sought to keep the Palestinian struggle free from all Arab governments. In the initial years, it advocated the liberation of all of Palestine, relying exclusively on armed struggle. After years of operating as clandestine cells, on 1 January 1965, Fatah began sabotage activities against Israel, and this event is marked as Fatah Day. Following the **June War of 1967**, the group operated from Jordanian soil, and on 21 March 1968, it joined hands with the Jordanian army at the battle of Karameh against Israel. In the wake of the **Black September Massacre**, the Fatah was forced out of **Jordan**. Thereafter it relocated itself to **Lebanon** and continued to operate against Israel. At the 1972 Congress, it revised its earlier policy and declared guerrilla warfare to be one of the means of Palestinian struggle.

In 1983, following the Israeli invasion of Lebanon and its aftermath, the Fatah faced internal rebellion backed by **Syria** and soon witnessed the formation of the breakaway factions **Fatah Revolutionary Council** and Fatah Revolutionary Council–Emergency Command. When the **Intifada** broke out in 1987, Fatah joined hands with the **Popular Front for the Liberation of Palestine** and the **Democratic Front for the Liberation of Palestine** to form the **Unified National Leadership of the Uprising**.

The **assassination** of key figures al-Wazir and Khalaf, coupled with internal dissent, thereafter significantly weakened the organization. The **Oslo Accords** exposed internal differences, yet despite their rejection of the accords, personal loyalty to Arafat prevented leaders such as Farouq al-Qaddumi (1935–), Khalid al-Hassan, and Hani al-Hassan from joining the opposition. The formation of the Fatah Hawks in April 1994 and other such factions are manifestations of continuing internal divisions within the organization.

During the first **Palestinian Legislative Council** elections in January 1996, Fatah captured 52 seats in the 88-member council, but at the same time, the rebels who fought as independents also won 12 seats. The rising fortunes of **Hamas** are further undermining Fatah, as shown by frequent clashes between the two, especially in the **Gaza Strip**. The emergence of new militant outfits associated with Fatah, such as **Tanzim** and the **Al-Aqsa Martyrs Brigades**, following the outbreak of the **Al-Aqsa Intifada** has showed Fatah's desire to imitate the militant campaigns of Hamas that evoke popular support and approval. Following the death of Yasser Arafat in November 2004, his deputy **Mahmoud Abbas** was elected leader of Fatah, and in the popular elections held on 9 January 2005, Abbas was also elected president of the **Palestinian National Authority**.

Within the framework of the **Cairo Dialogue**, in March 2005 various Palestinian factions, including Fatah dissidents, agreed to a lull in fighting (*tahidiyeh*). In the municipal elections held in the **West Bank** and Gaza Strip in May, Fatah faced tough competition from Hamas but managed to secure the largest number of seats. Under pressure from Fatah, in June 2005, Abbas postponed the elections to the Palestinian parliament slated for July 2005. The completion of the **Gaza Withdrawal Plan** in August 2005 witnessed an increased rivalry between different factions of Fatah. *See also* SUICIDE ATTACKS.

FATAH REVOLUTIONARY COUNCIL (FRC). In 1974, Sabri Khalil al-Banna, better known as Abu Nidal (1937–2002), broke away from **Fatah** and established this anti–**Yasser Arafat** faction. Also known as the Abu Nidal Organization, it was responsible for a number of attacks in Europe and was believed to have operated as the Black September Organization. An **assassination** attempt against **Mahmoud Abbas** led to its expulsion from the **Palestine Liberation Organization** (PLO), and Abu Nidal was sentenced to death in absentia. For many years, Abu Nidal operated from Libya, and the FRC was held responsible for the assassination of a number of Palestinian moderates, including the second in command of the PLO, Abu Iyad

(Salah Khalaf), in January 1991 in Tunis. In simultaneous attacks carried out on 27 December 1985 against the Israeli national airline El Al counters in Rome and Vienna airports by members of the Abu Nidal group, 20 civilians were killed and more than 100 injured, most of the victims being non-Israeli tourists. Israel reacted by urging all countries that maintain diplomatic ties with the PLO to suspend their relations and expel the PLO mission in their countries. Since the early 1990s, the FRC has been less active. Abu Nidal spent his last years in **Iraq**, where he was found dead in Baghdad in August 2002. *See also* BLACK SEPTEMBER MASSACRE; MUNICH MASSACRE.

FATAH UPRISING. Backed by **Syria**, in 1983 a Palestinian faction led by Sa'id Mussa Muragha, alias Abu Mussa, formed the National Salvation Front, which rebelled against **Palestine Liberation Organization** (PLO) chairman **Yasser Arafat** and unsuccessfully sought to oust the Palestinian leader. This move followed the expulsion of the PLO and Arafat from **Lebanon** in the wake of the 1982 Israeli invasion of that country (**Operation Peace for Galilee**).

FEDAYEEN. Literally "self-sacrificers," this term refers to Palestinian commandos who organized and conducted periodic raids into Israel from the neighboring Arab states. After the conclusion of the **armistice agreements** in 1949, threats to Israel emanated primarily from Fedayeen attacks from the **Gaza Strip** and the **West Bank**. In the early 1950s, these attacks often resulted in massive Israeli retaliations deep inside **Egypt** and **Jordan**. By the early 1960s, infiltration of Fedayeen forces into Israel and their attacks against Israeli military and civilian targets was the key element of the Palestinian struggle. *See also* KHAN YUNIS RAID.

FEDERAL PLAN. While making a number of unanimous recommendations, the **United Nations Special Committee on Palestine** (UNSCOP) was divided over the central issue of the future of the Palestine **Mandate**. Seven members of the committee recommended partition as the solution, and a three-member minority—India, **Iran**, and Yugoslavia—recommended the formation of a federal Palestine, with Arabs and Jews enjoying considerable internal autonomy. The majority's **Partition Plan** was acceptable to the Jewish leadership but not to the Arab–Palestinian leaders. Both sides, however, rejected the minority's Federal Plan and hence the **United Nations** never discussed it.

FEZ PLAN. An amended version of the **Fahd Plan** was accepted at the 12th summit meeting of the **Arab League** at Fez, Morocco, in November 1982, laying down guidelines for an Arab–Israeli settlement. Modifying the proposals put forward by Crown Prince Fahd of **Saudi Arabia** (1921–2005), the Fez Plan called for an Israeli withdrawal "from all occupied Arab territories" and the dismantling of **settlements** "in the Arab territories." Affirming the Palestinian right to self-determination, it recognized the **Palestine Liberation Organization** as "the sole legitimate representative" of the Palestinian people. While the Fahd Plan had affirmed "the right of all states in the region to live in peace," the Fez Plan merely proposed "a **United Nations** Security Council guarantee for the peace and security of all states in the region including a **Palestinian State**." Israel found these modifications less palatable than the Fahd Plan and rejected them. *See also* ABDULLAH PLAN.

FIDA. In March 1990, Yasser Abed-Rabbo (1945–) broke away from the **Democratic Front for the Liberation of Palestine** (DFLP) and formed FIDA (*Al-Ittihad ad-Dimuqrati Al-Filastini*, or Palestinian Democratic Union). In February 1993, it transformed itself into a political party. Advocating reforms and democratic pluralism, FIDA extends critical support to the **Oslo Process**. It contested the first Palestinian elections in January 1996 and secured two seats in the 1996 **Palestinian Legislative Council**. Its support base is largely confined to the **West Bank**. FIDA was represented in both the **Palestine Liberation Organization** Executive Committee and the **Palestinian National Authority** by Abed-Rabbo.

FIVE-STAGE ISRAELI PLAN. In response to the peace moves following the **Hussein–Arafat Accord** and the **Mubarak Plan**, in June 1985 Israeli prime minister **Shimon Peres** outlined a five-stage plan. It called for negotiations to be held between Israel, the **United States**, **Egypt**, **Jordan**, and Palestinian representatives who were not members of the **Palestine Liberation Organization** (PLO); the creation of an Israeli–Jordanian–Palestinian working group to prepare an **international conference** on the Middle East; the solicitation of support for such a conference from other permanent members of the

United Nations Security Council; the appointment of "authentic Palestinian representatives" from the **Occupied Territories** who "will represent the inhabitants and will be acceptable to all parties"; and the convening of an international conference within three months. The explicit exclusion of the PLO and the attempt to seek alternative leaderships made it unviable. *See also* PLO LAW.

FORCE 17. Shortly after their expulsion from **Jordan**, senior **Fatah** officers formed Force 17 to provide personal security to Chairman **Yasser Arafat** and other senior leaders of the **Palestine Liberation Organization** (PLO). Gradually, it evolved into an elite unit and played an active combatant role during the 1982 Israeli invasion of **Lebanon**. In August 1982, along with other PLO forces, Force 17 moved to Tunis. Following the **Oslo Accords**, the members of the force returned to the **autonomous areas** and transformed into the Presidential Security Unit, which was again responsible for Arafat's personal security. During the **Al-Aqsa Intifada**, Israel charged that members of Force 17 were responsible for a number of acts of **terrorism** against Israelis, including the killing of Kahane Hai leader Binyamin Kahane on 31 December 2000. Following a number of attacks on Jewish settlers in Hebron, Israeli helicopters raided the headquarters of Force 17 in Gaza and Ramallah on 29 March 2001, resulting in the death of three Palestinians and the wounding of 64 others. In February 2002, days after he lost the elections to **Ariel Sharon**, caretaker Israeli prime minister **Ehud Barak** ordered the **assassination** of Lt. Col. Massoud Ayad, a senior official in Force 17. *See also* KACH.

FOUR MOTHERS MOVEMENT. In the aftermath of the **She'ar Yashuv Accident** in February 1997, when 73 Israeli soldiers heading for the **security zone** were killed, opposition to the Israeli presence in southern **Lebanon** gathered momentum. Four women whose sons were serving in units of the **Israel Defense Forces** (IDF) in the security zone held a demonstration at the Machaniyan Junction in northern Israel. They then held similar protests in various parts of the country, and this gradually grew into a protest movement that took the name Four Mothers Movement. Despite its name, a host of men and women endorsed the principal goal of the movement, namely, Israeli withdrawal from southern Lebanon. It began to attract support from a wide spectrum of Israelis, including former IDF officers, academics, and politicians. As the Israeli casualties in the security zone increased, the movement gained widespread support, and Lebanon became a major issue in Israeli society. During the 1999 election campaign, **Labor Party** leader **Ehud Barak** pledged to get the IDF out of Lebanon within a year, and by the summer of 2000, Israel unilaterally completed its **Lebanese withdrawal**. The four Mothers Movement remains one of the most successful grassroots efforts in fundamentally altering Israel's security policy. *See also* OPERATION PEACE FOR GALILEE.

FOURTH GENEVA CONVENTION. Initiated by the International Committee of the Red Cross, the fourth Geneva Convention came into force on 12 August 1949. It prohibits an occupying power from resorting to collective punishments and reprisals, **deportations**, hostage taking, torture, or discriminatory treatment of the civilian population under its occupation. Israel maintains that the Convention did not apply to the **Occupied Territories** at the time of the **June War of 1967**, because **Jordan** and **Egypt** were not the sovereign powers of the **West Bank** and the **Gaza Strip**, respectively, but were themselves occupying powers of these areas. At the same time, it took upon itself to apply the "humanitarian provisions" of the Convention on a de facto basis. In December 2001, the Conference of High Contracting Parties to the Fourth Geneva Convention met in Geneva and unanimously decided that the Conventions did apply to the Occupied Territories. Both Israel and the **United States** boycotted the Conference. *See also* SECURITY FENCE.

FRANCE. The secret **Sykes–Picot Agreement** between France and **Great Britain**, aimed at dividing the Arab-dominated provinces of the Ottoman Empire after World War I, brought France into the Arab–Israeli conflict. Under this arrangement, France would take control of **Lebanon** and **Syria**, while **Iraq** and Palestine would go to Britain. Even though the Bolshevik Revolution in Russia compelled both parties to renounce the agreement, the postwar division of the Ottoman Empire nevertheless followed the Sykes–Picot arrangement. France briefly accepted Faisal (1883–1933), the son of Sharif Hussein (1852–1931) of Mecca, as the emir of Syria, but in July 1920 deposed him and established French supremacy in Syria.

The **League of Nations** granted the **mandate** over Palestine to Britain, which largely removed France from the emerging Arab–Jewish conflict. Though it voted for the **Partition Plan** in the **United Nations**, France delayed its recognition of the Jewish state because of its interests in the Arab world. Along with the **United States** and **Turkey**, France was elected to the United Nations **Palestine Conciliation Commission** in December 1948. After the conclusion of the **armistice agreements**, French officers also served in the UN peacekeeping missions. In May 1950, France joined the United States and Britain to issue the **Tripartite Declaration** that banned arms shipments to Israel and the Arab states.

The **nationalization of the Suez Canal** by President **Gamal Abdel Nasser** of **Egypt** dragged France solidly into the Arab–Israeli conflict. France joined hands with Britain, which had controlling interests in the **Suez Canal**, and Israel, which sought to contain the growing regional influence of Nasser, in planning the **Suez War**. On 23 October 1956, at a high-level meeting in a Parisian suburb, leaders of Britain, France, and Israel formally concluded the **Sèvres Conference** aimed at initiating military attacks against Nasser's Egypt. The parties set 29 October as D-day for the operations. Despite the intended illusion of not cooperating, France openly operated from its bases in Israel. Even though the Sèvres understanding was not made public at the time of the war, the veto exercised by Britain and France in the UN Security Council against the U.S. proposal for a cease-fire and general withdrawal, confirmed the premeditated nature of the tripartite aggression. Under intense pressure from the Eisenhower administration (1953–1961), the three attackers were forced to withdraw from the canal, the **Sinai Peninsula**, and the **Gaza Strip**. Still, the Suez Crisis witnessed the consolidation of Franco-Israeli strategic relations and the French agreement to build the Dimona nuclear reactor in the Negev.

The **June War of 1967**, however, marked a significant setback in Franco-Israeli relations, as France opposed the use of force to remove the **naval blockade** of the Strait of Tiran imposed by Nasser. In the wake of Israel's preemptive hostilities, French president Charles de Gaulle (1890–1970) imposed a total **French embargo** on arms supplies to the entire Middle East, and Israel became the principal victim of this policy. In December 1968, following the **Beirut Airport Bombings**, when an Israeli air raid destroyed a number of civil aircraft, France placed a total embargo on arms supplies specifically to Israel.

Since that time, Israeli–French relations have deteriorated, especially after France emerged as the key European player backing the **Palestine Liberation Organization** (PLO) and the PLO's entry into the United Nations. The frequent Israeli raids against Lebanon in response to Palestinian **Fedayeen** attacks further contributed to bilateral tensions. For its part, France adopted lukewarm, if not unfriendly, postures toward various U.S. peace initiatives in the Middle East, including the **Camp David Accords**, **Madrid Conference**, and **Oslo Process**.

Following his serious illness, in October 2004 Palestinian leader **Yasser Arafat** was moved to France for medical treatment. On 11 November, Arafat died in a military hospital in Paris.

FRENCH EMBARGO. In protest against Israeli preemptive strikes against Arab states in the **June War of 1967**, **France** imposed an arms embargo on Israel and refused to deliver 50 supersonic Mirage IV fighters that Israel had ordered and paid for. Israel retaliated by clandestinely obtaining the technical details of Mirage IV designs and developed its own Kfir fighters for domestic use and for export. The French embargo terminated the strategic cooperation between the two countries forged on the eve of the **Suez War** and had three distinct results: France ceased to be a close ally of Israel and was perceived to be sympathetic toward its former **Mandate** territories, **Syria** and **Lebanon**; the **United States** emerged as the principal arms supplier of Israel; and the embargo acted as a catalyst for Israel's arms industry.

– G –

GAHAL. *See* LIKUD.

GALILI DOCUMENT. In early 1973, Israeli minister without portfolio and close confidant of Prime Minister **Golda Meir**, Israel Galili (1910–1986), prepared a plan outlining the government's policy vis-à-vis the **Occupied Territories**. Approved by the **Labor party** on 3 September 1973, just weeks before the **October War of 1973**, it outlined plans for the development of the economy, infrastructure, and social services of the residents of the Occupied Territories and their closer integration with the Israeli economy. Encouraging Jewish set-

tlements in areas considered vital for security, the document largely reflected the parameters set by the **Allon Plan** in 1967. The proposal was overtaken by the October War, which exposed the limitations of Israel's military planning and the lack of foresight of the political leadership. *See also* GAZA WITHDRAWAL PLAN.

GAZA-JERICHO AUTONOMY AGREEMENT. *See* CAIRO AGREEMENT (1994).

GAZA RAID. In response to **Fedayeen** raids from the **Gaza Strip**, on 28 February 1955 Israeli paratroopers attacked an army position of **Eygpt** north of Gaza City. This occurred less than two weeks after **David Ben-Gurion** returned to the Israeli government and took over the defense portfolio. The raid also came just four days after the signing of the **Baghdad Pact**, which was vehemently opposed by Egyptian president **Gamal Abdel Nasser**. The raid was the most serious clash between Israel and Egypt since the signing of the **armistice agreement**. Thirty-six Egyptian soldiers and two civilians were killed, and another 31, including two civilians, were wounded; eight Israelis were killed during the raid. Subsequently, Nasser cited this attack as a motivating factor for the **Czech Deal**.

GAZA STRIP. Covering 363 square kilometers (140 square miles), the Gaza Strip is a narrow coastal plain bordering the southeastern Mediterranean Sea. This 45-kilometer-long, 8-kilometer-wide (28-mile by 5-mile) stretch was densely populated by Palestinians and, under the **Partition Plan** of 1947, was allotted to the Arabs. During the **Arab–Israeli War of 1947–1948**, it came under the control of **Egypt** and was thereafter administered by a military governor. During the **Suez War** of 1956, Israel captured the Gaza Strip, but was forced by the Eisenhower administration (1953–1961) to return it to Egyptian rule. Israel once again captured it during the **June War of 1967**.

Compared to the **West Bank**, the Gaza Strip suffers from a number of handicaps: high population density, meager economic resources, and growing religious extremism. The outbreak of the **Intifada** in 1987 underscored the security problems Gaza posed to Israel. As a result, since the late 1980s, a number of Israelis, especially right-wing Israelis, have advocated unilateral Israeli withdrawal from the Gaza Strip.

In 1970, Israel established the first **settlement** in Kfar Darom; since then, it has established 20 settlements. In the initial period of the **Oslo Process**, Israel advocated a "Gaza first" policy, whereby it would withdraw from much of the Strip. This was vehemently opposed by the Palestinian leadership; however, due to fears that Israel would try to hold on to the West Bank, Israel eventually agreed to include the West Bank town of **Jericho** in the first phase of Palestinian self-rule. Under the Interim Agreement of 1995, 219 square kilometers (85 square miles) of the Gaza Strip was transferred to the **Palestinian National Authority** but Israel still controlled 40 percent of the Strip.

The movement of people and goods from the Gaza Strip into Israel is controlled through the Erez Crossing on the northern edge of the Strip. Under the **Olso Accords**, the Erez Crossing, as well as Rafah, Sufa, Kissufim, and Karni Crossings in the Gaza Strip, were under the overall security control of Israel. As part of its **Gaza Withdrawal Plan**, in August 2005 Israel completely pulled out of the Gaza Strip and for the first time since the withdrawal of **Great Britain** in May 1948, the area came under the full control of the Palestinians. *See also* EVACUATION COMPENSATION BILL; GAZA TUNNELS; HAMAS; RAINBOW OPERATION.

GAZA TUNNELS. Over the years, Palestinians have built underground tunnels in the sand dunes surrounding the Palestinian town of Rafah in the southern **Gaza Strip** and used them to smuggle weapons, explosives, ammunition, and drugs from the **Sinai Peninsula** of **Egypt** into the Strip. Some of the tunnels run more than a kilometer (half a mile) on either side of the border, are well lit, and even contain food and water supplies. Citing smuggling activities, Israel periodically closes the Rafah crossing, the only access point for the residents of Gaza to Egypt and to the outside world. Under the **Oslo Accords**, Israel obtained a small strip of land along the border with Egypt known as the Philadelphi route, which it uses to prevent the illegal movement of people and goods into the Gaza Strip. Under the **Rainbow Operation** of 2004, pursued during the **Al-Aqsa Intifada**, the **Israel Defense Forces** (IDF) demolished a large number of houses along the Philadelphi road and expanded the zone.

GAZA WITHDRAWAL PLAN. On 28 May 2004, Israeli prime minister **Ariel Sharon** announced a four-stage disengagement plan, commonly known as the Gaza Withdrawal Plan. According to the plan, Israel would withdraw from the **Gaza Strip**, including all Israeli settlements; the **Israel Defense Forces** (IDF) would be **redeployed** outside the area of the Strip, with the exception of a military presence in the area adjacent to the border between Gaza and **Egypt** (the Philadelphi route); and Israel would also withdraw from four Jewish **settlements** in the **West Bank**, namely, Ganim, Kadim, Sa-Nur, and Homesh. Israel would remove all permanent military installations in the West Bank and, along with the international community, would help improve the transportation infrastructure in the West Bank. Even though a few Jewish settlements in the West Bank were also included, the plan was largely seen as an Israeli disengagement from the Gaza Strip.

While the proposal enjoyed widespread public support in Israel, Sharon faced considerable opposition from within his own party, and on 18 August 2004, the **Likud** Central Committee voted down Sharon's proposal and there were strong demands that Sharon should submit this plan to a **referendum**. Despite these difficulties, on 26 October, Sharon managed to secure Knesset approval of his unilateral plan. After the death of **Palestinian National Authority** (PNA) Chairman **Yasser Arafat** on 11 November 2004, there were suggestions that the plan could be transformed into a negotiated settlement with the post-Arafat Palestinian leadership. During the **Sharm al-Sheikh Summit** in February 2005, Sharon agreed to coordinate the withdrawal with the PNA, now headed by **Mahmoud Abbas**. In a bid to mitigate the opposition, Sharon enacted an **Evacuation Compensation Bill** in February 2005 to pay compensation to the settlers who were prepared to voluntarily move out of the settlements that would be evacuated under the withdrawal plan.

Amid growing protest from settlers and their supporters, in April 2005 the Knesset rejected a bill that demanded a referendum to decide on the pullout. In August, Israel evacuated all the Jewish settlements in the Strip and completed its withdrawal.

GENEVA CONFERENCE (1971). On 21 December 1971, the Geneva Peace Conference was formally opened by **United Nations** secretary-general Kurt Waldheim (1918–), with the foreign ministers of two superpowers—Henry Kissinger (1923–) of the **United States** and Andrei Gromyko (1909–1989) of the **Soviet Union**—acting as cochairs. The Arab states were eager to invite **Great Britain** and **France** but were overruled by the United States, Soviet Union, and Israel. **Syria** refused to participate, and the **Palestine Liberation Organization** was not invited. After the ceremonial opening, the conference was adjourned and was never reconvened. However, under its auspices, an Egyptian–Israeli Military Committee met on 26 December to discuss an agreement on the separation of forces on the **Sinai Peninsula**. *See also* GENEVA CONFERENCE (1973); GENEVA CONFERENCE (1983).

GENEVA CONFERENCE (1973). Resolution 338 of the **United Nations** Security Council, which brought about a cease-fire in the **October War of 1973**, called for the commencement of negotiations between Israel and its Arab neighbors "under appropriate auspices." Accordingly, the **United States** and **Soviet Union** cochaired a Middle East peace conference that opened in Geneva on 21 December 1973. It was attended by **Egypt**, Israel, and **Jordan**, as well as by the UN secretary-general. As at the **Geneva Conference of 1971**, the **Palestine Liberation Organization** was not invited. **Syria** was invited, but its participation was vetoed by Israel, which objected to the Syrian treatment of its prisoners of war. The first conference attended by Israel and its adversarial neighbors established working groups to discuss various issues, but did not make much progress. It was soon overshadowed by U.S. secretary of state Henry Kissinger's **shuttle diplomacy** and the determination of President **Anwar Sadat** of **Eygpt** to seek a U.S.-brokered peace with Israel. *See also* GENEVA CONFERENCE (1983).

GENEVA CONFERENCE (1983). Compelled by the stalemate in the Middle East and the inability of the **United Nations** Security Council to act decisively, the UN General Assembly took the initiative and organized an **international conference** on the Palestinian question. Backed by members of the Nonaligned Movement, the General Assembly was primarily concerned with the continued exclusion of the **Palestine Liberation Organization** (PLO)—despite its near-universal recognition as the "sole and legitimate" representative of the Palestinians—from any major peace initiative in the region. Convened in Geneva from 23 August to 7 September 1983, it was attended by 137 countries, but was boycotted by Israel and the **United States**. The Geneva Declaration adopted at the end of the meeting called for a peace conference under UN auspices with the full and equal participation of all parties to the conflict, including the PLO. On 13 December, this declaration was endorsed by the UN General Assembly and became part of the UN documents. *See also* GENEVA CONFERENCE (1971); GENEVA CONFERENCE (1973).

GENEVA CONVENTION. *See* FOURTH GENEVA CONVENTION.

GENEVA INITIATIVE. After months of negotiations, on 1 December 2003, Yossi Beilin (1948–), an Israeli peace activist and architect of the **Oslo Process**, and Yasser Abed Rabbo (1945–), a senior member of the Executive Committee of the **Palestine Liberation Organization**, unveiled a peace initiative in Geneva. Coming in the midst of the **Al-Aqsa Intifada**, this private, unofficial initiative sought to bridge some of the contentious issues that had resulted in the failure of the **Camp David Talks**. According to this understanding, the Palestinian **refugees** would give up their right of return and recognize Israel as a Jewish state. In return, Israel would withdraw to the **Green Line**, except for certain mutually recognized territorial adjustments and exchanges. The city of **Jerusalem** would be divided, with the Arab part of **East Jerusalem** becoming a part of the **Palestinian state**. The Temple Mount/*Haram al-Sharif* would be Palestinian but an international force would ensure freedom of access for visitors of all faiths, while the **Western Wall** would remain under Jewish sovereignty. Palestinians would prevent **terrorism** and incitement and disarm all militants. The Palestinian state would be demilitarized, and border crossings would be supervised by an international force. This understanding would replace all previous **United Nations** resolutions as well as earlier agreements. The opposition of the Israeli government headed by **Ariel Sharon** made the initiative a nonstarter.

GENEVA UNITED NATIONS SESSION. On 9 November 1988, **Palestine Liberation Organization** (PLO) chairman **Yasser Arafat** applied for a U.S. visa to attend the annual **United Nations** General Assembly session in New York. Due to pro-Israeli domestic political pressures within weeks of the **Algiers Declaration**, which proclaimed a **Palestinian state**, Secretary of State George Shultz (1920–) denied the request on 26 November. This move, in violation of the agreement between the United Nations and the **United States**, led the General

Assembly to call for a special plenary session in Geneva in December with the participation of Arafat. A resolution to this effect was adopted on 2 December, with 154 members voting in favor and only the United States and Israel voting against. The session was held during 13–15 December.

GLIDER ATTACK. On 25 November 1987, an armed man belonging to Ahmed Jibril's **Popular Front for the Liberation of Palestine– General Command** infiltrated northern Israel from **Lebanon** in a glider. Entering an army camp near the town of Kiryat Shmona, he killed a number of Israeli officers and soldiers. This was the first glider attack on Israel by Palestinians.

GOLAN ACCORD. *See* ISRAEL–SYRIA DISENGAGEMENT OF FORCES AGREEMENT.

GOLAN HEIGHTS. The Golan Heights, the mountainous area east of the Sea of Galilee adjoining Mt. Hermon, links Israel, **Jordan**, **Lebanon**, and **Syria**. Roughly 65 kilometers (40 miles) long and 25 kilometers (15 miles) wide, the area is sparsely populated. This sovereign Syrian territory is about 48 kilometers (30 miles) west of Damascus and overlooks the Damascus–Beirut highway. The plateau initially gave a strategic advantage to Syria, enabling it to shell Israeli villages along the Sea of Galilee.

During its negotiations with **France** demarcating the Palestine–Syria boundaries, **Great Britain** aspired to include parts of the Golan Heights within the Palestine **Mandate**, and an agreement to this effect was signed in December 1920 only to be renounced by the British in 1922. A small area on the Heights formed the demilitarized zone under the **armistice agreement** of 1949 following the **Arab–Israeli War of 1947–1948**. During the **June War of 1967**, Israel captured this Syrian territory and placed it under **military administration** along with other territories captured during the war. During the **October War of 1973**, Israel repulsed Syrian efforts to regain control over the Golan Heights and captured some additional territory, but under the **Israel–Syria Disengagement of Forces Agreement** of 1974, Israel returned this newly captured area.

In June 1967, Israel established the first Jewish **settlement** in Merom Golan, and since then the governments headed by both the

Labor Party and **Likud** have stepped up settlement activities. Since 1967, Israel has built 35 rural settlements and the urban center of Katzrin on the Golan Heights. The settlement drive increased following the **Camp David Accords** of 1978 when Israel agreed to return the **Sinai Peninsula** to **Egypt**. On 14 December 1981, the Knesset passed the **Golan Law** extending Israeli laws to the Heights, a move condemned by the international community and the **United Nations**.

Israeli willingness to apply **Resolution 242** and **Resolution 338** of the UN Security Council to the Golan Heights enabled Syrian participation in the **Madrid Conference** and subsequent peace negotiations with Israel. Amid indications of progress in January 1994, Israeli prime minister **Yitzhak Rabin** announced that any substantial territorial pullout from the Heights would be submitted to a **referendum**. According to a law passed by the Knesset on 26 January 1999, a majority vote in the Knesset would be needed if Israel were to withdraw from any parts of Israeli sovereign territory. Despite this, opinions in Israel differ about the legal status of the Golan Heights, and the claims of sovereignty are contested even in Israel.

During the June 1967 war, when Israel captured the Heights, most of the Druze residents fled to Syria. Israel offered citizenship to Druze residents of the Heights who were separated from their clan on the other side of the cease-fire line. Most of them remained indifferent to this offer and retained their citizenship of and loyalty to Syria. *See also* ASSAD, HAFEZ AL-; GREEN LINE; SHEPHERDSTOWN TALKS.

GOLAN LAW. On 14 December 1981, Prime Minister **Menachem Begin** surprised his colleagues by announcing his decision to annex the **Golan Heights**. Formally presented as an "extension of Israeli law," the move was approved by the cabinet. On the same evening, the Knesset passed the Golan Law by a majority of 63–21, with a number of opposition **Labor Party** members voting with the government. Israel had been building **settlements** on the Golan Heights since 1967, and the law merely revealed Israel's resolve to retain the Syrian territory. The international community, including the **United Nations** Security Council, swiftly condemned the move. An initiative by **Jordan** in January 1982 to impose a Security Council sanction upon Israel because of the Golan Law was vetoed by the **United States**.

GOOD FAITH AIDE MEMOIRE. An annexure to the **United Nations** secretary-general's report to the General Assembly on 20 November 1956 outlining the functions and jurisdictions of the **United Nations Emergency Force** (UNEF) to be deployed in the Sinai along the **Egypt**–Israel borders. Speaking at the General Assembly on 27 November, the Egyptian foreign minister declared that the General Assembly "could not request UNEF to be stationed or to operate on the territory of a given country without the consent of the Government of the country." This recognition of Egyptian permission for the continuance of the UNEF proved controversial and problematic in May 1967, when President **Gamal Abdul Nasser** of **Eygpt** demanded partial and later complete withdrawal of the peacekeeping force, which eventually led to the **June War of 1967**.

GOOD FENCE POLICY. A euphemism for the policy Israel adopted toward the Christian population in southern **Lebanon** following the outbreak of the Lebanese civil war (1975–1989). In early 1976, Israel began providing medical, economic, and subsequently limited military aid to Christian elements in southern Lebanon. This assistance was accelerated following the election of **Menachem Begin**, who transformed it into a cornerstone of his policy toward Israel's northern neighbor. This policy was meant to prevent **Syria** from invading Lebanon and to keep Palestinian militants from establishing independent **autonomous areas** north of Israel. This policy of "helping beleaguered Christians" eventually led to the formation of the **South Lebanese Army**.

GRAPES OF WRATH OPERATION. Code name for the Israeli military response to **Hezbollah** attacks on northern Israel in the spring of 1996. The government of **Shimon Peres** was already under domestic pressure following a spate of **suicide attacks** in **Jerusalem** and Netanya by Palestinians that had claimed more than 50 victims in February and March 1996. The Katyusha rocket attacks from southern **Lebanon** complicated the situation. Hezbollah began this latest barrage of missile and artillery exchanges in response to the alleged Israeli killing of two Lebanese children in the **security zone**. Already trailing in opinion polls following the suicide attacks, Peres was forced to take a tough stand vis-à-vis Hezbollah to restore public confidence as well as to increase his prospects in the May Knesset elections. In response to the rocket attacks, in early April 1996 Israel initiated aerial and ground strikes against suspected Hezbollah and **Popular Front for the Liberation of Palestine–General Command** targets.

When the rocket attacks increased, Israel escalated the conflict and began attacking Lebanese targets beyond the immediate vicinity, including bombing power stations near Beirut, the main north–south highway, and Beirut's international airport. During the operation, more than 400,000 Lebanese civilians were displaced. Israel sought to undermine the local support for Hezbollah through such measures and pressured the Lebanese government to act against and disarm the militants. On 18 April 1996, an Israeli shell accidentally landed on a **United Nations International Force in Lebanon** (UNIFIL) base in Kfar Qana and killed 105 Lebanese civilians who had sought refuge there. This attack changed the entire situation, resulting in strong international condemnation of Israel and compelling the **United States** and **France** to mediate.

On 26 April, a cease-fire agreement known as the Grapes of Wrath Understanding was reached. U.S. secretary of state Warren Christopher (1925–) announced that Israel and **Hezbollah** had agreed on terms that would end the fighting. According to this unsigned understanding, Israel would not fire at civilians or civilian targets in Lebanon, while Hezbollah agreed not to attack Israel. This was a reaffirmation of a similar understanding reached in July 1993, following the **Accountability Operation**. A five-member group made up of the United States, France, Israel, **Syria**, and Lebanon was formed to monitor the compliance and application of the understanding. This proved short lived when both sides accused each other of violating the agreement.

GREAT BRITAIN. Following the outbreak of World War I, Great Britain sought the help of Sharif Hussein ibn Ali of Mecca (1852–1931) to instigate a rebellion against the Ottoman Empire. Through the **Hussein–McMahon Correspondence** (July 1915–March 1916), the British facilitated the **Arab Revolt** (1916–1918) against the Ottomans and, in return, promised to create a unified Arab kingdom after the war, whose territorial limits remained vague and contentious. Simultaneously, in May 1916, Britain entered into a secret agreement with **France** (the **Sykes–Picot Agreement**) to divide the Arab provinces of the Ottoman Empire between themselves after the war. Meanwhile, in an attempt to gain the support of the **United States**, it promised support for the creation of a Jewish national home in Palestine through the **Balfour Declaration**.

After capturing Palestine during the war, Britain began trying to extricate itself from the conflicting promises regarding Palestine by, in April 1921, carving out areas east of the Jordan River and installing Sharif Hussein's second son, **Abdullah I**, as emir of **Transjordan**. The **Churchill White Paper** declared that the region west of Transjordan was exempted from any assurances in the Hussein–McMahon Correspondence. On 24 July 1922, the **League of Nations** recognized the British **mandate** over Palestine. Though a trust territory, Britain administered the territory without ever going to the League for approval or authorization.

Britain's contradictory promises to the Arabs and **Zionists** made the mandate unworkable. While the creation of a Jewish national home in Palestine largely depended upon *Aliya*, the Palestinians were vehemently opposed to Jewish immigration and land purchases. This resulted in periodic clashes between Jews and Arabs and in 1936 exploded into full-fledged violence, commonly known as the **Arab Revolt** (1916–1918). British attempts to secure Arab acquiescence to its pro-Zionist policy went nowhere, and in July 1937, the **Peel Commission**, for the first time, advocated partition as a solution to the irreconcilable situation. On the eve of World War II, Britain issued the **MacDonald White Paper**, which formally renounced the British commitments to the Balfour Declaration.

In April 1947, Britain handed over the Palestine problem to the newly founded **United Nations**, and the following month the United Nations appointed an 11-member **United Nations Special Commission on Palestine** (UNSCOP). On 1 September, UNSCOP submitted two recommendations: partition or a **Federal Plan**. On 29 November 1947, the United Nations approved the **Partition Plan**, and shortly afterward Britain declared that it would withdraw from Palestine on 15 May 1948.

Hours before the scheduled British withdrawal, on 14 May 1948, Zionist leaders met in Tel Aviv and declared the founding of the State of Israel, precipitating the **Arab–Israeli War of 1947–1948**. The **Arab Legion** of Transjordan, sponsored and supported by Britain, played a critical role in the war, successfully occupying the **West Bank** and **East Jerusalem**, which were annexed by **Jordan** in April 1950. On 25

May 1950, Great Britain joined hands with France and the United States to issue the **Tripartite Declaration**, which prohibited supplies of arms to belligerents in the Arab–Israeli conflict. Similarly, Britain played a significant role in the formation of the **Baghdad Pact** in 1955.

The **nationalization of the Suez Canal** by President **Gamal Abdul Nasser** of **Egypt** resulted in Britain, France, and Israel colluding to attack Egypt in what became the **Suez War** of 1956. Because of strong U.S. pressure, the successful assault was reversed and all foreign forces withdrew from the **Sinai Peninsula**.

Britain played an important role in the drafting of **Resolution 242** of the UN Security Council, which was adopted on 22 November 1967 following the **June War of 1967**. Since then, however, Great Britain has not been very prominent with regard to initiatives to settle the Arab–Israeli conflict. *See also* LONDON CONFERENCE; ST. JAMES CONFERENCE.

GREATER JERUSALEM. On 21 June 1988, the Israeli cabinet approved a proposal to create "Greater **Jerusalem**" by extending the municipal boundaries westward and incorporating the outlying towns. This move aimed at consolidating the Jewish majority within the city and also envisaged the creation of an "umbrella municipality" comprising eight Jewish **settlements** in the **Occupied Territories** bordering Jerusalem. *See also* CLINTON PLAN; MA'ALEH ADUMIM.

GREATER SYRIA. In return for his support of **Great Britain** against the Ottoman Empire during 1918–1920, Emir Faisal ibn Hussein (1883–1933), son of Sharif Hussein of Mecca (1852–1931), aspired to establish an Arab Syrian kingdom under his rule. With the active support of the British, Faisal proclaimed himself king of **Syria** in March 1920 and then sought to include and unify **Lebanon**, Palestine, and **Transjordan** under his rule. His reign proved to be short lived, and he was soon driven out of Damascus. The British subsequently installed him as the monarch of **Iraq**. *See also* FRANCE.

GREEN LINE. The frontier between Israel and the neighboring Arab states of **Egypt**, **Jordan**, **Lebanon**, and **Syria** as established by the **armistice agreements** of 1949. The Green Line delineated Israel's borders on the eve of the **June War of 1967**, assuming this nomenclature because it was drawn on the maps with a green marker. Also referred to as the "4 June borders," the Green Line ceased to exist on official Israeli maps following the 1967 war.

The governments headed by the **Labor Party** and **Likud** were vehemently opposed to any Israeli withdrawal back to the Green Line. Weeks after the signing of the peace treaty with Egypt, Israeli prime minister **Menachem Begin** told the Herut Party Conference in April 1979 that the "green line no longer exists, it has vanished forever." Nevertheless, it briefly resurfaced following the 1987 **Intifada** and was institutionalized in the 1990s when Israel sought to prevent Palestinians from entering Israel, especially after acts of **terrorism**. Even though Israeli citizens are not prevented from crossing over the Green Line, the movement of Palestinian residents of the **Occupied Territories** into Israel is severely restricted. *See also* SETTLEMENT/S.

GULF WAR. *See* KUWAIT WAR.

GUSH EMUNIM. Gush Emunim ("Bloc of the Faithful") became active after the **June War of 1967**, seeking to promote Jewish **settlements** in the **Occupied Territories**. Driven by messianic zeal, it relies on biblical Jewish claims to **Judea and Samaria**. Following the **October War of 1973**, Gush Emunim organized itself into a political movement opposed to any territorial concessions. Seeking to promote Israeli sovereignty over the Occupied Territories, it promotes legal as well as illegal settlement activities, which often result in confrontations with the Palestinians. Rabbis identified with the movement have issued religious edicts opposing Israeli withdrawal from the **West Bank** and **Gaza Strip**. Rabbi Moshe Levinger (1935–), leader of the **Kiryat Arba** settlement near Hebron, was one of the founding members and the most influential figure in Gush Emunim.

Even though its first formal settlement plan was submitted to the **Likud** government in 1978, the group was active during the previous **Labor Party** governments. In defiance of the official policy, but with the backing of Defense Minister **Shimon Peres**, Gush Emunim began establishing settlements after April 1975 beyond the strategically important areas identified by the **Allon Plan**. One such settlement it established was **Ma'aleh Adumim**, northeast of **Jerusalem**, which subsequently became the largest Jewish settlement in the Occupied Territories.

The extraparliamentary religious **Zionist** movement advocates the extension of Israeli sovereignty over the West Bank and Gaza Strip as a vital move toward the realization of Zionist dreams. Initially, Gush Emunim was affiliated to the National Religious Party; then, moving further to the right, it actively cooperated with other right-wing parties such as **Kach**, Kahane Hai, and Herut Leumi. Some of its members were also active in the **Jewish Underground**, which emerged in the late 1980s and 1990s. In 1978, Gush Emunim established **Amana** to promote settlement activities. In 1982, it was active in opposing the Israeli withdrawal from the **Sinai Peninsula** and the demolition of the Yamit settlement.

– H –

HABASH, GEORGE (1926–). Born into a Greek Orthodox family in Lydda (currently Lod in Israel) in 1926, George Habash is a radical Palestinian leader and a cofounder of the **Popular Front for the Liberation of Palestine** (PFLP). In the **Arab–Israeli War of 1947–1948**, Habash was expelled from Lydda during the **Dalet Plan** operation and became a **refugee**. Initially he lived in Amman.

In December 1967, as a result of the **June War of 1967**, Habash joined with Ahmad Jibril (1939–), Nayef Hawatmah (1934–), and others to form the PFLP, which in 1972 joined the **Palestine Liberation Organization** (PLO). Meanwhile, in late 1968, Jibril, a senior army officer in **Syria**, had broken away from the PFLP and formed the **Popular Front for the Liberation of Palestine–General Command** (PFLP–GC).

In 1970, Habash's PFLP hijacked a number of Western civilian aircraft and blew them up in **Jordan**, which precipitated significant Jordanian–Palestinian tension and the **Black September Massacre**. As a result, Habash was later vehemently opposed to any reconciliation or political dialogue with the Hashemite kingdom.

In November 1988, Habash endorsed the **Algiers Declaration**, which recognized the **Partition Plan** of the **United Nations**. At the same time, he opposed the decision of PLO chairman **Yasser Arafat** to accept **Resolution 242** and **Resolution 338** of UN Security Council, which merely recognized the **refugee** rights of the Palestinians and not their political rights. Following the **Madrid Conference**, Habash joined other Palestinian factions based in Syria and formed the **Rejectionist Front**. He also opposed the **Oslo Process** and the establishment of the **Palestinian National Authority** under the **Cairo Agreement** of 1994. In April 2000, Habash resigned as secretary-general of the PFLP and was briefly replaced by **Abu Ali Mustafa**.

HAGANAH. Literally "defense," Haganah refers to the **Jewish Underground** force established in 1920 with the explicit purpose of defending "Jewish life, property, and honor" in the wake of Arab violence, especially in the Jewish quarters of **Jerusalem**. Consisting of volunteers, the self-defense force formed the rudimentary beginning of the **Israel Defense Forces** (IDF). In 1941, amid growing attacks and the abandoning of the **Balfour Declaration** by **Great Britain**, Haganah formed an elite strike force called **Palmah**. On 31 May 1948, Haganah ceased to exist following the establishment of a unified IDF. Most of the future officers of the IDF came from Haganah or had served in its Palmah units. *See also* ARAB–ISRAELI WAR of 1947–1948; RABIN, YITZHAK.

HAMAS. The acronym for *Harakat al-Muqawama al-Islamiyya* (Islamic Resistance Movement), Hamas is a militant Islamic political party that subscribes to the view that the whole of Palestine is an Islamic *waqf* in perpetuity, and hence no part can be ceded to or shared with non-Muslims. It advocates the spread of Islam toward the establishment of an Islamic state in Palestine. While endorsing a temporary truce due to tactical considerations, Hamas is opposed to making peace with Israel because such a course would mean giving up parts of the land of Palestine. Its nonnegotiable maximalist approach toward peace has precluded Hamas from acting as a negotiating partner in the Middle East peace process.

For many years, Hamas functioned as a social welfare organization among the Palestinians and sought to bring about an Islamic state through Islamization of the Palestinians. Since 1967, it has functioned as an arm of the **Muslim Brotherhood**, the mother of most contemporary Islamic movements in the Middle East. As such, the welfare activities of the Mujamma'al-Islami (Islamic Center) were tolerated by Israel, which perceived it to be an effective counterweight to the growing influence of **Fatah**. The Islamic activities of the Center appeared less threatening to Israel than the nationalist activities of the **Palestine Liberation Organization** (PLO).

The outbreak of the **Intifada** in 1987 and the popular support it evoked compelled the movement to reexamine itself. Transforming itself into a political party, in August 1988 Hamas issued a covenant that declared all of Palestine to be an Islamic trust and proclaimed a jihad, or holy war, against Israel. **Sheikh Ahmed Yassin** was one of the founding leaders of Hamas. Working independently of the Fatah-dominated **Unified National Leadership of the Uprising**, Hamas issued separate calls for protest actions against Israel.

To cleanse itself of past associations with Israeli authorities, Hamas launched a militant campaign against Israel and established a separate military wing named after the Muslim Brotherhood leader who conducted military campaigns against the **Mandate** authorities, **Izzeddin al-Qassem**. On 18 June 1989, Israel declared Hamas to be an illegal organization, and on 16 October 1991, Sheikh Yassin was convicted and given a life sentence. The kidnapping and execution of an Israeli border police officer in December 1992 led to the Israeli **deportation** of 415 suspected Hamas members to **Lebanon**, but due to persistent international pressure, Israel eventually agreed to their return a year later.

Vehemently rejecting peace with Israel, Hamas opposed the **Oslo Process** and criticized the Palestinian leadership for its capitulation to the **Zionists**. Emerging as a strong critic of the peace process, it refused to participate in the January 1996 elections to the **Palestinian Legislative Council**. However, aware of the popular support for elections, Hamas refrained from issuing a boycott call.

Capitalizing on its role in promoting religious zeal, its members have conducted virulent **suicide attacks** against Israel, especially after the onset of the Oslo Process. The Israeli counteroffensive against the suicide bombings and the delayed implementation of the **Oslo Accords** significantly eroded the support base for **Yasser Arafat** while correspondingly increasing and reinforcing the popularity of Hamas and its militant campaign.

In September 1997, following the botched **Masha'al Affair**, an **assassination** attempt against Hamas leader Khalid Masha'al (1956–) in Amman, Israel, was forced to release Sheikh Yassin from prison. Since the outbreak of the **Al-Aqsa Intifada**, Hamas has been active in its militant campaign against Israel and has claimed responsibility for a number of suicide attacks inside Israel. The formation of Fatah-linked militant groups to organize suicide attacks against Israel during the Al-Aqsa Intifada was the result of the growing Palestinian endorsement of suicide **terrorism** against Israel. In response to increased violence, Israel resorted to assassination of Hamas personalities, a policy known as **targeted killing**. In a deliberate policy of targeting the political leadership of Hamas in March 2004, Israel assassinated Sheikh Yassin as he was coming out of the Gaza Mosque. Shortly afterward, **Abdel Aziz al-Rantisi**, who briefly took over as Hamas chief, was also assassinated by Israel. On 26 September 2004, Israeli agents assassinated Hamas leader Izz el-Deen Sheikh Khalil (c. 1964–2004) in Damascus.

Hamas did not participate in the Palestinian elections held on 9 January 2005 in which **Mahmoud Abbas** was elected president of the **Palestinian National Authority**. However, it did take part in the May elections for the municipal councils and made impressive gains and has expressed its desire to participate in the national elections originally slated for July. Partly because of the visible manifestation of the popularity of Hamas, Abbas came under intense pressure from Fatah and others and, citing need for additional time to change the election laws, in June Abbas postponed the parliamentary elections to January 2006. *See also* CAIRO DIALOGUE; QASSEM II.

HASHOMER. Hashomer ("Guard") was an association of Jewish guards who were employed in defending the Jewish **settlements** in the Palestine **Mandate**. Active since 1909, it was disbanded following the formation of **Haganah** in 1920. *See also* PALMAH.

HAYCRAFT COMMISSION. The first in the series of commissions appointed by **Great Britain** to investigate periodic violence that occurred in the Palestine **Mandate**. Headed by Sir Thomas Haycraft, chief justice of Palestine, the commission inquired into the May 1921 riots and attributed the Arab violence to the pro-**Zionist** position of the British administration, dismissing suggestions of the Zionist leaders that the Arab property owners instigated the disturbances due to their fears of losing their status and because of their resentment of the British. *See also* LEAGUE OF NATIONS.

HEBRON MASSACRE (1929). Tensions between Jews and Muslims over the **Western Wall** in the Old City of **Jerusalem** reverberated into major communal violence in the historic southern city of Hebron. On 24 August 1929, 64 unarmed Jewish men, women, and children were slaughtered by an Arab mob. This resulted in the complete evacuation of the Jewish population from Hebron, where the Tomb of the Patriarchs is located. Jewish life in Hebron was renewed after the **June War of 1967** when the first **settlement** was established in April 1968. *See also* HEBRON MASSACRE (1994).

HEBRON MASSACRE (1994). On 25 February 1994, Baruch Goldstein, a resident of the Jewish **settlement** of **Kiryat Arba** near Hebron, opened fire on Muslim worshippers in the Ibrahimi Mosque in Hebron (also known as Tomb of the Patriarchs), killing 29 and wounding more than 100 others. The survivors killed Goldstein. The Israeli government and all the political parties in the Knesset condemned the attack. Israeli prime minister **Yitzhak Rabin** appointed a commission of inquiry, headed by the president of the Supreme Court, Justice Meir Shamgar (1925–), that also included, for the first time, an Arab member, Nazareth District Court Justice Abd el-Rahman Zoabi (1933–). On 26 June 1994, the commission submitted its findings and ruled out the presence of any organization behind the massacre, concluding that Goldstein acted alone in committing this "base and murderous" massacre. The attack stalled the Israeli–Palestinian negotiations toward the conclusion of the 1994 **Cairo Agreement** and led to the formation of the **Temporary International Presence in Hebron**, an unarmed multilateral European observer unit. As a follow-up measure, on 13 March 1994 the Israeli government declared **Kach** and Kahane Hai to be "**terrorist** organizations" and proscribed them; a number of key functionaries of these two groups were also identified. *See also* CAIRO AGREEMENT (1994); HEBRON PROTOCOL.

HEBRON PROTOCOL. On 15 January 1997, Israeli prime minister **Benjamin Netanyahu** and **Palestinian National Authority** chairman **Yasser Arafat** met at the Erez Checkpoint in the presence of U.S. Middle East coordinator Dennis Ross and agreed on the Hebron Protocol. Signed by Dan Shomron (1937–) and Saeb Erakat (1955–), the agreement called for an Israeli withdrawal from 80 percent of the city within

10 days. It also provided for an Israeli withdrawal from rural areas of the **West Bank** in three stages, the last to be completed by mid-1998. Both sides agreed that within two months after the signing of the protocol, they would begin the **Permanent Status Negotiations**, to be completed by 4 May 1999. This was the first peace agreement signed by a **Likud** government with the Palestinian leadership. Opposing the move, Minister of Science Benny Begin (1943–) resigned from the cabinet.

In accordance with the **Taba Agreement** of 1995, Israel had begun withdrawing from Palestinian towns and population centers on 25 October 1995. However, the religious significance of Hebron and the political opposition it evoked had prevented the **Labor Party**–led government of **Shimon Peres** from contemplating an Israeli withdrawal from the city. Netanyahu's erstwhile opposition to the **Oslo Process** and making peace with Arafat further delayed an agreement on Hebron. By the Hebron Protocol, Israel agreed to withdraw from most of the city, while retaining control of a **settlement** enclave for a period of at least two years. The area under Israeli control, designated as H-2, consisted of 450 settlers and 35,000 Palestinians and contained the Tomb of the Patriarchs/Ibrahimi Mosque. The first phase of the withdrawal was delayed due to differences about the extent of the territory to be handed over to the Palestinians. The **United States** was in favor of handing over 13.1 percent of the land to the Palestinians, which Israel refused to accept.

HERUT. *See* LIKUD.

HEZBOLLAH. Hezbollah, meaning "Party of God," is a Shia Muslim movement, militia, and political party in **Lebanon**. Inspired by the Islamic revolution in **Iran** and following the 1982 Israeli invasion of Lebanon (**Operation Peace for Galilee**), a group of members led by Sheikh Mohammed Hussein Fadlallah (1935–) broke away from the **Amal** militia and formed Hezbollah. Radical in its outlook, it offered itself as an alternative to Amal and sought the establishment of an Islamic state in Lebanon along the Iranian model. This objective was gradually diluted as Hezbollah joined the Lebanese political process and contested the 1992 parliamentary elections. It enjoys the patronage of Iran as well as **Syria**.

Since 1983, Hezbollah has launched a militant campaign against the West and Israel, which has often taken the form of **suicide attacks**.

Its attacks against the U.S. Embassy, the U.S. Marine headquarters, and the French headquarters in Beirut in 1983 resulted in the hasty pullout of American and French forces from Lebanon. Since the late 1980s, Hezbollah has been active in the **security zone** and had led the Lebanese resistance against the Israeli occupation. Its militant campaign against Israel with Katyusha attacks against northern Israel often led to retaliatory strikes from Israel. At times, the crisis escalated into major Israeli offensives, for example, the **Accountability Operation** in 1993 and **Grapes of Wrath Operation** in 1996.

The mounting military casualties in southern Lebanon and resultant domestic pressures eventually resulted in Israel's unilateral **Lebanese withdrawal** from the security zone, which was completed in May 2000. New disputes over the status of **Sheba'a Farms** bordering Israel, Syria, and Lebanon, however, renewed the low-level hostilities between Hezbollah and the **Israel Defense Forces**. Following the withdrawal of the Syrian forces from Lebanon, parliamentary elections were held in May–June 2005, in which Hezbollah made impressive gains in the Shia-dominated Southern Lebanon. *See also* BEIRUT AIRPORT BOMBINGS; FRANCE; TANNENBAUM AFFAIR.

HINDAWI AFFAIR. An unsuccessful attempt on 17 April 1986 to blow up an El Al plane en route from Heathrow Airport in London to Tel Aviv. A young, pregnant Irish woman was the innocent courier of an explosive device, timed to explode an hour after departure. It was discovered during a routine security check by El Al officials prior to departure. A day later, Scotland Yard police arrested Nizar Hindawi, the Jordanian journalist boyfriend of the Irish woman to whom he had given the explosive device without revealing its contents. Hindawi carried a Syrian diplomatic passport, and this led to a brief severance of diplomatic relations between **Great Britain** and **Syria**.

HIRAM OPERATION. During the **Arab–Israeli War of 1947–1948**, Israel launched the 29–31 October 1948 Hiram Operation, which resulted in the Israeli penetration of **Lebanon**. Israel reached the Litani River and along the way destroyed a number of units belonging to Lebanon and **Syria**, as well as the **Arab Liberation Army**. The Israeli withdrawal from 14 Lebanese villages captured during the operation resulted in the Israel–Lebanese **Armistice Agreement** signed on 23 March 1949.

HOPE-SIMPSON COMMISSION. In 1930, **Great Britain** asked Sir John Hope-Simpson to inquire into the recommendations of the **Shaw Commission**, which had investigated the **Western Wall Riots** of September 1929. Hope-Simpson submitted his report in August, and it was published in October 1930. Focusing on the economic conditions of Palestine, the report concluded that there was no surplus land in Palestine and that the Arab rural population in fact suffered from an acute *shortage* of land. Beyond this, the commission felt that the Jewish national institutions in Palestine were causing unemployment among the Arabs due to their policy of employing only Jewish labor. Hence, it advocated a temporary halt to the immigration of Jewish laborers until the problem of Arab unemployment was resolved. The Hope-Simpson Report formed the basis of the **Passfield White Paper** of October 1930, which recommended restrictions upon *Aliya* and land purchase. *See also* LEAGUE OF NATIONS; MANDATE, PALESTINE.

HOREV OPERATION. On 22 December 1948, Israel launched a major offensive in the **Arab–Israeli War of 1947–1948** on the **Egypt**–Negev front south of Beersheba. The operation, which lasted until early January, witnessed Israeli forces for the first time crossing the international boundary into Egyptian territory. On 7 January 1949, the last day of operations, Israel shot down five reconnaissance planes belonging to **Great Britain** and drew widespread criticism for this act. The operation was seen as the catalyst for Egyptian willingness to directly negotiate with Israel, and formal talks began at Rhodes on 13 January 1949 leading to an **armistice agreement**.

HUSSEIN, KING (1935–1999). As the ruler of **Jordan**, King Hussein ibn Talal was the longest reigning monarch in the Middle East. Born in Amman in 1935, Hussein was educated in **Great Britain** and graduated from Sandhurst Military Academy. He was with his grandfather King **Abdullah I** when the latter was assassinated near the Al-Aqsa Mosque in **Jerusalem** in July 1951. After his father Talal, who succeeded Abdullah, was dethroned on grounds of mental illness in May 1953, Hussein became king of Jordan. After that, Hussein survived a number of internal crises, **assassination** attempts, and regional conflicts.

Amid growing Arab nationalism spearheaded by President **Gamal Abdul Nasser** of **Egypt**, in March 1956 Hussein dismissed Gen.

Glubb Pasha (1897–1986) as the commander of the **Arab Legion** and renamed the legion the Jordanian Armed Forces. Fearing threats to his newly born son Prince Abdullah (later King **Abdullah II**), King Hussein in 1965 named his younger brother Prince Hassan (1947–) crown prince and hence next in the line of succession. This hierarchy was maintained until 1999, when Hussein suddenly and without any prior hint changed his earlier decision and named his son Abdullah as crown prince and successor.

Due to domestic pressure and regional tensions, Hussein signed a defense pact with Egypt on 30 May 1967 and was thereby dragged into the **June War of 1967** through false information claiming Egyptian successes in the early stages of the war. As a result of Israeli retaliation, Jordan lost control over **East Jerusalem** on 7 June 1967 and subsequently the rest of the **West Bank** as well.

From the time he ascended the throne, King Hussein competed for leadership of the Palestinians. The formation of the **Palestine Liberation Organization** (PLO) in 1964 and the loss of the West Bank in 1967 did not dampen his interest. When the PLO and its **Fedayeen** threatened Hashemite rule in 1970, however, Hussein responded with a massive crackdown, known as the **Black September Massacre**. In the process, he not only secured public order in Jordan but also succeeded in expelling the PLO and its militia from the country.

On 25 September 1973, only days before the **October War of 1973**, King Hussein secretly but unsuccessfully warned Israeli prime minister **Golda Meir** of an impending coordinated military campaign by Egypt and **Syria**.

Despite his opposition, in October 1974 the **Rabat Arab Summit** declared the PLO to be the "sole and legitimate representative" of the Palestinian people, which resulted in the admission of the PLO to the **United Nations** in an observer status. Afraid that the **Intifada**, which broke out in December 1987, would spill over into Jordan, in June 1988 he announced the **Jordanian disengagement** from the **Occupied Territories**.

King Hussein never lost hope of regaining some control over the West Bank. Despite periodic rapprochements such as the **Hussein–Arafat Accord**, relations between Jordan and the PLO, especially with **Yasser Arafat**, always remained tense. The Israeli **Labor Party**'s favorable approach toward the **Jordan Option** and its determination to circumvent the PLO and **Fatah** suited him well. On 11 April 1987, Hussein concluded the **London Agreement**, which sought an enhanced role for Jordan in resolving the Palestinian problem, but this was vetoed by **Likud** leader **Yitzhak Shamir**.

Domestic pressures, especially from the Palestinian population, forced King Hussein to support President Saddam Hussein (1937–) of **Iraq** during the **Kuwait War**. This considerably weakened his standing and influence among his regional friends and Western allies. Seeking to regain his previous influence, he became the foremost supporter of the new Middle East peace initiative of U.S. secretary of state James Baker (1930–). In October 1991, the Palestinians agreed to be part of the joint Jordanian–Palestinian delegation that went to the **Madrid Conference**.

Initially King Hussein was surprised by Israel's desire to negotiate directly with the PLO and to conclude the **Oslo Accords**, but he was determined to capitalize on the new opening. Having maintained clandestine relations with Israel since the 1950s, he was quick to sign the **Washington Declaration**, a day after the **Declaration of Principles** between Israel and the PLO was signed on the White House lawn. This resulted in the **Israel–Jordan Peace Treaty** signed on 26 October 1994. He managed to secure a special role for Jordan over religious sites in the Old City of Jerusalem.

Hussein developed a close personal friendship with Israeli prime minister **Yitzhak Rabin**, and in November 1995, the king attended and delivered a moving eulogy at Rabin's funeral in Jerusalem. His relations with **Benjamin Netanyahu**, however, were tense. The Israeli attempt to assassinate a **Hamas** leader in Amman in September 1997 sparked one of the worst exchanges between the two leaders. The incident, known as the **Masha'al Affair**, ended with Israel releasing **Sheikh Ahmed Yassin** from prison. Despite this, in October 1998, King Hussein came back from his hospital bed in Rochester, Minnesota, to help Netanyahu and Arafat conclude the **Wye Memorandum**. After a long battle with cancer, on 7 February 1999, King Hussein passed away and was succeeded to the throne by his son Abdullah II.

HUSSEIN–ARAFAT ACCORD. After the **Black September Massacre** of 1970, relations between **Jordan** and the **Palestine Liberation Organization** (PLO) remained tense. Reconciliation efforts by **Egypt** finally proved successful when the Palestine National Council met in Amman in November 1984 and paved the way for negotiations between King **Hussein** of Jordan and PLO chairman **Yasser Arafat**. On 11 February 1985, they reached an agreement, calling for complete Israeli withdrawal from the **Occupied Territories** and the right of self-determination of the Palestinians. Both leaders also agreed that Palestinians would exercise their inalienable right of self-determination toward the formation of the "proposed confederated Arab states of Jordan and Palestine." Proposing an **international conference** on the Middle East, the accord suggested a joint Jordanian–Palestinian delegation. In July 1985, at the request of the **United States**, Hussein forwarded seven names suggested by Arafat for the possible Jordanian–Palestinian delegation. The list, which comprised senior and middle-level PLO functionaries, was rejected by Israel.

Arafat's insistence on U.S. recognition of the right of self-determination for Palestinians in return for the acceptance by the PLO of **Resolution 242** and **Resolution 338** of the **United Nations** Security Council led to the failure of another round of talks between Hussein and Arafat in Amman on 8 February 1986. Soon, each accused the other of reneging on previous agreements. In a nationwide address on 22 February 1987, King Hussein declared that Jordan was "unable to continue to coordinate politically with the PLO" and hinted that Palestinians should look for an alternative leadership.

HUSSEIN–MCMAHON CORRESPONDENCE. During the early years of World War I, the high commissioner of **Great Britain** in Cairo, Sir Henry McMahon (1862–1949), exchanged correspondence with Sharif Hussein ibn Ali of Mecca (1852–1931) concerning the future of the Ottoman Empire. Between 14 July 1915 and 30 March 1916, they exchanged 10 letters wherein **Great Britain** urged the sharif to launch a rebellion against Turkish rule and in return promised to support the establishment of an independent Arab kingdom under his leadership. Based on this assurance, in June 1916 Sharif Hussein launched the **Arab Revolt** (1916–1918) and declared Arab independence from Ottoman rule.

The two sides, however, disagreed over the territorial limits of the Arab state that was to be created out of the Ottoman Empire, especially over the inclusion of Palestine in the proposed state. The British commitments concerning the inclusion of Palestine in the proposed

Arab state under Hussein have remained contentious since then. In a bid to dispel the Arab claims, Secretary of State for the Colonies Winston Churchill (1874–1965) produced the **Churchill White Paper** in 1922 and clarified that the "whole of Palestine West of the Jordan [River] was excluded from Sir Henry McMahon's pledge" to Sharif Hussein. Arabs and Palestinians tend to differ with this interpretation, and in 1939, the British government admitted that the language in which the exclusion of Palestine "was expressed was not so specific and unmistakable as it was thought to be at the time." *See also* FAISAL–WEIZMANN AGREEMENT; MANDATE, PALESTINE.

– I –

INTERNATIONAL CONFERENCE. In early 1986, both King **Hussein** of **Jordan** and President **Hosni Mubarak** of **Egypt** floated the idea of an international conference on the Middle East with the participation of both the superpowers, the **United States** and the **Soviet Union**. This received warm endorsement of the **Labor Party** component of Israel's national unity government (1984–1990), but was opposed by the **Likud**. The issue was revisited during the preparatory stage for the **Madrid Conference** of 1991, but the format was tailored to Israeli demands whereby the inaugural session in the Spanish capital would be followed by bilateral negotiations between Israel and its Arab partners.

INTERNATIONAL CRIMINAL COURT (ICC). Since its establishment, Israel has supported the idea of an international regime to try individuals charged with crimes against humanity, aggressions, genocide, and war crimes. Over the years, however, the growing anti-Israeli positions of the **United Nations** and other regional and international organizations and groups compelled Israel to reexamine its position. It became apprehensive that such a court would be politicized and loaded against the Jewish state. Hence, when the Rome Conference approved the statute of the ICC on 17 July 1998, Israel voted against it.

INTIFADA (1987–1993). On 9 December 1987, four Palestinians were killed in a traffic accident in Gaza involving an Israeli vehicle. The funeral of the workers of the Jabaliya **refugee** camp resulted in violent protests against Israeli security forces, who responded with live ammunition leading to the deaths of three more youths. The unrest soon spread to the **West Bank** and transformed into a popular uprising against Israeli occupation. The spontaneous outburst was initially led by Palestinian youths. The scope and intensity of protest surprised both Israel and the Palestinian leadership. Soon the **Unified National Leadership of the Uprising** (UNLU), consisting of various **Palestine Liberation Organization** (PLO) factions as well as **Islamic Jihad**, began coordinating the movement. Through periodic pamphlets, the UNLU issued calls for protest actions.

With notable exceptions, often associated with **Hamas**, the Intifada remained a nonviolent mass movement supported by most segments of the Palestinian population. Except for stone throwing, the resistance to occupation manifested itself primarily as various forms of noncooperation, including strikes, a boycott of Israeli goods, and similar moves. The heavy-handed Israeli responses—the prolonged closure of **Occupied Territories**, preventive detentions, **deportation** of Palestinians, house demolitions, travel restrictions, and other forms of collective punishment—not only fueled the rebellion but also undermined the Israeli position among Western countries. The image of sling-waving young Palestinians taking on the Israeli military might presented the Palestinians as the new David taking on the mighty Goliath.

The Intifada brought the Palestinian question, marginalized by the prolonged Iran–Iraq War, back to center stage and projected it as the prime destabilizing factor in the Middle East. By 1990, the Intifada had run its course, and the outbreak of the **Kuwait War** gradually shifted international focus away from the Palestinian problem. In 1993, it formally ended with the signing of the **Oslo Accords**. According to Israeli human rights watch group B'tselem, 1,346 Palestinians, including 276 children, and 256 Israeli civilians, including 18 children, were killed during the Intifada. *See also* AL-AQSA INTIFADA; ALGIERS DECLARATION; JORDANIAN DISENGAGEMENT.

INTIFADA, AL-AQSA. *See* AL-AQSA INTIFADA.

IRAN. The involvement of Iran in the Arab–Israeli conflict began in 1947, when it was nominated to the 11-member **United Nations Special Commission on Palestine**. Along with India and Yugoslavia, Iran presented a **Federal Plan** as a solution to the Palestine problem. On 29 November 1947, it joined other Islamic countries in the **United Nations** in voting against the **Partition Plan**. However, on 6 March 1950, Iran recognized the Jewish state. As a part of his policy in support of the **United States**, Reza Shah Pehlavi (1919–1980) developed close ties with Israel and even supplied oil to the Jewish state.

The Islamic revolution in February 1979 brought about a fundamental shift in Iran's policy toward Israel, and opposition to Israel became a cornerstone of Iranian foreign policy. Under the leadership of Ayatollah Ruhollah Khomeini (1912–1989), the Islamic republic recognized the **Palestine Liberation Organization** (PLO) and called for the liberation of all Palestinian lands, including **Jerusalem**, from Israeli control. Since then, Iran has opposed any reconciliation with Israel and emerged as a prime opponent of the **Oslo Process**. Critical of Palestinian leader **Yasser Arafat**'s peaceful approach to Israel, Iran increased its support of **Hamas**. Iran was suspected of involvement in several incidents of **terrorism** against Israel, including the **Buenos Aires Bombing**. In January 2002, in the *Karine* **Affair**, Israeli naval commandos seized the *Karine-A*, a Lebanese-registered freighter, in the international waters of the Red Sea. It was carrying about 50 tons of weapons, including rockets and missiles, which Israel claimed were supplied by Iran for the **Palestinian National Authority**.

Similarly, Iran was also instrumental in the formation and growth of **Hezbollah** in **Lebanon**, which in the 1980s and 1990s conducted a militant campaign against the Israeli presence in the **security zone** in southern Lebanon. Since late 2002, disclosures of the Iranian nuclear weapons program and its development of long-range missile capabilities have increased tensions between the two countries. The election of Mahmoud Ahmadinejad (1956–) as president in June 2005 witnessed increased anti-Israeli rhetoric from Tehran.

IRAQ. The **Hussein–McMahon Correspondence** marked the formal entry of Iraq into the Arab–Israeli conflict. The high commissioner of **Great Britain** in **Egypt**, Sir Henry McMahon (1862–1949), and Sharif Hussein (1852–1931) of Mecca exchanged letters during the early years of World War I, in which **Great Britain** urged the sharif to launch a rebellion against Ottoman Empire rule. In return, Britain promised to support the establishment of an independent Arab kingdom under Sharif

Hussein. Based on this assurance and aimed at creating an independent Arab kingdom comprising Hijaz, **Syria**, and Iraq, Sharif Hussein of Mecca proclaimed Arab independence on 10 June 1916 and called on his followers to rebel against Ottoman rule. This proved short lived, however, and Hussein was defeated and driven out by the al-Sauds.

Meanwhile, under a secret arrangement known as the **Sykes–Picot Agreement**, Great Britain and **France** had agreed to divide the Arab provinces of the Ottoman Empire after World War I. Under this plan, France would control **Lebanon** and Syria, while Iraq and Palestine would go to Britain. Czarist Russia approved the agreement in return for British and French recognition of its own territorial ambitions, but in November 1917, the plan was published and repudiated by the Bolsheviks. Even though both parties sought to distance themselves from the agreement, the final distribution of the Ottoman Empire partially reflected the Sykes–Picot Agreement.

In March 1920, in return for the support of Sharif Hussein against the Ottoman Empire and with active British support, Hussein's son Emir Faisal ibn Hussein (1883–1933) proclaimed himself king of Syria. He aspired to include and unify Lebanon, Palestine, and **Transjordan** under his rule, but he was soon driven out of French-controlled Damascus. The British then installed him as the monarch of Iraq, where the increasing *Aliya* and Arabization of the Palestinian issue also brought forth nationalist pressures.

As a founding member of the **Arab League**, Iraq vehemently opposed the partition of Palestine. On 15 May 1948, the day after Israel was established, Iraqi forces joined the other Arab armies in invading Israel and fought alongside the **Arab Legion** on the eastern front. At the end of the **Arab–Israeli War of 1947–1948**, acting **United Nations mediator** Ralph J. Bunche (1904–1971) requested that Iraq join the armistice negotiations at Rhodes. On 13 February 1949 (two weeks prior to the signing of the Egypt–Israeli **Armistice Agreement**), Iraqi foreign minister A. Hafid informed the **United Nations** that "the terms of armistice which will be agreed upon by the Arab State neighbors of Palestine, namely, Egypt, Transjordan, Syria and Lebanon will be regarded as acceptable" to Iraq. This explicit Iraqi willingness to recognize and accept the armistice agreements between Israel and its Arab neighbors is often ignored.

As part of its policy of containing the **Soviet Union**, the **United States** succeeded in encouraging Iraq and **Turkey** to sign a mutual defense treaty in 1955. Gradually Great Britain, **Iran**, and Pakistan were brought into a larger agreement, popularly known as the **Baghdad Pact**. This arrangement drew widespread criticism from other countries of the region, especially Egypt, and the pact became a rallying cry for **Gamal Abdel Nasser** to discredit conservative monarchs who opposed him and his radical pan-Arabism. The overthrow of the monarchy in Iraq in July 1958 by a coup led by Gen. Abdul Karim Qassem (1914–1963) reduced the fortunes of the Baghdad Pact and, following the Iraqi withdrawal in March 1959, the alliance was renamed the Central Treaty Organization (CENTO).

As part of the preemptive strike against Arab air forces on 5 June 1967 at the beginning of the **June of War of 1967**, Israel also attacked H-2 and H-3 airfields in Western Iraq, but Iraq did not take part in the war. Iraq was an active participant during the **October War of 1973**, however, when the Arab oil-exporting countries decided to institute an oil embargo (the **oil crisis**) against the United States and its allies for their support for Israel. Similarly, in response to Israel adopting the **Jerusalem Law** in August 1980, Iraq joined **Saudi Arabia** and threatened to sever economic and diplomatic ties with any country that recognized **Jerusalem** as Israel's capital.

Iraq was vehemently opposed to the peace initiatives of President **Anwar Sadat** of Egypt and considered them a violation of Arab unity and the resolutions adopted at the **Khartoum Arab Summit** in 1967. Baghdad became the rallying point for anti-Sadat forces in the region. Iraq played a pivotal role in the isolation of Egypt and its temporary expulsion from the Arab League and the Organization of the Islamic Conference.

Correspondingly, while supporting the Palestinian cause and the leadership of the **Palestine Liberation Organization** (PLO), Iraq also played host to a number of radical Palestinian groups, some of which were opposed to the leadership of **Yasser Arafat** and were accused of involvement in **terrorism**. One such group was the **Arab Liberation Front**, a militant, pan-Arabist, and left-leaning Palestinian group sponsored, based, and directed by the Iraqi military. Similarly, the country also hosted the **Palestine Liberation Front** (PLF), which was linked to the *Achille Lauro* **Affair**; PLF leader Abu Abbas (1948–2004) was captured by Allied forces in Iraq in April 2003 and died while in allied custody in 2004. Another Palestinian military group, the **Fatah Revolutionary Council**, headed by Abu Nidal, also enjoyed some Iraqi patronage; in August 2002, Abu Nidal was found dead in Baghdad under mysterious circumstances.

For its part, Israel long pursued an anti-Iraqi policy. Besides the preemptive air strike during the June War of 1967, Israel conducted an air raid on 7 June 1981 on a nearly completed nuclear reactor close to Baghdad in Osiraq. Constructed with French cooperation, the reactor was under the full-scope safeguards of the International Atomic Energy Agency (IAEA), the international nuclear regulatory body. The **Osiraq Bombing** was seen as a sign of Israeli determination to prevent any of its adversaries in the region from acquiring nuclear capabilities. Israel justified its raid on the Iraqi reactor on the basis that a state of war still existed between the two countries because of Iraq's refusal to sign an armistice agreement in 1949—ignoring Foreign Minister Hafid's February 1949 statement accepting the armistice agreements.

If the prolonged Iran–Iraq War marginalized the Palestinian cause, the Iraqi invasion of Kuwait on 2 August 1990 posed new challenges. Iraqi president Saddam Hussein (1937–) linked his actions in Kuwait to the Palestinian problem and demanded Israeli withdrawal from the **Occupied Territories** as a precondition for his withdrawal from Kuwait. The endorsement of this position by the Palestinian leadership proved counterproductive, alienating Arafat from oil-rich countries such as **Saudi Arabia** and Kuwait and resulting in the expulsion of tens of thousands of Palestinian workers from these countries.

On 17 January 1991, a day after the United States launched its military campaign against Iraq, Iraq launched a Scud missile against Israel. Saddam Hussein (1937–) hoped to break the U.S.-led international coalition against Iraq by dragging Israel into the conflict. However, U.S. pressure and strategic calculations stopped Israel from responding to the 39 Scuds that were eventually launched against it.

Following the **Kuwait War**, the United States relaunched the Middle East peace process. Having supported the losing side, Arafat's options were limited, and he agreed to the idea of sending a Palestinian delegation to the **Madrid Conference** as a joint delegation with **Jordan**. Since the late 1990s, the U.S. desire to weave an anti-Iraq coalition resulted in the United States promoting a number of half-hearted peace initiatives, such as the **Bush Plan** and the **Middle East Road Map**, aimed at placating the Arab world. With the American invasion in 2003, Iraq ceased being a major player in the Arab–Israeli conflict.

IRGUN. At times referred to as **Haganah** Bet (Haganah-B), Irgun Tz-vail Leumi was a Jewish military organization in the Palestine **Mandate** associated with the Revisionist stream of the **Zionist** movement. It was established and headed by Avraham Tehomi and was organized with strict military discipline. An attempt in 1937 at a merger between Irgun and Haganah led to a split in the movement.

Based on the teachings of Vladimir Ze'ev Jabotinsky (1880–1940), the architect of Revisionism, Irgun believed that an armed Jewish force was a precondition for the realization of a Jewish state, and it was committed to establishing such a state on both sides of the Jordan River. This radical position and its refusal to abide by the decisions of the **Jewish Agency** brought Irgun into conflict with the *Yishuv* leadership. Until the publication of the **MacDonald White Paper** in 1939, the military actions of Irgun were focused against the Arabs, but thereafter the Mandate authorities became the prime target of Irgun. Meanwhile, not satisfied with the policies of Irgun, in 1940, Avraham Stern broke away and founded the **Stern Gang**.

In December 1943, **Menachem Begin** took over as the commander of Irgun and remained in that position until its dissolution following the establishment of Israel. Irgun conducted a militant campaign against the interests of **Great Britain** and, on 22 July 1946, blew up the Mandate headquarters in the **King David Hotel Explosion** in **Jerusalem**. On 10 April 1948, Irgun forces joined hands with the Stern Gang and carried out the **Deir Yassin Massacre** in which scores of Arab civilians were butchered.

The organization was active even after the formation of the State of Israel and independently sought to import arms for its operations during the **Arab–Israeli War of 1947–1948**. However, on 20 June 1948, the *Altalena*, a ship carrying arms supplies for Irgun, was sunk off the coast of Tel Aviv on the orders of Israeli prime minister **David Ben-Gurion** in what became known as the *Altalena* **Affair**. Eventually on 1 September 1948, Irgun was disbanded and most of its members joined the **Israel Defense Forces**.

ISLAMIC JIHAD. In the 1980s, Abdul Aziz Oudeh and Fathi Shiqaqi (?–1995) split from the **Muslim Brotherhood** and founded this militant Islamic faction. Oudeh headed the movement until his **deportation** in 1988, and he was then succeeded by Shiqaqi, who was killed in Malta on 26 October 1995 by Israeli commandos. Following the **assassination** leadership of the group went to Ramadan Abdullah Salah. Islamic Jihad advocates armed struggle for the liberation of Palestine, which it considers a precondition for the Islamization of society, and calls for the establishment of an Islamic state that would replace Israel. However, unlike **Hamas**, Islamic Jihad does not perceive itself to be a rival to the **Palestine Liberation Organization**, and during the **Intifada** (1987–1993), it actively cooperated with the **Unified National Leadership of the Uprising**. Islamic Jihad was vehemently opposed to the **Oslo Process**, and since the early 1990s, it has claimed responsibility for various **suicide attacks** inside Israel. Following the outbreak of the **Al-Aqsa Intifada**, it has renewed its militant campaign against Israel, including suicide bombings. Nevertheless, Islamic Jihad took an active part in the **Cairo Dialogue** aimed at temporarily stopping the suicide attacks and, in March 2005, joined other military groups in agreeing to a *tahidiyeh* (a temporary lull in fighting, as opposed to an actual cease-fire or *hudna*).

ISMAILIA SUMMIT. On 26 December 1977, President **Anwar Sadat** of **Egypt** and Israeli prime minister **Menachem Begin** met in the Egyptian town of Ismailia. Both sides agreed to institutionalize the periodic meetings of military and political committees. The first meeting of the political committee was formally inaugurated in **Jerusalem** on 17 January 1978. Prime Minister Begin, Egyptian foreign minister Muhammad Ibrahim Kamel (1927–2001), and U.S. secretary of state Cyrus Vance (1917–2002) participated in the committee meeting in Jerusalem. *See also* JERUSALEM VISIT.

ISRAEL DEFENSE FORCES (IDF). Israel's land, air, and sea forces operate under the unified command of the Israel Defense Forces. With a civilian as its head, the Ministry of Defense is in charge of the IDF. Over the years, a number of former generals, including **Moshe Dayan**, **Yitzhak Rabin**, **Ehud Barak**, and **Ariel Sharon**, have held the position of defense minister. The chief of the General Staff is the commander of the IDF and has the rank of lieutenant general. He is formally appointed on the defense minister's recommendation for three years, although the government can extend his service to four (and in rare occasions even five) years.

The chief of the General Staff reports directly to the defense minister and indirectly to the prime minister and the government.

The origin of the IDF can be traced to prestate paramilitary security organizations such as **Hashomer**, **Haganah**, and **Palmah**. On 27 June 1948, Prime Minister and Defense Minister **David Ben-Gurion** unified the military arm of the *Yishuv*, and the IDF came into being right in the middle of **Arab–Israeli War of 1947–1948**. The IDF played a critical role in consolidation of the Jewish state that had been proclaimed on 14 May 1948 as well as in expanding its territorial limits beyond those areas allotted by the **Partition Plan** of the **United Nations**.

Since its foundation, the IDF has relied heavily on conscription. Men and women are drafted at the age of 18, serve for three and two years, respectively, and are liable for annual reserve duty until the age of 45 and 24, respectively. While the draft was made compulsory for Druze citizens, **Israeli Arabs** are not required to serve but they can. The IDF plays an important role in the absorption of new immigrants.

Following the **June War of 1967**, when Israel captured the **West Bank**, **Gaza Strip**, **Golan Heights** and **Sinai Peninsula**, the operative responsibility of the IDF increased considerably. The **military government**'s treatment of the Palestinian population in the **Occupied Territories** has often not only brought the IDF into serious differences with the Israeli government but also resulted in increased international criticism, especially during the **Intifada** (1987–1993) and the **Al-Aqsa Intifada**.

The intelligence arm of the IDF, Aman, occupies an important role in Israel's security and strategic doctrine. Its failure to accurately read the intelligence information proved costly during the **October War of 1973**. Similarly, the IDF's involvement in **Lebanon** following **Operation Peace for Galilee** was painful and protracted. This resulted in its unilateral **Lebanese withdrawal** that was completed in the summer of 2000.

On the operational level, the IDF is divided into four branches, namely Ground Forces, Air Force, Navy, and Military Intelligence. IDF units operate as small units relying on swift movement, and its policy is based on preemptive strategy. The IDF is considered to be one of the most advanced armies in the world. The bulk of its military hardware is supplied by the **United States**, but Israel also has a robust domestic military industry that includes leading firms such as

Israel Aircraft Industries, Israel Miliary Industry, Elbit, El-Op, Rafael, Soltam, and dozens of smaller firms.

In terms of territorial jurisdiction, the IDF is divided into three commands: northern, central, and southern. A new Home Front command was created during the **Kuwait War**. IDF units also undertake various counter**terrorism** operations, including the **Entebbe Operation**. Special units such as **Sayeret Matkal** have carried out distant military operations such as the **Tunis Raid** and **Osiraq Bombing**. Over the years, the IDF has mastered the art of rescue missions and has been active in different parts of the world affected by earthquakes and other natural calamities. *See also* MILITARY ADMINISTRATION; TARGETED KILLING.

ISRAELI ARABS. After the outbreak of hostilities in the **Arab–Israeli War of 1947–1948**, a large number of Palestinians opted to stay behind in areas that became the State of Israel and are popularly called Israeli Arabs. The nomenclature underscores their dual identities and dilemmas. They are citizens of Israel but belong to the larger Arab–Palestinian nation. Due to security considerations, until 1966 Israel placed the Arab-dominated areas under **military administration**.

In 1948, Israeli Arabs numbered 150,000, and by 2002, the figure stood at about 1,000,000. They predominantly inhabit the Galilee area, northern Israel, and coastal plains. A substantial Arab population lives in cities and towns such as **Jerusalem**, Haifa, Jaffa, Acre, and Nazareth. Due to distinct religious and cultural identities, the Israeli Arabs are subdivided into Muslim Arabs, Christian Arabs, Druze, and Bedouins.

Free and equal before the law, Israeli Arabs enjoy all political rights in Israel and participate in, contest, and are elected to the Knesset as well as local councils. At the same time, numerous legal and quasi-legal impediments and deprivations hamper their aspirations for equality in Israeli society. The exclusive Jewish identities of Israel and unique legislation such as the **Law of Return** and discriminations associated with conscription are resented by the Israeli Arabs.

The **Intifada** (1987–1993) rekindled the Palestinian consciousness of the Israeli Arabs and was manifested in the formation of exclusive Arab political parties. The Arab leaders have supported the demand for a **Palestinian state** for a long time, as well as the need for Israel to recognize and negotiate with the **Palestine Liberation Organization**.

Their support from the back bench ensured the survival of the **Labor Party** government headed by **Yitzhak Rabin** and **Shimon Peres** in 1992–1996 and enabled it to pursue the peace process with the Palestinians.

The outbreak of the **Al-Aqsa Intifada** once again brought them to the forefront and, in October 2000, Israeli Arabs held demonstrations in various Arab towns and villages. During clashes with the police, 13 Israeli Arabs were killed. This incident played a critical role in the Israeli Arabs abandoning the Labor Party during **Ehud Barak**'s re-election campaign in February 2001. *See also* ARD, AL-; JERUSALEM PALESTINIANS; KFAR KASSEM MASSACRE; LAND DAY; NAQBA, AL-.

ISRAEL–JORDAN PEACE TREATY. On 14 September 1993, a day after the signing of the **Declaration of Principles**, Israeli and Jordanian delegations in Washington, D.C., initialed an agreement that set the agenda for a formal peace agreement between the two countries. This brought into the open the prolonged ties that had been maintained even before the formation of Israel. On 25 July 1994, King **Hussein** of **Jordan** and Israeli prime minister **Yitzhak Rabin** signed the Washington Declaration, which terminated the state of belligerency between the two countries. On 17 October 1994, Israel and Jordan initialed a peace agreement in Amman, and on 26 October, Prime Ministers Rabin and Abdul-Salam Majali (1925–) signed the formal peace treaty. A number of international leaders, including U.S. president **Bill Clinton** (1946–), attended the public ceremony in the Arava in the Jordan Valley. Chairman **Yasser Arafat**, who by then had become the head of the **Palestinian National Authority**, was not invited.

Consisting of 30 articles and five annexures, the treaty addressed a number of issues, including border demarcation, water rights, environmental issues, Palestinian **refugees**, and border crossing. It demarcated and formalized the international borders between the two countries based on the maps of **Mandate** Palestine. Jordan agreed to lease back for 25 years the farmland in the Arava returned to its sovereignty but cultivated by Israeli farmers. Israel recognized the "special interests" of Jordan in the Islamic holy places in **Jerusalem**. In November 1994, both countries agreed to establish full diplomatic relations. The **Al-Aqsa Intifada** temporarily weakened the Israeli–Jordanian ties, and Jordan did not nominate a new ambassador when the post fell vacant in late 2004, but at the **Sharm al-Sheikh Summit** in 2005, it agreed to return an ambassador to Tel Aviv. *See also* ARAB LEAGUE; ARAB LEGION; JERICHO CONFERENCE; NAHARAYIM SHOOTING.

ISRAEL–LEBANON AGREEMENT. Following its invasion of **Lebanon** in 1982, designated **Operation Peace for Galilee**, Israel sought a formal agreement with Lebanon. It hoped that its agreement with the Maronite Christian–dominated Lebanese government would ensure the withdrawal of all foreign forces from Lebanon. Prime Minister **Menachem Begin** conditioned the Israeli withdrawal from Lebanon upon a simultaneous withdrawal of the forces of **Syria** stationed in Lebanon following the Riyadh summit of the **Arab League** in October 1976. This idea gradually culminated in a peace agreement, similar to the one it had signed with **Egypt**.

On 11 October 1982, during the controversy over the **Sabra and Shatila Massacre**, the Israeli cabinet approved a working paper toward achieving a peace treaty with Lebanon. On 16 December, Defense Minister **Ariel Sharon** disclosed that a secret agreement had been reached with Lebanon, which would lead to political gains for Israel following the military campaign. As many as 35 sessions of negotiations were held in Khalde in southern Lebanon and Kiryat Shmona and Netanya in Israel between December 1982 and May 1983. Finally, on 17 May 1983, a formal agreement was signed in two separate ceremonies in Khalde and Kiryat Shmona.

Falling short of a peace treaty, it presented the modalities for Israel's withdrawal from Lebanon, in return for specific security arrangements in southern Lebanon and certain elements of normalization. It also formalized their border, and both sides agreed that "the existing international boundary between Israel and Lebanon is inviolable."

Though ratified by both sides, the willingness of the government of Amine Gemayel (1942–) to a sign such an agreement with Israel even while the latter was militarily occupying large parts of Lebanon considerably weakened the position of the Beirut government. Moreover, since the beginning of negotiations, the agreement had been vehemently opposed by Syria. On 5 March 1984, Lebanon formally abrogated the agreement. *See also* ASSASSINATION.

ISRAEL–SYRIA DISENGAGEMENT OF FORCES AGREEMENT. In May 1974, helped by the **shuttle diplomacy** of U.S. secretary of state Henry Kissinger (1923–), Israel and **Syria** reached an agreement that reaffirmed the cease-fire achieved at the end of the **October War of 1973**. It paved the way for the disengagement of Israeli and Syrian forces on the **Golan Heights** and the creation of disengagement zones between the two armies. On 31 May 1974, a new cease-fire line was established on the Golan Heights, slightly to the west of the post-1967 cease-fire line. As part of the agreement, Israel withdrew from the Syrian town of Quneitra.

ISRAEL–UNITED STATES MEMORANDUM OF UNDERSTANDING (MoU). As part of its Interim Agreement with **Egypt**, on 1 September 1975 Israel signed a memorandum of understanding with the **United States**, which formed part of the **Sinai II Agreement**. Through this MoU, Israel secured a number of politically significant concessions. The United States pledged:

- to be "fully responsive" to Israel's defense, energy, and economic needs, subject to congressional approval and availability of resources
- to consult with Israel, in case of military involvement of the **Soviet Union** in the Middle East
- to "coordinate" with Israel about the timing and format of the **Geneva Conference of 1973**
- not to recognize the **Palestine Liberation Organization** as long as the latter "does not recognize Israel's right to exist and does not accept Security Council **Resolutions 242** and **338**"
- to oppose any changes and modifications to Resolutions 242 and 338

It also guaranteed American support for ensuring Israel's freedom of navigation through the **Suez Canal**.

Since then, Israel has signed a number of similar understandings with the United States and consolidated its strategic ties with Washington. As part of the **Egypt–Israel Peace Treaty** on 26 March 1979, Israel and the United States signed a MoU that provided a number of economic and security guarantees to Israel. Signed by Foreign Minister **Moshe**

Dayan and U.S. secretary of state Cyrus Vance (1917–2002), it undertook to supply oil for 15 years should Israel find it difficult to procure it from the international market.

On 30 November 1981, Israeli defense minister **Ariel Sharon** and U.S. defense secretary Caspar Weinberger signed a MoU on strategic cooperation that provided the framework for joint military exercises between the two armed forces. This was the first formal security agreement between the two countries and sought to deter Soviet threats to the Middle East.

On 21 April 1988, U.S. president Ronald Reagan (1911–2004) and Israeli prime minister **Yitzhak Shamir** signed an MoU in Washington, D.C., that designated Israel as "a major non-NATO ally of the United States." Coming in the midst of the **Intifada** (1987–1993) and growing international criticism of Israel over its handling of the Palestinian uprising, it established a comprehensive framework for bilateral consultations.

On 31 October 1998, Israel and the United States signed a MoU on strategic cooperation. Unlike the previous ones, which were ministerial-level agreements, this one was signed by U.S. president **Bill Clinton** and Israeli prime minister **Benjamin Netanyahu**. *See also* RESOLUTION 242; RESOLUTION 338.

IZZEDDIN AL-QASSEM. The military wing of **Hamas**. It is named after **Muslim Brotherhood** member Sheikh Izzeddin al-Qassem (d. 1935), who preached jihad against the **Mandate** administration of **Great Britain** and the **Zionists**. He was killed by the British in a military operation near Jenin in 1935 and was buried in Haifa. The Hamas fighters have claimed responsibility for a number of **terrorist** attacks and **suicide attacks** inside Israel. It is a closely knit organization and has remained free from desertion or infiltration. However, since the outbreak of the **Al-Aqsa Intifada**, Israel pursued a policy of **assassination** and targeted killing against a number of militants belonging to the Izzeddin al-Qassem. The presence of distinct political and military wings impedes a number of Western countries from following the U.S. example and proscribing Hamas as a terrorist organization. *See also* OSLO PROCESS; QASSEM II.

– J –

JARRING MISSION. Following the recommendations of **Resolution 242** of the **United Nations** Security Council, on 27 December 1967 Gunnar Jarring (1907–2002), the Swedish ambassador to the **Soviet Union**, was appointed the special representative to the Middle East of the UN secretary-general. Jarring was entrusted with the task of implementing Resolution 242. Bound by the **Khartoum Arab Summit** resolution of the "three *no*'s," **Egypt** was reluctant to conduct direct negotiations with Israel aimed at securing the Israeli withdrawal from territories occupied during the **June War of 1967**. For its part, Israel was determined not to comply with the Arab demand without ensuring its recognition by its adversaries and security arrangements. The determination of both sides to place their demands as a precondition for negotiation precluded any progress. To circumvent the difficulties facing direct negotiations, in March 1969 Jarring submitted a list of questions to Israel and its Arab neighbors. However, the **War of Attrition** overtook this, and soon the Jarring Mission was suspended.

Jarring renewed his mission in February 1971, following the end of the War of Attrition and the changing of the guard in Egypt after the death of President **Gamal Abdul Nasser** of **Egypt**. Jarring demanded a complete Israeli withdrawal to the borders of **Mandate** Palestine and an Egyptian willingness to enter into a peace agreement with Israel. Refusal of both parties to accept such a proposal eventually led to the termination of the Jarring Mission. *See also* OCCUPIED TERRITORIES; ROGERS PLAN; UNITED STATES INITIATIVE.

JENIN CONTROVERSY. As a part of the **Defensive Shield Operation** in early April 2002, Israeli forces entered Jenin. This led to fierce resistance from its residents, especially in the adjacent **refugee** camps. The siege continued until 11 April, during which Israel conducted large-scale military operations described as a "clean-up," and Palestinians accused the **Israel Defense Forces** of organizing a massacre in Jenin. In response, the **United Nations** Security Council called for an international commission to investigate the claims—a move vehemently opposed by Israel. The report prepared by the UN commission, without any field investigation, dismissed Palestinian claims of a massacre even though 52 Palestinians were killed during the military operations. The presence of arms, training facilities, and a huge quantity of weapons found inside the refugee camps in the area run by the **United Nations Relief and Works Agency** raised doubts about the functioning of the refugee welfare organization.

JERICHO. Considered the oldest inhabited city in the world, Jericho lies northwest of the Dead Sea. Among other things, it is believed to be the place where Joshua led the Israelites to the Land of the Canaan and contains the Mount of Temptation, where Jesus Christ was said to have fasted after his baptism. The city was rebuilt several times and, in modern times, was rediscovered in 1907. It was at the **Jericho Conference** of December 1948 that the pro-Hashemite Palestinians met and asked the monarch of **Transjordan** to assume control over the **West Bank**. Following the signing of the **Cairo Agreement** of May 1994, the city, along with the **Gaza Strip**, came under the control of the **Palestinian National Authority** (PNA). Disagreements between Israel and the **Palestine Liberation Organization** over the size of the Jericho area partly contributed to delays in the implementation of the **Declaration of Principles** and the Israeli withdrawal from the Gaza-Jericho area. In the wake of the **Al-Aqsa Intifada**, Israel reoccupied Jericho, and the area remained under Israeli control until 16 March 2005, when the **Israel Defense Forces** handed over security control of the city to the PNA.

JERICHO CONFERENCE. On 1 December 1948, a congress of Palestinian Arabs comprising notables and mayors from the **West Bank** met in Jericho with Hebron mayor Mohammed Ali al-Jabri as president. It adopted a resolution calling on King **Abdullah I** of **Jordan** to "unite" the West Bank and **East Jerusalem**, which were controlled by **Transjordan**, with the Hashemite Kingdom. This was endorsed by the Transjordanian parliament on 13 December. A second conference of Palestinian notables was held in Nablus on 28 December 1948. In March 1949, the West Bank was brought under civilian rule. On 24 April 1950, the Jordanian House of Deputies and the House of Notables held a joint session in Jericho and adopted a resolution supporting the "complete unity between the two sides of the Jordan River and their union into one State, which is the Hashemite Kingdom of Jordan" with King Abdullah I as the monarch.

JERICHO PLAN. Promoted by Israeli minister Yigal Allon (1918–1980) in 1974, the Jericho Plan advocated a partial disengagement agreement with **Jordan** and the return of the **West Bank** city of **Jericho** and its environs to Jordanian rule. Meanwhile, the **Palestine Liberation Organization** (PLO) had emerged as a credible player and, despite King **Hussein**'s opposition, the **Rabat Arab Summit** declared the PLO to be "the sole and legitimate representative" of the Palestinian people. This hardened the traditional Israeli opposition toward the PLO and throttled any progress on the Jericho Plan.

JERUSALEM. Despite its large Jewish majority, on 27 June 1948 **United Nations mediator** Count Folke Bernadotte (1895–1948) suggested handing over the city of Jerusalem to the Kingdom of **Transjordan**. A month later, he visited Jerusalem and suggested the demilitarization of the city, a proposal vehemently rejected by Israel. The **Partition Plan** of 1948 advocated international status for Jerusalem and was reiterated in **Resolution 194** of the **United Nations** General Assembly, adopted in December 1948. On 9 December 1949, the General Assembly adopted Resolution 303 (IV) that declares that "the City of Jerusalem shall be established as a *corpus separatum* under a special international regime and shall be administered by the United Nations." It also asserts that the Trusteeship Council shall be designated to discharge the responsibilities of the Administering Authority. This move was vehemently opposed by Israel as well as Transjordan, which controlled much of the city. On 5 December 1950, Sweden unsuccessfully proposed a resolution in the General Assembly that called for an international regime for Jerusalem and the protection of the holy places.

On 2 August 1948, Israel, which controlled the western part of the city, declared Jerusalem to be Israel-occupied territory and temporarily appointed a military governor. On 30 January 1949, Israel abolished the governor and appointed a civilian administration. Following the elections to the first Knesset, on 14 February Israel's parliament met in Jerusalem and elected Chaim Weizmann (1874–1952) the first president of Israel. Following the adoption of Resolution 303, the Knesset met in Tel Aviv on 13 December and approved a governmental motion to move its seat and that of all government offices to Jerusalem. The Knesset held its first session in Jerusalem on 27 December, and soon other government offices were gradually moved to the city. While the Defense Ministry continues functioning from Tel Aviv, the Foreign Ministry moved to Jerusalem in 1953. Following the **June War of 1967**, the Knesset on 27 June 1967 "extended" Israel's jurisdiction to the Old City in **East Jerusalem** as well.

The **armistice agreement** of April 1949 signed between Israel and **Jordan** recognized the de facto partition of Jerusalem. Jordan, however, refused to honor its commitment under the agreement to ensure "free access to the Holy Places and to cultural institutions and use of the [Jewish] cemetery on the Mount of Olives." Jews were thus prevented from praying at the **Western Wall** until June 1967, when Israel captured the Old City as well as the **West Bank**. Until then even Israeli Muslims were denied access to the holy places.

Following the June War, on 15 August 1967 UN secretary-general U Thant (1909–1974) appointed Ernesto Thalmann of Switzerland to visit and examine the situation in Jerusalem following de facto annexation by Israel. In his report to the secretary-general, Thalmann recorded:

> It was made clear [by Israeli leaders] beyond any doubt that Israel was taking every step to place under its sovereignty those parts of the city which were not controlled by Israel before June 1967. . . . The Israel authorities stated unequivocally that the process of integration was irreversible and not negotiable.

Since the early 1990s, the Congress of the **United States** has been adopting nonbinding resolutions that recognize Jerusalem as the capital of the Jewish state, supported by an overwhelming majority of both Houses. Presidents, however, have used executive powers to avoid implementing these resolutions for diplomatic and strategic reasons.

On 21 March 2005, Prime Minister **Ariel Sharon** approved the construction of 3,500 new homes in a neighborhood that would link the largest settlement of **Ma'aleh Adumim** in the **West Bank** with Jerusalem. *See also* ABU DIS; ARAB–ISRAELI WAR OF 1947–1948; BEILIN–ABU MAZEN PLAN; BERNADOTTE PLAN; JERUSALEM LAW; JERUSALEM PALESTINIANS; ORIENT HOUSE; SECURITY FENCE.

JERUSALEM COMMISSION. On 6 May 1948, the Second Special Session of the **United Nations** General Assembly called on "the Mandatory Power [to] appoint . . . before 15 May 1948, a neutral acceptable to both Arabs and Jews, as Special Municipal Commissioner, who shall, with the cooperation of the community committees already existing in **Jerusalem**, carry out the functions hitherto performed by the Municipal Commission." Accordingly, a Philadelphia attorney named Harold Evans was appointed to the post, but before his arrival, the **Arab–Israeli War of 1947–1948** broke out. *See also* MANDATE, PALESTINE.

JERUSALEM LAWS. On 21 June 1967, the Israeli cabinet decided to expand the jurisdiction of **Jerusalem**, and on 27 June 1967, the Knesset amended two existing laws and brought the eastern part of Jerusalem captured during the **June War of 1967** within the municipal and administrative jurisdiction of the city. This move was aimed at consolidating the Jewish demography of the city. Israel never explicitly described this move as an "annexation," calling it merely an "extension" of Israeli laws to the eastern part. However, since 4 July 1967, when the **United Nations** General Assembly passed Resolution 2253 in its emergency session, this change in the status of Jerusalem has been vehemently denounced.

Reacting to the Israeli efforts to shift foreign embassies to Jerusalem, on 6 August 1980, **Saudi Arabia** and **Iraq**, the two principal Arab oil suppliers of the region, warned that they would sever economic and diplomatic ties with any country that recognized Jerusalem as Israel's capital. A number of states that previously had missions in Jerusalem moved their missions out of the city to Tel Aviv. However, since 1984, both Houses of the **United States** Congress have been pressing the U.S. administration to move its embassy from Tel Aviv to Jerusalem. Due to American pressure, Costa Rica (1982) and El Salvador (1984) moved their embassies to Jerusalem.

On 26 December 1994, the Knesset adopted the "Law Implementing Agreement on Gaza and **Jericho** Areas (Restrictions of Activity)," which sought to prevent the **Palestinian National Authority** from engaging in political, diplomatic, security, or other activities within the city limits of Jerusalem, including those areas annexed by Israel in 1968. Coupled with this legislation, Israel has periodically requested European leaders and envoys not to conduct any official meetings with the Palestinians in the eastern part of the city, lest it be construed as European recognition of their claims to **East Jerusalem** as the capital of the future **Palestinian state**. *See also* ORIENT HOUSE.

JERUSALEM MASSACRE. *See* TEMPLE MOUNT FAITHFUL.

JERUSALEM PALESTINIANS. Various peace plans in the late 1980s, such as the **Baker Plan**, the **Mubarak Plans**, and the **Shamir Plan**, proved to be nonstarters because of Israel's refusal to accept any role for the Palestinians who were residents of **Jerusalem**. In April 1993, the Israeli government headed by **Yitzhak Rabin** modified this stand. Faisal Husseini (1940–2001), who led the Palestinian negotiations with U.S. secretary of state James A. Baker (1930–) prior to the **Madrid Conference** on behalf of the Palestinians, was chosen as the leader of the Palestinian delegation. Until then, he had been part of the steering committee and, due to Israel's opposition, was not part of the bilateral talks that were taking place in Washington, D.C., following the Madrid Conference. Husseini led the eight rounds of talks, which began on 27 April 1993. The Israeli concession came in the midst of growing international criticism over the **deportation** of more than 400 suspected **Hamas** activists.

Jerusalem Palestinians took part in the January 1996 elections to the Palestinian Legislative Assembly. On 21 March 2005, Prime Minister **Ariel Sharon** approved the construction of 3,500 new homes in a neighborhood that would link the largest Jewish settlement in the **West Bank**, **Ma'aleh Adumim**, with Jerusalem. This move further dilutes the proportion of Palestinians living in areas beyond the **Green Line** that were annexed by Israel following the **June War of 1967**. *See also* PLO LAW; SECURITY FENCE.

JERUSALEM VISIT. On 19 November 1977, President **Anwar Sadat** of **Egypt** flew to Israel, met Israeli prime minister **Menachem Begin**, addressed the Knesset, and sowed the seeds for the **Egypt–Israel Peace Treaty**. This sudden move did not go down well within Egypt nor in the Arab world, and Foreign Minister Ismail Fahmi resigned in protest against the proposed visit. *See also* CAMP DAVID ACCORDS; ISMAILIA SUMMIT.

JEWISH AGENCY. The Jewish Agency was established in 1929 under the terms of the **mandate** for Palestine given to **Great Britain**. Article 4 of the **League of Nations** mandate called for the establishment of an appropriate "Jewish Agency . . . for the purpose of advising and cooperating" with the Mandate administration "in such economic, social, and other matters." It further stated that the administration "shall encourage, in co-operation with the Jewish Agency . . . close settlement by Jews, on the land, including State lands and waste lands not required for public purposes" (Art. 6). Until 1929, the **World Zionist Organization** (WZO) had acted as the body specified in the mandate.

The newly formed Jewish Agency consisted of both **Zionist** and non-Zionist Jews and became the worldwide organization responsible for the establishment of a Jewish national home. It became the de facto body responsible for various aspects of the *Yishuv* life, including immigration, settlement, and economic development. Besides representing the *Yishuv* before the Mandate administration, the agency was diplomatically active in promoting the Jewish home in Palestine.

Through diverse activities such as promoting *Aliya*, fund raising, social welfare activities, economic enterprises, and cultural activities, the Jewish Agency formulated and conducted the domestic and external policies of the *Yishuv*, and on the eve of the establishment of Israel, it emerged as an important governing structure of the *Yishuv*. In 1952, many of the internal functions of the Agency were transferred to the government of Israel, and the Agency thereafter concentrated much of its attention on Diaspora activities and encouraging *Aliya* to Israel.

JEWISH BRIGADE. During World War II, Jewish volunteers from Palestine served in the army of **Great Britain**, especially in the East Kent Regiment. By the outbreak of the war in September 1939, about 13,000 Jews from Palestine had registered with the British. This comes against the backdrop of the British **MacDonald White Paper** of 1939 and its formal abandonment of the **Balfour Declaration**. At one time, the number of Jews serving with the British rose to 26,000. The British government of Winston Churchill (1874–1965) decided to establish separate Jewish units of volunteers to fight against the Axis Powers. Three of the companies were separated and made into a Palestine Regiment and, in September 1944, it was converted into a Jewish Brigade under the command of Brig. Ernest Frank Benjamin. Following the war the brigade was disbanded in the summer of 1946 and most of the volunteers subsequently joined the **Israel Defense Forces**. *See also* JEWISH LEGION.

JEWISH LEGION. Following the outbreak of World War I, a small number of Jews living in Palestine sought to aid **Great Britain**. With the help of Captain Trumpeldor, they organized the Zion Mule Corps, which took part in the Dardanelles Campaign. This gradually expanded into the Jewish Legion. The **Zionist** movement encouraged and organized Jewish volunteers from **Great Britain**, the **United States**, and Palestine, as well as **Egypt**, to fight alongside the British. Organized into various battalions, the Jewish Legion, at its height, totaled around 6,400 fighting men. The experience in the legion during the war proved useful to the Jewish cause in Palestine when many joined the **Haganah**, which was formed in 1920. The participation of some members of the Jewish Legion in defense of the Jewish quarters against Arab violence in May 1921 led to its dismemberment. *See also* JEWISH BRIGADE.

JEWISH UNDERGROUND. In the early 1980s, a number of Jewish settlers in the **West Bank** carried out organized and violent attacks against the Palestinians, including grenade and bomb attacks. The clandestine Jewish groups operated under the names of Ya'al, Sikari, and Lifta. On 2 June 1980, members of the Jewish underground planted bombs in the cars of the mayors of the West Bank towns of Nablus, Ramallah, and Bireh. The mayor of Nablus lost both his legs, and the Ramallah mayor lost his foot; the third bomb was dismantled, but an Israeli sapper lost an eye. In 1984, a three-member Lifta group was arrested for a conspiracy to blow up the Dome of the Rock on the Temple Mount/*Haram al-Sharif* in the Old City of **Jerusalem**. They managed to bring a large quantity of arms into the courtyard of the mosque before they were discovered. They were arrested and convicted for their actions but were gradually released due to remission or clemency. In April 1984, the internal intelligence agency Shabak discovered and thwarted a plot to plant explosives on several Arab buses in the **Occupied Territories**. *See also* KARP REPORT; TEMPLE MOUNT FAITHFUL.

JOHNSON MISSION. In November 1961, the **Palestine Conciliation Commission** (PCC) appointed Joseph E. Johnson, president of the Carnegie Foundation, to explore the possibilities of seeking progress on the question of Palestinian **refugees**. In his interim report to the PCC submitted in November 1961, Johnson concluded, "No progress can be made on the Palestinian Arab refugees question apart from or in advance of, an overall settlement."

JOHNSON PLAN. A week after the cessation of hostilities in the **June War of 1967**, on 19 June 1967, U.S. president Lyndon Johnson outlined a five-point peace program for the region. It called for recognition of the fundamental right of every state in the region to exist, justice for the **refugees**, respect for the maritime rights of all states, the need to curb the dangerous arms race, and respect for the political independence and territorial integrity of all states. This was marginalized by the ongoing debates in the **United Nations** Security Council over the drafting of a resolution acceptable to all state parties. Some of the provisions of the Johnson Plan were incorporated into **Resolution 242** adopted on 22 November 1967.

JOHNSTON PLAN. On 16 October 1953, **United States** president Dwight D. Eisenhower (1890–1969) appointed Eric Johnston (1896–1963) as his special representative to undertake discussions with states along the Jordan River and recommend a comprehensive plan for the development of the Jordan Valley. At the same time, Israel constructed a National Water Carrier and diverted water from the Jordan River north of the Sea of Galilee to the Negev in the south. Johnston held intense but separate negotiations with all four riparian states and worked out a plan under which **Syria** and **Lebanon** would use 20 and 35 million cubic meters (mcm), respectively, from the Jordan River tributaries, the Baniyas and Hasbani rivers; Syria would use an additional 22 mcm from the Jordan. The remaining waters of the Jordan River would be used by Israel (around 375–450 mcm) and **Jordan** (about 100 mcm). From the Yarmouk River, Syria would receive about 90 mcm, Jordan around 380–430 mcm, and Israel around 25–40 mcm. The plan envisaged the Sea of Galilee as a reservoir for Israel and Jordan.

The plan was never implemented, as the Arab states ultimately refused to enter into any agreement with Israel. On 18 August 1955, the **Arab Higher Committee**, headed by the former mufti of **Jerusalem**, urged the Arab states to reject any schemes or projects connected with Israel, and in October 1955 the **Arab League** formally rejected the Johnston Plan. In 1964, Jordan and Syria sought to divert the Baniyas and Hasbani rivers and reduce the flow of water into the Sea of Galilee. Israel conducted air raids over the construction sites in early 1965 and forced the Arab states to abandon the diversion plan.

JOINT JORDANIAN–PLO COMMITTEE. Following the conclusion of the **Camp David Accords** in September 1978, Arab states opposed to the peace initiative of President **Anwar Sadat** of **Egypt** organized a summit meeting in Baghdad. During this eighth Arab summit, a joint Jordanian–**Palestine Liberation Organization** (PLO) Committee was formed to consolidate Palestinian opposition to the Camp David process, which had excluded the PLO. It set up a special fund, called Sumud or the Steadfastness Aid Fund, to provide financial assistance to the Palestinians living in the **Occupied Territories**. See also JERUSALEM VISIT; REJECTIONIST FRONT.

JORDAN. The Hashemite Kingdom of Jordan was established by **Great Britain** in 1921 as the semiautonomous Emirate of **Transjordan**, with Abdullah ibn Hussein (1852–1931), the son of Sharif Hussein of Mecca, as the emir. In 1946, Transjordan gained independence from Britain, and the emir became King **Abdullah I**. The country assumed the name of Jordan in 1950.

The involvement of the Hashemites in the Arab–Israeli conflict predates the establishment of Transjordan and can be traced to the **Hussein–McMahon Correspondence** of 1915–1916. In appreciation for the support of Sharif Hussein during the **Arab Revolt** (1916–1918), Britain partitioned Palestine in 1921 and created Transjordan.

Beginning in the mid-1940s, Emir Abdullah had close contacts with the *Yishuv* leadership, and this continued after the British decision to refer the Palestine **Mandate** to the **United Nations**. Though nominally opposed to the **Partition Plan**, Abdullah had strong territorial ambitions in Palestine. A day after the establishment of Israel in 1948, Arab states invaded Palestine. Jordan's **Arab Legion**, the strongest and best trained army in the region, fought mainly in areas that were allotted to the Arabs by the **United Nations**. The city of **Jerusalem** was an exception, and the legion captured the Old City, which houses the *Haram al-Sharif* or Temple Mount. By the time hostilities ended, Transjordan was in control of eastern Palestine. After the **Arab–Israeli War of 1947–1948**, Transjordan signed an **armistice agreement** with Israel on 3 April 1949, which consolidated and recognized its hold over the **West Bank** and **East Jerusalem**.

In December 1948, weeks after the formation of the **All Palestine Government**, Arab Palestinian notables who were sympathetic to King Abdullah met at the **Jericho Conference** and asked the Hashemite monarch to officially take over the West Bank, which was duly annexed in 1950. Consequently, the Palestinian residents of the West Bank as well as Palestinian **refugees** living in the West Bank were given full Jordanian citizenship.

The annexation of the West Bank by Jordan was strongly resented by other Arab states, and they even contemplated suspending Jordan from the **Arab League**. This popular resentment led to the **assassination** of King Abdullah near the Al-Aqsa Mosque in 1951 in **Jerusalem**. King **Hussein**, who assumed the throne in 1953 (following a brief stint by his father, Talal), faced a host of threats not only from his Palestinian subjects but also from Arab nationalists led by President **Gamal Abdel Nasser** of **Egypt**. The precarious domestic situation forced him to see the West and Israel as his potential allies.

The **June War of 1967** changed his fortunes. The compulsions of Arab nationalism and false information about military successes spread by Egypt induced King Hussein to ignore Israeli warnings, and Jordan joined the war. Capitalizing on the Jordanian offensive, Israel captured East Jerusalem as well as the West Bank. Afterward, Hussein's desire to regain control over these territories brought Jordan closer to Israel. On the eve of the **October War of 1973**, he unsuccessfully tried to warn Israeli prime minister **Golda Meir** of the impending coordinated attack by Egypt and **Syria**.

Meanwhile, the **Palestine Liberation Organization** (PLO), which had been formed in 1964, was gathering widespread support and began undermining Hussein's efforts to be the representative of the Palestinians. In 1970, the tension between the two was manifested in the form of widespread unrest, and Hussein responded with a large-scale crackdown, commonly referred to as the **Black September Massacre**. Under the **Cairo Agreement of 1970**, mediated by Nasser, the PLO leaders and militia were expelled from Jordan. Nevertheless, over Jordanian opposition, the **Rabat Arab Summit** in 1974 declared the PLO to be the sole and legitimate representative of the Palestinian people.

Seeking to isolate the PLO, Israel has often looked to Jordan as a possible solution for the problem posed by its occupation of the West Bank, as evidenced by the **Jordan Option** and **London Agreement**. The outbreak of the **Intifada** in December 1987 radically altered the situation, and in June 1988, King Hussein directed the **Jordanian disengagement**, formally severing Jordanian ties to the West Bank. At times, Hussein perceived **Hamas** to be an effective counterweight to the **Fatah**-led PLO.

Jordan's support for President Saddam Hussein (1937–) of **Iraq** during the **Kuwait War** resulted in its regional isolation and economic hardships. Afterward, seeking to regain its earlier influence with the West, Jordan became one of the earliest supporters of the new Middle East peace initiative of U.S. secretary of state James Baker (1930–). Jordan endorsed his idea of a joint Jordanian–Palestinian delegation to the **Madrid Conference**, which began on 30 October 1991.

After Israel and the PLO signed the **Declaration of Principles**, Jordan was prepared to formalize its close and clandestine relations with Israel. The **Washington Declaration** signed on 14 September 1993 soon resulted in the **Israel–Jordan Peace Treaty** signed in the Arava along the Israel–Jordan border in October 1994. Despite occasional tensions (for example, the **Masha'al Affair**), both Israel and Jordan have maintained close ties.

After the death of King Hussein on 7 February 1999, his eldest son **Abdullah II** ascended the throne. In June 2003, Abdullah organized the **Aqaba Summit**, where, in the presence of President **George W. Bush**, Prime Minister **Ariel Sharon**, and Palestinian prime minister **Mahmoud Abbas**, he formally accepted the **Middle East Road Map**. At the **Sharm al-Sheikh Summit** in 2005, King Abdullah agreed to return a Jordanian ambassador to Israel; the new envoy, Marouf Suleiman Bakhit, assumed office in March 2005. *See also* GREEN LINE; JERICHO PLAN; JOHNSTON PLAN; JOINT JORDANIAN–PLO COMMITTEE; JORDAN IS PALESTINE; OPEN BRIDGES POLICY; QIBYA RAID.

JORDANIAN DISENGAGEMENT. On 31 July 1988, King **Hussein** of **Jordan** announced that he was severing legal and administrative links with the **West Bank**. This was seen as a response to the ongoing **Intifada** (1987–1993) and his impatience with **Yasser Arafat**. The move formally ended four decades of a Jordanian quest for Palestinian allegiance and loyalty. Since the **Mandate** years, the Hashemites had coveted parts of Palestine, and the establishment of the **All Palestine Government** under the leadership of Mufti Hajj Amin al-Husseini (c. 1895–1974) had not inhibited King **Abdullah I** from annexing the West Bank. The formation of the **Palestine Liberation Organization** (PLO) in 1964 and its growing stature and influence did not diminish the Jordanian drive. Even after losing the territories during the **June War of 1967**, tacit Israeli concurrence enabled Jordan to wield considerable influence and control in the West Bank.

Bowing to the growing strength of the PLO, in November 1973, Jordan went along with other Arab states and recognized the PLO as "the sole legitimate representative of the Palestinian people." Still, opposition from Israel and the **United States** to according any role to the PLO, Arafat's failure to advance the Palestinian cause through diplomacy, and the rekindling of the **Jordan Option** by the Israeli **Labor Party** kept Hashemite interest in regaining the West Bank alive.

The July 1988 disengagement thus was the Jordanian response to growing international support for an independent **Palestinian state**. On 4 August, the Jordanian cabinet decided to dismiss all Palestinian employees in the West Bank commencing 16 August; reports put the number of dismissed former Jordanian employees at more than 20,000. On 23 August, Arafat signed the order signaling the PLO takeover of responsibilities for the West Bank and the **Gaza Strip**. This disengagement from the West Bank, however, did not prevent Jordan from securing a "special role" as the guardian of the Muslim holy sites in **Jerusalem** under the 1994 **Israel–Jordan Peace Treaty**.

JORDAN IS PALESTINE. Right-wing groups in Israel consider **Jordan** to be the solution to Israel's problems with the Palestinians. In their view, both the **Balfour Declaration** and the British **Mandate** were applicable to lands on both sides of the Jordan River, and hence the partition of Palestine and the formation of **Transjordan** in 1921 by **Great Britain** were a violation and injustice to the Jewish people and an illegitimate act. This position, espoused by Revisionist **Zionists**, persisted even after the formation of Israel, and the Israeli Right has continued to lay claims over the East Bank of the Jordan River.

According to this view, because of the predominant presence of the Palestinian population, Jordan is in fact a **Palestinian state**, even though it is ruled by the non-Palestinian Hashemite monarchy. Hence, it was argued that there was no need for a Palestinian state west of the Jordan River. As defense minister under **Menachem Begin**, **Ariel Sharon** used this slogan to attempt to resolve the Palestinian problem through Jordan. He even advocated Israeli contacts with the **Palestine Liberation Organization**, aimed at helping the latter take control of Jordan. Strongly espousing such positions, the party anthem of the **Likud** until 1990 referred to the East Bank as part of *Eretz Yisrael*. In September 1980, Foreign Minister **Yitzhak Shamir** told the **United**

Nations General Assembly, that Jordan is "a state which is the Arab state in Palestine." This position has been vehemently rejected by the Palestinians and Jordanians, as well as by the Israeli Left.

In the past, as part of his plan for unification of the **West Bank** and Jordan, King **Hussein** of Jordan sought to propagate the notion that Jordan is Palestine and Palestine is Jordan. This position changed, however, when the Israeli Right began to use similar arguments to undermine Hashemite rule. Such plans called for the expulsion of Palestinians in the West Bank into Jordan and hence caused apprehension about Israel's intentions among the Jordanian and Palestinian leadership.

The 1988 **Jordanian disengagement** from the West Bank and the **Oslo Accords** significantly eroded the popular appeal of the slogan "Jordan Is Palestine" in Israel. Therefore, the overwhelming endorsement of the **Israel–Jordan Peace Treaty** by the Israeli Knesset on 25 December 1994 did not go unnoticed and unappreciated in Amman. *See also* JORDAN OPTION.

JORDAN OPTION. Like its counterpart on the Right, the Israeli **Labor Party** also looked to **Jordan** as the means of resolving the Palestinian problems. While recognizing the sovereignty and independence of Jordan, the Hashemite kingdom was seen as the interlocutor in deciding the future status of the **West Bank**. As the power in control of the territories from 1949 to 1967, Jordan was keen to regain the West Bank. Capitalizing on this, the Labor Party sought to circumvent the difficult and thorny issue of the **Palestinian state** and instead pursued a Jordanian–Palestinian federation. The most visible articulation of this position was the **London Agreement** of April 1987, concluded between King **Hussein** of Jordan and Foreign Minister **Shimon Peres**. However, a host of developments such as the **Intifada** (1987), the **Jordanian disengagement** (1988), the **Oslo Process** (1993), and the **Israel–Jordan Peace Treaty** (1994) made the idea redundant and irrelevant.

JUDEA AND SAMARIA. These biblical names are used in Israel to denote the land west of the Jordan River that was occupied and subsequently annexed by **Transjordan** following the **Arab–Israeli War of 1947–1948**. The terminology acquired ideological connotations following Israel's capture of the **West Bank** in 1967. In 1979, residents of the West Bank and the **Gaza Strip** established a Council of Jewish

Communities in Judea, Samaria, and the Gaza Strip called Yesha ("Salvation"), which became an extraparliamentary group. In the letters exchanged as part of the **Camp David Accords**, with **Egypt**, Israel categorically stated, with U.S. acquiescence, that the term *West Bank* appearing in the Accords "is being and will be understood by the Government of Israel as Judea and Samaria." Israel for the first time used the expression "the West Bank" in the **Declaration of Principles** signed in September 1993. On 9 June 2005, the Israeli Supreme Court dismissed petitions challenging the **Gaza Withdrawal Plan** and ruled that these areas were not legally part of Israel. *See also ERETZ YIS-RAEL*; SETTLEMENT/S.

JUNE WAR OF 1967. The mounting tension between Israel and **Egypt** over the withdrawal of the **United Nations Emergency Force I** from the **Sinai Peninsula** and the imposition of the Egyptian **naval blockade** of the Strait of Tiran climaxed on 5 June 1967, when Israel launched a preemptive strike on 25 airfields in Egypt and **Syria**, as well as **Iraq**. A large portion of the Arab air forces was destroyed on the ground and runways were made nonoperational. During the first day of the conflict, more than 400 Arab aircraft were destroyed on the ground, giving air supremacy to the Israeli Air Force and depriving the Arab ground forces of any air cover. **Jordan** was initially spared the Israeli attack but, following the shelling of West **Jerusalem** later in the day, Israel expanded its military offensive to include Jordan.

A simultaneous ground offensive began against Egypt and Jordan, and by 7 June, Israel had captured the whole of the Sinai Peninsula and the **Gaza Strip** and reached the banks of the **Suez Canal**. On 8 June, a cease-fire came into effect on the Egyptian front. On the Jordanian front, **East Jerusalem**, including the Old City, was captured on 6 June, and the remaining portions of the **West Bank** came under Israeli control the following day. Israel initiated a ground offensive against Syria on 9 June, which lasted for 20 hours and captured the whole of the **Golan Heights**, including the Syrian town of Quneitra. When a general cease-fire came into force on 10 June, the Israeli forces were less than 50 kilometers (30 miles) from Amman, 60 kilometers (37 miles) from Damascus, and 110 kilometers (70 miles) from Cairo, and they controlled an area of 88,000 square kilometers (34,000 square miles) compared to about 20,250 square kilometers

(7,800 square miles) a week earlier. *See also ERETZ YISRAEL*; GREEN LINE; OCCUPIED TERRITORIES; RESOLUTION 242.

– K –

KACH. An extreme right-wing political movement in Israel founded and led by Rabbi Meir Kahane (1932–1990) until his **assassination** in New York on 5 November 1990. Though secular and nationalist, it sought to maintain the Jewish character of Israel and advocated the "**transfer**" or expulsion of its Arab citizens. As an extension of his Jewish Defense League, Kahane in 1971 established a political party, which adopted the name Kach when it decided to run for the 1973 Knesset elections. Its first electoral success came in 1984, when it crossed the threshold margin. That year, the Election Commission had sought to prevent Kach from contesting the Knesset elections because of its anti-Arab posture, but the Supreme Court quashed the ban. Gaining nearly 26,000 votes, Kach secured one seat, and Kahane entered the Knesset.

The extremism of Kach led the Knesset to introduce legislation in August 1986 that prevented groups with racist postures from contesting elections. Kach was thus proscribed from contesting the 1988 Knesset elections. The ban has remained in force since then.

Following Kahane's murder in 1990, Rabbi Avraham Toledano was chosen as the leader of Kach, but internal differences and personal rivalry have led to the formation of a breakaway faction called Kahane Chai ("Kahane Lives"), headed by Kahane's son Benjamin. On 25 February 1994, Baruch Goldstein, a member of the Kach movement, killed 29 Muslim worshippers in the **Hebron Massacre**. As result, the Israel government outlawed Kach and Kahane Chai on 13 March 1994. Despite the ban, the activists of both groups have virulently opposed the **Oslo Process** and territorial compromise with the Palestinians. On 30 December 2000, Benjamin Kahane, his wife, and five children were killed in an ambush by Palestinian gunmen near the **settlement** of Ofra.

KADESH OPERATION. *See* SUEZ WAR.

KAHAN COMMISSION. The **Sabra and Shatila Massacre** of Palestinian civilians in **refugee** camps in the Beirut area in September

1982 evoked widespread domestic and international criticism of Israel. Since the **Israel Defense Forces** (IDF) were in control of the areas, critics have argued that Israel must have been aware of the impending massacre and could have prevented it. Initially, the Israeli
government headed by **Menachem Begin**, sought to appoint a judicial commission to investigate, but due to growing domestic criticism, on 28 September 1982, the cabinet was forced to appoint a
commission of inquiry to examine "all the facts and factors connected with the atrocity carried out by a unit of the Lebanese forces"
against the residents of the refugee camps. On 1 October 1982, a
commission headed by the president of the Supreme Court, Justice
Yitzhak Kahan, was appointed; the other members were Justice
Aharon Barak and Yona Efrat, a reserve major general in the IDF.

On 7 February 1983, the commission submitted its final report,
which recommended that Maj. Gen. Yehoshua Saguy not continue as
director of military intelligence. It also found that division commander Brig. Gen. Amos Yaron "did not act properly" regarding the
operations of the **Phalange** forces in the camps and hence advised
that he no longer serve in the capacity of a field commander. It declined to make any recommendations against the IDF chief of staff,
Lt. Gen. Rafael Eitan (1929–2004), because of the government's decision against extending his tenure. Above all, the commission ruled
that, in view of his overall political responsibility, Defense Minister
Ariel Sharon should not be given any "sensitive" position in future.
On 13 February 1983, Sharon resigned as defense minister.

Subsequently, most of those mentioned in the Kahan Commission
have returned to prominence. Most notably, Sharon continued to
serve in government, first as minister without portfolio (October
1983–September 1984); then as minister of trade and industry (September 1984–February 1990), housing (June 1990–July 1992), and
national infrastructure (July 1996–October 1998); and then as foreign
minister (1998–1999). On 6 February 2001, Sharon was elected
prime minister of Israel in direct elections, and he retained this position following the **Likud** victory in January 2003.

After his retirement from the army, Eitan founded Tsomet and successfully ran in the 1988 elections. He also served as minister under
Yitzhak Shamir (1990–1992) and **Benjamin Netanyahu**
(1996–1999). Saguy joined the **Likud** and became a member of the

Knesset. Yaron was made director general of the Defense Ministry. Reacting to this, the Belgian Supreme Court used the findings of the Kahan Commission to rule that Yaron, despite being the director general, could be prosecuted and tried for war crimes over the Sabra and Shatila Massacre. *See also* OPERATION PEACE FOR GALILEE.

KARINE **AFFAIR.** In January 2002, Israeli naval commandos seized the *Karine-A*, a freighter registered in **Lebanon**, in international waters in the Red Sea. It was carrying about 50 tons of weapons, including rockets and missiles, which Israel claimed was cargo bound for the **Palestinian National Authority** in Gaza from **Iran**. Even though both denied the allegations, a lieutenant colonel of the Palestinian naval police was the ship's captain. The incident further emboldened the Israeli siege of Ramallah and brought the **United States** closer to the Israeli view of the irrelevance of **Yasser Arafat** in the peace process.

KARP REPORT. Acting on complaints about the activities of the Jewish settlers vis-à-vis Arab residents of the **Occupied Territories**, in 1981 Israel's attorney general Yitzhak Zamir appointed a committee headed by Judith Karp. The committee's report, published in February 1984, concluded that police investigations into Arab complaints against Jewish settlers were inadequate and incomplete. *See also* JEWISH UNDERGROUND.

KFAR KANA MASSACRE. On 18 April 1996, during the offensive against **Hezbollah** targets in **Lebanon** code-named the **Grapes of Wrath Operation**, an Israeli artillery shell landed on a **United Nations** compound where numerous Lebanese civilians were taking refuge. In that attack, more than 100 civilians were killed and scores of others injured. While Israel described it as a mistake, the **United Nations Interim Force in Lebanon** (UNIFIL) authorities argued that the camp had clear UN markings. The magnitude of the deaths compelled U.S. president **Bill Clinton** (1946–) to call for an immediate cease-fire, and the Israeli offensive ended on 26 April. The government formally expressed its sorrow over the attack. Israeli prime minister **Shimon Peres** was unable to capitalize on the offensive and reverse his dwindling popularity in the opinion polls in Israel. The Kfar Kana Massacre indeed worked against him, as many leaders of the **Israeli Arab** community accused the government of deliberately targeting the civilians and called for boycotting the closely contested prime ministerial elections slated for 29 May 1996.

KFAR KASSEM MASSACRE. On the eve of the **Suez War**, 49 **Israeli Arab** citizens were killed in the village of Kfar Kassem in central Israel on 29 October 1956. As in many other Arab areas, the village had been placed under curfew, and Israeli border policemen fired at the Arabs, who were returning to their homes without recognizing the curfew had been imposed. An official inquiry commission headed by a district judge found eight border policemen guilty of murder, and they were given long prison sentences. However, most of the sentences were reduced and the last convict was freed in 1960. Both the killings and the lenience shown to the policemen undermined the trust and confidence of the Arabs in the government of Israel.

KHAN YUNIS RAID. Frequent **Fedayeen** attacks from the **Egypt**-held **Gaza Strip** into Israel began to intensify in late August 1955 and culminated in large-scale attacks on the southern Israeli towns of Rehovot and Rishon le-Zion, just 16 kilometers (10 miles) south of Tel Aviv. In these attacks, which lasted for four days, 11 Israeli civilians were killed, scores of others were injured, and many installations were destroyed. In retaliation, on the night of 31 August, Israel attacked and destroyed the police headquarters in Khan Yunis and killed 72 Egyptians, wounding another 58. The Israeli attack was one of the largest against Egyptian positions in Gaza, resulting in a temporary lull in Fedayeen attacks.

KHARTOUM ARAB SUMMIT. From 29 August to 1 September 1967, members of the **Arab League** held a summit meeting in Khartoum, Sudan, to consider the impact and consequences of the **June War of 1967**. The leaders agreed on a unified effort "to eliminate the effects of the [Israeli] aggression" and to secure an Israeli withdrawal from the **Occupied Territories**. The summit, however, assumed prominence because of its "three *no*'s" with regard to Israel: "no peace with Israel, no recognition of Israel [and] no negotiations with [Israel]." The three *no*'s at Khartoum resulted in Israel complaining about not having an Arab peace "partner" to negotiate with. The detractors of **Egypt** subsequently adopted this position when President **Anwar Sadat** initiated a separate bilateral peace with Israel. *See also* CAMP DAVID ACCORDS; JERUSALEM VISIT.

KILOMETER 101. The location along the Cairo–Suez road where military commanders of **Egypt** and Israel met on 28 October 1973 to negotiate the implementation of **Resolution 338** of the **United Nations** Security Council. Gen. Abdul Ghani Gamassy and Gen. Aharon Yariv signed the agreement on 11 November 1973, and it paved the way for the **Sinai I Agreement** of 1974. The agreement formalized and stabilized the cease-fire following the **October War of 1973**. Mediated by Secretary of State Henry Kissinger (1923–) and Undersecretary of State Joseph Sisco (1923–) of the **United States**, the six-point agreement was the first to be signed between Israel and Egypt since the February 1949 **armistice agreement**.

KING–CRANE COMMISSION. The King–Crane Commission was the first formal U.S. political involvement in the Middle East. Following a meeting of the Big Four (**Great Britain**, **France**, the **United States**, and the **Soviet Union**) in March 1919, U.S. president Woodrow Wilson (1856–1924) suggested the formation of an international commission that would visit **Syria**, evaluate the prevailing opinion of the region, and report back to the forthcoming Versailles Peace Conference. Wilson appointed Henry C. King, president of Oberlin College, and manufacturer Charles R. Crane to visit the area. Imperial designs and rivalry in the region prevented Britain and France from participating in the mission.

In June 1919, the King-Crane Commission arrived in Palestine, conducted interviews, and studied reports and documents, and in August, it submitted its report to the U.S. delegation to the Versailles Conference. Coming less than a year after the **Balfour Declaration** and in the midst of a trickling *Aliya*, the commission warned against **Zionist** aspirations in Palestine. With the British forces in physical control of Palestine, though their future remained uncertain, the commission suggested the inclusion of Palestine within a larger Syrian mandate. The recommendations of the commission were largely ignored by the United States as well as its European allies. *See also* LEAGUE OF NATIONS.

KING DAVID HOTEL EXPLOSION. On 22 July 1946, the **Irgun**, commanded by **Menachem Begin**, blew up the southwest corner of the King David Hotel, where the civilian as well as the military headquarters of the Palestine **Mandate** administration were located. Ninety-one people—41 Arabs, 28 British, and 17 Jews—were killed in the attack, which was condemned by the mainstream leadership of the *Yishuv*. Irgun presented the attack as a demonstration of its ability and willingness to strike at the heart of the Mandate administration, and this resulted in a British crackdown against various militant Jewish groups in Palestine.

KINNERET OPERATION. The dispute between Israel and **Syria** over violations of their 1949 **armistice agreement** and Israeli complaints of Syrian harassment of its fishermen took a turn for the worse when, on the night of 11 December 1955, Israel launched a massive three-pronged attack on Syrian outposts on the eastern bank of the Sea of Galilee. Commanded by Col. **Ariel Sharon**, the operation involved a two-column attack from the north and south of the Syrian positions, with an amphibious attack from the water. In the short but powerful raid, Israel captured the entire shore strip and destroyed all Syrian fortifications. Thirty-seven Syrian soldiers and 12 civilians were killed in the operation, and another 30 were taken prisoner; Israel lost six men. While many were surprised by the timing and magnitude of the Israeli attack, the operation seemed to have resulted in Syrian noninvolvement when Israel launched its Sinai campaign a few months later. This was also known as Operation Olive Leaves.

KIRYAT ARBA. This Jewish **settlement** on the outskirts of Hebron was established in 1968 and since then has remained the nerve center of settler extremism and the **Gush Emunim** Movement. In February 1994, during the **Hebron Massacre**, Baruch Goldstein, a Jewish settler from Kiryat Arba, killed 29 Muslim worshippers in the Ibrahimi Mosque/Tomb of the Patriarchs.

KNESSET APPROVAL. Though lacking any legal sanction or requirements, Israeli prime ministers have sought the approval of the Knesset for any peace agreements signed with neighboring Arab countries. Normally, this precedent is attributed to Prime Minister

Menachem Begin, who sought Knesset endorsement of the **Camp David Accords**. However, it was **Golda Meir** who inaugurated this practice on 22 January 1974, when she placed the **Sinai I Agreement** before the Knesset and sought its approval; the agreement was approved 76–36. Since then, various Israeli leaders have sought and obtained Knesset approval for a number of peace agreements with the Arab states and the Palestinians, including the Interim Agreement between Israel and **Egypt** (3 September 1975, 70–43, with seven abstentions); **Camp David Accords** (27 September 1977, 84–19–17); **Egypt–Israel Peace Treaty** (21 March 1979, 95–18–2); **Declaration of Principles** (24 September 1993, 61–50–8); **Washington Declaration** (3 August 1994, 91–3–2); **Israel–Jordan Peace Treaty** (25 or 26 October 1994, 105–3–6); **Taba Agreement** (5 October 1995, 61–59); **Hebron Protocol** (16 January 1997, 87–17); and **Sharm al-Sheikh Memorandum** (8 September 1999, 54–23).

KUWAIT WAR. The invasion of Kuwait by **Iraq** on 2 August 1990 diverted the attention of the international community from the Arab–Israeli conflict to the Persian Gulf. On 12 August, after annexing Kuwait, President Saddam Hussein (1937–) of Iraq offered to withdraw from Kuwait if Israel did the same from the **Occupied Territories**. Although this increased his popularity among the Palestinians, who warmly greeted his proposal, it generated a negative image of the Palestinians in the Israeli peace camp and in the West and considerably weakened Palestinian influence in the region, especially among the oil-rich Arab states in the Persian Gulf.

In weaving an anti-Iraqi coalition, the George H. W. Bush administration (1989–1993) was keen to exclude Israel for political reasons and was determined to prevent its participation in any military confrontation. This was finally achieved through diplomatic cajoling, political pressure, and restricted military access.

On 17 January 1991, a day after the **United States** initiated its military campaign against Iraq, the Iraqis launched a Scud missile against Israel. During the duration of the conflict in the Persian Gulf, Iraq launched at least 39 Scud missiles against Israel. One Israeli was killed and 12 others died due to indirect consequences of the attacks, about 200 civilians were injured, and more than 4,000 buildings suffered severe damage. Despite some internal criticism and pressure, Israel maintained its restraint and did not retaliate. The withdrawal of Iraqi forces from Kuwait eventually resulted in the resumption of the Middle East peace process at the **Madrid Conference** in October 1991.

– L –

LABOR PARTY. This is the successor to Mapai, the left-wing **Zionist** Party that dominated the politics of both the prestate *Yishuv* and the State of Israel during the first three decades after its establishment. Socialist in orientation, Mapai focused on developing a Jewish national home rooted in agriculture and industrial economy and developing Hebrew culture. Unlike the Revisionist Zionists, it supported and cooperated with the **mandate** administration and **Great Britain**. This changed, however, following the publication of the **MacDonald White Paper** of 1939, which announced the reversal of the British support for a Jewish national home enshrined in the **Balfour Declaration**.

After the establishment of Israel, **David Ben-Gurion** of Labor became the first prime minister and a dominant figure. In June 1965, Ben-Gurion joined with **Moshe Dayan** and **Shimon Peres** to form a new party called Rafi. On the eve of the **June War of 1967**, Rafi joined the unity government formed by Prime Minister Levi Eshkol (1895–1969), with Dayan becoming defense minister. On 21 January 1968, Mapai merged with two other labor parties, Ahdut Haavoda and Rafi, to form the Israel Labor Party.

The policies of the Labor Party have included support for *Aliya*, establishment of a social welfare state, a state-planned and publicly regulated economy, full employment, a minimum wage, and the right to strike. The party stands for the separation of religion and state and supports equality for minorities, including the **Israeli Arabs**. In the initial years, it organized separate minority lists for Knesset elections but, since 1981, it has been placing Arab members of the party in one unified list. For many years, the *Histadrut* labor union was closely linked to the party and functioned as a strong support base.

The intelligence failure during the **October War of 1973** proved costly for the Labor Party. Though it managed to regain its dominant position in the December 1973 Knesset elections, in May 1977 Labor lost its monopoly to the **Likud** Party. During 1984–1990, 2001–2002, and

2005, it was government. Labor briefly returned to power in 1992 (under **Yitzhak Rabin**) and again in 1999 (under **Ehud Barak**), but since the 2001 elections, the party's support base has gradually dwindled and it has ceased to be the largest faction in the Knesset.

With regard to peace, having accepted the **Partition Plan** in 1947, the Labor Party has adopted a pragmatic and relatively moderate posture toward the Palestinians. Following the June War, in which Israel captured the **West Bank**, **Gaza Strip**, **Sinai Peninsula**, and **Golan Heights**, the Labor Party government began the construction of Jewish **settlements** in the **Occupied Territories**. The party was instrumental in the signing of the **armistice agreements**, **Sinai I Agreement**, and **Sinai II Agreement**. However, the honor of signing the first peace treaty with the Arab world went to its traditional rival Likud, which signed the **Camp David Accords** with **Egypt**. Reflecting the national consensus, until the early 1990s the Labor Party opposed the recognition of the **Palestine Liberation Organization** (PLO). During most of the 1980s, it toyed with the **Jordan Option** as means of resolving the dispute over the Occupied Territories.

In 1992, the Labor Party led by Rabin returned to power. The lack of progress in the peace negotiations following the **Madrid Conference** brought about a change in the attitude of the Labor Party. Its secret contacts with the PLO paved the way for the **Oslo Process** and culminated in the signing of the **Declaration of Principles** and other agreements. However, its failure to hasten the process and to fulfill some of the basic expectations of the Palestinians resulted in the failure of the **Camp David Talks** held in the summer of 2000. These developments and the controversial visit of the Likud leader **Ariel Sharon** to the Temple Mount/*Haram al-Sharif* resulted in the outbreak of the **Al-Aqsa Intifada** in September 2000. The violence undermined not only Israeli influence over the Palestinians but also the Labor Party's domestic support, bringing about a surge of popularity for right-wing parties and the victories of Sharon in the 2001 and 2003 elections. Labor briefly served in the unity government under Prime Minister Sharon in March 2001–November 2002 and January–November 2005. However, the party has been suffering from a crisis of leadership, identity, and lack of a meaningful role in the peace process.

In November 2005, *Histadrut* labor federation leader Amir Peretz (1952–) defeated Peres and became party chairman. Shortly afterward, the Labor Party pulled out of the unity government; Peres resigned from the party and joined the Kadima ("Forward") party floated by Sharon.

LAND DAY. On 30 March 1976, **Israeli Arabs** organized a general strike protesting against the confiscation of their lands by Israel. The protest was sparked by the official decision to expropriate 20,000 *dunums* (a *dunum* is 1,000 square meters or about a quarter of an acre) of Arab lands in Galilee. This resulted in six protestors being killed in Nazareth when soldiers opened fire. Since then, 30 March has been annually observed as Land Day. Over the years, Arabs in the **Occupied Territories** have joined to commemorate Land Day. While protests have generally remained peaceful, the day marked a new phase in the politicization and political participation of Israeli Arabs.

LANDLESS ARAB INQUIRY. The 1930 **Passfield White Paper** severely criticized *Aliya* and land purchases, as well as the Jews-only policy of the *Histadrut* labor federation. Most of these provisions were nullified through the **Black Letter** that British prime minister Ramsey MacDonald (1866–1937) sent to Chaim Weizmann (1874–1952) in February 1931. On the question of land purchases Lewis French was appointed to head the Landless Arab Inquiry, which concluded that fewer than 900 Arab claims were valid, thus enabling the *Yishuv* leadership to maintain that the **Zionist** settlement activities in Palestine had little or no impact upon the Arab peasant society or their landlessness. At the same time, the inquiry concluded that a number of leading Arab families were involved in selling land to the Jews. This disclosure consolidated Mufti Hajj Amin al-Husseini (c. 1895–1974) and his followers and gave rise to opposition to land sales. However, it did not impede the land purchases, and the Jews owned 456,000 *dunums* (four *dunums* make one acre) of land in 1920, with the figure rising to 1.3 million in 1939.

LAVON AFFAIR. In July 1954, an Israeli plot was designed to abort the Anglo-Egyptian agreement over the withdrawal of British troops from the **Suez Canal** zone. Israel viewed this as a security threat and had agents detonate bombs in **Egypt** targeting British and U.S. targets with the intension of creating popular discontent and distrust about the ability of **Gamal Abdul Nasser** to safeguard foreigners. The plan, which mainly involved Egyptian Jews, collapsed when the spy ring was caught. Of these, six members were given long prison terms, two were tried in absentia, and two were publicly hanged on 31 January 1955. Nasser, who had executed leaders of the **Muslim Brotherhood** for conspiracy, could not be lenient with the Israeli agents.

Prime Minister Moshe Sharett (1894–1965) initially took a cautious response to the incident. While Sharett had not been informed of the operations, the head of the Aman (Military Intelligence), Col. Binyamin Gibli, refuted the plea of ignorance of Pinhas Lavon (1904–1976), who had been defense minister at the time, and stated that Lavon had orally approved the bombing campaign. As a result, in February 1955 Lavon was forced to resign and was replaced by **David Ben-Gurion**, which resulted in the **Gaza Raid**.

Lavon was elected secretary-general of the *Histadrut* labor federation. In 1961, he was exonerated and the Israeli cabinet maintained that the operation was ordered without the knowledge of the defense minister, even though no responsibility was fixed for the bombing campaign in Egypt.

LAW OF RETURN. On 5 July 1950, the Knesset passed the Law of Return, bestowing an almost unlimited right of Jews to immigrate to Israel. Except for those who indulge in activities "directed against the Jewish people" or who might "endanger public health or the security of the state," this right is available to Jews everywhere. Though controversial, the Law of Return enjoys near-unanimous support among Israel's Jewish population. The Citizenship Law of 1952 grants automatic Israeli citizenship to any Jew who immigrates to Israel under the Law of Return. In 1977, Israel added the Extradition Law, which explicitly prevents the extradition of an Israeli citizen for crimes committed abroad before he or she became an Israeli citizen. On 19 March 1970, the Law of Return was amended to define a Jew as a person who is born to a Jewish mother or who has converted to Judaism and is not a member of any other religion. This unique and unparalleled law forms the basis for the large waves of *Aliya* that have occurred since the law's passage soon after the formation of Israel.

The presence of large numbers of non-Jews joining the massive *Aliya* from the **Soviet Union** in the late 1980s led to renewed calls for modification of the Law of Return. Religious circles are apprehensive that those who are not considered Jewish according to *halacha* are taking advantage of the Law of Return and bringing in non-Jewish spouses and children. This law remains one of the most contentious issues in the Arab–Israeli conflict because, while granting unrestricted immigration rights to Jews, Israel refuses to recognize the rights of Palestinians who had left their homes in 1948 and became **refugees**. *See also* RESOLUTION 194; WORLD ZIONIST ORGANIZATION; ZIONISM.

LEAGUE OF NATIONS. Established at the end of World War I, the League of Nations was an international organization that was a forerunner of the **United Nations**. It presided over the dismantling of the Ottoman Empire, including various Arab-dominated areas that were awarded as **mandates** to **France** and **Great Britain**. Based on the decisions of the **San Remo Conference** of April 1920, it placed **Syria** and **Lebanon** under the French mandate and Palestine and Mesopotamia (**Iraq**) under the British. On 24 July 1922, the League approved the Mandate of Palestine and made Britain responsible "for putting into effect" the **Balfour Declaration** of 1917 and for the formation of a **Jewish Agency** "for the purpose of advising and cooperating" the *Yishuv* with the Mandate administration. In the interim, in April 1921, Britain had carved off the East Bank of the Jordan River from Palestine and formed the Emirate of **Transjordan**. In September 1922, Britain informed the League that provisions pertaining to **Zionism** would not be applicable to Transjordan or areas east of the Jordan River. Despite Palestine being a mandate territory, Britain administered it without any reference to League. The outbreak of the World War II in September 1939 signaled the demise of the League.

LEBANESE WITHDRAWAL. As part of the national unity government platform, on 14 January 1985 the Israeli cabinet agreed to a three-stage unilateral withdrawal from **Lebanon**. In the first phase in February, Israel pulled out of the western sector, including Dison, the Litani River area, and the area around Nabatiya. In the second stage, Israel vacated Tyre on 29 April. In the final phase, it pulled out off the remaining areas, except for a small strip along the border in southern Lebanon, which it designated the **security zone**. This zone was to be controlled by the **South Lebanese Army** (SLA), with Israeli military, logistical, and financial support. Since its invasion in the **Litani Operation** in 1978, Israel had lost about 900 soldiers in Lebanon and the mounting casualties were primarily responsible for the increased and eventually successful demand for an Israeli pullout from Lebanon.

For its part, **Hezbollah** had lost more than 1,200 fighters since 1978. In addition, hundreds of Lebanese civilians were killed during periodic air raids, artillery exchanges, and other military offensives carried out by Israel from 1978 to 2000.

On 5 March 2000, the Israeli cabinet unanimously decided to pull out of the security zone in southern Lebanon and return to the international borders, even without an agreement with **Syria**. The withdrawal was to be completed by July 2000. Accordingly, fortified Israeli positions were gradually handed over to the SLA. However, deprived of the Israeli military presence and support, the SLA soon disintegrated, and its positions in the security zone were overrun by Hezbollah. This in turn accelerated the process of Israeli withdrawal, and Israel completed a disorganized withdrawal by 24 May. *See also* FOUR MOTHERS MOVEMENT; SHE'AR YASHUV ACCIDENT; SHEBA'A FARMS.

LEBANON. The role of Lebanon in the **Arab–Israeli War of 1947–1948** was limited and confined to small-scale operations in northern Israel. Following the end of hostilities, Israel–Lebanon negotiations were held in the border town of Rosh Hanikra and an **armistice agreement** was signed on 23 March 1949.

Even though Lebanon was not involved in the **June War of 1967**, under pressure from **Syria**, it refused to accept **Resolution 242** of the **United Nations** Security Council because the resolution recognized Israel's right to exist.

The **Black September Massacre** in **Jordan** in 1970 and the resultant expulsion of the Palestinian **Fedayeen** brought Lebanon to center stage of the Arab–Israeli conflict. Under the **Cairo Agreement of 1970**, the **Palestine Liberation Organization** (PLO) and its militia were relocated to southern Lebanon. The Lebanese government approved the establishment of "Fatahland," a state-within-a-state where the Palestinians could launch their military attacks against Israel. The arrangement enabled the Palestinians to bear arms, to conduct and administer their own affairs, and to oversee Palestinian **refugee** camps in Lebanon. However, this arrangement undermined Lebanese sovereignty, as the PLO challenged any attempts by the Lebanese government to regain control in southern Lebanon, and it ultimately sowed the seeds for the Lebanese civil war. Civil war raged in Lebanon from 1975 to 1989 and was brought to a close only by the country's division and occupation by Syrian and Israeli military forces.

The Palestinian militant campaign against Israel resulted in periodic Israeli counteroffensives against Lebanon. In March 1978, Israel launched the **Litani Operation**, a combined offensive against the PLO positions in Tyre and Sidon in Lebanon that sought to "wipe out" the PLO. The invasion resulted in the UN Security Council's adoption of **Resolution 425** and the formation of the **United Nations Interim Force in Lebanon** (UNIFIL).

This spiral of Palestinian violence (e.g., the **Ma'alot Massacre**) and Israeli retaliations (e.g., the **Beirut Airport Bombings** and **Beirut Raid**) eventually culminated in the Israeli invasion of Lebanon in 1982, designated **Operation Peace for Galilee**. This offensive resulted in the expulsion of the PLO from Lebanon and its relocation to Tunis. Taking advantage of its continued military presence in Lebanon, Israel sought and, on 17 May 1983, concluded a formal peace agreement with the Maronite Christian–dominated Lebanese government. Falling short of a peace treaty, the **Israel–Lebanon Agreement** delineated the criteria for Israeli withdrawal in return for specific security arrangements in southern Lebanon and contained certain elements of normalization. For example, both sides agreed that "the existing international boundary between Israel and Lebanon is inviolable." However, under vehement Syrian pressure, Lebanon abrogated the agreement on 5 March 1984.

In January 1985, the Israeli cabinet, as part of the policies of the national unity government, agreed to a three-stage unilateral withdrawal from Lebanon, and the last of these was completed in June of that year. Israel, however, retained control over a narrow strip in southern Lebanon bordering Israel, designated as the **security zone**, and handed it over to the **South Lebanese Army** (SLA). This arrangement proved insufficient to ensure Israel's security, though. Militant attacks from Palestinian groups, and later **Hezbollah**, against northern Israel often resulted in massive Israeli retaliations. On two occasions, these attacks led to full-scale military operations against Lebanon: the **Accountability Operation** in 1993 and the **Grapes of Wrath Operation** in 1996.

The presence of the **Israel Defense Forces** (IDF) in the security zone and the mounting casualties gradually became domestically unpopular in Israel. As a result, on 5 March 2000, the Israeli cabinet unanimously decided to pull out of the security zone, declaring that the **Lebanese withdrawal** would be carried out even without an agreement with Syria and would be completed by July 2000. The sudden collapse of the SLA, however, accelerated the process, and on 24 May 2000, Israel completed a hasty withdrawal. On 16 June, UN secretary-general Kofi Annan (1938–) informed the Security Council that Israel had completely withdrawn from Lebanon and had complied with the demands of Resolution 425. Differences, however, exist over the status of **Sheba'a Farms**, which Israel had captured from Syria during the June War.

In June 2005, the Lebanese government announced its decision to allow Palestinian refugees born in Lebanon to legally work at manual and clerical jobs in the country. This removed restrictions that had prevented the Palestinians from working in more than 70 professions. *See also* AMAL; FATAH UPRISING; GOOD FENCE POLICY; KFAR KANA MASSACRE; PHALANGE; PRISONER EXCHANGE; SABRA AND SHATILA MASSACRE.

LEHI. *See* STERN GANG.

LIKUD. Formally established on the eve of the December 1973 Israeli Knesset elections, the Likud is the ideological successor of Herut, a right-wing **Zionist** Party that had existed since the formation of the State of Israel. Founded by **Menachem Begin**, Herut was modeled on the ideology of Ze'ev Jabotinsky (1880–1940). In 1965, Begin merged Herut with the Liberal Party and formed Gahal, which took part in the national unity government established on the eve of the **June War of 1967**.

In the 1977 Knesset elections, Likud defeated the **Labor Party** and ended the monopoly on power the latter had enjoyed since 1948. Since then, it has emerged as a dominant political force in Israel. Until his resignation in 1983, the Likud was headed by Begin, and the party won the Knesset elections in 1981, 1996, and 2003. Since 1977, Likud prime ministers have been Begin (1977–1983), **Yitzhak Shamir** (1983–1984 and 1986–1992), **Benjamin Netanyahu** (1996–1999), and **Ariel Sharon** (2001–). In 1984–1990, 2001–2002, and 2005, Likud had joined hands with Labor to form a unity government. Through careful political maneuvers and alliances with religious parties, the Likud has emerged as the largest political party in Israel.

As a right-of-center party, Likud is strongly nationalist and follows an assertive foreign policy. For a long time, it was opposed to Palestinian statehood and maintained that "**Jordan is Palestine**." In 1986, the Likud was instrumental in the adoption of the **Palestine Liberation Organization (PLO) Law**, which prevented any contacts between Israel and members of the PLO. When in power, it actively pursued and accelerated **settlement** activities in the **West Bank** and **Gaza Strip**. Until 1990, the party anthem carried references to the East Bank of the Jordan River as being part of the *Eretz Yisrael*.

The visit of President **Anwar Sadat** in November 1977 and the conclusion of the **Camp David Accords** in 1978 and the **Egypt–Israeli Peace Treaty** the following year were the highlights of the Likud administration. Peace with Egypt, however, did not enjoy the unanimous support of the party. Influential figures such as Moshe Arens (1925–) and Shamir were opposed to the Camp David Accords. Responding to internal opposition, Prime Minister Begin enacted the **Golan Law** in 1981 and brought the **Golan Heights** under Israeli rule.

The Likud portrayed its **Operation Peace for Galilee**, the code name for the Israeli invasion of **Lebanon**, as "a war of choice," but in the process exposed serious differences inside the country. It was, however, responsible for the Israeli restraint during the **Kuwait War** (1990–1991) and its decision not to respond to Scud missiles fired by **Iraq**. After the war, Prime Minister Shamir led the Israeli delegation to the **Madrid Conference**. Overshadowed by the **loan guarantee** controversy with the **United States**, the party lost the 1992 elections to the Labor Party.

In the wake of the **Oslo Process** initiated by Prime Minister **Yitzhak Rabin**, Likud led the Israeli opposition to the peace process. It perceived the establishment of the **Palestinian National Authority** (PNA) as a forerunner of an independent **Palestinian state**. Following his 1996 election victory, Prime Minister Netanyahu was forced to negotiate with the PNA and its leader **Yasser Arafat**, concluding the **Hebron Protocol**. This in turn brought about internal divisions within the Likud and resulted in the victory of Labor leader **Ehud Barak**. In September 2000, the controversial visit of Likud leader Sharon to the Temple Mount/*Haram al-Sharif* sparked the **Al-Aqsa Intifada**. Capitalizing on the failure of Barak, the Likud won the February 2001 prime ministerial and January 2003 Knesset elections. The **Gaza Withdrawal Plan** announced by Sharon in May 2004 created strong tension and opposition to the party. In November 2005, Sharon resigned from the Likud and floated a new party called

Kadima ("Forward"); the following month, Netanyahu was again elected the leader of the Likud.

LITANI OPERATION. In the early hours of 15 March 1978, Israel launched this military offensive against **Palestine Liberation Organization** (PLO) positions in Tyre and Sidon in **Lebanon**. It came four days after a **terrorist** attack, when an 11-member Palestinian commando unit hijacked two Israeli buses on the Haifa–Tel Aviv route, resulting in the deaths of 37 people, with injuries to more than 75. Israel responded with a full-scale invasion of Lebanon with an explicit intention of "wiping out" the PLO. The **Israel Defense Forces** (IDF) occupied a 10-kilometer-wide (6-mile) strip north of the Israeli border to the south of the Litani River. In this operation, more than 1,000 Lebanese and Palestinian civilians were killed and more than 200,000 fled their homes.

On 19 March, without any reference to the hijacking and killings, the **United Nations** Security Council unanimously adopted **Resolution 425**, which called on Israel to "immediately . . . cease its military action against Lebanese territorial integrity and withdraw forthwith its forces from all Lebanese territory." The resolution also established the **United Nations Interim Force in Lebanon** (UNIFIL) "for the purpose of confirming the withdrawal of Israeli forces." Israel pulled out of the area on 13 June 1978, following the formation of UNIFIL, but handed over its positions to its right-wing Christian militia allies, the **South Lebanese Army**, rather than to UNIFIL. This led to the continued presence of UNIFIL even after the Israeli pullout. *See also* OPERATION PEACE FOR GALILEE.

LOAN GUARANTEES. During the **Kuwait War** against **Iraq**, Israeli leaders floated the idea of the **United States** providing a loan to fund infrastructure programs for the absorption of the new wave of Jewish immigrants from the former **Soviet Union**. As Scuds were falling on Israel, U.S. secretary of state James A. Baker (1930–) signed a $400 million loan guarantee, which gradually grew to guarantees of $10 billion. Even though the George H. W. Bush administration (1989–1993) was inclined toward the idea, it wanted to use the economic largesse to influence Israel's **settlement** policy in the **Occupied Territories**. The **Yitzhak Shamir** government's lack of transparency over settlements in **Jerusalem** beyond the **Green Line** led to acrimonious relations between the Israeli government and the United States and partially contributed to the election of the **Labor Party** in the 1992 elections.

On 11 August, the newly elected Israeli prime minister, **Yitzhak Rabin**, met President Bush in Kennebunkport, Maine, and worked out a formula that satisfied both sides. Rabin's assurance of a "partial" freeze of settlement activities and "change of priorities" enabled the United States to agree to a $10 billion loan guaranteed over a five-year period. The United States would determine the amount that would be deducted from the guarantees spent by Israel for settlement activities. On 13 December 1996, the Israeli government headed by **Benjamin Netanyahu** rescinded the restrictions and established the pre-1992 policy of official subsidies and other concessions for the settlements.

Though the dollar-for-dollar penalty warranted much larger deductions, the United States often deducted symbolic amounts to convey its displeasure over Israel's settlement activities. In 1997, it deducted only $60 million, even though it identified Israel as having spent $307 million. The administration ruled that the $247 million spent on **bypass roads** and other expenses were incurred to implement the **Oslo Accords** and, hence, were exempted.

LOD MASSACRE. On 30 May 1972, three members of the Japanese Red Army, acting on behalf of the **Popular Front for the Liberation of Palestine**, attacked passengers arriving on an Air France flight at Israel's Lod (later Ben-Gurion) International Airport outside Tel Aviv with machine guns and hand grenades. Thirty people, including two of the hijackers, were killed, more than 70 were injured. The sole surviving attacker, Kozo Okamoto, was arrested and tried in Israel. His release was demanded during some of the post-1972 Palestinian hostage-takings against Israel, including the **Munich Massacre** of 1972 and **Entebbe Operation** of 1976. Okamoto was eventually released in 1985 due to proved insanity. The Lod attack marked the first coordinated Palestinian attempt to enlist the support of non–Middle Eastern **terrorist** groups in support of their cause.

LONDON AGREEMENT. On 11 April 1987, Foreign Minister **Shimon Peres** held a secret meeting with King **Hussein** of **Jordan** in London, and both leaders agreed on a six-point plan that outlined the purposes and format of an **international conference**. Subsequently termed the

London Document, it was discussed by Israel's inner cabinet in May and was vehemently opposed by Israeli prime minister **Yitzhak Shamir**. On 30 September, Peres outlined his agreement with King Hussein before the **United Nations** General Assembly. Among other things, it called for an international conference that would neither impose any settlements nor veto any agreements concluded by the parties. The resolution of the Palestinian problem "in all its aspects" would be accomplished "in negotiations between the Jordanian–Palestinian delegation and the Israeli delegation." The inability of Peres to secure the backing of the prime minister not only stymied any progress, however, but also raised doubts among the Arab leaders of the wisdom of reaching agreements with only a section of the Israeli government.

LONDON CONFERENCE. On 1 March 2005 Prime Minister Tony Blair of **Great Britain** hosted a conference in London to promote Middle East peace. It was attended by U.S. secretary of state Condoleezza Rice (1954–), **United Nations** secretary-general Kofi Annan (1938–), British foreign secretary Jack Straw (1946–), and the newly elected president of the **Palestinian National Authority** (PNA), **Mahmoud Abbas**. The meeting was boycotted by Israel, however, and hence was transformed into a conference urging the Palestinian leadership to pursue "reforms." It strongly condemned the 25 February 2005 suicide bombing in Tel Aviv and called on the PNA to pursue sustained actions against **terrorism**.

– M –

MA'ALEH ADUMIM. A Jewish **settlement** in the **West Bank** on the outskirts of **Jerusalem** established in 1975. Ma'aleh Adumim was recognized and legalized through a cabinet decision of 26 July 1977 and since then has become the largest Jewish settlement in the **Occupied Territories**. At the end of 2003, its population stood at 25,000. On 21 March 2005, Prime Minister **Ariel Sharon** approved the construction of 3,500 new homes in a neighborhood that would link Ma'aleh Adumim with Jerusalem.

MA'ALOT MASSACRE. On 13 May 1974, a three-man **Palestine Liberation Organization** team took hostage 85 students and teachers of

Nativ Meir School in the Upper Galilee township of Ma'alot. Holding them for ransom, the hijackers demanded the release of 20 of their comrades held in Israeli prisons and their safe passage to Damascus. Israel agreed to release the prisoners, but refused to concede to the demand of the militants to take the hostages to **Syria**. Following the impasse, Israel ordered a commando raid on the school, and during the operation, 21 children, all three Palestinian hostage-takers, and a soldier were killed.

MACCABEE OPERATION. On 1 May 1948, during the **Arab–Israeli War of 1947–1948**, Jewish forces launched an offensive on the Hulda–Latrun road, which formed a part of the Tel Aviv–**Jerusalem** road. After intense fighting, on 16 May, the Hulda–Jerusalem road was opened for Jews living in western Jerusalem. This was one of the decisive phases of the war.

MACDONALD WHITE PAPER. Responding to mounting opposition to its policy in Palestine, which was perceived to be pro-**Zionist**, on 17 May 1939 the government of **Great Britain** came out with a white paper named after its author, Colonial Secretary Malcolm MacDonald (1901–1981). Having failed to satisfy its contradictory commitments to Arabs and Jews, the government opted to revise its policy following the **Balfour Declaration**. The policy paper called for a unitary state in Palestine to be established gradually over the next 10 years. It imposed severe restrictions upon *Aliya* and stipulated that for the next five years, Jews would be admitted at the rate of 15,000 per year; the total number for the entire period was not to exceed 75,000—and any illegal entrants into Palestine would be deducted from that figure. Any additional *Aliya* into Palestine would require the consent of the Arab community. The white paper also imposed restrictions upon the Jewish purchase of land in Palestine.

In addressing the two key Arab complaints against the **Mandate** authorities—immigration and land purchase—the white paper angered Zionists, who regarded it as a reversal and abandonment of the **Balfour Declaration** and a betrayal of the decision of the **League of Nations** to award the mandate to **Great Britain**. Coming against the backdrop of mounting tensions following the advent of Nazism, the Zionists coined a strategy "to fight the war [against Nazism] as if there is no White Paper and to fight the White Paper as if there is no war." Thus, the white paper marked a distinct phase in Zionist–Mandate relations and consolidated anti-British sentiments in the *Yishuv*. *See also* ST. JAMES CONFERENCE.

MADRID CONFERENCE. The Middle East Peace Conference opened in Madrid on 30 October 1991, under the cochairmanship of the **United States** and the **Soviet Union**. It was attended by Israel, **Egypt**, **Lebanon**, **Syria**, **Jordan**, and Palestinians. This was the most visible and positive outcome in Arab–Israeli relations following the **Kuwait War**, which had taken place earlier that year. This was made possible by prolonged diplomatic initiatives of U.S. secretary of state James A. Baker (1930–), who undertook as many as eight trips to the Middle East to convince the participants to attend.

The format of the conference satisfied all the key participants. Though not sponsored by the **United Nations**, the international nature of the conference satisfied the long-standing Arab demand for a multinational forum and guarantees for peace with Israel. The Arab willingness to negotiate directly satisfied Israel's aspirations of recognition and acceptance. Weakened by its support for Saddam Hussein (1937–) during the Kuwait War, the Palestinian leadership was content just to be invited and agreed to be part of a joint Jordanian–Palestinian delegation.

All the Middle East participants agreed that **Resolution 242** and **Resolution 338** of the UN Security Council would be the basis for any peace settlement. It was also agreed that all bilateral negotiations would be conducted independently and that progress on one track would not be linked to or conditional upon progress on other tracks. Adjourned after three days, the participants went to Washington, D.C., on 9 December for follow-up bilateral negotiations. The 10 rounds of bilateral talks during 1991–1993 did not produce any meaningful progress.

Under the Madrid format, **multilateral talks** began in Moscow on 28 January 1992. Five separate working groups were formed on the multilateral front, devoted to water, the environment, arms control and regional security, **refugees**, and regional economic development. Even though progress from the conference has been minimal, it established a procedure and direct communication between both sides. *See also* OSLO PROCESS; SHAMIR, YITZHAK.

MANDATE, PALESTINE. At the end of World War I, the **League of Nations** dismantled the Arab-dominated areas of the Ottoman Empire and awarded them as a mandate to **France** and **Great Britain**.

Based on the decisions of the **San Remo Conference** of April 1920, it placed **Syria** and **Lebanon** under the French Mandate and Palestine and Mesopotamia (**Iraq**) under the British. In none of these cases was the consent of the inhabitants sought.

The Palestine Mandate was approved by the League of Nations on 24 July 1922, and the League made Britain responsible for "putting into effect" the **Balfour Declaration** of 1917. It called for the formation of a **Jewish Agency**, "for the purpose of advising and cooperating" with the mandate administration in its relations with the Jewish population of Palestine. The mandate came into force formally on 29 September 1923. Meanwhile, in April 1921, the East Bank of the Jordan River had been carved out of Palestine to form the Emirate of **Transjordan**. On 16 September 1922, Britain informed the League of Nations that the provisions pertaining to **Zionism** would not be applicable to Transjordan or areas east of the Jordan River.

The British proposals in the 1920s and 1930s for the creation of an elected legislative council met with strong opposition from the Arabs, due to differences over representation for the Jews and Arabs. When Britain was first granted the mandate, the Arabs constituted 92 percent of the population and owned 98 percent of the land in Palestine.

Despite the formal authority of the League, Britain ruled Palestine as a Crown Colony and administered it through the Colonial Office. On 1 July 1920, even before the conferment of the mandate, Sir Herbert Samuel was appointed the first high commissioner of Palestine. Under the mandate, most of the political, economic, social, and military institutions and state structures of the future State of Israel were established. With a view to implementing the Balfour Declaration, the mandate authorities initially favored and facilitated *Aliya* to and Jewish land purchases in Palestine. As Arab opposition to these two measures grew, Britain gradually modified and, through the **Macdonald White Paper** of 1939, reversed its sympathetic attitude toward the establishment of a Jewish national home in Palestine.

Unable to reconcile its contradictory promises to the Arabs and Jews, in April 1947 Britain expressed its inability to continue with the mandate and asked the new **United Nations** to find a political settlement. Upon the approval of the partition resolution by the UN General Assembly, Britain announced its decision to terminate its presence in Palestine on 15 May 1948. Hours before this deadline, the Zionist leaders met in Tel Aviv and announced the establishment of the Jewish state. *See also* ARAB REVOLT (1936–1939); CHURCHILL WHITE PAPER; HOPE-SIMPSON COMMISSION; HUSSEIN–MCMAHON CORRESPONDENCE; KING DAVID HOTEL EXPLOSION; MORRISON–GRADY PLAN; NABI MUSA RIOTS; PASSFIELD WHITE PAPER; SHAW COMMISSION; WESTERN WALL; WOODHEAD COMMISSION; UNITED NATIONS SPECIAL COMMITTEE ON PALESTINE.

MAPAI. *See* LABOR PARTY.

MASHA'AL AFFAIR. On 25 September 1997, Israeli agents made an unsuccessful **assassination** attempt on Khalid Masha'al (1956–), the **Hamas** Political Bureau chief in Amman, **Jordan**. The capture of two Israeli agents with false Canadian passports led to a serious diplomatic crisis between Israel and **Jordan**, as well as between Israel and Canada. The affair was amicably ended when Prime Minister **Benjamin Netanyahu** agreed to provide an antidote against the lethal chemical used in the attack and to release Hamas spiritual leader **Sheikh Ahmed Yassin** from prison. Israel also promised not to use Jordanian territory for such attacks in future. An official Israeli inquiry commission, headed by Joseph Ciechanover, criticized the technical aspects of the operation and questioned the wisdom of approving such an operation in Jordan. In February 1998, Danny Yatom (1945–) resigned as Mossad chief, and this was seen as an attempt to placate King **Hussein** of Jordan who expressed his public anger over the affair. Following the election of Prime Minister **Ehud Barak** in 1999, Yatom returned to diplomacy as a senior aide to Barak and played an important role in relations with Jordan. *See also* TARGETED KILLING.

MAY 17 AGREEMENT. *See* ISRAEL–LEBANON AGREEMENT.

MEIR, GOLDA (1898–1978). A leading Israeli politician, Golda Mabovitch served as Israel's first and only woman prime minister, from March 1969 to June 1974. Born on 3 May 1898 in Kiev, Ukraine, Meir immigrated to the **United States** in 1906 and studied in Milwaukee, Wisconsin. In 1917, she married Morris Meyerson; in 1956, she Hebraicized her name and came to be known as Golda Meir.

Meir made *Aliya* to Palestine in 1921 and became active in the *Histadrut* labor federation. After holding senior positions in the trade union, in 1946 she replaced Moshe Sharett (1894–1965) as acting head of the political department of the **Jewish Agency**. In that capacity, in April 1948, she held secret talks with King **Abdullah I** of **Transjordan** over the **Partition Plan** for Palestine. Weeks before Israel's formation, she also conducted a highly successful fund-raising campaign in the United States.

In June 1948, Meir was appointed Israel's first ambassador to the **Soviet Union**, holding that position until her election to the Knesset in 1949. During 1949–1956, she served as minister of labor and national insurance. In June 1956, she took over as foreign minister until January 1966, initiating and consolidating Israel's relations with the newly independent countries of Africa. Between 1966 and 1968, Meir served as secretary-general of the Mapai Party and later headed the newly formed Labor Alignment, both forerunners of the **Labor Party**.

In March 1969, after the death of Levi Eshkol (1895–1969), Meir became Israel's prime minister. She presided over Israel's debacle in the **October War of 1973** and managed to lead the party to victory in the December 1973 Knesset elections. Even though the **Agranat Commission** appointed to inquire into the October War absolved her of any direct responsibility for the Israeli unprepardness, in April 1974 Meir resigned as prime minister and was succeeded by **Yitzhak Rabin**. She withdrew from public life but was present when President **Anwar Sadat** of **Egypt** visited **Jerusalem** in November 1977. Meir died on 8 December 1978.

MIDDLE EAST AND NORTH AFRICA (MENA) ECONOMIC SUMMITS. The first Middle East and North Africa (MENA) Economic Summit Conference was held in Casablanca, Morocco, from 30 October to 1 November 1994. Believed to be the initiative of **Shimon Peres**, the economic summit was intended to complement the political aspects of the peace process and to facilitate Israel's eventual integration into the Middle East. Reflecting the existing enthusiasm over the **Oslo Process**, the Casablanca Summit was attended by representatives from 64 countries.

The second MENA Summit was held in Amman 29–31 October 1995. The political climate in the region following the 1996 electoral victory of **Benjamin Netanyahu** led to **Egypt** downgrading the third meeting that took place in Cairo on 12–15 November 1996 to a lower level. The fourth and last MENA Conference was held in Doha, Qatar, 16–18 November 1997, with only six Arab participants. Most of the key members of the region, including the **Palestinian National Authority**, boycotted the conference due to lack of progress in the peace process.

MIDDLE EAST PEACE CONFERENCE PROPOSAL. On 6 December 1976, Israel presented a proposal to the **United Nations** General Assembly, calling for the immediate convening of a Middle East peace conference to resume negotiations toward implementing **Resolution 242** and **Resolution 338** of the UN Security Council. Under the proposal, **Egypt**, Israel, **Jordan**, and **Syria** would participate in the conference under the cochairmanship of the **United States** and the **Soviet Union**. However, a number of countries belonging to the Non-aligned Movement introduced an amendment and called for the participation of the **Palestine Liberation Organization** in the proposed conference, and as a result, Israel formally withdrew its first draft proposal ever submitted to the United Nations on 9 December.

MIDDLE EAST ROAD MAP. Formally unveiled on 30 April 2003, the Middle East Road Map was aimed at reviving the peace process, which had been stalled since the outbreak of the **Al-Aqsa Intifada** in September 2000. It was the result of the protracted efforts of the "Quartet"—the European Union, **Russia**, the **United Nations**, and the **United States**. Projected as "performance-based and goal driven," the Road Map demanded specific and time-bound commitments from Israel and the **Palestinian National Authority**. It also formally endorsed the two-state solution, whereby Israel and a sovereign, independent, democratic, and viable **Palestinian state** would coexist side by side.

During the first phase, the Road Map required unconditional cessation of Palestinian violence and the withdrawal of the Israeli forces to positions held prior to the outbreak of the Al-Aqsa Intifada. It also called on the Palestinians to undertake political reforms and to resume security cooperation with Israel. In the second phase, an independent Palestinian state with provisional boundaries would be created in 2003. And in the third phase, Israeli–Palestinian negotiations aimed at concluding a permanent status agreement would be reached in 2005.

The continued violence and refusal of either party to fulfill the commitments expected of it undermined progress with the Road Map. The appointment of the **Mahmoud Abbas** as the first Palestinian prime minister in March 2003 was the only positive outcome. *See also* BUSH PLAN.

MILITARY ADMINISTRATION. In 1948, as an emergency measure during the **Arab–Israeli War of 1947–1948**, Israel established a military administration to govern its Arab citizens. Arabs and Druze living in Galilee and its environs, the Negev, and the towns of Ramleh, Lod, Jaffa, Ashkelon, and **Jerusalem** were brought under this administration. This minority-targeted, nonterritorial arrangement was seen as essential to prevent the Arab citizens of Israel from acting against the state and collaborating with its enemies. The arrangement imposed severe restrictions on the civil rights and movements of the **Israeli Arabs** and hence was criticized both inside and outside Israel. In 1962, following their classification as a separate minority, the Druze population was excluded from the military administration. Even though it was formally abolished in 1966, some of the emergency regulations could still be enforced by the heads of various military commands of the **Israel Defense Forces**.

MILITARY GOVERNMENT. Following the **June War of 1967**, Israel established a military government headed by a serving military officer to govern and administer the **West Bank** and the **Gaza Strip**. The governor was responsible for the overall security as well as civic administration of the **Occupied Territories** and was aided by an array of serving military officials, who looked after both the military and civilian aspects of the administration. This dual role often created frictions inside the government as well as the military establishment. Officially termed "coordinator of activities in the Territories," this arrangement continued until the **Oslo Accords** were implemented and the **Palestinian National Authority** was put in place.

MITCHELL COMMITTEE REPORT. On 17 October 2000, following the outbreak of the **Al-Aqsa Intifada**, U.S. president **Bill Clinton** and President **Hosni Mubarak** of **Egypt** organized the **Sharm al-Sheikh Summit**, attended by the leaders of Israel, **Jordan**, the **Palestinian National Authority** (PNA), the **United Nations**, and the

European Union. The conferees decided to establish a committee to investigate the ongoing violence and the events leading to the Al-Aqsa Intifada and to suggest measures to prevent its recurrence, to rebuild mutual confidence, and to resume the negotiations. Subsequently, Sen. George J. Mitchell (1933–) was named head of the committee, which also consisted of former senator Warren Rudman (1930–), former Turkish president Suleiman Demirel (1924–), former EU foreign policy chief Javier Solana (1942–), and Norwegian foreign minister Thorbjorn Jagland (1950–).

On 30 April 2001, the committee completed its report, which was published on 20 May. Refraining from apportioning blame for the intifada, it ruled out the controversial visit of Israel's leader of the opposition, **Ariel Sharon**, to the Temple Mount/*Haram al-Sharif* area as the cause for Palestinian violence. It also rejected the Israeli government's position that the PNA and **Yasser Arafat** had orchestrated the Palestinian violence. The report called for a complete freeze on **settlement** activities and an end to the economic blockade imposed upon Palestinian areas. It also requested the PNA to make greater efforts to prevent **terrorism** against Israeli civilians.

While the PNA accepted the report and called for its implementation, the Israeli government declined to accept its recommendations—especially its call for a total freeze of settlements. Israel argued that linking the settlement freeze to an end to Palestinian violence would reward terrorism. Gradually the **United States** diluted the linkage between cessation of Palestinian violence and Israeli confidence-building measures. *See also* TENET PLAN.

MIXED ARMISTICE COMMISSIONS (MAC). Following the conclusion of the **armistice agreements** in 1949, four Mixed Armistice Commissions were established to maintain and consolidate the agreements between Israel and the four neighboring Arab countries **Egypt, Jordan, Lebanon**, and **Syria**. Chaired by a **United Nations** official serving with the **United Nations Truce Supervision Organization**, each of these commissions was composed of equal numbers of Israeli and Arab military or police representatives. The initial hopes for these MACs to turn into avenues for border political exchanges between the two sides did not materialize, and the MACs were primarily confined to addressing issues concerning local border policing.

MORRISON–GRADY PLAN. The disagreements between U.S. president Harry S. Truman (1884–1972) and Prime Minister Ernest Bevin (1881–1951) of **Great Britain** over the recommendations of the **Anglo-American Committee** announced on 30 April 1946 compelled Bevin to suggest a new cabinet-level committee to discuss the implications of the report. Headed by British deputy prime minister Herbert Morrison and U.S. ambassador to London Henry Grady, this second committee reached an agreement in July 1946 that largely nullified the recommendations of the Anglo-American Committee. It advocated a federal solution for Palestine, recommending the establishment of semiautonomous Arab and Jewish cantons. Under this arrangement, the British **mandate** would be converted into a trusteeship and would be divided into two provinces, Arab and Jewish, plus two districts, **Jerusalem** and the Negev. On the contentious issue of the entry of 100,000 Jews into Palestine, the Morrison–Grady Plan concluded that this should be undertaken only if acceptable to both Arabs and Jews.

In September, this plan was discussed at the Round Table Conference in London, where it was rejected by the Palestinian delegation, which advocated a unitary Palestine with adequate civil rights for Jews. Though initially favorable to the plan, Truman came under pressure from **Zionists** to stick to his earlier demand for the immediate admission of 100,000 Jewish refugees from Europe into Palestine. Facing an election in November, Truman disassociated himself, thereby forcing Bevin to reject the U.S. demand, and the plan subsequently collapsed.

MUBARAK, HOSNI (1928–). A former air force officer and politician, Hosni Mubarak has been the president of **Egypt** since 1981. He was born on 4 May 1928, in the village of Kafr al-Musaliha, northeast of Cairo. He graduated from the Egyptian Air Force Academy in 1950. During the **June War of 1967**, he commanded the Western Air Base in Cairo, and he became chief of air staff in 1969. In 1972, President **Anwar Sadat** appointed him commander of the air force and deputy minister of war, a position he held during the **October War of 1973**. He became vice president of Egypt in April 1975 and vice president of the ruling National Democratic Party (NDA) four years later. After the **assassination** of Sadat, Mubarak became president on 6 October 1981. The following year he took over the leadership of the NDA. Since then Mubarak has successively won all the presidential elections held in Egypt.

A supporter of Sadat's peace overtures toward Israel, Mubarak presided over the implementation of the **Camp David Accords** and the Israeli withdrawal from the **Sinai Peninsula** in April 1982. During much of the 1980s, he played an active role in seeking a settlement of the Palestinian question and engaged Israel over Prime Minister **Menachem Begin**'s **Autonomy Plan**. He also mended fences with the Arab countries, healed the rift over Egypt's peace with Israel, and managed to secure the return of Egypt to the **Arab League** and the Organization of the Islamic Conference. Mubarak played a pivotal role in securing Arab endorsement of the **United Nations**-backed military action against **Iraq** during the **Kuwait War**.

Having contributed to the inauguration of the **Madrid Conference**, Mubarak played an important part in the continuation of the **Oslo Process** and in bridging differences between the Israeli leaders and **Yasser Arafat**. He periodically hosted negotiators from both sides and facilitated the conclusion of the **Taba Agreement** in September 1995 and the **Sharm al-Sheikh Memorandum** in September 1999 as well as the **Cairo Dialogue** between **Hamas** and the **Palestinian National Authority** (PNA).

At the same time, Mubarak has been the architect of the Egyptian–Israeli "cold peace." With the sole exception of his last-minute decision to attend the funeral of slain Israeli prime minister **Yitzhak Rabin** in November 1995, Mubarak has refused to visit Israel. He not only has limited political and economic contacts with Israel but also twice recalled the Egyptian ambassador to Israel (in June 1982 and November 2000). After the electoral victory of **Benjamin Netanyahu** in 1996, Mubarak called for Israel's isolation in the Middle East. The onset of the **Al-Aqsa Intifada**, the Israeli policy of **targeted killing**, and its periodic incursions into territories held by the PNA have only heightened the tension between the two countries.

Egypt played a key role in the eventual conclusion of the Cairo Dialogue, whereby various Palestinian militant groups agreed to a lull in their militant attacks against Israel. In February 2005, during the **Sharm al-Sheikh Summit**, Prime Minister **Ariel Sharon** and PNA president **Mahmoud Abbas** declared a joint cease-fire. During that summit, Mubarak also agreed to the return of an Egyptian ambassador to Tel

Aviv. *See also* BAKER PLAN; MUBARAK PLAN (1985); MUBARAK PLAN (1989); SHAMIR PLAN; SHARM AL-SHEIKH SUMMIT (1996).

MUBARAK PLAN (1985). In an interview published in the *New York Times* on 25 February 1985, President **Hosni Mubarak** of **Egypt** called for direct negotiations between Israel and a joint delegation of **Jordan** and the Palestinians. The **Hussein–Arafat Accord** of 11 February and Israeli prime minister **Shimon Peres**'s remarks that the agreement and the tacit acceptance by the **Palestine Liberation Organization** (PLO) of **Resolution 242** of the **United Nations** Security Council marked a significant departure from the resolutions of the **Khartoum Arab Summit** provided the framework for this plan. But the Israeli opposition to any involvement of the PLO made the plan a nonstarter.

MUBARAK PLAN (1989). In a bid to bridge the gap between Israel and the **Palestine Liberation Organization** over peace negotiations, in July 1989 President **Hosni Mubarak** of **Egypt** came up with a new plan. Formally communicated to Israel on 15 September, it focused on the most contested aspect of the Israeli position: Palestinian elections. Mubarak's plan called for Israeli acceptance of the results of the elections, international supervision, complete immunity for elected representatives, withdrawal of Israeli forces from voting stations, an Israeli guarantee to start "a dialogue on the final status of the '**Occupied Territories**' by an appropriate date," a freeze on **settlement** activities, complete freedom of election campaigning, and barring Israelis from entering the **West Bank** and the **Gaza Strip** on election day. It also stated that residents of **Jerusalem** "may participate" in the election and that

> Israel must accept the four principles of the American policy in the Middle East: the solution must be based on **Resolution 242** of the UN Security Council and **Resolution 338** of the UN Security Council, trading land for peace, a guarantee of security of all countries in the region and acknowledgement of Palestinian political rights.

While **Yasser Arafat** endorsed the Egyptian format for the elections, **Yitzhak Shamir** found it unacceptable and the cabinet rejected the proposal on 6 October due to **Likud** opposition. Meanwhile, U.S. secretary of state James A. Baker (1930–) suggested a five-point bridging proposal, the **Baker Plan**, which also failed to break the deadlock. *See also* INTIFADA; RABIN PLAN; SHAMIR PLAN; SHULTZ PLAN.

MULTILATERAL TALKS. As a follow-up to the **Madrid Conference** of October 1991, Moscow hosted the inaugural session of a round of multilateral talks on 28 January 1992. The desire to participate in the multilateral talks influenced countries such as China and India to normalize relations with Israel on the eve of the Moscow conference. The conference was cosponsored by the **United States**. Five separate working groups were formed, devoted to water, the environment, arms control and regional security, **refugees**, and regional economic development. Citing a lack of progress, **Syria**—and by extension **Lebanon**—boycotted the meeting, as well as all subsequent sessions. The Palestinian delegation boycotted the inaugural meeting, protesting against the U.S. refusal to accept the participation of Diaspora Palestinians.

MULTINATIONAL FORCE AND OBSERVERS (MFO). Reflecting growing disapproval of the **Camp David Accords**, in July 1979 the **United Nations** Security Council decided against renewing the mandate of the **United Nations Emergency Force II**. Therefore, as provided for by the Camp David Accords, **Egypt**, Israel, and the **United States** reached an agreement to create the Multinational Force and Observers, which would monitor the security arrangements in the **Sinai Peninsula** following the Israeli withdrawal slated for April 1982. As part of an arrangement to secure Israeli withdrawal from the Sinai passes and the Abu Rodies oil fields, Egypt agreed to the presence of U.S. civilian technicians in the Sinai. This was seen as a means of strengthening the Interim Agreement and eventually paved the way for the multinational force. The initial Egyptian demand for a UN presence was rejected by Israel.

An agreement to this effect was concluded in late 1981. Speaking for the European Economic Community (EEC), Foreign Secretary Lord Carrington (1919–) of **Great Britain** declared that European states would participated in the MFO only within the context of the **Venice Declaration** of 1980, which, inter alia, recognized the Palestinian right to self-determination.

MUNICH MASSACRE. On 5 September 1972, an eight-member Black September Organization (BSO) team attacked a group of 13 Israeli athletes participating in the Munich Summer Olympic Games. While two escaped and two were killed, the remaining nine Israeli athletes were taken hostage. In exchange for their release, the group demanded the release of 234 Palestinian prisoners held in Israel and West Germany, threatening to execute the hostages otherwise. Subsequently, they demanded a plane to carry them and the hostages to Cairo. While they were boarding the plane, a German anti**terrorism** unit conducted a botched rescue operation in which all the athletes and five of the eight terrorists were killed. The three hijackers who were captured alive during the raid were subsequently released when another BSO group hijacked a Lufthansa plane on 29 October 1972.

Responding to the terrorist attack, Prime Minister **Golda Meir** authorized the **assassination** of those responsible for the Munich massacre. Several Palestinian terrorists were subsequently killed, but one such operation ended disastrously. In July 1973, Ahmed Bouchikhi, an innocent Moroccan waiter, was mistakenly killed by a special Israeli antiterrorism unit in Lillehammer, Norway. Israel expressed "remorse" for his death, but refused to accept legal and financial responsibility for the killing. Norway was not allowed to interrogate former Mossad operative Mike Harari regarding his involvement in the killing of Bouchikhi, who was mistaken for the **Palestine Liberation Organization** intelligence chief Hassan Salameh (1948–).

MUSKETEER OPERATION. Following the decision of President **Gamal Abdul Nasser** of **Egypt** for the **nationalization of the Suez Canal, Great Britain** and **France**—who jointly owned, controlled, and operated the canal—sought to reverse the move. In an attempt to militarily regain control over the canal, a joint military staff was established in August 1956 in London under the command of British general Sir Charles Keightley and French vice admiral Pierre Barjot. Under the plan, the hostilities were to be initiated jointly on 15 September, while Britain simultaneously organized diplomatic moves by hosting a conference of signatories to the **Constantinople Convention** of 1888. The entry of Israel into the crisis and the conclusion of the **Sèvres Conference** in October 1956 expanded the scope of the military operations against **Egypt** during the **Suez War**.

MUSLIM BROTHERHOOD. The Muslim Brotherhood (Ikhwan al-Muslimin) is the source of most of the present-day fundamentalist politico-religious Islamic groups in the Middle East and elsewhere.

Established by Sheikh Hassan al-Banna in **Egypt** in 1928, it provided a strong inspiration for anti-Western feelings in the region. Through well-organized networks of mosques and educational institutions, the movement soon swept throughout Egypt and spread to other parts of the region, including **Syria**, **Iraq**, **Jordan**, and **Saudi Arabia**. The relations between the Brotherhood and the governments have often been strained and resulted in violence and suppression. The Palestinian branch of the Muslim Brotherhood was founded in 1942 and, following the outbreak of the 1987 **Intifada**, it transformed itself into the militant group **Hamas**. *See also* ISLAMIC JIHAD; YASSIN, SHEIKH AHMED.

MUTUAL RECOGNITION. In an interview on ABC-TV in August 1988, the deputy of Palestinian leader **Yasser Arafat**, Abu Iyad (1934–1991), called for a mutual recognition of Israel and the **Palestine Liberation Organization** (PLO). The realization of this suggestion had to wait until 9 September 1993, four days before the signing of the **Declaration of Principles**, when Israel and the PLO accorded one another mutual recognition.

– N –

NABI MUSA RIOTS. In 1920, the Nabi Musa ("Prophet Moses") festival in Palestine coincided with Passover and Easter. During the festivities on 4–5 April, the growing tension between the Arabs and Jews over immigration manifested itself into an attack on the Jewish Quarter in Old **Jerusalem** by Muslims in which a number of Jews and Muslims were killed and wounded. Similar rioting took place the following year, when a number of Jewish settlements came under attack and the **Mandate** authorities resorted to air attacks on the Arab rioters. In the ensuing violence, 47 Jews and 48 Arabs were killed and more than 200 Jews and Arabs were wounded. These were two of the major incidents of intercommunal violence in the Palestine Mandate.

NACHSHON OPERATION. During the **Arab–Israeli War of 1947–1948**, **Jerusalem** was virtually cut off from the coastal plains by late March 1948, and with the impending end of the **Mandate**, the

Jewish forces sought to establish access to the city. A plan code-named the Nachshon Operation called for creating an access route to Jerusalem that would be a 10 kilometers (6 miles) wide in the coastal plain and 3 kilometers (2 miles) wide in the mountains. The road would be secured by the occupation of high ground and nearby Arab villages. On 6 April, a convoy of 60 trucks carrying civilian and military supplies slowly moved toward Jerusalem. On the night of 7/8 April at Castel, Arab volunteers led by Abd al-Qader al-Husseini (1907–1948) ambushed the convoy. After six days of fighting, al-Husseini was killed and Castel fell into the hands of the Jewish forces. The success of the operation was short lived, however, and on 20 April, the Arab forces reinforced the blockade and brought Jerusalem under siege. A similar operation called the **Dalet Plan** eventually secured the access to Jerusalem.

NAHARAYIM SHOOTING. A soldier from **Jordan** opened fire on a group of Israeli students visiting a Jordanian enclave near the Israeli territory of Naharayim on 13 March 1997, in the midst of growing tensions between Israel and Jordan. During the shooting, seven Israeli girls were killed and a number of others were injured. On 16 March, King **Hussein** of Jordan visited all seven families and offered his condolences. The soldier, Lance Cpl. Ahmed Mousa (al-) Daqamseh, was tried and given a life-term prison sentence.

NAQBA, AL-. This Arabic term, meaning "catastrophe," is used by Arabs to describe the exodus of Palestinians from the Palestine **Mandate** during the **Arab–Israeli War of 1947–1948**. Coined by Constantine Zurayk, a professor of history at the American University of Beirut, the term refers to the onset of the Palestinian **refugee** problem. Palestinians fled areas of the mandate that became the State of Israel. Since then, Palestinians mark 15 May—the day **Great Britain** formally withdrew from Palestine—as Al-Naqba Day.

NASSER, GAMAL ABDUL (1918–1970). Widely popular in the Arab world, Gamal Abdul Nasser was an Arab nationalist who ruled **Egypt** until his death in 1970. Born in Alexandria on 15 January 1918, he graduated from the Royal Military Academy in 1938 and joined the Egyptian Army. From 1942 to 1948, he formed the nucleus of the Society of Free Officers which led the revolution that deposed King Farouq (1920–1965) on 23 July 1952. As a young soldier, Nasser also took part in the **Arab–Israeli War of 1947–1948** and was deeply affected by the poor performance of the Arab armies.

After staying behind the scenes for a while, in April 1954 Nasser became prime minister, and later that year he took over as president of Egypt. In April 1955, he attended the **Bandung Conference** of Afro-Asian Nations and gradually forged close personal relations with Prime Minister Jawaharlal Nehru (1889–1964) of India and President Josip Tito (1892–1980) of Yugoslavia. These three leaders were instrumental in the formation of the Nonaligned Movement in 1961.

Nasser's nationalist position and his opposition to conservative monarchs and the Cold War–related military blocs in the Middle East raised regional tensions. He emerged as the strongest critic of the **Baghdad Pact**, and in 1955, through the **Czech Deal**, obtained large quantities of arms from Eastern Europe. He also allowed the Palestinian **Fedayeen** to conduct military raids against Israel from the Egypt-held **Gaza Strip**. All these developments raised his popularity among the Arab masses and brought him into confrontation with Israel.

Having failed to secure the promised Anglo-American funding for the **Aswan Dam** project, on 26 July 1956 Nasser announced the **nationalization of the Suez Canal**. The anger and disappointment of **Great Britain** and **France**, who operated the **Suez Canal**, offered an opportunity to Israel to work toward curtailing Nasser's regional influence. As agreed at the **Sèvres Conference**, Israel invaded the **Sinai Peninsula** on 23 October 1956 and was joined later by the forces of Britain and France. Under **United States** and **United Nations** pressure, the tripartite assault was reversed, and the Sinai and Gaza Strip returned to Egyptian control. The **Suez War** and the military defeat at the hands of Israel and its Western allies enhanced Nasser's regional position, influence, and popularity. He was seen as someone who could stand up to the military might of the imperial powers and their regional ally, Israel. At the end of the war, **United Nations Emergency Force I** (UNEF I) was deployed on the Egyptian side of its border with Israel.

In January 1964, Nasser convened the first summit meeting of the **Arab League**, which has since become a standard reaction to crises. Shortly afterward, in May 1964, with Nasser's backing, the **Palestine Liberation Organization** (PLO) was formed. Though initially under the patronage and control of Nasser, the PLO gradually established its autonomy and independence from the Arab states.

In May 1967, tensions along Israel's borders with **Syria** heightened over media reports of increased Israeli military activities. As an ally of Syria, Nasser could not remain indifferent. Bowing to criticism from his Arab detractors that he was "hiding behind the UN's skirts," on 16 May Nasser demanded a partial withdrawal of UNEF I from Sharm al-Sheikh. This was unacceptable to UN secretary-general U Thant (1909–1974), and hence, on 18 May, Nasser demanded the complete withdrawal of the peacekeeping forces. Four days later, he closed the Strait of Tiran to Israeli shipping. International indifference to these measures heightened Israeli security concerns and anxieties, and on 6 June Israel launched a preemptive air strike against the Arab air forces, including Egypt's. The **June War of 1967** ended in a disaster for the Arabs, with Egypt losing the whole of the Sinai as well as its control over the Gaza Strip. Taking personal responsibility for the military debacle, Nasser offered his resignation on 9 June, but it was overwhelmingly rejected by massive popular demonstrations.

Nasser played a critical role in the **Khartoum Arab Summit**, which declared a policy of the "three *no*'s" toward Israel. Having accepted **Resolution 242** of the UN Security Council, he sought a peaceful resolution concerning the **Occupied Territories**, but neither the **Jarring Mission** nor the **Rogers Plan** yielded any meaningful results. Toward the end of his tenure, Nasser initiated the **War of Attrition**, which sought to harass Israeli positions on the eastern side of the Suez Canal, and in August 1970 he accepted U.S. secretary of state William Rogers's proposal for a cease-fire. After the **Black September Massacre** of Palestinians in **Jordan**, Nasser arranged a truce between the warring sides (the **Cairo Agreement of 1970**). Within hours after securing an agreement, Nasser died on 20 September 1970 and was succeeded by **Anwar Sadat** as president. Despite his many failings, Nasser's name continues to evoke strong support and admiration both in Egypt and in the larger Arab world. *See also* AL-PHA PLAN; GAZA RAID; OMEGA OPERATION.

NATIONALIZATION OF THE SUEZ CANAL. On 26 July 1956, President **Gamal Abdel Nasser** of **Egypt** declared the nationalization of the **Suez Canal**, in retaliation for the Anglo-American decision to reverse their earlier commitment to fund the **Aswan Dam**

project. Announcing his move through a public statement in Alexandria, he pledged to adhere to the **Constantinople Convention**, which guarantees nondiscriminatory freedom of navigation of the canal both in peacetime and during war. *See also* SUEZ WAR.

NAVAL BLOCKADE. Within days after the outbreak of hostilities with the newly founded State of Israel in May 1948, **Egypt** imposed a blockade against Israel-bound shipping through the **Suez Canal**. The blockade continued even after the conclusion of the **armistice agreement** between the two countries in February 1949. The blockade was formalized on 6 February 1950 through a royal decree and was gradually extended to the Strait of Tiran, whose entrance Egypt controls through the islands of Tiran and Sanafir. The blockade was partially lifted in the spring of 1957 following the **Suez War**. In January 1957, Israel conditioned its withdrawal from the **Sinai Peninsula** and the **Gaza Strip** on international recognition of its freedom of navigation in the Strait of Tiran and the Suez Canal. Even though no formal understanding was reached, the closure of the Strait was interpreted as the *casus belli* for the Israeli response. The reimposition of a naval blockade in the Strait of Tiran on 23 May 1967 heightened the tension created following the withdrawal of the **United Nations Emergency Force I** from the Sinai Peninsula and led to the **June War of 1967**. *See also* ARAB BOYCOTT OF ISRAEL.

NAVAL COMMANDO DISASTER. On 5 September 1997, 11 Israeli naval commandos were killed, four were wounded, and another was missing and presumed dead during a botched predawn raid between Sidon and Tyre in south **Lebanon**. The operation was believed to be aimed at kidnapping Khalik Harb, the head of the military wing of the **Hezbollah**. At a crowded press conference in Beirut, Hezbollah leader Sheikh Hassan Nasrallah (1953–) declared that his organization had parts of the body of the missing soldier, Petty Officer Third Class Itamar Ilya, and that Hezbollah explosive devices and gunfire and the detonation of explosives they carried had killed the commandos. This led to renewed calls for a unilateral Israeli **Lebanese withdrawal**. *See also* SECURITY ZONE.

NETANYAHU, BENJAMIN (1949–). A politician and leader of the **Likud**, Benjamin Netanyahu was Israel's first directly elected prime minister, holding this position from June 1996 to July 1999. Born in Tel Aviv on 21 October 1949, he is the younger brother of Jonathan Netanyahu, who commanded the **Entebbe Operation** in July 1976. After studying at the Massachusetts Institute of Technology and Harvard University, Netanyahu served in the **Sayeret Matkal** anti-**terrorism** unit of the **Israel Defense Forces** from 1967 to 1972. After a brief stint in business, in 1982 he began his diplomatic career and served as Israel's deputy chief of mission under the Israeli ambassador to the **United States**, Moshe Arens (1925–). From 1984 to 1988, Netanyahu was Israel's permanent representative to the **United Nations**. In November 1988, he was elected to the Knesset on the Likud platform and became deputy foreign minister. During the **Kuwait War**, when the Iraqi Scud missiles were falling over the country, Netanyahu became Israel's most articulate spokesperson to the outside world.

After the Likud's defeat in the 1992 Knesset elections, Netanyahu was elected leader of the Likud. In the wake of the **Oslo Process**, he emerged as a hardened critic of the peace process and was often held responsible for the rising right-wing extremism in Israel against Prime Minister **Yitzhak Rabin**. In the direct election for prime minister held in June 1996, he narrowly defeated **Shimon Peres** and became Israel's youngest prime minister. After weeks of hesitation, he met Palestinian leader **Yasser Arafat** in October 1996 and renewed peace negotiations; in January 1997, they concluded the **Hebron Protocol**. Citing Palestinian violations and noncompliance, however, he repeatedly stalled the implementation of further Israeli **redeployment**. Under international pressure, Netanyahu concluded the **Wye Memorandum** in October 1998, but two months later, owing to internal pressures, he suspended the agreement.

Netanyahu's tenure also witnessed increased tensions in Israel's relations with **Egypt** and **Jordan**. The **Tunnel Controversy** brought about by his decision to reopen the historic Hasmonean Tunnel in the Old City of **Jerusalem** in September 1996 sparked widespread violence in the **Occupied Territories**. In October 1997, the **assassination** attempt on a senior member of **Hamas** in Amman resulted in a rapid deterioration of relations with Jordan. The incident, known as the **Masha'al Affair**, was resolved peacefully when Netanyahu released the spiritual leader of Hamas, **Sheikh Ahmed Yassin**, who had been imprisoned in Israel.

On 17 May 1999, Netanyahu was convincingly defeated by **Labor party** leader **Ehud Barak**. Netanyahu then resigned as Likud leader and from the Knesset. In 2001, though, he returned to politics and was again elected to the Knesset. Following the withdrawal of the Labor party from the unity government headed by **Ariel Sharon**, Netanyahu became foreign minister in November 2002, and in February 2003, he was shifted to the Finance Ministry. In his bid to regain party leadership, Netanyahu actively campaigned against the **Gaza Withdrawal Plan** outlined by Sharon, and he eventually resigned from the cabinet in August 2005, days before the Israeli withdrawal from the **Gaza Strip**. In the wake of Sharon's decision to leave the Likud and form a new party called Kadima ("Forward") in December 2005, Netanyahu was again elected leader of the Likud.

NETUREI KARTA. Neturei Karta (Aramaic for "Guardians of the City") is an extremist Jewish religious group that inhabits the Mea Shearim neighborhood of **Jerusalem** and Bnei Brak. Following a strict Orthodox lifestyle, it is vehemently opposed to **Zionism**, believes that the redemption of the Jewish people and the establishment of a Jewish state can be brought about only by God, and refuses to recognize the State of Israel and its numerous manifestations, such as its currency, the Hebrew language, its education system, or social welfare programs. It does not seek or accept any social security benefits from the state. Though marginal in Israel, it has widespread publicity outside and is seen as a manifestation of ultraorthodox opposition to Zionism. The Palestinian leadership has courted it. The **Palestine Liberation Organization** (PLO) had considered Neturei Karta to be the representative of the "Palestinian Jews" and accommodated them in the Palestine National Council. In 1994, a member of Neturei Karta was included in the Palestinian cabinet headed by Chairman **Yasser Arafat**.

NILI. Nili (an acronym of *Netzah Israel lo yeshaker*, "The glory of Israel will not fail") was a Jewish underground intelligence group that was formed in the spring of 1915 to help **Great Britain** conquer *Eretz Yisrael* from the Ottomans during World War I. By 1919, following the death of a number of its leading figures, Nili had ceased to exist. The group was opposed by the official leadership of the *Yishuv*, who perceived Nili to be adventurous, irresponsible, and even dangerous to the Jewish community in Palestine, but in 1967, the services of its members were formally recognized.

NINE-POINT ISRAELI PEACE PLAN. In a bid to break the stalemate in the **Jarring Mission** and to circumvent Arab demands for an unconditional withdrawal from the territories Israel had occupied during the **June War of 1967**, on 8 October 1968 Israeli foreign minister Abba Eban (1915–2002) outlined a nine-point peace plan before the **United Nations** General Assembly. It called for a cease-fire, to be followed by "a just and lasting peace, duly negotiated and contractually expressed"; secured and recognized borders; security arrangements to avoid the vulnerable situation that preceded the June War; freedom of navigation through international waterways; a comprehensive settlement to the **refugee** problem through integration and rehabilitation; Israeli recognition of Christian and Islamic rights to their respective holy places; "acknowledgement and recognition of sovereignty, integrity and right to national life"; and regional cooperation. The prevailing climate in the Middle East, however, especially the resounding Arab defeat in the **June War of 1967**, was not conducive to any progress.

NUCLEAR NONPROLIFERATION TREATY (NPT). Coming into force on 5 March 1970, the NPT prohibits the transfer by nuclear weapon states of nuclear weapons or technology to any non–nuclear weapon states. It also prohibits the receipt by non–nuclear weapon states of any transfer, manufacture, or acquisition of nuclear weapons or other nuclear explosive devices. It recognizes the five states that had nuclear weapons as of 1 January 1967—the **United States**, the **Soviet Union**, **Great Britain**, **France**, and China—as nuclear weapon states. By entering into the NPT, signatories agree to give up their nuclear ambitions and abide by the international nonproliferation regime.

Israel remains the only state in the Middle East that has refused to sign the NPT. It is recognized as a country with a significant nuclear weapon capability and has adopted a policy of nuclear ambiguity. Its refusal to reconsider its position dominated the international debate in the early years when the NPT was extended indefinitely. Combined with its nuclear ambiguity, as articulated by the Begin Doctrine, Israel has vowed to prevent any hostile country in the Middle East from acquiring a nuclear capability and for this reason carried out the **Osiraq Bombing** to destroy the Osiraq Nuclear Reactor in

Iraq in June 1981. In 1995, at the time of international negotiations for the indefinite extension of the NPT, **Egypt** threatened to oppose the move unless Israel became a party to the nonproliferation regime, but backtracked due to a U.S. threat to withhold annual economic aid. Since early 2003, international suspicions over the nuclear ambitions of **Iran** have rekindled the nonproliferation debate in the Middle East. *See also* BIOLOGICAL WEAPONS CONVENTION; CHEMICAL WEAPONS CONVENTION; PLUMBAT OPERATION.

– O –

OCCUPIED TERRITORIES. Those territories captured by Israel during the **June War of 1967**, namely, the **West Bank**, including **East Jerusalem**; the **Sinai Peninsula**; the **Gaza Strip**; and the **Golan Heights**. Under the **Camp David Accords**, Israel returned the entire Sinai Peninsula to **Egypt**. Thereafter, the Occupied Territories consisted of 5,698 square kilometers of the West Bank, 349 square kilometers of the **Gaza Strip**, and 1,864 square kilometers of the Golan Heights.

From June 1967, the Occupied Territories were controlled and administered through a **military administration**. In September 1981, the Israeli cabinet approved Defense Minister **Ariel Sharon**'s plan to separate the military from the **civil administration** in the Occupied Territories and the appointment of Menachem Milson as the new civilian administrator. While the Palestinian residents were subjected to the amended pre-1967 laws of **Jordan** and the Mandatory Emergency Regulations of 1945, Israeli settlers living in the Occupied Territories are subjected to Israeli laws and the regulations of the Interior Ministry.

The expression "Occupied Territories' has not been very popular in Israel, hence expressions such as "Administered Territories" or merely "Territories" are commonly used. Since 1967, Israel has maintained that the **Fourth Geneva Convention** of 1949 is not applicable to the Occupied Territories because of their unresolved legal status between 1948 and 1967, when the West Bank was occupied and subsequently annexed by Jordan. Nevertheless, Israel undertook to voluntarily apply the humanitarian rules of the Geneva Convention on the Occupied Territories. In December 2001, a Conference of High Contracting Parties to the Convention was held in Geneva, and it reiterated that the Geneva Convention *does* apply to the Occupied

Territories and urged Israel to implement the provisions in the Occupied Territories, including East Jerusalem.

On 21 March 2005, Prime Minister **Ariel Sharon** approved the construction of 3,500 new homes in a neighborhood that would link the largest settlement in the West Bank, **Ma'aleh Adumim**, with Jerusalem. Dismissing petitions challenging the **Gaza Withdrawal Plan**, on 9 June 2005 the Israeli Supreme Court ruled that the Occupied Territories were not legally part of Israel and were "seized" during the **June War of 1967**. In August, Israel completed its withdrawal from the Gaza Strip and from four isolated settlements in the northern West Bank. *See also* JUDEA AND SAMARIA; SECURITY FENCE.

OCTOBER WAR OF 1973. Also known as the Yom Kippur War or Ramadan War, this conflict broke out on 6 October 1973 when, in coordination with **Syria**, **Egypt** launched a surprise offensive against Israel. With about 70,000 troops, five Egyptian divisions crossed the **Suez Canal** and overpowered the 500-odd Israelis who were defending the **Bar-Lev Line**. By 8 October, most of the defensive Israeli fortifications in the **Sinai Peninsula** were either captured by the Egyptians or abandoned by the Israelis. On the same day, Israel launched an unplanned counteroffensive and suffered heavy losses. Meanwhile, after some initial setbacks, Israel was able to push the Syrian forces back from the **Golan Heights** and, by 10 October, actually made further territorial gains.

The initial Egyptian strategy revolved around crossing the canal, establishing a foothold on the eastern bank, and holding onto its position. Following urgent pleas from Syria, however, on 11 October, President **Anwar Sadat** of Egypt ordered an offensive strategy aimed at capturing the strategic Mitla and Gidi passes about 50 kilometers (30 miles) from the canal. This exposed the Egyptian rear when Israel regrouped and launched a counteroffensive on the night of 15/16 October. Israeli forces encircled the Egyptian Third Army, crossed the Suez Canal, and cut off supplies. This compelled Egypt to accept an immediate cease-fire that it had rejected earlier.

When the cease-fire finally came into effect on 22 October, as called for by **Resolution 338** of the **United Nations** Security Council, Egypt was holding about 1,000 square kilometers (400 square miles) of territory east of the Suez Canal, while Israel had managed to capture 1,600 square kilometers (600 square miles) of territory west of the canal. On the Syrian front, Israel had captured about 600 square kilometers (230 square miles) of additional Syrian territory. Both sides suffered enormous casualties in the war, with combined Egyptian and Syrian casualties estimated at 15,000, while 2,700 Israelis were killed and another 5,000 wounded.

The war witnessed a massive airlift of U.S. weapons to Israel, beginning on 14 October. As an expression of solidarity with Egypt and Syria, **Saudi Arabia** imposed an embargo upon the **United States** and the Netherlands on 16 October. This was soon followed by other oil-exporting Arab states, and the resulting **oil crisis** affected a number of Western states and Japan, compelling them to modify their position on the Arab–Israeli conflict.

The war is remembered for the Israeli failure to read intelligence signals regarding Egyptian intentions and the failure of their strategic concept. The war resulted in the complete overhaul of Israeli political-military leadership and eventually contributed to the erosion of the Mapai/**Labor Party** monopoly. The subsequent **Agranat Commission** severely criticized the government for the intelligence failure that led to the war. The surprise offensive enabled Egypt, despite its loss, to shatter the myth of Israeli invincibility and subsequently enabled Sadat to come to terms with Israel's existence and make peace. *See also* BLUE-WHITE OPERATION.

OIL CRISIS. During the **October War of 1973**, Arab oil-exporting countries met in Kuwait and agreed to cut production, while Abu Dhabi decided to halt its oil exports to the **United States**. These moves were part of the Arab displeasure with countries that were supporting Israel during the war. This policy partly influenced a number of European allies of the United States to deny refueling/overflight facilities for the massive U.S. airlift of military supplies to Israel during the war. Only the Netherlands was willing to provide transit facilities.

The production cuts and dislocation resulted in a massive oil price increase. As a result, in early November 1973, the European Council called for an Israeli withdrawal from the **Occupied Territories** and endorsed the legitimate rights of the Palestinians. Its dependency upon the Middle East for its energy requirements also compelled Japan, a key ally of the United States, to modify its Middle

East policy. Israel called such shifts surrender to Arab "blackmail." Even though similar proposals have been made subsequently, oil was never used again as a political tool in the Arab–Israeli conflict.

OMEGA OPERATION. By March 1956, Anglo-American frustrations over the failure of the **Alpha Plan** led to their desire to isolate and undermine President **Gamal Abdul Nasser** of **Egypt**. Growing contacts between Nasser and the **Soviet Union** increased their apprehensions. Where the Alpha Plan involved positive inducements for Egypt, Omega contained veiled but real threats to harm Egyptian interests. These included threats to suspend Anglo-American financing of the **Aswan Dam**, to encourage anti-Nasser conservative Islamic forces, and to engage in economic warfare against the cotton industry of Egypt. Great Britain and the **United States** even contemplated taking "more drastic actions" to influence Nasser. *See also* CHAMELEON OPERATION.

OPEN BRIDGES POLICY. Following the **June War of 1967**, Israel and **Jordan** agreed to use the Allenby Bridge (also known as the King **Hussein** Bridge), north of the Dead Sea, and the Damia Bridge in the Jordan Valley to link the **Occupied Territories** to the outside world. Introduced by Israeli defense minister **Moshe Dayan**, the Open Bridges Policy provided access for the Palestinians to the Arab world and enabled the export of Palestinian produce and the migration of Palestinian laborers to the Gulf countries. At the same time, through various security measures directed against Palestinians of age 20–40, it encouraged Palestinian emigration from the Occupied Territories. Following the implementation of the **Cairo Agreement** in 1994, nominal control of the western end of the Allenby Bridge went to the **Palestinian National Authority**, with Israel maintaining a security presence. Since the outbreak of the **Al-Aqsa Intifada**, Jordan has been apprehensive of massive Israeli **deportations** of Palestinians, and in June 2001, it imposed severe restrictions on the entry of Palestinians from the **West Bank** and the **Gaza Strip**.

OPERATION PEACE FOR GALILEE. On 6 June 1982, Israel launched a massive offensive against the **Palestine Liberation Organization** (PLO) in **Lebanon**. An **assassination** attempt on 2 June 1982 on Israel's ambassador in London, Shlomo Argov (1929–2003), by radical Palestinian groups opposed to **Yasser Arafat** provided the spark. Since its expulsion from **Jordan** following the **Black September Massacre**, the PLO had frequently attacked Israel from southern Lebanon. Determined to put Galilee out of the reach of Palestinian shelling, Israel, through this operation, sought to remove the military threats posed by the PLO.

The offensive was sudden, and Israeli forces swiftly moved deep into Lebanese territory and captured and destroyed numerous PLO positions. Within weeks, thousands of Palestinians were either killed or captured in southern Lebanon. The quick military advances gradually expanded the objectives of Israeli invasion, and by mid-June, Beirut came under virtual Israeli siege. On 1 August, the **Israel Defense Forces** (IDF) captured the Beirut International Airport. On 12 August, PLO leader Arafat gave in to the Israeli conditions and agreed to withdraw his forces under supervision of a multinational force. The first contingent of PLO fighters bound for Cyprus, Jordan, and **Iraq** left Beirut aboard a Greek ship on 21 August 1982. By end of the month, the Palestinian combatants had evacuated Beirut and headed for various Arab states. In December, Arafat himself left Lebanon for Tunis.

In the midst of this operation, Bashir Gemayel (1947–1982) was elected president of Lebanon on 23 August. His inauguration was scheduled for 23 September, but on 14 September, he was assassinated by Palestinian elements. With the knowledge and approval of the IDF, right-wing Christian **Phalangist** elements then entered the Palestinian **refugee** camps on 16 September and retaliated against the Palestinians in the **Sabra and Shatila Massacre**.

Operation Peace for Galilee exposed serious domestic divisions in Israel regarding the invasion, the expanding military objectives, and the massacre at Sabra and Shatila, and there were widespread public protests in Israel. In May 1983, the country managed to sign the **Israel–Lebanon Agreement**, but due to persistent opposition from **Syria**, Beirut abrogated it by the following March. The domestic opposition inside Israel, mounting casualties in Lebanon, and the inability to find an interlocutor who would sign a formal agreement eventually compelled Israel to conduct a unilateral **Lebanese withdrawal**. On 10 June 1985, Israel evacuated its forces from most of the Lebanese territory, but retained a narrow strip in southern

Lebanon as a self-declared **security zone**. It was estimated that the whole exercise cost Israel about $3.5 billion. In November 1983, Israel released 4,500 prisoners it had captured during Operation Peace for Galilee in a **prisoner exchange** for six IDF members held by PLO factions in northern Lebanon. *See also* BELGIUM LAW; FOUR MOTHERS MOVEMENT; KAHAN COMMISSION.

ORIENT HOUSE. The property of the Husseini family, the Orient House in **East Jerusalem** was built in 1897. During 1949–1950, it functioned as the headquarters of the **Palestine Conciliation Committee** and **United Nations Relief and Works Agency**, and subsequently it was operated as a hotel. Following the **June War of 1967**, when Israel captured East Jerusalem, it was converted into a private residence. In 1983, the Arab Studies Societies headed by Faisal al-Husseini (1940–2001) rented a portion of the House. During the **Intifada**, citing security reasons, Israeli authorities briefly closed it on 28 July 1988. In early 1991, the Orient House emerged as the effective headquarters of the Palestinian delegation to the **Madrid Conference** and hosted preconference negotiations with the **United States**. Since then, it has hosted meetings with foreign diplomats, journalists, and occasionally junior officials from other countries.

As part of the **Oslo Process**, on 11 October 1993 Israeli prime minister **Yitzhak Rabin** sent a letter to Norwegian foreign minister Johan Jorgen Holst (1937–1994) stating that Israel would not change the status of economic, social, educational, and cultural institutions operating in Jerusalem. However, the conduct of what was seen as diplomatic activities became controversial in the domestic Israeli agenda. Citing such activities as a violation of the **Declaration of Principles**, on 26 December 1994 the Israeli government enacted the Orient House Law, which restricted political activities at the House and prohibited the establishment of any institution connected to the **Palestinian National Authority** in East Jerusalem. The law enables the Israeli government to act against Palestinian political activities in the Orient House or in any other institution located in East Jerusalem.

Days before the May 1999 Knesset elections, Israel sought to close three Palestinian offices located in the Orient House but was stopped by the Supreme Court from enforcing its law. Despite this legislation, the Israeli government followed a hands-off policy vis-à-vis the Orient House until August 2001. In the midst of the **Al-Aqsa Intifada**, responding to a suicide attack in West **Jerusalem** in which 15 Israelis were killed, on 9 August Israeli forces stormed the building; confiscated computers, data, files, and other materials and sealed the building.

OSIRAQ BOMBING. On 7 June 1981, Israel conducted an air raid on a nearly completed nuclear reactor near Baghdad, **Iraq**. Constructed with cooperation of **France**, the reactor—known as Tammuz I to the Iraqis and Osiraq to the French—was under the full-scope safeguards of the International Atomic Energy Agency, the international nuclear regulatory body. The attack was seen as the ushering in of what is often termed the Begin Doctrine. Under this doctrine, Israel expressed its determination to prevent any of its adversaries in the region from acquiring nuclear weapon capabilities.

Even though Israel is not a signatory of the **Nuclear Nonproliferation Treaty** (NPT), it accused Iraq—which is a signatory—of deviating from peaceful nuclear means and pursuing a weaponization program. Israel justified its preemptive strike by clarifying that it would be the prime target of a nuclear Iraq. The international community was critical of Israel, and the **United Nations** Security Council unanimously condemned the raid. The **United States**, on the other hand, only mildly rebuffed the raid on the nuclear facility south of Baghdad and briefly suspended the delivery of four F-16 jet fighters. Even though the Reagan administration (1981–1989) admonished Israel and joined the international condemnation of Israel, a decade later the United States used the same arguments to partly justify its campaigns against Baghdad in the **Kuwait War**. *See also* ARMISTICE AGREEMENT/S.

OSLO ACCORDS. This expression refers to all the agreements between Israel and the Palestinian leadership, including the **Declaration of Principles** (1993), **Cairo Agreement** (1994), **Paris Agreement** (1994), **Taba Agreement** (1995), **Wye Memorandum** (1998), and **Sharm al-Sheikh Memorandum** (1999). *See also* OSLO PROCESS.

OSLO PROCESS. This nomenclature refers to the peace talks that began in Oslo, Norway, between the officials of Israel and the **Palestine Liberation Organization** (PLO) and the various **Oslo Accords** concluded between the two sides as a follow-up to such talks. In late 1992, Israel and the PLO initiated secret negotiations to circumvent the impasse in the bilateral talks that were taking place in Washington. These talks, held within the framework of the **Madrid Conference** peace process, formally excluded the PLO; the Palestinians were represented as part of the joint Jordanian–Palestinian delegation. Controversy over the **deportation** of more than 400 suspected **Hamas** activists in December 1992 provided another impetus to resolve the stalemate.

Back-channel diplomacy initiated by two Israeli academics gradually became official with the involvement of Deputy Foreign Minister Yossi Beilin (1948–) and Foreign Minister **Shimon Peres**. The talks were held in Oslo, where Norwegian foreign minister Johan Jorgen Holst (1937–1994) played host. After many drafts, the **Declaration of Principles** was secretly initialed on 20 August 1993. On 9 September 1993, Israel and the PLO exchanged letters, signed by Israeli prime minister **Yitzhak Rabin** and PLO chairman **Yasser Arafat**, that granted **mutual recognition**. The PLO formally accepted Israel's right to exist, and Israel recognized the PLO as "the representative of the Palestinian people." The PLO also committed to **annulling** clauses in its Covenant (also known as the **PLO Charter**) that challenged Israel's existence.

OSLO TIMETABLE. *See* DECLARATION OF PRINCIPLES.

OSLO II AGREEMENT. *See* TABA AGREEMENT.

– P –

PACT OF MUTUAL COOPERATION. *See* BAGHDAD PACT.

PALESTINE CONCILIATION COMMISSION (PCC). Resolution 194 of the **United Nations** General Assembly, passed on 11 December 1948, established the three-member Palestine Conciliation Commission to take over the functions and responsibilities of **United Nations mediator** Count Folke Bernadotte (1895–1948), who had been killed in September. The five permanent members of the UN Security Council were authorized by the resolution to recommend the commission's members, and they nominated **France, Turkey**, and the **United States**.

On 27 April 1949, the PCC convened a meeting in Lausanne, Switzerland, attended by Israel and neighboring Arab states. By then, Israel had signed **armistice agreements** with **Egypt, Lebanon**, and **Jordan** and had begun negotiations with **Syria** for a similar agreement. Nevertheless, the Arabs refused to participate in direct negotiations with Israel, so the PCC held separate consultations with both sides. Based on its consultations, the PCC developed the Protocol of Lausanne, which set out a number of principles for future resolution of the Arab–Israeli conflict. Signed on 12 May 1949, the protocol recognized the **Partition Plan** and the accompanying map that outlined the territorial jurisdiction of Jewish and Arab states in the Palestine **Mandate** as "*a basis* for discussion with the Commission."

In late 1950, the PCC sought to resolve the **refugee** question through a three-pronged approach: repatriation to Israel; resettlement in Arab countries; and absorption by other countries. However, differences between parties over the territorial issue and the refugee problem prevented any agreement, and in November 1951, the commission conceded its inability to function and fulfill its mandate.

Years later, the commission tried to revive its refugee proposal. To investigate the possibility of such an option, in 1961 the PCC sent a team to the region, headed by Joseph E. Johnson. The **Johnson Mission** submitted its final, negative report in September 1962. The PCC was never formally dissolved and still periodically submits reports to the United Nations about its nonactivity.

PALESTINE LIBERATION ARMY (PLA). This military branch of the **Palestine Liberation Organization** (PLO) was established by **Yasser Arafat** in 1964 and consisted of three brigades. Their autonomy and independence were severely curtailed, however, and the PLA units were absorbed into the armies of the host countries: *Ein Jalut* under the control of the army of **Egypt**, *Qadisiyya* under **Iraq**, and *Hittin* under **Syria**. Following the **Arab–Israeli War of June 1967**, *Qadisiyya* brigade was transferred to **Jordan** and renamed *al-Badr*. Apprehensive of Israeli retaliation, the PLA units were prohibited from organizing, assisting, or supporting any commando raids against Israel. Following the signing of the **Taba Agreement** in May 1994, some units returned to the **Occupied Territories** and were deployed as the police force of the **Palestinian National Authority**.

PALESTINE LIBERATION FRONT (PLF). Following a split from the **Popular Front for the Liberation of Palestine** and the **Popular Front for the Liberation of Palestine–General Command**, Mohammed Zeidan (aka Abu Abbas, 1948–) formed this militant group in April 1977. It subsequently split into three factions, two supported by **Syria** and the one led by Abu Abbas, which was supported by **Iraq**. At one time, Abu Abbas was a member of the **Palestine Liberation Organization** (PLO) Executive Committee and headed the Department of **Refugees**. In the 1980s, his group was held responsible for a number of **terrorist** incidents, including the *Achille Lauro* **Affair** in 1985. On 30 May 1990, the PLF launched an unsuccessful commando raid on the beaches of Tel Aviv, and this led to the suspension of the **United States**–PLO dialogue that had began in December 1988. Despite its opposition to the **Madrid Conference** and **Oslo Process**, the PLF is still represented in the PLO Executive Committee. During the Allied invasion of **Iraq** in 2003, Abu Abbas was captured in South Baghdad on 15 April, and the following March he died while still in allied custody.

PALESTINE LIBERATION ORGANIZATION (PLO). An umbrella organization set up in 1964 to represent the dispersed Palestinian people and to enable them to liberate their homeland and shape their destiny. A decision to this effect was made at the first **Arab League** summit in Cairo in January 1964. Subsequently, the PLO held its first **Palestine National Congress** in May 1964 in **East Jerusalem**, then under the control of **Jordan**, and adopted the **PLO Charter**. Veteran Arab diplomat Ahmad Shuqeiri (1908–1980) was chosen as the first chairman of the PLO.

The first Palestinian Congress also set up the Palestinian National Council (PNC), the PLO Executive Committee, a National Fund, and the **Palestine Liberation Army** (PLA). The PLO created a number of organizations to provide education, health, and relief services and formed a quasi-government with a security apparatus, financial system, information offices, and diplomatic missions. Since 1967, the PLO has strengthened its organizational, social, financial, educational, propagandist, and political activities. Its successful guerrilla campaign helped consolidate its support base among Palestinian **refugees** as well as the Arab masses elsewhere. At its height, the PLO functioned inside the areas controlled by Israel, along Israel's borders, and against Israeli interests around the world.

From its inauguration in 1964, the PNC functioned as the Palestinian parliament in exile. Normally the PNC met once a year. Its membership was allocated to the various component bodies of the PLO, as well as to affiliated mass organizations representing workers, students, women, teachers, doctors, and others; the membership included representatives from the **Occupied Territories** and the Palestinian diaspora in Jordan, **Syria**, **Lebanon**, and the Gulf States. The 1964 PLO Covenant (also known as the PLO Charter) called for the establishment of a secular and democratic **Palestinian state** in the whole of Palestine, as it existed under the **mandate**.

The **Arab Higher Committee**, headed by former **Jerusalem** mufti Hajj Amin al-Husseini (c. 1895–1974), was not in favor of creating the PLO. Similarly, Jordan, which annexed the **West Bank** in 1951, was opposed to the formation of a separate nonterritorial entity to represent the Palestinians. To mitigate this opposition, the Palestinian demand for independent statehood carefully excluded those parts of Palestine occupied by Jordan and **Egypt** during 1948–1967. However, this distinction became irrelevant following the Israeli occupation of the West Bank and the **Gaza Strip** in 1967 and hence was removed from the PLO Covenant in 1968.

While the performance of the Arab armies had been dismal in the **June War of 1967**, the **Fedayeen** operations were relatively successful. In July 1968, the fourth PNC in Cairo clearly stated, "Armed struggle is the only way to liberate Palestine." That session of the PNC transformed the PLO from being merely a political representation of the Palestinians into an umbrella organization of various military and civilian Palestinian groups, with the guerrilla groups at its core.

Fatah, established in 1959, has been a prominent component of the PLO; its other major components are the **Popular Front for the Liberation of Palestine** (PFLP) and the **Democratic Front for the Liberation of Palestine** (DFLP). At the fifth session of the PNC in February 1969, Fatah seized control of the PLO and gained the majority in the 13-member executive. **Yasser Arafat**, the leader of the Fatah, became the chairman and held that position until his death in November 2004.

In September 1970, a violent confrontation erupted between the PLO and the Jordanian army, culminating in the **Black September Massacre**. The confrontation arose from the apprehensions of King **Hussein** that the PLO would try to take over Jordan. At the end of the crisis, Jordan ceased to be a base for the operations of the PLO against Israel; the organization was ousted from Amman and transferred to Beirut.

In June 1974, the PLO moved toward the idea of establishing a Palestinian state in the Occupied Territories as the first step toward the total liberation of the Palestine Mandate. Despite Jordanian opposition, the Arab League recognized the PLO in 1974 as the "sole and legitimate" representative of the Palestinian people. This was followed by similar recognition by a number of Third World countries. Following an address by Arafat at the **United Nations** General Assembly on 22 November 1974, the world body recognized the PLO as "the representative of the Palestinian people" and reaffirmed the Palestinian right to self-determination and national independence. Since then, the PLO has been participating in all UN deliberations concerning Palestinians.

Most of the PLO activities against Israel have emanated from the Occupied Territories, southern Lebanon, Jordan (until the Black September crackdown), Syria (until the 1975 separation of forces agreement), or Egypt (until Sadat's peace initiative in 1978). At one time or another, its guerrilla tactics against Israel put the PLO at odds with all those countries, although its financial dependence upon oil-rich Arab states made the PLO vulnerable to pressure tactics. More than its diplomatic successes, the PLO gained international attention and recognition primarily through its guerrilla campaigns against Israel and its interests in the Middle East.

After the Israeli invasion of Lebanon in June 1982 in **Operation Peace for Galilee**, the PLO, its commandos, and the PLA troops were evacuated from Beirut and were dispersed to various Arab countries. On 17 September 1982, **Phalange** militants entered the Palestinian refugee camps in Lebanon and committed the **Sabra and Shatila Massacre**, in which nearly 2,000 Palestinians, including women and children, were killed. The PLO headquarters, which was moved to Tunis as part of the evacuation from Lebanon, was raided by Israel on 1 October 1985, resulting in the death of more than 70 people, with Arafat making a providential escape.

The outbreak of the **Intifada** in the Gaza Strip in December 1987 once again brought the PLO to the forefront. Though the uprising was spontaneous, the PLO quickly took control of the situation and became part of the **Unified National Leadership of the Uprising**. Capitalizing on international attention and support, the PNC adopted the **Algiers Declaration** on 15 November 1988 and proclaimed the establishment of the State of Palestine, with Arafat as its president. In a historical shift, it accepted the **Partition Plan** of 1947, renounced the use of violence to achieve the aims of the PLO, and became reconciled to the idea of Palestinian self-determination in coexistence with Israel. Meanwhile, responding to the Intifada, **Jordanian disengagement** cut off all its administrative links with the West Bank. Following these developments and Arafat's renunciation of violence, in 1988, the **United States** initiated a dialogue with the PLO, only to suspend it in July 1990 after an aborted terrorist attack against Israel by the **Palestine Liberation Front** headed by Abu Abbas (1948–2004).

The Iraqi invasion of Kuwait in August 1990 and the Palestinian endorsement of Saddam Hussein (1937–) brought the PLO into conflict with the prevailing Arab consensus. Oil-rich countries such as Kuwait and **Saudi Arabia**, the principal benefactors of the PLO, resented Palestinian approval of the Iraqi linkage between the **Kuwait War** and the future of the **Occupied Territories**. Arafat became persona non grata in the Arab world. Following a series of negotiations with U.S. secretary of state James Baker (1930–), however, the PLO backed the idea of a peaceful and negotiated settlement with Israel and agreed to attend a Middle East peace conference. When the Israelis balked, the PLO agreed to form a joint Jordanian–Palestinian delegation for the **Madrid Conference**, which opened on 30 October 1991. Even though the negotiations were supposedly conducted with the Palestinians based in the Occupied Territories, the Tunis-based PLO leadership was deeply involved. The bilateral talks, however, did not make any progress.

After his election as prime minister in July 1992, **Labor Party** leader **Yitzhak Rabin** expressed Israel's commitment to a land-for-peace policy, and in January 1993, Israel repealed the **PLO Law**. These moves set off the **Oslo Process** between Israel and the PLO. On 9 September 1993, Prime Minister Rabin and Chairman Arafat exchanged letters of **mutual recognition**. On 13 September, the **Declaration of Principles** (DoP), signed on the White House lawn in the presence of President **Bill Clinton** (1946–) and other international leaders, outlined the terms of reference for achieving a negotiated settlement.

The DoP was transformed into a working document in May 1994, when both parties agreed to the establishment of the **Palestinian National Authority**, delineated the geographical and functional limits of autonomy, and agreed on a framework for **Permanent Status Negotiations**. In July 1994, the PLO and Arafat moved to the Gaza Strip from Tunis to administer Gaza and **Jericho**. By 1995, Israel completed its **redeployment** from Palestinian towns.

In January 1996, a popular vote was held to elect the president of the PNA and an 88-member **Palestinian Legislative Council**. This was not acceptable to a number of Palestinian groups, however, including some affiliated with the PLO, and they launched a **Rejectionist Front** in Damascus. They often staged protest rallies and demonstrations against the Oslo Process. The most violent protest against the peace process came from the **Hamas** Islamic radicals, who conducted a series of **suicide attacks** against and often inside Israel.

On 24 April 1996, a few weeks before crucial parliamentary elections in Israel, the PNC met in Gaza and passed a resolution declaring that "the articles [of the Covenant] that are contrary to the [9 September 1993] letters of Mutual Recognition" were null and void. This declaration, approved 504–54 (with 14 abstentions), was nevertheless rejected by many Israelis as vague, imprecise, and insufficient. On 10 December 1998, the PNC met in the Gaza Strip and by 81–7 (with seven abstentions) voted to revoke the specific clauses of the Covenant. The PNC again ratified this decision on 14 December, with President Clinton witnessing this decision, which was adopted by a show of hands rather than a formal vote.

After the death of Arafat on 11 November 2004, **Mahmoud Abbas** was elected leader of the PLO. The following month he visited Kuwait, met members of the ruling family, and offered an apology for the policies pursued by the Palestinian leadership during the Kuwait War. *See also* QUREI, AHMED.

PALESTINE MANDATE. *See* MANDATE, PALESTINE.

PALESTINE NATIONAL CONGRESS. With the intention of liberating Palestine, President **Gamal Abdul Nasser** of **Egypt** led an **Arab League** initiative and organized a conference in September 1963. At that conference, a Palestinian entity to be led by Ahmad Shuqeiri (1908–1980) was set up, and a resolution calling for the formation of the **Palestine Liberation Organization** (PLO) was adopted. Known subsequently as the first Palestine National Congress, it established the Palestine National Fund and the **Palestinian National Council** and adopted a national Palestinian covenant. *See also* PLO CHARTER.

PALESTINE NATIONAL FRONT (PNF). A secret body set up by the Palestine National Council in January 1973 to organize Palestinian resistance in the **Occupied Territories** against Israel and to weaken the influence of **Jordan** in the **West Bank**. Israeli and Jordanian efforts to circumvent the influence of the **Palestine Liberation Organization** (PLO) in the Occupied Territories compelled the PLO to strengthen its influence. As a follow-up to the 11th Palestinian National Council, the PNF was established in 1973 to function as a PLO-guided framework for all nationalist activities in the **West Bank** and **Gaza Strip**. Members of the PNF were harshly persecuted by the Israeli military authorities for their "subversive" activities. In 1976, the PNF contested the local elections conducted by the Israeli **military administration** and won a number of seats. Its growing popularity caused concerns not only for Israel and **Jordan** but also for the Beirut-based PLO leadership, which sought to exercise greater control over the PLF's activities. In May 1980, Israel **deported** some of the key leaders of the PNF, including the mayors of Hebron and Halhul, to **Lebanon**. The PNF was outlawed by Israel and the newly formed **Committee for National Guidance** became the principal organ of nationalist activities in the West Bank.

PALESTINE NATIONAL SALVATION FRONT (PNSF). On 25 March 1985, a number of anti–**Yasser Arafat** groups supported by **Syria** organized themselves into the Palestinian National Salvation Front to oppose the **Hussein–Arafat Accord** of February 1985. The PNSF was led by Khalid al-Fahum, the head of the **Palestine Liberation Organization** Central Council. The faction backed by Syria had earlier boycotted the Palestinian National Council (PNC) meeting held during 22–29 November 1984. At that meeting, the PNC decided to remove al-Fahum as its speaker and replace him with Abd al-Hamid al-Sayyeh.

PALESTINE PEOPLE'S PARTY (PPP). In February 1982, Bashir al-Barghouti founded the Palestine Communist Party in the **Occupied Territories**. Following the disintegration of the **Soviet Union** and the end of the Cold War, this party discarded the Leninist ideology and relaunched itself as the Palestine People's Party. The PPP was one of the constituent members of the **Unified National Leadership of the Uprising** during the **Intifada**. It pioneered the Israeli–Palestinian dialogue and advocated a two-state solution. The PPP supported the **Oslo Process** and was the only organized political party besides **Fatah** to contest the January 1996 elections to the **Palestinian Legislative Council**. Though the PPP was unsuccessful, its leader Barghouti was appointed a minister in the **Palestinian National Authority**. The PPP calls for the reorganization of the **Palestine Liberation Organization** and political dialogue with opposition factions.

PALESTINIAN COMMITTEE. During the 1975 annual session, the **United Nations** General Assembly formed a 20-member committee (later increased to 24) to devise plans for the implementation of Palestinian "self-determination and national independence." The current members are Afghanistan, Belarus, Cuba, Cyprus, Guinea, Guyana, Hungary, India, Indonesia, Laos, Madagascar, Malaysia, Mali, Malta, Namibia, Nigeria, Pakistan, Romania, Senegal, Sierra Leone, South Africa, Tunisia, **Turkey**, and Ukraine. The committee periodically meets and organizes various conferences on the Palestinian question.

PALESTINIAN LEGISLATIVE COUNCIL (PLC). The **Taba Agreement** stipulated that upon the completion of Israeli "**redeployment**" from major Palestinian towns, Palestinians in the **Occupied Territories** would directly elect an 82-member Legislative Council and the chairman of the **Palestinian National Authority** (PNA). Israeli redeployment from six Palestinian towns in the **West Bank** was completed by late 1995. Between 12 November and 12 December 1995, voter registration was undertaken in the West Bank and the **Gaza Strip**, and 1,013,235 Palestinians were registered as eligible voters. A Central Election Commission headed by **Mahmoud Abbas** was appointed on 22 December.

Due to internal demands, **Palestine Liberation Organization** chairman **Yasser Arafat** increased the size of the council from 82 seats to 88. The West Bank and the Gaza Strip were divided into the 16 multimember electoral districts: Balah (5 seats), Bethlehem (4), Deir Nablus (8), Gaza (12), Hebron (10), Jabaliya (7), Jenin (6), **Jericho** (1), **Jerusalem** (7), Khan Yunis (8), Qalqilya (2), Rafah (5), Ramallah (7), Salfit (1), Toubas (1); and Tulkaram (4). Out of the 88 seats, seven were reserved for religious minorities: one each in Gaza and Ramallah and two each in Bethlehem and Jerusalem were reserved for Christians, and one seat was allotted for the 400-member Samaritan community of Deir Nablus.

The elections, which were held on 20 January 1996, witnessed a high voter turnout of 79 percent. **Fatah** fielded the highest number of candidates, an d the **Palestine People's Party** was the only other organized political party to contest the elections. A number of important Palestinian groups and parties—including **Hamas**, the **Popular Front for the Liberation of Palestine**, the **Democratic Front for the Liberation of Palestine**, and **Islamic Jihad**—boycotted the elections, primarily because of their disapproval of and opposition to the **Oslo Process**. Fatah won 52 seats, and 12 seats went to former members of Fatah who contested as rebels. Of the others, 16 seats went to independents, two to **FIDA**, four to independents affiliated with Islamists, one to Samaritans, and one to Arafat, who was elected president of the PNA.

The Palestinian Legislative Council held its first session on 7 March 1996, and **Ahmed Qurei** was elected Speaker of the Council. The members of the PLC were automatically made members of the Palestinian National Council. The PLC is responsible for drafting a Palestinian constitution and any other legal and regulatory framework, all of which require a formal approval from Israel. However, the PLC lacks foreign policy powers. Following the death of Chairman Arafat on 11 November, Speaker of the PLC Rawhi Fattouh (1949–) became interim head of the PNA.

The elections for the new council were slated for July 2005, but following internal tensions between Fatah and other militant groups, President **Mahmoud Abbas** postponed the national elections to January 2006. In June 2005, the PLC adopted new election laws under which the strength of the parliament was raised to 132 seats; out of this, 66 members would be elected in constituency-based regional elections and the other 66 would be elected through proportional representation.

PALESTINIAN NATIONAL AND ISLAMIC FORCES (PNIF). This umbrella organization was the product of the **Al-Aqsa Intifada**. It consists of members of the **Palestine Liberation Organization**, **Hamas**, and **Islamic Jihad**.

PALESTINIAN NATIONAL AUTHORITY (PNA). The PNA was established in the wake of the **Declaration of Principles** with the explicit purpose of governing Palestinian affairs in the self-rule area. The terms and conditions were established under the **Cairo**

Agreement of May 1994. The initial contingent of Palestinian police arrived in the **Gaza Strip** in May 1994 and **Yasser Arafat** made a triumphant entry on 1 July.

Initially, the name "Palestinian National Authority" had been given to the Palestinian self-government entity established to implement this accord. Subsequently, it was used to describe the Palestinian body administering the **West Bank** and the Gaza Strip. Despite its limited powers, the PNA is responsible for the entire **Occupied Territories**, including those areas under nominal Israeli security control.

In the beginning, the PNA took over the responsibilities for tourism, education, health, taxes, and social welfare. On 20 August 1995, it assumed the administration of commerce and industry, agriculture, local government, gas and petrol, postal services, labor, insurance, and statistics.

The **Taba Agreement** of 1995 provided for the election of 82 (subsequently increased to 88) representatives to a **Palestinian Legislative Council** and the formation of an Executive Authority under a *ra'ees* (chairman or president). The elections were held on 20 January 1996, and the Palestinian cabinet was formed during March–June 1996. Although subject to all agreements signed with Israel, the PNA lacks foreign relations powers but is empowered to conduct **Permanent Status Negotiations**. However, since the outbreak of the **Al-Aqsa Intifada** and especially during the **Defensive Shield Operation** in 2002, Israel has systematically destroyed the physical as well as administrative infrastructure of the PNA.

Under pressure from the **United States** in March 2003, Arafat created the post of prime minister and appointed **Mahmoud Abbas** to the position. However, due to differences with Arafat, Abbas resigned in September and was replaced by **Ahmed Qurei**. After the death of Arafat on 11 November 2004, Speaker of the Council Rawhi Fattouh (1949–) became interim head of the PNA. In August 2005, Israel completed its **Gaza Withdrawal Plan** and the PNA took control of the Gaza Strip.

PALESTINIAN STATE. Since the end of the **mandate**, the Palestinians have declared independence on two occasions. In September 1948, the grand mufti of **Jerusalem**, Hajj Amin al-Husseini (c. 1895–1974), proclaimed the **All Palestine Government**. It was recognized by all the Arab countries except **Transjordan**, but the attempt soon fizzled out. Similarly, amidst the **Intifada**, on 15 November 1988, the Palestinian National Council proclaimed the State of Palestine. Though recognized by more than a hundred countries—mostly those belonging to the Third World and the Nonaligned Movement—it lacked all the attributes of a state. Under the **Declaration of Principles**, the final status of the **Occupied Territories** was to be resolved by September 1999. As the deadline neared, Palestinian leader **Yasser Arafat** threatened to again unilaterally declare statehood, but he was dissuaded by the international community from such an action. On 12 March 2002, the **United Nations** Security Council unanimously adopted (with **Syria** abstaining) the **United States**–sponsored Resolution 1397, which for the first time affirmed the "vision" of a Palestinian state. *See also* ALGIERS DECLARATION; UNILATERAL DECLARATION OF INDEPENDENCE.

PALMAH. In 1941, the Palmah was established as the "striking force" of **Haganah** and was headed by Yitzhak Sadeh. It gradually became the principal force of Haganah, and on the eve of Israel's formation consisted of 3,000 men in 15 companies organized into four battalions, one of which consisted of special units. Highly trained and motivated, the Palmah played a crucial role in Israel's victories in the **Arab–Israeli War of 1947–1948**. After the formation of the **Israel Defense Forces**, the Palmah was disbanded in October 1948 as the government decided not to allow any independent military command. Most members of the Palmah, including **Yitzhak Rabin**, joined the regular army. *See also ALTALENA* AFFAIR; IRGUN; STERN GANG.

PARIS AGREEMENT. As part of the Interim Agreement, Israel and the **Palestine Liberation Organization** (PLO) negotiated the terms and conditions of an economic arrangement between the Jewish state and the **Palestinian National Authority**. The dialogue began in Paris on 13 October 1993, and after five months of negotiations, a formal agreement called the "Protocol on Economic Relations between the Government of Israel and the PLO" was signed in Paris on 29 April 1994 by Israeli finance minister Avraham Shochat (1936–) and his Palestinian counterpart, **Ahmed Qurei**. It was subsequently incorporated as an annexure to the **Taba Agreement** signed in May 1994.

PARTITION PLAN. Acting on the recommendations of the **United Nations Special Committee on Palestine** (UNSCOP), the **United Nations** General Assembly voted on 29 November 1947, 33–13 with 10 abstentions, to pass Resolution 181 and partition Palestine. The **Peel Commission** had first floated the idea of partition in July 1937. The UN plan granted 56.47 percent of the Palestine **Mandate** to the Jews and 43.53 percent to the Arabs. At that time, the Jews owned less than 7 percent of the land in Palestine and constituted 30 percent of the total population. Under this plan, the Jewish state would have a 58 percent Jewish population (498,000 Jews, 325,000 Arab Muslims, and 90,000 Bedouins), while the Arab state would be 99 percent Arab (807,000 Arab inhabitants and 10,000 Jews). The Partition Plan called for an internationalized sector (*corpus separatum*) for the city of **Jerusalem** and its environs, with guaranteed free access to places holy to Christians, Jews, and Muslims. About 100,000 Jews and 105,000 Arabs resided in Jerusalem.

Modifying UNSCOP's majority plan in favor of the Jews, the plan allotted the Negev to the Jewish state and granted access to the Red Sea through the port of Eilat. The plan was welcomed by the **Zionists** but was completely rejected by the Arab and Palestinian leadership. On the eve of the decision by **Great Britain** to withdraw from Palestine, the General Assembly convened a special session to discuss a **United States** proposal to temporarily suspend the partition resolution, but it was preempted by the unilateral declaration of independence by the Zionist leadership. *See also* ARAB–ISRAELI WAR OF 1947–1948; FEDERAL PLAN; NAQBA, AL-; WORLD ZIONIST ORGANIZATION.

PASSFIELD WHITE PAPER. As a follow-up to the **Shaw Commission** report, in October 1930, **Great Britain** came out with the Passfield White Paper. Addressing the key Arab demands of the **Mandate** authorities, it called for a halt to the *Aliya* and Jewish land purchases. This indirect repudiation of the **Balfour Declaration** evoked strong protest from the *Yishuv* and the **Zionist** leadership. On 13 February 1931, Prime Minister Ramsay MacDonald (1866–1937) of **Great Britain** sent a letter—known to Palestinians as the **Black Letter**—to Chaim Weizmann (1874–1952), the president of the **World Zionist Organization**, nullifying the objectionable clauses of the White Paper. *See also* LEAGUE OF NATIONS.

PEACE NOW. In 1978, a group of 350 reserve army officers made an appeal to Israeli prime minister **Menachem Begin** urging him to pursue the road to peace. This gradually swelled into an extraparliamentary nonpartisan movement that helped to promote peace with Israel's neighbors. This group organized a number of rallies and demonstrations to keep up the pressure and eventually became the embryonic peace bloc in Israel. It transformed into an organized peace group, *Shalom Achshav* ("Peace Now"), following the Israeli invasion of **Lebanon** in 1982. On 25 September 1982, in the wake of the **Sabra and Shatila Massacre**, it organized the largest demonstration in the Middle East, which eventually compelled the government to institute the **Kahan Commission** to inquire into the massacre. Not a pacifist movement, Peace Now adopts much of the mainstream Israeli position concerning the indivisibility of **Jerusalem** and opposition to complete Israeli withdrawal to the **Green Line**. Among other things, Peace Now has been advocating a territorial compromise with the Palestinians and monitoring **settlement** activities in the **Occupied Territories**. *See also* FOUR MOTHERS MOVEMENT.

PEEL COMMISSION. In 1936 **Great Britain** appointed a royal commission headed by Sir Robert Peel to investigate the causes of the disturbances in the Palestine **Mandate**, which subsequently transformed into prolonged rebellion and violence. The report of the commission was published on 7 July 1937. It concluded that the British government had given contradictory promises and hopes to Arabs and Jews and that the events since 1922 indicated the mandate's unworkable nature. It found no scope for cooperation between the two communities and ruled out the possibility of their coexistence in one state. Hence, the Peel Commission called for partitioning Palestine as a solution to the Jewish–Arab tension and violence. It called for an independent Jewish state and the incorporation of the remaining territories into **Transjordan**.

As a follow-up measure, another commission was appointed in 1938 to work out the technical details of the partition recommended by the Peel Commission. This Palestine Partition Commission, headed by Sir John Woodhead—known as the **Woodhead Commission** —submitted its report in November 1938.

The **Zionists** adopted a rather circumspect position. While many viewed it as a departure from the commitments of the **Balfour**

Declaration, the idea of an independent state was seen as a positive development. Despite disagreements over the exclusion of **Jerusalem** and limited territories allotted to the proposed states, the *Yishuv* leadership was eventually favorable to the idea.

The Arabs, however, vehemently rejected the idea of an independent Jewish state in Palestine, and contrary to its intentions, the Peel Commission aggravated the **Arab Revolt** (1936–1939) and compelled the British to abandon the proposed partition. Instead, two years later, the Mandate authorities came out with the **MacDonald White Paper**, which formally distanced **Great Britain** from the Balfour Declaration. *See also* LEAGUE OF NATIONS; PARTITION PLAN.

PERES, SHIMON (1923–). A leading Israeli politician, Shimon Peres twice served as prime minister. Born Shimon Perksy in Poland on 16 August 1923, he made *Aliya* to Palestine when he was 11. Active in the Kibbutz movement, in 1943 he was elected secretary of the Labor-**Zionist** youth movement. In the late 1940s, he joined the **Haganah** and was made responsible for manpower and arms procurement, a position he held during and after the **Arab–Israeli War of 1947–1948**. In 1952, Peres joined the Ministry of Defense as deputy director-general and became director-general the following year at the young age of 29, holding this position until 1959. He was instrumental in a number of strategic projects, including the Dimona nuclear reactor and the founding of Israel Aircraft Industries. In 1956, he played an important role in the **Sèvres Conference** when Israel forged close ties with **Great Britain** and **France** prior to the **Suez War**.

In 1959, Peres was elected to the Knesset, and he continues to be a member. From 1959 to 1965, he served as deputy defense minister. In the wake of the rift within the Mapai, Peres joined **Moshe Dayan** and **David Ben-Gurion** in 1965 and formed Rafi. Three years later, he was instrumental in Rafi rejoining with Mapai to form the **Labor Party**. From 1969 to 1974, Peres served as a minister under **Golda Meir**, and after the resignation of Prime Minister **Yitzhak Rabin** in 1977, he briefly served as acting prime minister. In the wake of the defeat of the Labor Party in the 1977 Knesset elections, Peres was elected leader of the party, a position he held until 1992.

Under the national unity government (1984–1990), Peres served as prime minister from 1984 to 1986 and later as foreign minister (1986–1988) and finance minister (1988–1990). In the internal party elections held on the eve of the 1992 Knesset elections, Peres lost the leadership race to Rabin, his longtime rival. Under Rabin, Peres served as foreign minister (1992–1995) and played an active role in the inauguration of the **Oslo Process** and the conclusion of the **Declaration of Principles**. He soon emerged as the troubleshooter in the negotiations. Peres shared the 1994 Nobel Peace Prize with Rabin and **Yasser Arafat** for his contributions to the peace process.

After the **assassination** of Rabin in November 1995, Peres again became prime minister and concurrently held the defense portfolio. In the subsequent direct election of the prime minister held in May 1996, he narrowly lost to **Likud** leader **Benjamin Netanyahu**. In July 1999, Peres became minister for regional cooperation under **Ehud Barak**, and in July 2000 he unsuccessfully contested the presidential election against Moshe Katsav (1945–). In March 2001, Peres joined the national unity government headed by **Ariel Sharon** as foreign minister, but due to differences over the peace process, he and other Labor ministers resigned from the unity government in October 2002.

After the Labor Party's defeat in the January 2003 Knesset elections, Peres replaced Amram Mitzna (1945–) as chairman. In November 2005, he lost to Amir Peretz (1952–) for the leadership of the party, and shortly afterward, Peres resigned from Labor and joined Kadima ("Forward"), a new party floated by Prime Minister Sharon. *See also* GRAPES OF WRATH OPERATION; GUSH EMUNIM; JORDAN OPTION; KFAR KANA MASSACRE; KIRYAT ARBA; LONDON AGREEMENT; SEVEN-POINT ISRAELI PLAN; SUICIDE ATTACKS.

PERMANENT STATUS NEGOTIATIONS. Under the **Taba Agreement** signed on 26 September 1995, Israel and the **Palestinian National Authority** agreed to commence Permanent Status Negotiations in early 1996, with May 1999 as the target date for an agreement. Accordingly, on the eve of the 1996 Israeli elections, Israeli prime minister **Shimon Peres** and **Palestine Liberation Organization** chairman **Yasser Arafat** met in **Taba** under the sponsorship of President **Hosni Mubarak** of **Egypt** and symbolically inaugurated the Permanent Status Negotiations. Due to the impending Israeli elections, both sides agreed to establish a negotiating group to work out the specifics. However, the victory of **Likud** leader **Benjamin Netanyahu** reversed the whole process and the Permanent Status Negotiations were stalled forever.

PHALANGE. Inspired by the Nazi Youth Movement, Christian leader Pierre Gemayel (1905–1984) of **Lebanon** established the Phalange in 1936. Both a political party and a militia, it attracted widespread support among Maronite Christians and sought to promote the idea that Lebanon constitutes a separate historic identity that can be traced back to the Phoenicians. While recognizing Lebanon's cultural linkages with the Arabs, the Phalangists deny political attachment to and unity with the Arab world. On the eve of the Lebanese Civil War (1975–1989), the Phalangists were the bastion of Christian military power and were headed by Pierre Gemayel's son Bashir (1947–1982). On 14 September 1982, before his inauguration as president of Lebanon, Bashir Gemayel (1945–1982) was assassinated. In retaliation, Phalangist militia entered the Palestinian **refugee** camps in West Beirut and killed hundreds of Palestinian civilians in the **Sabra and Shatila Massacre**. Elie Hubeika (1956–2002), who headed the Phalange's secret service, reportedly commanded the militia. Following the end of the civil war, the Phalange was transformed into a political party and agreed to dismantle its militia. *See also* ASSASSINATION; OPERATION PEACE FOR GALILEE; SOUTH LEBANESE ARMY.

PLO CHARTER. The **Palestine Liberation Organization** Charter (also known as the PLO Covenant) was adopted at the first Arab Palestine Congress convened in the Old City of **Jerusalem** on 28 May 1964. Consisting of 29 articles, it not only outlined the Palestinian problem but also set the territorial limits of the Palestinian struggle. It declared Palestine to be "a regional indivisible unit" as it existed at the time of the **mandate**. Recognizing the Palestinian right to a homeland, it identified three mottoes, "national unity, national mobilization and liberation." The charter proclaimed the **Balfour Declaration**, the mandate, and "all that has been based upon them" to be a "fraud" and portrayed **Zionism** as "a colonialist movement in its inception, aggressive and expansionist in its goal, racist and segregationist in its configurations and Fascist in its means and aims." Accommodating the position of **Jordan** with regard to the **West Bank**, the charter declared that it would not operate in "the West Bank in the Hashemite Kingdom of Jordan, in the **Gaza Strip** or the Himmah area." The latter was captured by **Syria** during the **Arab–Israeli War of 1947–1948**.

The charter underwent substantial revision following the **June War of 1967**, when Israel captured the West Bank from Jordan and thereby controlled the entire territory of the Palestine Mandate. The change in the regional political environment compelled the PLO to reexamine its position and revise its 1964 charter. Meeting in Cairo from 10 to 17 July 1968, the **Palestine National Congress** adopted a new and revised charter comprising 33 articles. Retaining most of the provisions of the earlier document, it removed references to the West Bank, Gaza Strip, and Himmah areas and declared its determination to assume "its full role in liberating Palestine." As demanded by the **Oslo Accords**, those provisions that called for the destruction of Israel and contravened peace efforts led to their **annulment** from the charter in December 1998.

PLO LAW. In 1986, the Knesset adopted a law that banned any contact between Israeli citizens and members of the **Palestine Liberation Organization** (PLO) and other "**terrorist** organizations." The measure had been proposed by the national unity government (1984–1990) comprising the **Labor Party** and **Likud**. The so-called PLO Law and the circumstances surrounding it precluded any progress in the host of proposals floated in the mid-1980s, as it precluded any role for the PLO in any peace plans. This law did not stop Israeli peace activists from meeting with PLO functionaries, however, often under the ambit of international meetings or academic conferences. The impasse in the **Madrid Conference** process and the recognition of the centrality of the PLO in any negotiation compelled Israel to reexamine its opposition to the PLO, and the PLO Law was repealed on 19 January 1993. This move, coming in the midst of the controversial Israeli **deportation** of more than 400 suspected **Hamas** activists to southern **Lebanon**, paved the way for formal but secret dialogues with the PLO that became the **Oslo Process**. *See also* BAKER PLAN; BEGIN PLAN; MUBARAK PLAN (1985); MUBARAK PLAN (1989); RABIN PLAN; SHAMIR PLAN; SHULTZ PLAN.

PLUMBAT OPERATION. A covert operation that Israel undertook to buy and smuggle large quantities of "yellowcake," or uranium oxide, for the Dimona nuclear reactor. In 1968, through a complex operation conducted through a host of front companies, Israel smuggled 200 tons of yellowcake obtained from a Belgian company based in Antwerp. It took Euratom, the nuclear agency of the European Economic Community, more than six months to discover the "disappearance" of the yellowcake, a key component for making nuclear bombs. *See also* NUCLEAR NONPROLIFERATION TREATY; OSIRAQ BOMBING.

POPULAR FRONT FOR THE LIBERATION OF PALESTINE (PFLP). George Habash, who was expelled from Lydda in 1948, and Hani al-Hindi, a volunteer from **Syria** who fought in the **Arab–Israeli War of 1947–1948**, founded the Arab Nationalist Movement in 1951, when both were studying in Beirut. This eventually grew, and on 11 December 1967, Habash established *Al-Jabha al-Sha'biyya li-Tahrir Filastin* (Popular Front for the Liberation of Palestine), which gradually adopted a Marxist-Leninist approach toward the Palestinian problem and portrayed it as part of a larger revolution in the entire Arab world. Though headquartered in Damascus, the PFLP acts independently of the Syrian army as well as the Ba'athist ideology. The rank and file of the PFLP largely came from **refugee** camps in **Jordan**, **Lebanon**, and Syria. In 1968, one group split from the PFLP and formed the **Popular Front for the Liberation of Palestine–General Command** and in 1969, another split led to the formation of the **Democratic Front for the Liberation of Palestine**.

In the early 1970s, the PFLP acquired widespread notoriety when its military wing, the Red Eagles, headed by Wadi Haddad, carried out a number of airplane hijackings. On 30 May 1972, together with members of the Japanese Red Army, the PFLP carried out an attack at Israel's Lod International Airport; the **Lod Massacre** resulted in the death of 30 people, including two hijackers.

While such acts focused international attention on the Palestinian cause, the spate of hijackings and an unsuccessful **assassination** attempt on King **Hussein** of Jordan led to the expulsion of the **Palestine Liberation Organization** (PLO) from Jordan.

Since 1973, the PFLP has moderated its position but was often at odds with **Yasser Arafat** and the PLO. It withdrew from the PLO Executive Committee from 1974–1981 and 1983–1987. The PFLP vehemently opposed the reconciliation talks with Jordan in the early 1980s as well as the **Fez Plan** of 1982, but during the 1987 **Intifada**, it joined the **Unified National Leadership of the Uprising**. Despite its opposition to the **Oslo Accords**, it remains a member of the PLO Executive Committee. The PFLP advocates the establishment of a democratic **Palestinian state** in all of Palestine where all, including Jews, would be treated as equal citizens.

Owing to its opposition to the policy of the PLO in seeking a political settlement with Israel, the PFLP refused to participate in the January 1996 elections to the **Palestinian Legislative Council**. With Israeli concurrence and approval, the deputy head of the PFLP, **Abu Ali Mustafa**, returned to areas controlled by the **Palestinian National Authority** in September 1999. In July 2001, following Habash's resignation, Ali Mustafa took over as head of the PFLP, but on 27 August 2001, he was assassinated by Israel. This revived the organization, and it responded by assassinating a senior Israeli cabinet minister, Rehavam Ze'evi (1926–2001), on 17 October 2001. Acting under pressure from Israel and the **United States** to arrest those responsible for the killing, Chairman Arafat arrested the new PFLP chief, Ahmed Sadaat, for his purported role in Ze'evi's killing. On 3 June 2002, the Gaza High Court ordered the release of Sadaat, but it was overruled by Arafat. *See also* TARGETED KILLING.

POPULAR FRONT FOR THE LIBERATION OF PALESTINE– GENERAL COMMAND (PFLP–GC). In late 1968, under the leadership of Ahmed Jibril (1939–), a senior army officer from **Syria**, a faction broke away from the **Popular Front for the Liberation of Palestine** (PFLP) and formed the PFLP–GC. Consisting of secret cells, it has been based in Damascus and, unlike the PFLP, had close links with the Syrian military, intelligence, and Ba'ath Party. Militantly pro-Syrian, the PFLP–GC led the anti-**Yasser Arafat** factions within the **Palestine Liberation Organization** (PLO) in 1983. Committed to armed struggle and guerrilla warfare, it opposed any peace settlement with Israel and was involved in numerous attacks against Israel. However, unlike the PFLP, this group lacks popular support and does not appear to have a significant support base in the **Occupied Territories**. It is also not represented in the PLO Executive Committee. In the early 1990s, the PFLP–GC emerged as a key player in the Damascus-based Palestinian groups opposed to the **Oslo Accords**, and in January 1996, it refused to participate in the **Palestinian Legislative Council** elections.

PRISONER EXCHANGE. At the time of the Entebbe hostage crisis, Israel resolved not to negotiate with hostage takers or groups it identified as **terrorists**. Despite this policy, Israel has often released prisoners in return for the safe passage of its citizens and soldiers held by militant Palestinian and Lebanese groups. In November 1983, Israel released 4,500 prisoners it had captured during **Operation Peace for Galilee** in return for six Israeli soldiers held by **Palestine Liberation Organization** (PLO) factions in northern **Lebanon**. On 20 May 1985, Israel also agreed to release 1,150 prisoners it had captured in Lebanon in return for the freedom of nine Israeli soldiers held by the **Popular Front for the Liberation of Palestine–General Command**. On 14 June 1985, a group of Lebanese militia hijacked a TWA flight from Athens to Rome and diverted it to Beirut. The group demanded the release of 766 Lebanese prisoners, mostly Shias, in return for the lives of 39 American passengers. After lengthy political deliberations and tension, Israel released 31 Lebanese prisoners on 24 June and the hostages were released on 30 June. Similarly, in February 2004, Israel released a large number of Lebanese citizens held in Israeli prisons, including members of **Hezbollah**, in exchange for the return of the remains of three Israeli soldiers and the release of an Israeli businessman. *See also* AZZAM AFFAIR; ENTEBBE OPERATION; MASHA'AL AFFAIR; TANNENBAUM AFFAIR; YASSIN, SHEIKH AHMED.

PROTECTION OF HOLY PLACES. The status of and access to holy places in the **Jerusalem** area is a sensitive issue in the Arab–Israeli conflict. This concern was reflected in the recommendations of the **United Nations Special Committee on Palestine** and the **Partition Plan** to declare Jerusalem to be an international city, or *corpus separatum*. On 27 June 1967, the Knesset passed the Protection of Holy Places Law, which guaranteed the protection of holy places "from desecration and any other violation" and mandated a seven-year prison term for violators.

– Q –

QASSEM II. A rudimentary short-range missile developed by **Hamas**. The first Qassem II rocket was launched against Israel on 10 February 2002, and since then, more than 300 rockets have been fired toward Israel. Their range is 3–10 kilometers (2–6 miles), and it is suggested that the Palestinians are working on a new Qassem IV with a possible range of 17 kilometers (10.5 miles). Even though the military significance is limited, Hamas has launched a number of missiles at Jewish **settlements** in the **Gaza Strip** and occasionally into the Israeli territories bordering Gaza. This could be seen as an imitation of the tactics of **Hezbollah**, which intimidated the Israeli civilian population with its Katyusha rockets during the Israeli occupation of **Lebanon**. Palestinian militants continued to fire Qassem rockets against Israel even after it completed the **Gaza Withdrawal Plan** in August 2005.

QIBYA RAID. In retaliation for an infiltration from **Jordan** that resulted in the deaths of three civilians, including two children, in the Israeli village of Yehud on 14–15 October 1953, a special anti**terrorist** squad conducted a military operation against the Jordanian village of Qibya. The raid, carried out by **Unit 101** under the command of **Ariel Sharon**, was the first major Israeli military operation against Jordan. Twelve Jordanian soldiers were killed, along with 60 civilians. The operation was carried out despite opposition from Israeli prime minister Moshe Sharett (1894–1965), but the Unit was never court-martialed for challenging and overruling the civilian authority. Though it led to a temporary lull in infiltrations from Jordan, the raid evoked strong criticism and condemnation by the **United Nations** Security Council. However, the action appeared to have compelled the **Arab Legion**, led by Gen. Glubb Pasha (1897–1986), to exercise greater control over infiltration into Israel and resulted in the temporary reduction of tensions between Israel and Jordan.

QUNEITRA. Quneitra is a town on the **Golan Heights** established by the Ottoman Empire. During the **June War of 1967**, it was captured by Israel, which forced the residents to flee. The ghost town witnessed heavy fighting during the **October War of 1973**. Under the 1974 **Disengagement Agreement**, Israel agreed to pull out and return it to **Syria**. Before withdrawing from Quneitra, Israel dynamited and destroyed all the houses in the town. As a result, Syria keeps this ruined city as a symbol of Israeli atrocities.

QUREI, AHMED (1937–). Better known as Abu Ala, Ahmed Qurei is a Palestinian leader who served as prime minister of the **Palestinian National Authority** (PNA). Born in the **Jerusalem** suburb of **Abu**

Dis in 1937, Qurei and his family became **refugees** in the wake of the **Arab–Israeli War of 1947–1948**. In the late 1960s, he joined the **Fatah** wing of the **Palestine Liberation Organization** (PLO). He came to prominence in the mid-1970s when he took over the economic and production activities of the PLO in **Lebanon**. In 1982, he accompanied **Yasser Arafat** when the Palestinian leadership was exiled to Tunis from Beirut following **Operation Peace for Galilee**. Qurei was elected to the Fatah Central Committee in 1989.

In 1991, Qurei coordinated the Palestinian delegation to the **Madrid Conference**, and he headed the Palestinian delegation during the secret negotiations with Israel that led to the **Oslo Accords** in September 1993. He was the chief Palestinian negotiator at the economic talks with Israel that resulted in the signing of the **Paris Agreement** in April 1994. The following year he negotiated the **Taba Agreement**, which outlined further Israeli **redeployment** from the **Occupied Territories**. During 1994–1996, he served as a minister in the PNA, and after the Palestinian elections in January 1996, Qurei was elected speaker of the **Palestinian Legislative Council**. In September 2003, he succeeded **Mahmoud Abbas** as prime minister of the PNA.

– R –

RABAT ARAB SUMMIT. At its summit meeting held in Rabat, Morocco, in 1974, the members of the **Arab League** voted to recognize the **Palestine Liberation Organization** (PLO) as "the sole legitimate representative" of the Palestinian people and to endorse their right to return to their country and determine their own future. This move, adopted on 25 October 1974, was opposed by **Jordan**, which had controlled the **West Bank** from 1948 to 1967. It ended any Jordanian aspirations to regain the West Bank and paved the way for the admission of the PLO into the **United Nations** the following month. *See also* JORDANIAN DISENGAGEMENT.

RABIN, YITZHAK (1922–1995). An Israeli general and politician, Yitzhak Rabin served as Israeli prime minister during 1974–1977 and 1992–1995. Born in **Jerusalem** on 1 March 1922, Rabin studied at the Kadourie Agriculture High School. In 1941, he joined the **Palmah** and became its deputy commander in October 1947. During the **Arab–Israeli War of 1947–1948**, Rabin commanded the Harel Brigade, which fought to keep the Tel Aviv–Jerusalem road open and to free Jerusalem from the Arab siege. In the June 1948 *Altalena* **Affair**, he commanded the unit that sank the ship *Altalena*, which was carrying arms for the Jewish underground group **Irgun** headed by **Menachem Begin**. Following the war, Rabin briefly took part in the negotiations with **Transjordan** but objected to the **armistice agreement** signed on 3 April 1949.

After the formation of the **Israel Defense Forces** (IDF), Rabin held senior positions, and in 1962, he became the chief of staff. He established the IDF training doctrine and introduced the preemptive doctrine implemented during the **June War of 1967**. Even though Defense Minister **Moshe Dayan** took the credit for that spectacular military victory, Rabin was instrumental in the war preparations. In January 1968, after serving 26 years in the military, he retired from the IDF. Later that year, he was appointed Israel's ambassador to the **United States**, returning to Israel in March 1973.

In December 1973, Rabin was elected to the Knesset on the **Labor Party** platform and became minister of labor in the government headed by **Golda Meir**. After Meir's resignation in June 1974, Rabin became prime minister. A controversy surrounding his wife's U.S. bank accounts led to his resignation in May 1977. After the victory of the **Likud** in the 1977 Knesset elections, Rabin lost the chairmanship of the Labor Party to his archrival **Shimon Peres**.

During the tenure of the national unity government from 1984 to 1990, Rabin served as Israel's defense minister and presided over the brutal Israeli response to the first Palestinian **Intifada** (1987–1993). In 1992, Rabin was elected leader of the Labor Party, and in June, he successfully led the party to victory. Breaking with past Israeli practice, Prime Minister Rabin was prepared to negotiate with the **Palestine Liberation Organization** (PLO), which ushered in the **Oslo Process** that culminated in the **Declaration of Principles** signed in Washington, D.C., on 13 September 1993. Despite initial misgivings, he wholeheartedly embraced Palestinian leader **Yasser Arafat** as his peace partner and continued to pursue a tough but accommodative policy toward the Palestinians. The following year, he concluded the **Israel–Jordan Peace Treaty** and periodically interacted with King **Hussein** of **Jordan** and President **Hosni Mubarak** of **Egypt**. In 1994, Rabin shared the Nobel Peace Prize with Peres and Arafat. He also actively pursued negotiations with **Syria** over the **Golan Heights**; though no formal agreements were reached, Rabin was prepared for a complete but conditional Israeli withdrawal from the Heights.

Rabin was confronted by the onset of the **suicide attacks** unleashed by **Hamas** and by increased domestic opposition to the peace process. Neither Palestinian **terrorism** nor internal incitement prevented Rabin from concluding the **Cairo Agreement** of 1994, the **Paris Agreement**, and the **Taba Agreement**. Following the **Hebron Massacre** in March 1994, Rabin banned the right-wing Jewish group **Kach**.

On 4 November 1995, Rabin was assassinated by Yigal Amir (1970–), an observant Jewish student of Bar-Ilan University, at a peace rally in Tel Aviv. Amir was motivated by his strong views over Rabin's peace policies, especially his "concessions" toward the Palestinians. Citing religious arguments, he justified his **assassination** by saying that by agreeing to part with *Eretz Yisrael*, Rabin had turned against his own people. On 27 March 1996, Amir was given a life sentence without parole. A section of the Israeli right has been campaigning to commute the sentence and to secure his early release. An official investigation headed by a former president of the Supreme Court, Justice Meir Shamgar (1925–), concluded that Amir had acted alone. Rabin's funeral at the Mt. Herzl military cemetery in Jerusalem was attended by a number of world leaders including U.S. president **Bill Clinton**, King Hussein, President Mubarak, and ministers from Oman and Qatar. *See also* ACCOUNTABILITY OPERATION; DALET PLAN; DEPORTATION; RABIN PLAN.

RABIN PLAN. Against the backdrop of the **Intifada** and the **United States'** decision to initiate a substantive dialogue with the **Palestine Liberation Organization** (PLO), in January 1989 Defense Minister **Yitzhak Rabin** outlined a peace proposal, which he termed "extended autonomy." Unlike the earlier suggestions, this called for the election of Palestinian delegates who would negotiate with Israel concerning the final status of the **Occupied Territories** and the suspension of the uprising for six months. Through elections of local leaders, the plan sought to isolate and marginalize the influence of the PLO in the Occupied Territories. The plan was derailed due to internal differences in Israel over the rights of the **Jerusalem Palestinians** to contest and vote in such elections. *See also* BAKER PLAN; MUBARAK PLAN (1985);

MUBARAK PLAN (1989); PLO LAW; SHAMIR PLAN; SHULTZ PLAN.

RAINBOW OPERATION. On 18 May 2004, Israel launched a large-scale military operation in the **Gaza Strip** with the stated objective of removing the infrastructure used for **terrorism**, including the underground **tunnels** in the **Gaza Strip** through which weapons were smuggled from **Egypt**. The operation was sparked by the killing of 13 Israeli soldiers in the Gaza Strip. Israel alleged that missiles and rockets stored on the Egyptian side of the border were to be smuggled in through the tunnels. During the operation, which lasted until 1 June, more than 50 Palestinians, including 12 civilians, were killed.

RAMADAN WAR. *See* OCTOBER WAR OF 1973.

RANTISI, ABDEL AZIZ AL- (1947–2004). A leader of **Hamas**, Abdel Aziz al-Rantisi, was born in Yebna (now Yavneh) near Ashkelon. As a baby during the **Arab–Israeli War of 1947–1948**, he became a **refugee** along with his family, which moved to the **Gaza Strip**, and he grew up in a refugee camp. In the 1970s, Rantisi pursued his studies in **Egypt** and became a trained pediatrician. During this period, he was attracted to the **Muslim Brotherhood**, an Islamic movement outlawed by President **Gamal Abdul Nasser** of **Egypt**, and became active in the movement's Gaza branch.

Following the outbreak of the **Intifada** in December 1987, Rantisi joined with **Sheikh Ahmed Yassin** and others to transform the social activist movement into a political force, Hamas. He was often identified as one of the seven founding members of the militant Islamic movement and was frequently arrested by the **Israel Defense Forces** during the Intifada.

Rantisi came to prominence following the Israeli **deportation** of more than 400 suspected Hamas activists to southern **Lebanon** in December 1992. He emerged as the spokesperson of the deportees in their camp, Marj al-Zahour. When the two-year deportation period ended, he returned to Gaza. Reflecting the prevailing position of Hamas, he vehemently opposed the **Oslo Process** and emerged as a hardened critic of the **Palestinian National Authority** (PNA). In 1998, PNA chairman **Yasser Arafat** ordered his brief incarceration.

Frequently appearing in the international media, Rantisi explained and justified **suicide attacks** conducted by the Hamas. As the **Al-Aqsa Intifada** progressed, the Israeli government under **Ariel Sharon** changed its policy and began **targeting killings** of political and non-militant leaders of Hamas and **Islamic Jihad**. After the Israeli **assassination** of Yassin in March 2004, Rantisi was named leader of Hamas. On 17 April, Rantisi was killed when an Israeli missile struck his vehicle in Gaza City. Hamas refrained from disclosing his successor.

REAGAN PLAN. On 1 September 1982, weeks after the Israeli invasion of **Lebanon** and the evacuation of the **Palestine Liberation Organization** (PLO) from Lebanon, **United States** president Ronald Reagan (1911–2004) unveiled an initiative to resolve the Arab–Israeli conflict. In a public address, Reagan called for the need to "reconcile Israel's legitimate security concerns with the legitimate rights of the Palestinians." Calling for Israeli "magnanimity, vision, and courage," Reagan admitted that the Palestinian cause was "more than a question of **refugees**" but reiterated U.S. opposition to recognizing the PLO until it accepted **Resolution 242** and **Resolution 338** of the **United Nations** Security Council.

The Reagan Plan called for a five-year transition period, beginning with free elections for a self-governing Palestinian authority and the freezing of Israeli **settlement** activities in the **Occupied Territories**. Opposed to the idea of an independent **Palestinian state**, it instead visualized a Palestinian entity in confederation with **Jordan**. The final status of **Jerusalem**, which "must remain undivided," would be decided through negotiations.

Israel was not consulted prior to Reagan's speech, and the plan was immediately rejected by Israeli officials. They objected to the right of Palestinians in **East Jerusalem** to participate in any elections, the handing over of internal security to an interim Palestinian authority, and the settlement freeze. On 8 September, the Arabs responded with the **Fez Plan**. *See also* BREZHNEV PLAN; OPERATION PEACE FOR GALILEE.

REDEPLOYMENT. First appearing in the **Declaration of Principles** in 1993, *redeployment* is the formal Israeli euphemism for the withdrawal of **Israel Defense Forces** (IDF) units from the **Occupied Ter-**

ritories to positions worked out through mutual consultation and agreement with the Palestinian leadership. The abandoned Israeli military positions and bases were to be either formally handed over to the **Palestinian National Authority** (PNA) or dismantled and shifted to other locations in the Occupied Territories. The term *withdrawal* does not appear in any official Israeli agreement signed with the Palestinians. In practice, redeployment actually meant a gradual change in the status of the areas in question; from complete Israeli control, they were transferred to partial, joint, or complete Palestinian control. Israel withdrew from Jenin on 25 October 1995, and the IDF completely pulled out of all Palestinian population centers (except Hebron) by the end of that year. However, these areas were reoccupied by the IDF following the outbreak of **Al-Aqsa Intifada**. Israel handed over the security control of Jenin to the PNA in March 2005. *See also* GAZA WITHDRAWAL PLAN.

REFERENDUM. Following the Geneva meeting between Presidents **Bill Clinton** of the **United States** and **Hafez al-Assad** of **Syria** in January 1994, Israeli prime minister **Yitzhak Rabin** declared that any agreement with Syria involving a "substantial" territorial withdrawal from the **Golan Heights** would be put to a referendum. This commitment was gradually extended, as **Labor Party** leaders pledged to refer the question of a **Palestinian state** to popular approval. The entire practice has no legal standing in Israel and indeed was never resorted to when Israel initiated a number of military operations as well as controversial political moves, such as the annexation of the Golan Heights or **East Jerusalem**. Referendum pledges are seen as another legal mechanism to delay and even preclude any territorial concessions to the Arabs. Even a decade after the proposal, Israel did not establish the necessary legal mechanism for a referendum.

REFUGEE/S. The refugee problem remains the most complicated and controversial issue in the Arab–Israeli conflict. The outbreak of hostilities in Palestine following the adoption of the **Partition Plan** in November 1947 led to the first flight of refugees, which only increased following the establishment of Israel. Israel has been accused of pursuing a deliberate policy of expulsion of Arab civilians during the **Arab–Israeli War of 1947–1948** or at least of not preventing the flight of Arabs from areas it had captured during the conflict. Brutal incidents such as the **Deir Yassin Massacre** had contributed to the departure of Arabs from areas captured by Israel. The lack of Arab Palestinian leadership inside Palestine during this critical period also contributed to the mass exodus.

The fate of the Palestinian refugees has become the prime focus of a number of peace proposals by the **United Nations** and others, such as the **Bernadotte Plan**, **Johnson Mission**, and **Johnston Plan**. The most significant move in this direction was the formation of the **United Nations Relief and Works Agency** (UNRWA), which was established to assist the Palestinians who had become refugees following the 1948 war. UNRWA has operated 59 registered refugee camps in the Middle East for anyone who was a resident of Palestine for at least two years before the 1948 conflict and who fled following the outbreak of hostilities. In 1950, the number of refugees registered with UNRWA was 914,221. An additional 300,000 were made homeless following the **June War of 1967**; by the end of that year, the number of UNRWA-registered refugees stood at just under four million.

Meanwhile, on 11 December 1948, **Resolution 194** of UN General Assembly was adopted, recognizing the right of Palestinian refugees to return to their homes or to be paid compensation. This resolution dominates the Israeli–Palestinian negotiations on the refugee question. While the Palestinians reiterate their right to return, Israel argues that it would cease to be a Jewish state if the resolution were to be implemented in toto. *See also* NAQBA, AL-; SABRA AND SHATILA MASSACRE.

REJECTIONIST FRONT. At periodic intervals, various Palestinian groups opposed to any compromise with Israel have organized themselves into loose partnerships. They normally include groups such as the **Popular Front for the Liberation of Palestine** (PFLP), the **Popular Front for the Liberation of Palestine–General Command** (PFLP–GC), the Popular Struggle Front, and the **Palestine Liberation Front**. Depending upon their specific national interests, countries such as Algeria, **Iraq**, Libya, **Syria**, and South Yemen have sometimes supported these efforts as well.

On 26 September 1974, protesting against the Palestinian participation in the Geneva Peace Conference, PFLP leader **George Habash** resigned from the **Palestine Liberation Organization** (PLO) Executive Committee and joined hands with the PFLP–GC and the **Arab Liberation Front** and formed the Rejectionist Front. A similar front was formed on 1 October 1977 in response to President **Anwar Sadat**'s peace initiatives toward Israel. On 2 December, less than two weeks after Sadat's visit to **Jerusalem**, leaders of Algeria, Iraq, Libya, South Yemen, and Syria and PLO chairman **Yasser Arafat** met at the **Tripoli Conference** in Libya to coordinate their opposition.

Arab states that often opposed any Middle East peace talks organized themselves into a Front of Steadfastness (*Jabhat al-Sumud*) and articulated their position. In the mid-1970s, it consisted of Iraq, Libya, Syria, Algeria, South Yemen, and the PLO. Due to its differences with Syria, in December 1977, **Iraq** walked out of the Front of Steadfastness. In the 1990s, the **Oslo Process** led to another Rejectionist Front but, unlike the past, this time it comprised Palestinian groups opposed to Arafat and his peace efforts toward Israel.

RESOLUTION 194. On 11 December 1948, amidst the temporary cease-fire in the **Arab–Israeli War of 1947–1948** but before the conclusion of any **armistice agreements** between Israel and its Arab neighbors, the **United Nations** General Assembly adopted Resolution 194, which outlined a number of guidelines for the conclusion of the conflict. The resolution established a three-member **Palestine Conciliation Commission** to take over and implement the functions and responsibilities of **United Nations mediator** Count Folke Bernadotte (1895–1948) who had been killed in September. Reiterating the internationalization of **Jerusalem** by the partition resolution, Resolution 194 also recognized the rights of the Palestinians who had become **refugees** following the outbreak of hostilities between the newly formed State of Israel and the neighboring Arab countries to return to their homes or, should the refugees decide against returning, to be paid compensation. The operative part of the resolution reads:

> The refugees wishing to return to their homes and live at peace with their neighbors should be permitted to do so at the earliest practicable date, and that compensation should be paid for the property of those choosing not to return and for the loss of or damage to property which, under principles of international law or in equity, should be made good by the Governments or authorities responsible.

This resolution dominates the Israeli–Palestinian negotiations concerning the refugee question. While the Palestinians reiterate their right to return, Israel argues that if they were to return in large numbers, it would cease to be a Jewish state. Resolution 194 thus became the most contentious issue in the Arab–Israeli conflict concerning the refugees and was incorporated into General Assembly Resolution 273 of 11 May 1949, which admitted Israel into the **United Nations**. *See also* NAQBA, AL-; UNITED NATIONS MEMBERSHIP.

RESOLUTION 242. On 22 November 1967, more than six months after the cease-fire that ended the **June War of 1967**, the **United Nations** Security Council adopted Resolution 242 sponsored by **Great Britain**. Intense diplomatic negotiations and deliberate ambiguity ensured its unanimous approval by the Council. The resolution proclaimed the "inadmissibility of the acquisition of territory by war," the right of every state in the region to "live in security" and "to live in peace within secure and recognized borders" free from acts or threats of force, and the need for "a just settlement of the **refugee** problem." It furthermore called for the withdrawal of Israel from territories occupied during the **June War of 1967**, termination of "all claims or states of belligerency," recognition of the "sovereignty, territorial integrity and political independence of every state" in the Middle East, guarantees of freedom of navigation through international waterways, assurance of "the territorial inviolability and political independence of every State" in the region, and the establishment of "demilitarized zones."

The principal players of the June War—Israel, **Egypt**, and **Jordan**—all accepted the plan. However, the recognition of Israel's right to exist prevented **Syria** and its ally **Lebanon** (though not involved in the conflict) from accepting the resolution. The portrayal of the Palestinian question as a "refugee" problem also precluded the Palestinian leadership, especially the **Palestine Liberation Organization**, from accepting it. In October 1973, the Security Council adopted **Resolution 338**, calling for the implementation of Resolution 242.

Despite the initial reservations expressed by Syria and Palestinians, since the October war of 1973, all Arab countries and Palestinians have been demanding the implementation of Resolution 242. In calling for its complete implementation, both Israel and the Arab parties have been exploiting the resolution's vagueness to suit their respective national interests. For example, Israel has been arguing that the resolution calls for withdrawal "from territories *occupied in the recent conflict*," not "from *the* territories," and hence it does not require a complete Israeli pullout from the **Occupied Territories**. The reference to the right of all states in the region to live "within secure and recognized" borders is also used by Israel to reiterate its opposition to withdrawal to the pre–June 1967 position.

The resolution's declaration of the "inadmissibility of territorial conquest" was also applicable to Jordan, which annexed the **West Bank** in 1950 (this argument was nullified following the July 1988 **Jordanian disengagement** from the West Bank), as well as Syrian encroachment on Palestinian territories beyond the 1948 Armistice lines. The reference to "recognized" borders precludes the possibility of unilateral moves by any party, including Israel. The Arabs argue that by refusing to withdraw to the pre–June 1967 position, Israel has violated the resolution.

As provided for by Resolution 242, in November 1967 the United Nations appointed a special representative to implement the resolution, selecting Gunner Jarring (1907–2002), the Swedish ambassador in Moscow. The rigid position adopted by all the parties prevented any progress by the **Jarring Mission**. The resolution nevertheless provided the framework for future negotiations between Israel and its Arab neighbors as it established land-for-peace as the guiding principle for peace in the Middle East.

The **Venice Declaration** of 1980 was the first significant move toward the recognition of the political rights of the Palestinians. Meeting in Italy, the leaders of the European Council declared that the Palestinian problem was more than "simply one of refugees" and recognized the right of the Palestinian people "to exercise fully its right to self-determination." This was followed by a similar move by the **United States** when the **Reagan Plan** admitted that the Palestinian cause was "more than a question of refugees."

The willingness of the Arab countries and Palestinians to attend the **Madrid Conference** in 1991 was conditional upon Israeli willingness to recognize Resolution 242 as the basis for any Middle East peace settlement. The **multilateral talks** that began in **Russia** in January 1992 as a follow-up to the Madrid Conference set up a separate working group devoted to the refugee question. Likewise, the **Declaration of Principles** recognized the importance of the refugee question and placed it on the agenda of the **Permanent Status Negotiations** between Israel and the Palestinians. The failure of the **Camp David Talks** of 2000 was largely due to the difficulties facing both sides in resolving the refugee issue. While Israel was prepared to accept a limited number of refugees within the framework of "family reunion," it demanded that the Palestinians give up their right of return to their erstwhile homes that they had left during the **Arab–Israeli War of 1947–1948**. The **Clinton Plan**, which was unveiled days before U.S. president **Bill Clinton** left office in January 2001, proposed that the Palestinian refugees would have the right to return to their Palestinian homeland but not to their original homes in Israel; refugees who did not exercise this right would be entitled to compensation and resettlement. However, the demand for the refugees to give up their right of return was a nonstarter. *See also* GREEN LINE.

RESOLUTION 338. On 22 October 1973, amidst the **October War of 1973**, the **United Nations** Security Council unanimously adopted Resolution 338, which called on all parties in the Middle East to implement **Resolution 242** and to accept and enforce an immediate cease-fire, which came into force on 24 October. The resolution explicitly called for negotiations "between the parties" toward establishing "a just and durable peace in the Middle East." It also called for "appropriate auspices," a tacit reference to the **international conference** demanded by the Arabs.

Syria and **Lebanon**, which did not formally accept **Resolution 242**, accepted Resolution 338 and thus, by extension, Resolution 242. Resolution 338 provided the basis for postwar military disengagement negotiations among Israel, **Egypt**, and Syria. Since 1973, Resolutions 242 and 338 remain the core basis in the search for Middle East peace.

As called for in the resolution, the Geneva Peace Conference was convened, on 21 December 1973. Israel, Egypt, and **Jordan**, with the **United States** and the **Soviet Union** acting as cochairs, attended it. The **Palestine Liberation Organization**, by then recognized as "the sole representative of the Palestinian nation" at the Algiers **Arab League** Summit of November 1973, was not invited, and Israeli opposition over the treatment of its prisoners of war precluded Syrian participation. Only meager progress was achieved in Geneva.

RESOLUTION 425. On 19 March 1978, the **United Nations** Security Council adopted Resolution 425, which called for "strict respect for the territorial integrity, sovereignty, and political independence" of **Lebanon**. Coming days after the Israeli incursion into Lebanon on 15 March (the **Litani Operation**), the resolution called on Israel "to cease its military action against Lebanon" and to withdraw "its forces from all Lebanese territory." It also established the **United Nations Interim Force in Lebanon** (UNIFIL) to confirm Israeli compliance with the UN demand.

Citing the presence of the army of **Syria** in Lebanon since the onset of the Lebanese civil war in 1975, Israel argued that its compliance would be conditional upon the withdrawal of the Syrian troops as well as the **Palestine Liberation Organization** from Lebanon. Subsequent governments headed by both the **Labor** and **Likud** parties adhered to this position, especially following the 1982 Israeli invasion (**Operation Peace for Galilee**).

In early 1998, the government headed by **Benjamin Netanyahu** declared Israel's willingness to negotiate the withdrawal of its forces from Lebanon based on Resolution 425. Due to the continued Lebanese refusal to negotiate with Israel without Syrian involvement, however, on 5 March 2000 Israel decided on a unilateral **Lebanese withdrawal**. On 16 June, UN secretary-general Kofi Annan (1938–) informed the Security Council that Israel had withdrawn from Lebanon and complied with the demands of its Resolution 425. A number of countries did not accept this assessment, but the Security Council endorsed Annan's report on 18 June and, on 24 July, the secretary-general informed the Security Council that Israel had rectified all the violations along the Israel-Lebanon border and complied with Resolution 425.

Differences, however, persist between Israel and Lebanon over **Sheba'a Farms**. While Israel maintained that it was Syrian territory when it captured the **Golan Heights** during the **June War of 1967**— and hence would be discussed in any peace agreement with Syria— Lebanon claimed that it was Lebanese territory. Based on UNIFIL maps, the United Nations agreed with the Israeli position. Despite the Israeli withdrawal and UN acceptance of Israeli compliance, UNIFIL continues to operate in southern Lebanon. *See also* FOUR MOTHERS MOVEMENT; GRAPES OF WRATH OPERATION; HEZBOLLAH; SHE'AR YASHUV ACCIDENT; SOUTH LEBANESE ARMY.

RESOLUTION 3210. On 14 October 1974, the **United Nations** General Assembly overwhelmingly approved Resolution 3210, which was sponsored by countries belonging to the Nonaligned Movement. With only Israel, **United States**, Bolivia, and the Dominican Republic voting against and 20 countries abstaining, 105 countries voted to recognize the Palestinian people as "the principal party to the question of Palestine" and decided to invite the **Palestine Liberation Organization** (PLO) "to participate" in General Assembly deliberations on "the question of Palestine." This paved the way for the participation of the PLO in all UN deliberations concerning the Palestine question.

RESOLUTION 3236. In response to growing support for the Palestinians, on 22 November 1974, the **United Nations** General Assembly by a 95–17 vote adopted Resolution 3236, which recognized that the "Palestinian people is entitled to self-determination" and "to regain its right by all means in accordance with the purposes and principles" of the UN Charter. The latter provision was a tacit UN recognition of the then prevailing Palestinian strategy of armed struggle against Israel. For a long time, Israel and its supporters viewed this as international acquiescence in violence and **terrorism** perpetrated by certain Palestinian groups against Israel and its Western allies.

Resolution 3236 also granted observer status to the **Palestine Liberation Organization** (PLO). Citing similar moves by the World Food Conference and the World Population Conference, the General Assembly voted to invite the PLO "to participate in the sessions and the work of all **international conferences**" convened by the United Nations. Since then, the PLO has been participating in all UN deliberations pertaining to the Palestinian question.

On 7 July 1998, the General Assembly voted to upgrade the observer status of the PLO and to confer upon it "additional rights and privileges." The move was passed almost unanimously, with only Israel, the **United States**, Micronesia, and the Marshall Islands voting against. *See also* ARAFAT, YASSER.

RESOLUTION 3379. On 27 June 1975, the International Women's Year Conference in Mexico City adopted a resolution that called for the elimination of "colonialism and neo-colonialism, foreign occupation, **Zionism**, apartheid, racial discrimination in all forms as well as recognition of peoples and their rights to self-determination." This formulation was subsequently used by the **United Nations** General Assembly, which on 10 November 1975 adopted the nonbinding Resolution 3379 that, inter alia, declared that Zionism "is a form of racism and discrimination." Sponsored by a number of Arab and Islamic countries, Resolution 3379 was adopted by a vote of 72–35, with 32 abstentions, and demonstrated Israel's deteriorating relationship with the United Nations and its increasing international isolation.

On 16 December 1991, shortly after the **Madrid Conference**, the General Assembly adopted a statement revoking Resolution 3379. This was supported by 111 countries, many of which had voted for the original resolution. A number of Arab and Islamic countries either voted against the revocation or were absent during the vote.

ROAD MAP. *See* MIDDLE EAST ROAD MAP.

ROGERS PLAN. Due to the impasse of the **Jarring Mission** caused by the **War of Attrition** that was going on on the **Sinai Peninsula**, on 9 December 1969, addressing an Adult Education Conference in Washington, D.C., U.S. secretary of state William Rogers (1913–2001) announced a two-pronged initiative: first, a cease-fire agreement between **Egypt** and Israel along the **Suez Canal**; and second, progress of Israel's negotiations with Eygpt and **Jordan** be based on **Resolution 242** of the **United Nations** Security Council. While Egypt and Jordan welcomed the initiative, the Israeli cabinet formally rejected the Rogers Plan on 22 December because it believed that if the American ideas were implemented, Israel's "security and peace" would be in grave danger.

In January 1970, Rogers came out with a new set of proposals, often referred to as Rogers II. It primarily sought to reactivate the mediatory efforts of the **United Nations** envoy Gunnar Jarring. Rogers reactivated the Jarring Mission and sought to mediate an interim agreement between Egypt and Israel and to reopen the Suez Canal in return for a partial Israeli withdrawal. However, Egypt demanded a full withdrawal, while Israel was not prepared to contemplate any moves without direct negotiations with Egypt.

On 19 June, Rogers outlined another plan aimed at ending the War of Attrition. It called for a 90-day cease-fire by both parties and a military standstill zone on either side of the Suez Canal. After prolonged efforts and consultations, all parties accepted the proposal and the cease-fire came into being on 7 August 1970.

In December, Rogers outlined a similar proposal on the Israel–Jordan front that called for an Israeli withdrawal to the 1949 armistice lines; equal religious, civil, and economic rights for Israel and Jordan in the unified city of **Jerusalem**, whose political status was to be determined through negotiations; and a settlement of the **refugee** problem. While Jordan accepted the proposal, Israel rejected it. *See also* NASSER, GAMAL ABDUL; UNITED STATES INITIATIVE.

RUSSIA. As the primary successor state to the **Soviet Union**, Russia cochaired the **Madrid Conference**, but its role was limited. In January 1992, Moscow hosted the **multilateral talks** of the Madrid Conference, at which five separate working groups were formed: water, environment, arms control and regional security, **refugees**, and regional economic development. Since the mid-1990s, most of these working groups have remained dormant.

Preoccupied with its domestic difficulties, Russia has remained a marginal player in the Middle East. The ongoing violence in the Arab–Israeli conflict, especially the **Al-Aqsa Intifada**, has rekindled the hopes of a Russian reentry in the Middle East peace process through the **Middle East Road Map** unveiled in early 2003. *See also* SYKES–PICOT AGREEMENT.

– S –

SABRA AND SHATILA MASSACRE. On 14 September, during the Israeli occupation of Beirut following its invasion of **Lebanon** in **Operation Peace for Galilee**, Lebanese President-elect Bashir Gemayel (1947–1982) was killed. In retaliation, Christian forces of **Phalange** affiliated with Gemayel's political party—reportedly commanded by Elie Hubeika (1956–2002), who headed the Phalange secret service—moved into Palestinian **refugee** camps in Sabra and Shatila on the outskirts of Beirut. Despite being aware of the prevailing mood for vengeance, Israeli forces, which were in control of the areas, did not prevent the entry of the Phalangists. During 16–18 September, hundreds of unarmed innocent Palestinian men, women, and children in the refugee camps were massacred.

The killings evoked widespread condemnation in the Middle East and elsewhere, and on 25 September, Tel Aviv witnessed an enormous demonstration against the massacre. Initially the Knesset voted against a judicial committee, but President Yitzhak Navon (1921–)

threatened to resign, and on 28 September, bowing to public pressure, Israeli prime minister **Menachem Begin** appointed an official commission of inquiry headed by the chief justice of the Supreme Court, Yitzhak Kahan. While absolving the **Israel Defense Forces** of any direct responsibility, the **Kahan Commission** severely criticized the top brass and ruled that Defense Minister **Ariel Sharon** should not be given any "sensitive" position in the cabinet. Protesting against the carnage, **Egypt** withdrew its ambassador from Israel (2000–2005), but continued with its oil exports as stipulated by the **Egypt–Israel Peace Treaty**. *See also* BELGIUM LAW.

SADAT, ANWAR (1918–1981). As president of **Egypt**, Anwar Sadat was the first Arab leader who recognized and sought peace with the State of Israel. Born in Menofia in the northeast of Cairo on 25 December 1918, Sadat graduated from the Egyptian Military Academy in 1938 and joined the army. In the wake of the July 1952 Revolution by the Free Officers, Sadat held numerous minor positions in the government and in the ruling Revolution Command Council. In 1960, he was elected Speaker of the parliament, and in 1964, President **Gamal Abdul Nasser** appointed Sadat to the visible but relatively powerless position of vice president. After the death of Nasser in September 1970, Sadat was appointed president and, in October, was reaffirmed through a referendum.

In a calculated attempt to regain the **Sinai Peninsula**, which Egypt had lost during the **June War of 1967**, Sadat sought a limited conflict with Israel that would trigger Great Power involvement. Moving away from Nasser's policies, he distanced himself from the **Soviet Union** and, in July 1972, expelled Soviet experts stationed in Egypt. Coordinating his moves with President **Hafez al-Assad** of **Syria**, Sadat launched a surprised attack on Israel on 6 October 1973, initiating the **October War of 1973**. Though the war eventually ended in Israel regaining its initial losses and the Egyptian Third Army being encircled in the Sinai by a small unit headed by **Ariel Sharon**, Sadat managed to shatter the image of Israeli invincibility. The war also revealed the Israeli dependence on the urgent airlift of military supplies from the **United States**. Helped by the **shuttle diplomacy** of U.S. secretary of state Henry Kissinger (1923–), Sadat thereafter concluded the **Sinai I** and **Sinai II Agreements** with Israel.

In the wake of the victory of the **Likud** in the 1977 Israeli Knesset elections, Sadat surprised the world by offering a **Jerusalem visit** in pursuit of peace. This eventually resulted in Sadat addressing the Knesset on 20 November 1977, which was followed by the **Camp David Accords** in 1978 and the **Egypt–Israel Peace Treaty** in 1979. Egyptian efforts toward securing Palestinian rights through the **Autonomy Plan**, however, proved futile. In 1978, Sadat shared the Nobel Peace Prize with Israeli prime minister **Menachem Begin**.

Sadat's determination to move away from the resolutions of the **Khartoum Arab Summit** of 1967 and to pursue a separate peace with Israel angered the Arab world. Radical states, led by Syria and **Iraq**, organized the **Rejectionist Front** aimed at isolating Egypt. In 1979, Egypt was expelled from the **Arab League** and the Organization of the Islamic Conference, and the League headquarters were moved from Cairo to Tunis.

Sadat's peace with Israel also angered the Egyptian public and some of his senior colleagues. On 6 October 1981, while he was watching a military parade commemorating the October War, Sadat was assassinated by a member of a militant Islamic group; following the **assassination**, **Hosni Mubarak** took over as president. Sadat's funeral was attended by many Western and Israeli leaders but was largely boycotted by the Egyptian masses. Despite his widespread support and endorsement in Israel and in the West, Sadat continues to evoke a negative image in Egypt and in the rest of the Arab world.

ST. JAMES CONFERENCE. On 7 February 1939, **Great Britain** organized this round table conference in London. It sought to secure **Zionist** acceptance of the need for an Arab agreement on future *Aliya* to Palestine. Pending a compromise formula, it delayed the publication of the **MacDonald White Paper**, which formally repudiated British commitments to the **Balfour Declaration**.

SAIQA. Saiqa was a Syrian-backed pan-Arabist commando unit of the **Palestine Liberation Organization** (PLO) established by Yousef Zu'ayyin in February 1968. The name is an Arabic acronym for the Vanguard of the Popular War of Liberation. Strongly influenced by the Syrian Ba'athist ideology, it saw the liberation of Palestine within a broader pan-Arab context under the leadership of **Syria**. Like the

Popular Front for the Liberation of Palestine, it sought to balance pan-Arab ideology with Palestinian specificity. After coming to power in November 1970, President **Hafez al-Assad** purged Saiqa and brought the military as well as political wings under the complete control of the Syrian Army. Though the second largest Palestinian guerrilla organization, its presence was limited to Syria and **Lebanon**. In 1983, Saiqa withdrew from the PLO due to differences with the policies of **Yasser Arafat** and opposed the **Madrid Conference** and **Oslo Process**. Some of its leaders, including Zuheir Muhsen and Mohammad al-Mu'aita, were killed because of internal violence, and Issam al-Qadi took over as leader of Saiqa.

SAN REMO CONFERENCE. At the end of the World War I, Japan, **Great Britain**, **France**, and Italy met in the Italian town of San Remo 16–20 April 1920 to consider the future of the Middle Eastern territories that had been under Ottoman rule prior to the war. This conference discussed and ratified some of the secret decisions that had been made during the wartime negotiations between Britain and France, especially the **Sykes–Picot Agreement** of May 1916 to divide the Turkish territories in the Middle East. Accordingly, France was to be given mandatory rights in **Lebanon** and **Syria**, while Britain would obtain similar rights to Palestine and Mesopotamia (**Iraq**). A second San Remo Conference eight months later delineated the boundaries of these areas. Despite the eventual repudiation of the Sykes–Picot Agreement by both signatories, the Palestine **Mandate** outlined in this agreement was formally approved by the **League of Nations** on 22 July 1922 and came into force on 29 September 1923.

SAUDI ARABIA. Since the days of its founder ibn Saud, Saudi Arabia has been actively championing the Palestinian cause, perceiving it to be an important political tool to promote its influence in the region. However, Saudi Arabia has also been careful not to jeopardize its close ties with the West, especially with **Great Britain** and later the **United States**, by adopting radical positions with regard to the Palestinian question.

Although it was a party to the decision of the **Arab League** to offer political, diplomatic, and military support in preventing the realization of the Jewish national home in Palestine, Saudi involvement in the **Arab–Israeli War of 1947–1948** was minimal. Its contingents played some role in southwestern Palestine. At the end of the war, acting **United Nations mediator** Ralph J. Bunche (1904–1971) invited Saudi Arabia to participate in the armistice negotiations at Rhodes. Declining the invitation, Saudi Arabia informed the **United Nations** on 8 February that it would accept "the decisions which have already been adopted, or which may be adopted by the Arab League, in respect of the situation in Palestine."

Since then, the Saudi role in the Arab–Israeli conflict has been passive. The growth of radical Arab nationalism and the popularity of President **Gamal Abdul Nasser** of **Egypt** prevented Saudi Arabia from pursuing an activist Palestine policy. The defeat of the Arab armies in the **June War of 1967** and the subsequent decline of Nasser rekindled Saudi hopes for a regional order more inclined to religious conservatism. Capitalizing on the **Al-Aqsa Fire** that destroyed portions of the Al-Aqsa Mosque in the Old City of **Jerusalem**, King Faisal (c. 1903–1975) of Saudi Arabia joined hands with King Hassan II (1929–1999) of Morocco to organize a summit meeting of heads of state and government of Islamic countries. The Rabat summit of September 1969 witnessed the formation of the Organization of the Islamic Conference (OIC), where Saudi Arabia continues to play a pivotal role.

The **October War of 1973** witnessed a more assertive Saudi policy, and as an expression of solidarity with Egypt and **Syria**, Saudi Arabia on 16 October imposed an oil embargo on the United States and the Netherlands because of their pro-Israeli policy. The oil embargo continued until March 1974 and created an **Oil Crisis** in the West. Similarly, Saudi Arabia sought to utilize its influence when Israel sought the transfer of foreign embassies from Tel Aviv to Jerusalem. On 6 August 1980, Saudi Arabia and **Iraq**, the two principal oil suppliers of the region, warned that they would sever economic and diplomatic ties with any country that recognized Jerusalem as Israel's capital. As a result, a number of states that already had missions in Jerusalem moved their diplomats out of the city.

The peace initiatives of President **Anwar Sadat** of **Egypt** toward Israel posed a serious challenge to Saudi Arabia, and it joined the rest of the Arab countries in isolating Egypt and suspending diplomatic ties with Cairo. On 7 August 1981, Crown Prince (later King) Fahd (1921–2005) outlined an eight-point plan to resolve the Arab–Israeli conflict. The **Fahd Plan** came against the background of the failure of the **Camp David Accords** to make progress on the Palestinian front, Egyptian isolation in the Middle East, and the **assassination** of Sadat. Among other things, the Saudi proposal called for Israeli withdrawal from territories captured in 1967, the dismantling of Jewish **settlements**, a guarantee of freedom of worship for all faiths in Jerusalem, recognition of the Palestinian right to return or to be paid compensation, a UN mandate for the **Occupied Territories**, establishment of a **Palestinian state** with **East Jerusalem** as its capital, and ensuring the rights of Palestinians and the states in the region to live in peace. The last point accorded tacit recognition to Israel and made the plan controversial in the Arab world. The attempts to secure Arab endorsement at the Fez summit in November 1981 ended in failure.

In November 1982, an amended version of the Fahd Plan was endorsed by the Fez Arab summit, which laid down certain guidelines for an Arab–Israeli agreement. While the Fahd Plan affirmed "the right of all states in the region to live in peace," the **Fez Plan** merely proposed "a UN Security Council guarantee for the peace and security of all states in the region including a Palestinian state."

The Saudi relationship with the Palestinian leadership, especially the **Palestine Liberation Organization** (PLO) and its chairman, **Yasser Arafat**, became increasingly strained. Following the formation of **Hamas** in 1988, Saudi Arabia emerged as that organization's principal supporter due to the ideological proximity between Hamas and the Sunni Wahhabism of Saudi Arabia. Arafat's political support of Iraqi president Saddam Hussein (1937–) during the **Kuwait War** infuriated the Saudis and contributed to Arafat's alienation from the oil-rich Arab countries, which also resulted in the expulsion of tens of thousands of Palestinian workers from these countries. Even though the **Oslo Process** has somewhat mitigated the situation, Saudi Arabia continues to be sympathetic toward Hamas.

Amidst the **Al-Aqsa Intifada** in early 2002, Crown Prince (now King) Abdullah (1923–) unveiled an initiative that called on Israel to withdraw completely from all the Arab territories it had occupied during the June 1967 war. The **Abdullah Plan** called for the establishment of a Palestinian state with East Jerusalem as its capital in return for a collective Arab normalization of relations with Israel. A slightly diluted proposal was adopted unanimously by the Beirut

Arab summit in March 2002. As part of its efforts to secure membership in the World Trade Organization, **Saudi Arabia** in November 2005 agreed to lift its economic embargo against Israel.

SAYERET MATKAL. This elite reconnaissance unit controlled by Israel's General Staff has been responsible for several special operations carried out by Israel. A number of leading Israeli personalities, including **Ehud Barak** and **Benjamin Netanyahu**, have served in Sayeret Matkal. Its activities have included the **assassination** of Abu Jihad in Tunis in April 1988.

SCISSORS OPERATION. The code name for the military operation to capture the mixed Arab-Jewish city of Haifa in the north during the **Arab–Israeli War of 1947–1948**. On 21 April 1948, the forces of **Great Britain** evacuated their positions and moved to the Haifa port for their impending departure. Mounting an attack from the high ground of Mount Carmel, the Jewish forces surprised the Arab population and trifurcated the city, eventually capturing it. As the Arab commander fled to neighboring **Lebanon**, the Arab fighters were outnumbered and outmaneuvered. When the city surrendered to the Jewish forces, most of the Arab population of Haifa fled eastward as **refugees**.

SECURITY FENCE. In an attempt to prevent Palestinian militants from entering Israel from the **West Bank** and to reduce **suicide attacks**, in June 2002 Israel decided to erect a physical barrier that would separate Israel from the West Bank. Though the idea was not new, **Ariel Sharon** sought the fence as an effective counterterrorism measure.

The barrier mostly consists of an electronic fence equipped with electronic sensors with dirt paths, barbed wire, and trenches on both sides, with an average width of 60 meters (200 feet). In some areas, a wall 6–8 meters (20–25 feet) high has been erected in place of the barrier system. Though built generally along the **Green Line**, it does not follow it strictly but instead incorporates significant Palestinian territories of the West Bank on the Israeli side and imposes new movement restrictions upon the Palestinians living near the barrier's route.

On 1 October 2003, the government approved the new route proposed by the defense establishment covering 270 kilometers (168 miles). On 30 June 2004, responding to a petition, the Israeli High

Court ruled against the separation barrier northwest of **Jerusalem** because it harms Palestinians living along the route. This forced the government to make slight modifications.

On 9 July 2004, acting on a request from the **United Nations** General Assembly, the International Court of Justice (ICJ) ruled that the construction of the barrier inside the **Occupied Territories** was forbidden under the **Fourth Geneva Convention** and that it violates the rights of the Palestinian residents. Rejecting Israel's arguments about security requirements, it ruled that "the infringement of Palestinian human rights cannot be justified by military exigencies or by the requirements of national security or public order." The ICJ felt that the construction constitutes various breaches of Israel's obligations to international humanitarian law and human rights. However, since the construction of the fence, the number of **terrorist** attacks, especially from the West Bank, has decreased considerably. About 225 kilometers (140 miles) of the fence had been completed by March 2005.

SECURITY ZONE. The territory in southern **Lebanon** that remained under Israeli occupation from 1983 to 2000. Due to the mounting casualties and international criticism of **Operation Peace for Galilee**, Israel drew back 30 kilometers (18 miles) on 3–4 September 1983 and established a new line along the Awali River, south of the coastal city of Sidon. In the process, the **Israel Defense Forces** (IDF) withdrew from Beirut, the Beirut–Damascus highway, and the Shouf Mountains. Israel withdrew its "legation" from Beirut on 25 July 1984.

On 14 January 1985, the Israeli cabinet decided in favor of a three-stage **Lebanese withdrawal**. In the first stage, the IDF would pull out from the Sidon area and deploy in the Litani-Nabatiya region; in the second stage, it would be deployed in the Nabatiya region on the east; and in the third, the IDF would withdraw to international borders but would maintain a "zone in southern Lebanon where local forces [namely, the **South Lebanese Army**, or SLA] will operate with IDF backing." The first stage was completed on 16 February 1985, and Sidon was handed over to local Lebanese forces. In the second phase, completed on 11 April 1985, the IDF pulled out of the Beka'a Valley and sections in the central sector, but Israel still controlled 20 percent of the Lebanese territory.

On 21 April 1985 the Israeli cabinet authorized the beginning of the third stage of the unilateral withdrawal from most of the Lebanese territory while retaining a small portion along Israel's international borders with its northern neighbor. This narrow security zone corridor extended 5–15 kilometers (3–9 miles) into southern Lebanon and was manned by the SLA, which was sponsored, armed, and financed by Israel. The purpose was to protect northern Israeli towns and villages from militant attacks by the Palestinian forces, particularly Katyusha missile attacks by **Hezbollah**. During the period from 1985–2000, 256 soldiers were killed in combat and 840 were injured. The continued Israeli casualties eventually compelled Israel to reexamine its policy and resulted in a unilateral Israeli withdrawal, a process that was completed in the summer of 2000. *See also* FOUR MOTHERS MOVEMENT.

SEPARATION OF FORCES AGREEMENT. *See* SINAI I AGREEMENT; SINAI II AGREEMENT.

SETTLEMENT/S. In the context of the Arab–Israeli conflict, the term *settlements* refers specifically to Jewish settlements established in territories that Israel captured during the **June War of 1967**—that is, in the **West Bank**, **East Jerusalem**, the **Gaza Strip**, the **Sinai Peninsula**, and the **Golan Heights**. The first settlement after the war was established in Gush Etzion in September 1967, and since then more than 150 settlements have been established in the West Bank and the Gaza Strip. Following the **Camp David Accords**, Israel withdrew its settlements and destroyed the town of Yamit on the northeastern edge of the Sinai. On the Golan Heights, the first settlement was built in 1967, and since then Israel has established 32 settlements and the town of Katzrin. After the annexation of East Jerusalem following the June War, Israel established a number of large Jewish neighborhoods east of the **Green Line**. At the end of 2002, as many as 208,000 Jews were living in 139 settlements in the West Bank and the Gaza Strip and another 17,000 resided in the Golan Heights. By mid-2004, the number in the West Bank and Gaza had risen to 230,000. Moreover, more than 170,000 Israelis live in 13 areas in the eastern part of **Jerusalem** beyond the Green Line.

Both the **Labor** and **Likud** governments have pursued a policy of unhindered settlement activities. However, while Labor focused on establishing Jewish settlements in areas considered vital for Israel's security, the Likud sought to promote settlement activities as a means of preventing Palestinian territorial continuity and thereby inhibiting the creation of a **Palestinian state**. The settlement activities have been promoted by the Israeli government as well as by the Settlement Department of the **Jewish Agency** and **World Zionist Organization**. In an effort to encourage the settlement activities, Israelis living in the **Occupied Territories** have been offered a host of financial subsidies, concessions, tax rebates, and other incentives.

The settlement policy of Israel has remained the most controversial issue in Israel–Palestinian as well as Israel–U.S. relations. The international community, including the **United States**, has portrayed the settlements in the Occupied Territories as a violation of the **Fourth Geneva Convention**. Efforts by various U.S. administrations to freeze the settlements, however, have proved futile and ineffective. In 1992, the Israeli government headed by **Yitzhak Rabin** agreed to a limited and partial freeze in return for $10 billion worth of U.S. **loan guarantees**, but settlement activities continued unhindered. Under the **Declaration of Principles**, Israel agreed to discuss the question of settlements during the **Permanent Status Negotiations** with the Palestinians, but even though the negotiations were formally initiated in the summer of 1996, no progress was made on the settlements issue.

On 21 March 2005, Prime Minister **Ariel Sharon** approved the construction of 3,500 new homes in a neighborhood that would link **Ma'aleh Adumim**, the largest settlement in the West Bank, with Jerusalem. Dismissing petitions challenging the **Gaza Withdrawal Plan**, the Israeli Supreme Court ruled on 9 June 2005 that the Occupied Territories were not legally part of Israel and were "seized" during the **June War of 1967**, making the legal status of the settlements questionable. *See also* GUSH EMUNIM; SECURITY FENCE; SHARON PLAN.

SEVEN-POINT ISRAELI PLAN. On 21 October 1985, speaking before the **United Nations** General Assembly shortly after the **Tunis Raid**, Israeli prime minister **Shimon Peres** outlined a seven-point peace plan. It called for negotiations between Israel and the Arab states toward concluding peace treaties and resolving the Palestinian issue. Such negotiations would be direct and unconditional and would be based on Security Council **Resolution 242** and General Assembly **Resolution 194**. If necessary, it would be supported by a mutually agreed upon international forum to be held within three months. On the sensitive Palestinian question, Peres proposed that negotiations "between Israel and **Jordan** are to be conducted between an Israeli delegation on the one hand and a Jordanian- or a Jordanian–Palestinian delegation on the other, both comprising delegates that represent peace, not terror."

The explicit noninclusion of the **Palestine Liberation Organization** made the process a nonstarter. Nonetheless, it was this format of a joint delegation that enabled both Israel and the Palestinians to attend the **Madrid Conference** six years later. Similarly, the Arab states that attended the October 1991 meeting agreed to pursue direct and unconditional negotiations with Israel, based on Resolution 242 and **Resolution 338** of the Security Council.

SÈVRES CONFERENCE. The nationalization of the **Suez Canal** by President **Gamal Abdul Nasser** of **Egypt** generated intense diplomatic activities in Europe and elsewhere. At a high-level meeting in the Parisian suburb of Sèvres, **Great Britain**, **France**, and Israel agreed on a plan to launch military attacks against Egypt. Under the formal agreement signed on 23 October, Israel would initiate a limited military operation that would represent "an actual threat to the Canal." Following the Israeli attack, Britain and France would issue a time-bound "call" for a cease-fire. The parties anticipated that Egypt would reject the call for a cease-fire while Israeli forces were occupying its territories, and hence, Anglo-French forces would attack the Suez Canal zone area with the intention of "ensuring freedom of navigation." The parties set 29 October as D-day for the operations.

Britain, because of its interests in the Arab world and colonial possessions in the Persian Gulf, sought to pretend that it was not a party to the Israeli aggression, but France was less pretentious about its involvement and operated from its bases in Israel. Even though the Sèvres agreement was not made public at the time of the **Suez War**, the veto exercised by Britain and France in the **United Nations** Security Council against the proposal by the **United States** for a cease-fire and general retreat confirmed the premeditated nature of the tripartite aggression. Israel's collusion with the imperial powers severely undermined its position among Third World countries.

SHAMIR, YITZHAK (1915–). Right-wing Israeli politician Yitzhak Shamir twice served as prime minister, during 1983–1984 and 1986–1992. Born Yitzhak Yzernitzky in Poland on 15 October 1915, he joined the Revisionist youth movement Betar at the age of 14. In 1935, he left Warsaw and made *Aliya* to Palestine. Two years later, he joined the Revisionist underground organization **Irgun**. In 1940, Shamir joined with Avraham Stern and formed the Irgun splinter group called the **Stern Gang**, which was held responsible for a number of acts of **terrorism** and **assassinations**, including the killing of **United Nations mediator** Count Folke Bernadotte in September 1948. After the establishment of Israel, he joined the secret service and held senior positions in the Mossad, the agency responsible for external intelligence.

In 1970, Shamir joined the **Herut** Party headed by **Menachem Begin** and was elected to the Knesset in 1973, a position he held for 23 years. Following the victory of the **Likud** in 1977, he became the Speaker of the Knesset and then served as foreign minister from 1980 to 1983. In the wake of Begin's resignation in October 1983, Shamir became prime minister. Under the national unity government (1984–1990) with the opposition **Labor Party**, he first served as foreign minister (1984–1988) and later as prime minister (1986–1988). He continued in that post after the Labor Party left the government in March 1990.

Adopting an intransigent and uncompromising position toward the **Palestine Liberation Organization**, Shamir strongly opposed various peace efforts undertaken by the **United States** during the 1980s. Bowing to international pressure, in 1989 he outlined a five-year transitional arrangement for the Palestinians in the **Occupied Territories** known as the **Shamir Plan**. The plan bogged down due to differences over the participation of **Jerusalem Palestinians**. Shamir also vetoed the **London Agreement** that Foreign Minister **Shimon Peres** had worked out with King **Hussein** of **Jordan**.

During the **Kuwait War**, as **Iraq** was firing Scud missiles at Israel, Shamir reversed the traditional Israeli policy of retaliation and decided not to respond to missile attacks. At end of the war, he led Israel to the **Madrid Conference** that began on 30 October 1991. Toward the end of his tenure, Shamir was involved in a bitter controversy with the United States over **loan guarantees** and severely undermined Israel's relations with Washington. After Likud lost the

1992 Knesset elections, Shamir stepped down from party leadership and, in 1996, retired from the Knesset. *See also* BAKER PLAN; BUS 300 AFFAIR; JORDAN IS PALESTINE; MUBARAK PLAN (1985); MUBARAK PLAN (1989); RABIN PLAN.

SHAMIR PLAN. Against the background of increased international criticism over Israel's handling of the **Intifada** (1987–1993), Israeli prime minister **Yitzhak Shamir** met U.S. president George H. W. Bush (1924–) and Secretary of State James A. Baker (1930–) in Washington, D.C., in April 1989 and outlined a four-point plan. It called for

1. the **Camp David Accords** to be the foundation of the peace process
2. the ending of Arab hostility and belligerency against Israel
3. multilateral efforts to resolve the problem of Arab **refugees**
4. the election of Palestinian delegates to "negotiate an interim period of self-governing administration"

The Shamir Plan was rejected by **Yasser Arafat** as well as by Palestinians in the **Occupied Territories**, who viewed it as an attempt to circumvent the **Palestine Liberation Organization** (PLO). Since the whole process was based on the Camp David Accords, the plan, if implemented, would give personal and not territorial autonomy to the residents. In the domestic area, it raised a number of unresolved questions, such as whether elections would be municipal or political, the provision of international supervision, the size of the self-governing authority, and the linkage between the interim and final settlement.

On 14 May 1989, the Israeli cabinet approved a modified version of the Shamir Plan. Its salient features were that the Camp David Accords would be the basis for peace; there would be no **Palestinian state**; Israel would not negotiate with the PLO; there would be no change in the status of the Occupied Territories; there would be a five-year transition period of "interim agreement" followed by a "permanent solution"; and during this transition period, Palestinians would have self-rule while Israel would retain control over defense, foreign affairs, and "all matters pertaining to Israeli citizens" living in the Occupied Territories. The Knesset approved the plan a couple of days later. The following month, 95 U.S. senators signed a letter addressed to Secretary Baker urging the administration to be "fully supportive" of the Israeli initiative. However, endorsing the position of the PLO that elections should be held only after Israeli withdrawal from the Occupied Territories, the Casablanca **Arab League** summit rejected the Israeli initiative in May 1989.

Meanwhile, Shamir's own **Likud** Party was opposed to the plan and sought to tighten it by bringing in additional restrictions on elections. In July, the Likud Central Committee demanded that **East Jerusalem** Arabs be excluded from the electoral process and that the uprising cease before negotiations begin. Such conditions, however, were rejected by the cabinet, which resolved to continue with the 14 May initiative. *See also* BAKER PLAN; MUBARAK PLAN (1985); MUBARAK PLAN (1989); PLO LAW; RABIN PLAN; SHULTZ PLAN.

While the Israeli cabinet failed to decide on the **Shultz Plan**, in March 1988, Prime Minister Shamir outlined a six-point plan aimed at pacifying and containing the Intifada. This plan was first discussed during his meeting with President Ronald Reagan (1911–2004) in March and proposed an international event hosted and sponsored by both superpowers, direct talks, no role for the PLO, an Israeli veto over the composition of the Palestinian representation, plans for refugee rehabilitation, and the entire process to be based on the Camp David Accords.

SHARM AL-SHEIKH MEMORANDUM. On 4 September 1999, newly elected Israeli prime minister **Ehud Barak** and Palestinian chairman **Yasser Arafat** signed this agreement at the resort Sharm al-Sheikh in **Egypt**. Witnessed by Secretary of State Madeleine Albright (1937–) of the **United States**, President **Hosni Mubarak** of **Egypt**, and King **Abdullah II** of **Jordan**, it paved the way for the implementation of the **Wye Memorandum** of October 1998. In Sharm al-Sheikh, both sides agreed on a further Israeli **redeployment** from 11 percent of the **Occupied Territories** in a two-phase withdrawal of transferring areas from full or partial Israel control to partial or full Palestinian control implemented in three stages: on 5 September 1999, to transfer 7 percent from Area C to Area B; on 15 November 1999, to transfer 2 percent from Area B to Area A and 3 percent from Area C to Area B; and on 20 January 2000, to transfer 1 percent from Area C to Area A and 5.1 percent from Area B to Area A. No official map was attached to the Sharm al-Sheikh Memorandum, and Israel was given the discretion to determine the specific areas from which it would withdraw. The agreement further stipulated that Israel would release about 350 Palestinian prisoners held in Israeli jails; open a safe passage between the West Bank and the Gaza Strip to become operational from 1 October; and commence the **Permanent Status Negotiations** on 13 September 1999. It called for a framework for a permanent settlement to be reached by February 2000 and a final peace agreement by September 2000.

Israel completed the first stage of its withdrawal on 10 September 1999. After protracted negotiations and differences, on 21 March 2000 Israel redeployed from another 6.1 percent of the Occupied Territories. *See also* TABA AGREEMENT.

SHARM AL-SHEIKH SUMMIT (1996). In 1996, Israel was reeling from a spate of **suicide attacks** by **Hamas** militants that had rocked the country beginning on 25 February. As many as 59 Israelis were killed and nearly 200 injured in four suicide attacks in **Jerusalem**, Ashkelon, and Tel Aviv. These attacks not only eroded the popularity of the **Shimon Peres** government but also instilled a sense of fear among ordinary Israelis over their personal safety. In order to shore up public support for the Israeli government that was facing renewed challenges from the Right, and to provide a political response to the militant campaign, it was decided to host a summit meeting at the resort Sharm al-Sheikh in **Egypt**. Presented as the "Summit of Peace Makers," this meeting was attended by a number of world leaders, including President **Bill Clinton** of the **United States**, President Jacques Chirac (1932–) of **France**, King **Hussein** of **Jordan**, German Chancellor Helmut Kohl (1930–), Prime Minister Victor Chernomyrdin (1938–) of **Russia**, Prime Minister John Major (1943–) of **Great Britain**, **Palestine Liberation Organization** chairman **Yasser Arafat**, and representatives from 13 Arab states. On 13 May 1996, the leaders vowed not to allow **terrorism** to scuttle the hopes of the peoples of the Middle East for peace.

SHARM AL-SHEIKH SUMMIT (2000). In 2000, the intensification of the **Al-Aqsa Intifada** appeared to be torpedoing the slow and painstaking gains made since the **Madrid Conference**. In a bid to stem the cycle of violence, on 17 October President **Hosni Mubarak** of **Egypt** hosted a summit in Sharm al-Sheikh attended by U.S. president **Bill Clinton**, Israeli prime minister **Ehud Barak**, Palestinian leader **Yasser Arafat**, and King **Abdullah II** of **Jordan**. All the participants agreed to work toward controlling violence. The meeting agreed to appoint a fact-finding committee to look into the causes of the violence and to suggest ways of renewing the peace process. On 7 November, Clinton appointed a three-member committee headed by former senator George Mitchell. *See also* MITCHELL COMMITTEE REPORT.

SHARM AL-SHEIKH SUMMIT (2005). Within days after his election as the president of the **Palestinian National Authority** (PNA), **Mahmoud Abbas** held a summit meeting with Prime Minister **Ariel Sharon** in Sharm al-Sheikh. Hosted by President **Hosni Mubarak** of **Egypt**, it was also attended by King **Abdullah II** of **Jordan**. Following their deliberations, Sharon and Abbas declared a joint ceasefire and renewed a call for reducing the violence that had been raging since the outbreak of **Al-Aqsa Intifada**. Sharon also agreed to coordinate the **Gaza Withdrawal Plan** with the PNA. Furthermore, they agreed to set up four committees to implement confidence-building measures, including prisoner release, responding to problems of **deportees**, and improving Israeli–Palestinian coordination. Egypt and Jordan decided to return ambassadors to Israel; Egypt had withdrawn its ambassador from Tel Aviv in October 2000, while Jordan had delayed the appointment of a new envoy to Israel.

SHARON, ARIEL (1928–). Known as "Arik" to his admirers, Ariel Sharon is a colorful but controversial Israeli politician who became prime minister in March 2001. Born on 27 February 1928 in Kfar Malal, in Palestine **Mandate**, he joined the **Haganah** in 1945 at the tender age of 14. During the **Arab–Israeli War of 1947–1948**, he commanded an infantry company. After the war, he joined the newly established **Israel Defense Forces** (IDF). In 1953, Sharon founded and led **Unit 101**, a special commando force that conducted a series of retaliatory operations against Palestinian guerrillas who were operating from **Jordan**. In one such attack, known as the **Qibya Raid** in October 1953, 12 Jordanian soldiers and 60 civilians were killed. The operation, which was carried out over the opposition of Prime Minister Moshe Sharett (1894–1965), successfully reduced the level of infiltrations from Jordan.

In 1956, Sharon was appointed commander of a paratrooper brigade and fought in the **Suez War**. Afterward, he held various senior positions in the IDF, including head of the Southern Command, but he was never made the chief of staff, apparently due to his political leanings. Disappointed at the treatment meted out by the Mapai/**Labor Party** leadership, Sharon resigned from the army in 1973. When the **October War of 1973** broke out, however, he was recalled to active military duty and commanded an armored division. His small unit successfully crossed the **Suez Canal**, encircled the Third Army of **Egypt**, and brought about a spectacular victory for Israel.

In December 1973, Sharon was elected to the Knesset, but he soon resigned his seat and briefly served as security adviser to Prime Minister **Yitzhak Rabin**. During the 1977 Knesset elections, he played an active role in the victory of the **Likud** and served as minister of agriculture under **Menachem Begin**. During this time, he promoted the **Sharon Plan** toward annexing most of the **West Bank**. Sharon became defense minister in 1981 and in that capacity bulldozed the cabinet into agreeing to his military operations against the **Palestine Liberation Organization** (PLO) in **Lebanon**, which eventually resulted in the June 1982 Israeli invasion of Lebanon commonly known as **Operation Peace for Galilee**. The war, especially the **Sabra and Shatila Massacre**, made Sharon extremely unpopular both inside and outside the country. The **Kahan Commission**, which looked into the massacre, concluded that Sharon should not be given any "sensitive" positions in the government again. As a result, from 1983 to 1990, he held minor portfolios in government; in 1990, he became minister of construction and housing under **Yitzhak Shamir**.

In the aftermath of the victory of **Benjamin Netanyahu** in 1996, Sharon returned to prominence. He became minister of national infrastructure and, following a cabinet crisis in October 1998, was made foreign minister. In that capacity, he attended the peace negotiations in the **United States** and played a critical role in the conclusion of the **Wye Memorandum**. The defeat of Netanyahu in the May 1999 elections saw the emergence of Sharon as leader of the Likud. In February 2001, he defeated **Ehud Barak** in the elections and, on 7 March, became prime minister. After a series of cabinet crises, he ordered a snap poll in January 2003 and returned to power.

Throughout his political career, Sharon pursued an aggressive **settlement** policy in the **Occupied Territories**. With the explicit intention of breaking up the territorial continuity of any future Palestinian entity, he established Jewish settlements in the vicinity of Palestinian population centers. Vehemently opposed to the **Oslo Process** and the creation of the **Palestinian National Authority** (PNA), Sharon maintained his opposition to directly negotiating with Chairman **Yasser Arafat**. In their brief meeting during the Wye Plantation negotiations in October 1998—the only occasion when the archrivals ever met—Sharon refused to shake hands with Arafat even in private. His controversial visit to the Temple Mount/*Haram al-Sharif* on 28 September 2000 led to the **Al-Aqsa Intifada**. In the wake of increased violence and **suicide attacks**, he initiated the **siege of Yasser Arafat** in December 2001 and publicly regretted that he had not killed the Palestinian leader during the Lebanese operations when the IDF encircled and eventually forced Arafat to leave Lebanon in 1982. Pressured by the United States, he reluctantly avoided physically harming or expelling Arafat from Ramallah.

Such restraint, however, was not extended to others. After assuming office in 2001, Sharon stepped up the military campaign against suspected Palestinian militants in the Occupied Territories and elsewhere. His policy of **targeted killing** was partly responsible for the failure of the **Cairo Dialogue**, wherein **Hamas** and the PNA had offered partial and conditional suspension of suicide attacks against Israel. Clearly departing from past Israeli practice, Sharon started targeting political as well as military leaders of Hamas, and this resulted in the **assassination** of **Sheikh Ahmed Yassin** and **Abdel Aziz al-Rantisi**. In a bid to reduce violence, in June 2002, Sharon authorized the construction of a controversial **security fence** in the West Bank.

Because of the growing violence in the **Gaza Strip** and the precarious nature of the Jewish settlements there, in May 2004, backed by U.S. president **George W. Bush**, Sharon offered the **Gaza Withdrawal Plan**. This plan, received with skepticism by the Palestinians and others, exhibits a different side of Sharon. Though an architect of settlement activities, Sharon was instrumental in completing the Israeli withdrawal from the **Sinai Peninsula** as demanded by the **Camp David Accords**. As defense minister in April 1982, he presided over the demolition of the last Israeli settlement in Yamit. Sharon's right-wing critics thus perceived the Gaza Withdrawal Plan as a reenactment of the Yamit example. Similarly, in 1997 Sharon played a central role in resolving tensions with Jordan following the **Masha'al Affair**, when Israeli agents sought to assassinate the leader of Hamas in Jordan.

In February 2005, during the **Sharm al-Sheikh Summit**, Sharon and PNA president **Mahmoud Abbas** declared a joint cease-fire. Just a month later, however, Sharon approved the construction of 3,500 new homes in a neighborhood that would link **Ma'aleh Adumim** in the West Bank with **Jerusalem**.

In November 2005 the protracted internal tension and schism within the Likud resulted in Sharon leaving the party and creating a new party called Kadima ("Forward"), which attracted sizable support from former Likud members as well as Labor Party members such as **Shimon Peres**. As a result of the massive stroke he suffered in January 2006, Sharon went into a coma and in April was formally declared unable to function as prime minister. His responsibilities were transferred to his deputy Ehud Olmert (b. 1945–). *See also* BELGIUM LAW; VILLAGE LEAGUE.

SHARON PLAN. In the late 1970s and early 1980s, Likud leader **Ariel Sharon** advocated a plan that would facilitate Israeli annexation of most of the **West Bank**. In contrast to the **Allon Plan**, which preferred Jewish **settlement** in areas along the **Jordan** Valley vital for Israeli security, Sharon sought to hasten settlements on the mountain plateau before the conclusion of the **Autonomy Plan** of Prime Minister **Menachem Begin**. Both as agricultural minister (June 1977–August 1981) and later as defense minister (August 1981–February 1983), Sharon pursued settlement activities that sought to keep enclaves of Palestinian population centers outside Israeli control. Even though the plan did not explicitly call for the annexation of the West Bank, it rejected any territorial compromise over it. *See also* GAZA WITHDRAWAL PLAN.

SHAW COMMISSION. In September 1929, Sir Walter Shaw was appointed to head a commission to inquire into the **Western Wall** Riots. The report attributed the riots to Arab apprehensions over *Aliya* and land purchases by the **Zionists**. In the commission's view, the Arab–Jewish conflict was rooted in the contradictory promises by **Great Britain** to both the communities. Among other things, it called on the British government to clearly articulate its policy, including its measures to safeguard the interests of the non-Jewish majority. *See also* LEAGUE OF NATIONS; MANDATE, PALESTINE.

SHE'AR YASHUV ACCIDENT. On 4 February 1997, 73 Israeli soldiers and airmen were killed when two U.S.-made CH-53 helicopters collided in midair over the settlement of She'ar Yashuv in northern Israel. The soldiers were being ferried to the **security zone** when the accident occurred. An official inquiry blamed the accident on lax security procedures, ambiguous flight instructions, and miscommunication. The accident and the large number of casualties resulted in a domestic debate over the continued Israeli military presence in southern **Lebanon.** *See also* FOUR MOTHERS MOVEMENT; LEBANESE WITHDRAWAL.

SHEBA'A FARMS. Located on the triborder of **Syria, Lebanon,** and Israel, the status of this 25-square-kilometer (10-square-mile) enclave remains controversial. Following the Israeli **Lebanese withdrawal** in 2000, **Hezbollah** and the Lebanese government, supported by Syria, demanded the Israelis also withdraw from Sheba'a Farms. However, Israel maintains that this Syrian territory was captured along with **Golan Heights** during the **June War of 1967**, and hence its fate can be decided only in Israeli–Syrian negotiations. Based on the maps of the **United Nations Interim Force in Lebanon**, the **United Nations** endorsed the Israeli position that Sheba'a Farms was a Syrian territory at the time of the June War. The Arab states and Hezbollah maintain that Syria "transferred" Sheba'a Farms to Lebanese control after the June War. Since the Israeli withdrawal, Hezbollah has periodically carried out limited military operations in the disputed enclave, including the kidnapping of Israeli soldiers serving there. *See also* SOUTH LEBANESE ARMY; TANNENBAUM AFFAIR.

SHEPHERDSTOWN TALKS. On 3 January 2000, the leaders of Israel and **Syria** met in Shepherdstown, West Virginia, for talks. In the presence of U.S. president **Bill Clinton,** Israeli prime minister **Ehud Barak** and Syrian foreign minister Farouq al-Shara (1938–) met and discussed the Israeli–Syrian negotiations, which had been stalled since early 1996 and were resumed only when Barak and al-Shara had met in Washington, D.C., on 15 December 1999. The structured Shepherdstown Talks failed to make progress over the Syrian insistence on prior Israeli commitments regarding withdrawal from the **Golan Heights.**

SHIP OF RETURN AFFAIR. In early 1988, the **Palestine Liberation Organization** (PLO) planned to organize the return to their homeland of Palestinians **deported** by Israel as a symbolic move to highlight the problem. On 15 February, the *Ship of Return*, which was to take on a small number of deportees, was sabotaged and crippled at Limasol, Cyprus. A day earlier, three PLO functionaries who had purchased the vessel on behalf of the PLO were killed in the same port city. Both these activities were attributed to Israeli commando raids.

SHULTZ PLAN. On 4 March 1988, U.S. secretary of state George Shultz (1920–) sent a formal letter to Prime Minister **Yitzhak Shamir** outlining a new American initiative to resolve the Palestinian problem. Prior to this, he had already held discussions with the leaders of Israel, **Egypt**, and **Syria**; the Palestinians had boycotted his planned meeting with them on 26 February in **East Jerusalem**. According to Shultz's proposal, negotiations between Israel and its neighbors would start on 1 May and would be based on **Resolution 242** and **Resolution 338** of the **United Nations** Security Council. Two weeks before negotiations commenced, an **international conference** would be held at the invitation of the UN secretary-general, which was not to impose solutions or veto agreements. The key component of the Shultz Plan was the negotiations between Israel and a joint Jordanian–Palestinian delegation, to conclude within six months an agreement for a five-year interim autonomy. The Palestinians rejected the proposal.

Israel's national unity government was divided over the Shultz Plan and Israeli prime minister Shamir's opposition revolved around the idea of an international conference and his insistence on an Israeli veto over the Palestinian representation. Differences between the coalition partners in the national unity government precluded any decision concerning the plan. Suggesting modifications, on 29 March 1988 Shamir outlined a six-point counterproposal. *See also* BAKER PLAN; MUBARAK PLAN (1985); MUBARAK PLAN (1989); PLO LAW; RABIN PLAN; SHAMIR PLAN.

SHUTTLE DIPLOMACY. At the end of the **October War of 1973**, U.S. secretary of state Henry Kissinger (1923–) shuttled between Israel and various Arab capitals in the hope of reaching **disengagement agreements** between Israel and its neighbors. The first such agreement was the **Sinai I Agreement** signed with **Egypt** on 18 January 1974. That was followed by the **Israel–Syria Disengagement of Forces Agreement** on 31 May 1974. *See also* SINAI II AGREEMENT.

SIEGE OF BETHLEHEM. As part of its **Defensive Shield Operation**, Israeli tanks moved into Bethlehem, and in the ensuing fighting on 2 April 2002, more than 100 Palestinian policemen and militants, mostly Muslims, took refuge in the Church of the Nativity along with clerics and noncombatants. Israeli troops encircled the church and launched a prolonged siege, which continued until 10 May. Under a plan worked out through European and U.S. mediation, the **Palestinian National Authority** agreed to transfer 26 gunmen who were holed up in the Church to Gaza and the 13 other higher-level cadres to permanent exile in various European Union member states. The compliance of **Yasser Arafat** with the **deportation** evoked strong criticism among the Palestinian public. *See also* AL-AQSA INTIFADA.

SIEGE OF YASSER ARAFAT. Against the backdrop of the **Al-Aqsa Intifada**, on 4 December 2001 Israeli tanks encircled and fired on Chairman **Yasser Arafat**'s headquarters in Ramallah, and a few days later, Prime Minister **Ariel Sharon** declared that the Palestinian leader was "irrelevant" to the political process. Earlier, Israel had disabled the helicopter fleet of Arafat stationed in Gaza. Not only did Sharon prevent Arafat from attending the Christmas celebrations in Bethlehem but his determination to stop Arafat from returning to Ramallah also prevented the Palestinian leader from attending the Beirut **Arab League** summit in March 2003. The siege continued until October 2004, when Arafat was shifted to Paris for medical treatment. On 11 November 2004, he succumbed to his illness and the following day he was buried in his Ramallah headquarters.

SINAI I AGREEMENT. With the **shuttle diplomacy** mediation of U.S. secretary of state Henry Kissinger (1923–), on 18 January 1974 Israel and **Egypt** signed the Sinai I Agreement on the disengagement of both their armies in the **Sinai Peninsula**. While Israel was allowed to retain its control of the Mitla and Gidi passes, Egypt agreed to restrict its military presence east of the **Suez Canal** to 7,000 troops and 30 tanks. This separate agreement between Egypt and Israel formally ended Egypt's prewar military alliance with **Syria**. As part of the agreement, the **United States** was able to persuade the Arab states to end their oil embargo against Israel's Western allies imposed during the **October War of 1973**.

Israel and Egypt concluded an agreement that paved the way for a partial Israeli withdrawal from the eastern banks of the Suez canal. Under the new armistice line, Israel withdrew 32 kilometers (20 miles) east of the canal, which eventually resulted in the reopening of the Suez Canal in June 1975. As part of the agreement brokered by Kissinger, Egypt agreed to restore diplomatic relations with the United States, broken off in 1973. On 1 September 1975, Israel and Egypt concluded a second agreement on Sinai, the **Sinai II Agreement**, which paved the way for further Israeli withdrawals east of the Mitla and Gidi passes, as well as from the oil fields in the Gulf of Suez. *See also* MULTINATIONAL FORCE AND OBSERVERS; UNITED NATIONS EMERGENCY FORCE II.

SINAI II AGREEMENT. On 4 September 1975, **Egypt** and Israel signed the Sinai II Agreement in Geneva, helped by the intensive **shuttle diplomacy** of U.S. secretary of state Henry Kissinger (1923–). Sinai II consisted of three published agreements and four secret documents. The accords widened the buffer zone between the two countries created by the **Sinai I Agreement**, and Egypt formally renounced the use of force against Israel. Of the secret annexures, one assured Egypt of U.S. construction of an early warning station on the **Sinai Peninsula** and American assurance of consultation in the event of an Israeli violation. The remaining three, comprising the **Israel–United States Memorandum of Understanding**, concerned promises to Israel of American assistance to maintain Israel's military superiority, an assured supply of oil in the event of an Egyptian embargo against Israel, and an American commitment not to recognize or negotiate with the **Palestine Liberation Organization** until the latter recognized Israel's right to exist. *See also* OCTOBER WAR OF 1973.

SINAI PENINSULA. Surrounded by the Gulf of Suez and the **Suez Canal** in the west, the Gulf of Aqaba in the east, and the Mediterranean Sea in the north, the Sinai Peninsula links the continents of Asia and Africa. Spread over 53,000 square kilometers (about 20,500 square miles), this territory of **Egypt** was briefly occupied by Israel during the **Suez War** in 1956 but was returned to Egypt in 1957 under pressure from the **United States**. Israel recaptured the Sinai in the **June War of 1967** but completely withdrew from the peninsula in 1982 following the **Camp David Accords**. During its occupation of the Sinai, Israel depended upon the Abu Rudeis oil fields in the Sinai Desert for nearly 50 percent of its oil needs. *See also* SINAI I AGREEMENT; SINAI II AGREEMENT; TABA; TABA TERROR ATTACK.

SINAI WAR. *See* SUEZ WAR.

SOUTH LEBANESE ARMY (SLA). The origin of this right-wing Christian militia force, which operated in southern **Lebanon** for more than two decades, can be traced to the **Litani Operation** of 1978. Following its withdrawal in June, Israel handed over its positions to the newly formed South Lebanese Army, then commanded by Maj. Sa'ad Haddad (1937–1984). After his death in 1984, Maj. Antoine Lahad (1929–) succeeded him. The SLA was armed, trained, paid, funded, and supplied by Israel. The members of the SLA and their families were provided easy access to Israeli markets as well as employment opportunities. On the eve of its withdrawal, Israel left a quantity of arms and ammunition as a "farewell gift"; however, this proved insufficient to prevent the SLA's quick disintegration after the Israeli pullout. At the time of the May 2000 unilateral **Lebanese withdrawal**, Israel absorbed about 6,000 members of the SLA, including its leader Lahad, while about 1,500 fighters surrendered to the **Hezbollah** and Lebanese police.

SOVIET PROPOSAL FOR THE MIDDLE EAST. Sidelined by its exclusion from the Interim Agreement and the dormant idea of the **Geneva Conference**, the **Soviet Union** on 7 October 1976 outlined a four-point proposal for the Middle East, calling for

1. complete Israeli withdrawal from the territories occupied in 1967
2. recognition and realization of Palestinian rights to self-determination and the establishment of an independent **Palestinian state**
3. recognition of the existence and security of all states including Israel through international guarantees
4. cessation of the state of war between Israel and its Arab neighbors

The reluctance of the principal players—**Egypt**, Israel, and the **United States**—to agree to Soviet involvement in the peace efforts hindered progress on the proposal.

SOVIET UNION. Even though it was one of the first countries to recognize the State of Israel, since the early 1950s the USSR emerged as the staunchest supporter of the Arabs in their conflict with Israel. The conclusion in 1955 of the military deal between its East European ally Czechoslovakia and President **Gamal Abdul Nasser** of **Egypt** was a landmark in Soviet Middle East policy. The **Czech Deal** included the supply of a wide range of offensive arms, ammunition, and support systems, including tanks, armored personnel carriers, howitzers, artillery pieces, antitank guns, antiaircraft guns, fighter jets, bombers, transport planes, radar installations, destroyers, minesweepers, torpedo boats, and six submarines. This was one of the largest single military transactions in the world and hence caused considerable anxiety in Israel. It also sowed the seeds of an Israeli desire to topple Nasser before he could pose a military threat and eventually led to the **Suez War**.

The **June War of 1967** exposed the limitations of the Soviet military equipment supplied to Egypt and **Syria**. The war also underscored the limitations of Soviet political influence. Partly to regain its lost prestige, in June 1967 Moscow and its East European allies broke off diplomatic ties with Israel and emerged as its harshest critic. The renewal of Soviet military supplies played an important role in the prolongation of the **War of Attrition**.

At the same time, the ongoing détente between the Soviet Union and the **United States** largely influenced President **Anwar Sadat** of **Egypt** to initiate a limited military campaign against Israel in 1973. Following the **October War of 1973**, Sadat sided with Israel in preventing any role for the Soviet Union in the peace negotiations. Even the regional opposition to the **Camp David Accords** did not improve the Soviet position. At the political level, the growing Soviet support contributed to various international bodies such as the **United Nations** adopting a host of anti-Israeli resolutions. This trend peaked in November 1975 when the UN General Assembly declared **Zionism** to be a form of racism. Soviet support also played a critical role in the international political and diplomatic recognition of the Palestinian leader **Yasser Arafat**. On 7 October 1976, the Soviets unveiled a four-point **Soviet Proposal for the Middle East**, which failed to gather momentum.

The end of the Cold War and the disintegration of the Soviet Union in 1991 fundamentally altered the situation in the Middle East. After its willingness to endorse the U.S. lead during the **Kuwait War**, Moscow played a secondary role in the **Madrid Conference** of October 1991. Days before the conference, it restored diplomatic ties with Israel. Since the collapse of the Soviet Union, **Russia** has had a much reduced role in the Arab–Israeli conflict.

SPECIAL MUNICIPAL COMMISSIONER FOR JERUSALEM. On 6 May 1948, the **United Nations** General Assembly formally asked the Palestine **Mandate** power to appoint "before 15 May 1948, a neutral acceptable to both Arabs and Jews" as a special municipal commissioner for **Jerusalem**. With the cooperation of both communities, he was to "carry out the functions hitherto performed by the Municipal Commission." **Great Britain** appointed Harold Evens as the commissioner, but he never had a chance to take up his duties. *See also* PARTITION PLAN.

STERN GANG. The Stern Group—also referred to as Lehi (short for Lohamei Herut Yisrael, "Fighters for the Freedom of Israel") and known to the British as the Stern Gang—was a **Jewish Underground** force that broke away from **Irgun**. Founded by Avraham Stern (1907–1942) in 1940, the Stern Gang was held responsible for a number of violent anti-British incidents both inside and outside the Palestine **Mandate**. The mainstream *Yishuv* leadership, as represented by the **Jewish Agency** and its military arm **Haganah**, as well as Irgun, was critical of Stern.

In February 1942, the British killed Stern, and other leaders were rounded up. However, a three-member team comprising Nathan Friedmann-Yelling, Yitzhak Yzernitsky (later **Yitzhak Shamir**), and Israel Scheib (Eldad) took over the leadership of the Stern Gang and pursued a policy of **assassination** and **terrorism**. Members of the Stern Gang assassinated Minister for Middle Eastern Affairs Lord Moyne (1880–1944) of **Great Britain** in Cairo on 6 November 1944. The group was also responsible for a number of attacks against British interests in Palestine, including military installations, business and government offices, military and police personnel, military vehicles, and the oil refinery in Haifa.

In April 1948, members of the Stern Gang raided an Arab village and killed more than 200 unarmed civilians, including women and children, in the **Deir Yassin Massacre**. Following the formation of the State of Israel, the group was disbanded and its fighters were incorporated into the **Israel Defense Forces**. On 18 September 1948, former members of the Stern Gang assassinated **United Nations mediator** Count Folke Bernadotte (1895–1948) due to strong differences over his peace plan, which advocated significant territorial concessions to Arabs. The membership and service in Lehi were subsequently recognized by the state and former members were given pensions similar to army service personnel. *See also ALTALENA* AFFAIR; BERNADOTTE PLAN.

STOCKHOLM DECLARATION. In December 1988, amid the controversy over U.S. denial of his visa request to attend the **United Nations** General Assembly session in New York, **Yasser Arafat** met five leading American Jewish leaders in Stockholm. With the participation of Swedish foreign minister Sten Andersson, on 7 December both sides agreed on a four-point statement, including

1. the recognition by the **Palestine Liberation Organization** (PLO) of **Resolution 242** and **Resolution 338** of the UN Security Council
2. recognition of Israel's right to exist
3. rejection and condemnation of all forms of terrorism
4. a resolution of the Palestinian refugee problem "in accordance with international law and practices and relevant UN resolutions"

This move enabled the **United States** to abandon its erstwhile opposition (as stipulated by the September 1975 **Memorandum of Understanding** with Israel) to negotiating with the PLO. Following additional clarification, on 14 December, during the **Geneva United Nations Session**, President Ronald Reagan (1911–2004) authorized the State Department "to enter into a substantive dialogue with the PLO representatives." The U.S. ambassador in Tunis, Robert Pelletreau (1935–), carried out initial contacts with the PLO.

SUEZ CANAL. The 101-kilometer-long (63-mile) Suez Canal linking the Mediterranean and Red seas was opened on 17 November 1869. The government of **Egypt** had a substantial share in the venture built by **France** but sold its shares to the British in 1875. The canal zone came under British control following **Great Britain**'s occupation of **Egypt** in 1882. In 1888, the major maritime powers met and signed the **Constantinople Convention**, which guaranteed that the canal would be "always free and open in time of war as in time of peace, to every vessel of commerce or of war, without distinction of flag." This provision was tested when Egypt, as part of the **Arab boycott of Israel**, prevented use of the Suez Canal for cargos to or from the Jewish state.

After protracted negotiations, **Great Britain** agreed to withdraw its forces from the Suez Canal zone in October 1954, completing the process in July 1956. On 26 July, President **Gamal Abdul Nasser** of Egypt announced the **nationalization of the Suez Canal**, which precipitated the **Suez War**. The canal was briefly closed during the war but reopened in January 1957. It was closed for a second time following the **June War of 1967** and **War of Attrition**. It was reopened for international shipping only on 5 June 1975, following the Egypt–Israel **Disengagement Agreement** of 1974 and the Interim Agreement of 1975. Under Article 5 of the **Camp David Accords**, Egypt agreed to keep the canal open for Israeli cargo, and the first Israeli freighter passed through the canal on 30 April 1979.

SUEZ WAR. Amid tensions between **Egypt** and the government of **Great Britain** and **France** over the **nationalization of the Suez Canal**, on 29 October 1956 Israel initiated its Sinai Campaign. Based on the agreement reached with the British and French at the **Sèvres Conference**, it launched a military attack on the **Sinai Peninsula** with the stated objectives of preventing guerrilla attacks from the **Gaza Strip** and opening the **Suez Canal** to Israeli shipping. It also exploited the crisis to pursue its desire to seek a foothold at the mouth of the Strait of Tiran and to capture Sharm al-Sheikh. Within 100 hours, Israeli forces routed the Egyptian forces in the Sinai Peninsula as well as their positions in Gaza. Meanwhile, as agreed, Great Britain and France issued an ultimatum on 31 October for both Israel and Egypt to "withdraw" 16 kilometers (10 miles) from the canal. At this time, Israeli forces were about 48 kilometers (30 miles) east of the canal and therefore still needed to advance another 32 kilometers (20 miles) into the Sinai to comply with the ultimatum. When President **Gamal Abdul Nasser** of Egypt refused, British planes from Cyprus attacked Egyptian airfields while French planes took off from their bases in Israel for similar raids. When the **United Nations** demanded an immediate cease-fire on 3 November, Israel was in complete control of the whole of the Sinai Peninsula except Sharm al-Sheikh, which it captured a few days later.

On 6 November, Britain and France agreed to a cease-fire. Following international pressure, especially from U.S. president Dwight D. Eisenhower (1890–1969), on 8 November the Israeli cabinet accepted the cease-fire demands "after suitable arrangements" were made with the newly formed peacekeeping force, the **United Nations Emergency Force I** (UNEF I). Israeli withdrawal from the Sinai began in November, but it made its withdrawal from the Sharm al-Sheikh area and the Gaza Strip conditional on Egypt ensuring freedom of navigation through the Strait of Tiran. This became a major friction point between Israel and the Eisenhower administration (1953–1961). Eisenhower's public statement against a reimposition of the **naval blockade** in the straits and the deployment of UNEF I to take over civilian administration of the Gaza Strip resolved the crisis. Israel completed its withdrawal from the Sharm al-Sheikh area and the Gaza Strip on 22 January 1957. On 11 March, Egypt replaced the civilian administration and appointed a military governor for the Gaza Strip.

SUICIDE ATTACKS. On 23 October 1983, a Lebanese volunteer belonging to **Hezbollah** rammed a truck fully loaded with TNT into a building at Beirut International Airport in **Lebanon** that was being used as a temporary headquarters, killing 241 **United States** Marines. This **Beirut Airport Bombing** came against the backdrop of a similar suicide truck bombing by a member of **Islamic Jihad** against the U.S. embassy in West Beirut on 18 April 1983, which resulted in the deaths of 49 people. These suicide attacks, especially the one against the barracks, led to the reevaluation of U.S. military involvement in Lebanon and resulted in the withdrawal in early 1984 of U.S. and French troops deployed in Lebanon to stabilize and contain growing sectarian violence.

Since the onset of the **Oslo Process**, especially after the signing of the **Declaration of Principles**, **Hamas** has used this strategy against Israeli civilians inside the **Green Line** to sabotage the Middle East peace process. Unlike **Islamic Jihad**, Hamas does not distinguish Israeli civilians from military personnel. The number of suicide attacks—described by Palestinians as "armed intifada"—increased following the outbreak of the **Al-Aqsa Intifada** and have dominated the current violence. As a result, some Palestinians have questioned the nomenclature *intifada* to describe the Palestinian protests against Israeli occupation.

Crowded buses, bus stops, restaurants, and shopping malls have been the prime targets of the suicide attacks, all of which have been carried out by one of four Palestinian groups: Hamas, Islamic Jihad, the **Popular Front for the Liberation of Palestine**, and **Fatah**, or by the Popular Resistance, a coalition of Fatah, Hamas, and Islamic Jihad. The emergence of groups such as the **Al-Aqsa Martyrs Brigade**, a group identified with the Fatah movement led by **Yasser Arafat**, signals public Palestinian support for such attacks. *See also* CAIRO DIALOGUE.

SYKES–PICOT AGREEMENT. A secret agreement was signed by **Great Britain** and **France** in May 1916 to divide the Arab provinces of the Ottoman Empire after World War I. It was named after its two architects, British orientalist Sir Mark Sykes (1879–1919) and former French consul general in Beirut François Georges-Picot. Under it, France would control **Lebanon** and **Syria**, while Mesopotamia (**Iraq**) and Palestine would go Britain. The agreement was approved in principle by Russia until the Bolshevik Revolution. Disclosing the secret agreement, the newly formed **Soviet Union** annulled its commitments and compelled both the signatories to renounce the agreement. However, following the war and the 1920 **San Remo Conference**, the Arab areas of the Ottoman Empire were divided along the lines suggested in the Sykes–Picot Agreement.

SYRIA. The involvement of Syria in the Arab–Israeli conflict began in March 1920 when Emir Faisal ibn Hussein (1883–1933), the son of Sharif Hussein of Mecca (1852–1931), proclaimed himself king of Syria. He aspired to include and unify **Lebanon**, Palestine, and **Transjordan** under his rule, but his reign proved to be short lived and he was driven out of Damascus; **Great Britain** subsequently installed him as the monarch of **Iraq**.

Despite being transformed into a mandate under **France** following World War I, Syria remained the prime ideological torchbearer of Palestinian nationalism. On the eve of the formation of Israel, Syria took over the responsibility of organizing, training, and arming the **Arab Liberation Army** (ALA). This irregular force played an important role in the **Arab–Israeli War of 1947–1948**, and Arab volunteers were recruited through centers set up in Damascus, Beirut, Baghdad, and Cairo. At the height of the 1947–1948 war, the ALA had a strength of 5,000 men and was active in northeast Palestine as well as in the **Jerusalem** area. At the end of the war, Syria, following the examples of other Arab neighbors, entered into armistice negotiations with Israel in April 1949. On 20 July, Syria became the last Arab country to sign an **armistice agreement**.

Israeli–Syrian disputes over violations of the armistice agreement and Israeli complaints of Syrian harassment of its fishermen took a turn for the worse when, on the night of 11 December 1955, Israel launched a massive three-pronged attack on Syrian outposts on the eastern bank of the Sea of Galilee, inflicting heavy Syrian casualties. This operation seems to have resulted in Syrian noninvolvement when Israel launched the **Suez War** a few months later.

On 6 June 1967, Israel launched a preemptive air strike against the Arab air forces, including Syria's, and crippled its air force. On 9 June, a day after the cease-fire in the **June War of 1967** came into force on the war front with **Egypt**, Israel initiated a ground offensive against Syria. Within 20 hours, Israeli forces captured the whole of the **Golan Heights**, including the Syrian town of **Quneitra**. Because of the clause recognizing Israel's right to exist, Syria refused to accept **Resolution 242** of the **United Nations** Security Council until 1972.

In a bid to regain the Golan Heights, Syria joined Egypt and launched a surprise offensive against Israel in the **October War of 1973**. After some initial setbacks, Israel was able to push the Syrian forces back from the Golan Heights, and by 10 October, it had made further territorial gains into Syria. When the cease-fire came into force on 22 October, Israel was in control of about 600 square kilometers (230 square miles) of additional Syrian territory. Shortly after the war ended, Syria accepted UN Security Council **Resolution 338**, which called for the implementation of Resolution 242.

Thanks to the **shuttle diplomacy** efforts of U.S. secretary of state Henry Kissinger (1923–), Israel and Syria reached an agreement in May 1974 that reaffirmed the cease-fire achieved at the end of the October 1973 war. The **Israel–Syria Disengagement of Forces Agreement** paved the way for the pullback of Israeli and Syrian forces on the Golan Heights and the creation of disengagement zones between the two armies. On 31 May 1974, a new cease-fire line was established on the Heights, slightly to the west of the post-1967 cease-fire line. As a part of the agreement, Israel withdrew from the Syrian town of Quneitra.

President **Hafez al-Assad** of **Syria** strongly opposed Egyptian president **Anwar Sadat**'s peace initiatives toward Israel and the conclusion of the **Camp David Accords**. Damascus emerged as the major critic of Sadat and his policies and the rallying point for groups opposed to peace with Israel. Damascus also became the main force behind a number of Palestinian groups opposed to Palestinian leader **Yasser Arafat**. The Israeli invasion of Lebanon (**Operation Peace for Galilee**) in 1982 offered new opportunities to Syria to support Lebanese groups such as **Amal** and **Hezbollah** in opposing the Israeli occupation of southern Lebanon. Similarly, Syrian pressures compelled Lebanon to abandon the peace agreement it had signed with Israel on 17 May 1983.

The end of the Cold War and disintegration of the **Soviet Union** removed the Syrian ability to pursue a military option against Israel. Deprived of its patron and having supported the efforts of the **United States** during the **Kuwait War**, Syria was persuaded to attend the **Madrid Conference**. The Israeli willingness to apply UN Security Council Resolutions 242 and 338 to the Golan Heights enhanced the Syrian position. However, citing the lack of progress, Syria and its client Lebanon boycotted the **multilateral talks**.

Following the Israeli launching of the **Grapes of Wrath Operation** in early 1996, Syria joined the United States and **France** in arranging a limited cease-fire agreement that involved Hezbollah. During the tenure of **Yitzhak Rabin** and **Shimon Peres** (1992–96), Israeli–Syrian negotiations showed signs of a breakthrough. However, disagreements over the time frame and security arrangements impeded any progress. In a bid to revive the negotiations, in January 2000 Israeli and Syrian leaders met in Shepherdstown, West Virginia. The **Shepherdstown Talks** proved to be unsuccessful. Meanwhile, on 5 March 2000, the Israeli cabinet unanimously decided to pull out of the **security zone** in southern Lebanon, which was completed by May 2000. This unilateral Israeli **Lebanese withdrawal** has significantly weakened any prospects of an agreement over the Golan Heights. *See also* AC-COUNTABILITY OPERATION; COHEN, ELI; FATAH UPRISING; GREEN LINE; HINDAWI AFFAIR; ISRAEL–LEBANON

AGREEMENT; KINNERET OPERATION; OCCUPIED TERRITO-
RIES; REJECTIONIST FRONT; SETTLEMENT/S; SHEBA'A
FARMS; TRIPOLI CONFERENCE.

– T –

TABA. This is a small area on the **Egypt**–Israel border southwest of the
Israeli town of Eilat along the Gulf of Aqaba. When Israel withdrew
from the **Sinai Peninsula** in 1982 in accordance with the **Camp
David Accords**, it refused to withdraw from Taba, challenging
Egyptian claims over Taba. After months of protracted negotiations,
both sides agreed to resolve the dispute through reconciliation talks.
When these efforts failed, on 12 January 1986 the Israeli cabinet resolved to refer the Taba dispute to an arbitration panel. On 11 September, Egypt and Israel formally agreed to the arbitration panel
comprising jurists from **France**, Sweden, and Switzerland. The five-
member international arbitration panel ruled in favor of Egypt on 29
May 1988, and on 15 March 1989, nearly seven years after its pullout from the rest of the Sinai, Israel completed its withdrawal from
the 700 square meters (one-sixth of an acre) of the Taba enclave.

TABA AGREEMENT. Also referred as the Oslo II Agreement, this accord was drawn up and initialed at the resort **Taba** in **Egypt** on 26
September 1996 by Israeli prime minister **Yitzhak Rabin** and Palestinian chairman **Yasser Arafat**. The agreement was formally signed
in Washington, D.C., on 28 September.

The Taba Agreement outlined the second stage of Palestinian autonomy and the gradual extension of Palestinian rule beyond the **Gaza
Strip** and **Jericho**. It comprised five main chapters and dealt with a
number of central issues, such as election of the **Palestinian Legislative
Council** (PLC) and its powers and responsibilities and Israeli **redeployment** from six Palestinian towns of Bethlehem, Jenin, Nablus,
Qalqilya, Ramallah, and Tulkaram. Concerning the sensitive question
of withdrawal from Hebron, the agreement provided for Israeli control
of 15 percent of the city, inhabited by 450 Jewish settlers. It also provided for an additional three-stage phased Israeli redeployment to be
completed within 18 months from the date of inauguration of the PLC.

It set October 1999 as the deadline for finalizing the **Permanent Status Negotiations**.

The Taba Agreement divided the **Occupied Territories** into three categories: Area A, territories with full Palestinian civil jurisdiction and internal security; Area B, territories with Palestinian civil jurisdiction but with joint Israeli–Palestinian security control; and Area C, territories where Israel enjoys complete civil and security control. In geographical terms, Area A would constitute 3 percent of the **West Bank**; Area B would include 450 small towns and villages constituting 27 percent of the West Bank; and Area C would made up the remaining 70 percent and would include Jewish **settlements** and Israeli military bases.

Israeli withdrawals from Arab population centers were completed by late 1995 and elections to the PLC were held in January 1996. Other provisions of the Taba Agreement were delayed considerably, and the withdrawal from Hebron was not completed until the conclusion of the **Hebron Protocol** in January 1997. The delays in the implementation of the Oslo II agreement, especially the additional redeployment, compelled both parties to sign the **Wye Memorandum** in October 1998.

TABA TERROR ATTACK. A total of 32 people were killed and more than 120 were wounded on 7 October 2004 in **terrorist** attacks on two holiday resorts in **Taba** on the **Sinai Peninsula**. These hotels were frequented by Israelis, and 12 Israelis were among the dead. Powerful explosions were caused by two separate car bombs, each containing about 200 kilograms (440 pounds) of explosives that were detonated in the lobby, causing the collapse of part of the Hilton Hotel, which bore the maximum damage and casualties. Jamaa al-Islamiya Al-Alamiya (World Islamist Group), a previously unknown group, claimed responsibility for the attack.

TANNENBAUM AFFAIR. Israeli businessman and reserve colonel Elhanan Tannenbaum, age 57, disappeared shortly before three soldiers of the **Israel Defense Forces** (IDF) were abducted by **Hezbollah** on 7 October 2000 in the disputed **Sheba'a Farms** in the trijunction of Israel, **Lebanon**, and **Syria**. It was not clear where Tannenbaum, who has business ties with the Arab world, was abducted. There was speculation that he was taken in Europe and handed over to Hezbollah. Israel denied claims by Hezbollah leader Sheikh Hassan Nasrallah

(1953–) that Tannenbaum was an agent of the Mossad, Israel's external intelligence agency. In January 2004, behind-the-scene mediation resulted in a **prisoner exchange** whereby Tannenbaum and the bodies of three Israeli soldiers were given to Israel in return for the release of 436 Arab prisoners to Hezbollah. Israel also handed over the bodies of 59 Lebanese fighters killed in the past. The swap was widely criticized inside Israel as Tannenbaum was suspected of links to the mafia.

TANZIM. The armed wing of **Fatah**, Tanzim was set up in 1995 as an attempt to counter the Islamic militants who opposed Chairman **Yasser Arafat** and the **Palestinian National Authority** (PNA). Most of its members were active during the **Intifada**. The November 1994 showdown between **Hamas** and the security forces of the PNA in Gaza City, which resulted in the death of 13 civilians, was seen as the inducement for the formation of this quasi-military force, which was supportive of and sympathetic to Arafat. It was also seen as a counterweight to the security forces belonging to the PNA but with mass appeal and grassroots support.

Members of Tanzim have been in the forefront of confrontation with Israeli forces and assumed a prominent role following the outbreak of the **Al-Aqsa Intifada** in September 2000. A number of attacks in the **Occupied Territories** against Israeli settlers and civilians have been attributed to Tanzim. Marwan Barghouti (1960–), a Palestinian from Ramallah and a member of the **Fatah Revolutionary Council**, has emerged as the principal leader of Tanzim. Initially, Barghouti filed his nomination paper from prison for the presidential elections held in January 2005 after the death of Arafat. Just days before the voting, however, he withdrew from the contest. *See also* ISLAMIC JIHAD.

TARGETED KILLING. The practice adopted by Israel to target and kill key Palestinians suspected of involvement in various acts of violence committed against Israel. Since the outbreak of the **Intifada** in 1987, the **Israel Defense Forces** (IDF) have killed several people accused of engaging in **terrorism**. The **Oslo Process** imposed a political price for such operations, but the targeted killings continued. The handing over of territories to the **Palestinian National Authority** posed logistical problems for such operations, but in January 1996 Israeli agents in Gaza killed Yahya Ayyash (popularly known as "The Engineer"), who was suspected of involvement in many **terrorist** acts against Israel.

The targeted killings and **assassinations** increased after the outbreak of the **Al-Aqsa Intifada**, and Israel killed a number of Palestinian militants as well as political leaders. Escalating its targeted killings in March 2004, Israel killed **Hamas** spiritual leader **Sheikh Ahmed Yassin** in Gaza City, and less than a month later **Abdel Aziz al-Rantisi**, who briefly succeeded Yassin, was also killed.

On 3 February 2005, a cabinet committee on security approved a decision to end the targeted killing of suspected Palestinian terrorists. Under the new policy guidelines, Israel would give a list of suspected militants to the Palestinian security officials. The suspects would then be located and offered amnesty by the Palestinian security officials if they renounced violence. However, following a series of incidents, in June 2005 senior officials of the IDF declared that targeted killing would be resumed. *See also* ALI MUSTAFA, ABU; CAIRO DIALOGUE.

TEL AVIV MASSACRE. On 11 March 1978, a group of 11 Palestinian militants penetrated Israel's coastal defenses and hijacked two buses. Israeli security forces stopped the group near Tel Aviv, and in the ensuing battle, 37 Israelis were killed and 76 were injured. This attack provided the excuse for the Israeli invasion of **Lebanon** called the **Litani Operation**.

TEMPLE MOUNT FAITHFUL. A religious messianic group committed to the reconstruction of the Jewish Temple in the Temple Mount area of the Old City of **Jerusalem**. Its periodic attempts to highlight its stated object often result in violent clashes in the Old City as well as in the **Occupied Territories**. On 8 October 1990, amidst the ongoing tension in the Persian Gulf in the wake of the **Kuwait War**, the Israeli High Court rejected a petition from the group to lay the cornerstone of the Third Temple. However, rumors spread of an impending move by the group to carry out its threat. In response, Arab youths began throwing stones from the Temple Mount/*Haram al-Sharif* area at the Jewish worshippers at the Western Wall below. This injured scores of Jewish worshippers and resulted in police firing at the rioters. The riots led to the deaths of 20 Palestinians and injuries to scores of others. The constraints of maintaining the anti-**Iraq** coalition led the **United States** to vote in favor of a **United Nations** Security Council Resolution 672, which denounced the Israeli action and called on Israel to receive a UN mission to investigate the killing. Israel refused to comply with the UN demand and instead appointed its own inquiry, which concluded that the police officers had acted in self-defense when they feared for their lives and the lives of other worshippers in the area. However, the report also criticized the police for not foreseeing the events, especially after the Temple Mount Faithful petitioned the High Court, and for not conveying the court's rejection of its appeal to the *Waqf* leaders.

TEMPORARY INTERNATIONAL PRESENCE IN HEBRON (TIPH). Responding to the **Hebron Massacre** of 18 March 1994, when 29 Muslims worshippers were killed in the Ibrahimi Mosque/Tomb of the Patriarchs by Baruch Goldstein, a member of **Kach**, the **United Nations** Security Council adopted a resolution that called for "a temporary international or foreign presence" to ensure "safety and protection" of the Palestinians in the **Occupied Territories**. On 31 March, Israeli and Palestinian negotiators reached an agreement in Cairo to set up an international observer unit in Hebron. Accordingly, Israel agreed to the formation of the 150-member TIPH, comprising unarmed observers from Norway, Denmark, and Italy. Later on, this was expanded to a 180-member contingent with the participation of observers from Sweden, Switzerland, and **Turkey**. The Security Council resolution, which was also supported by Israel, paved the way for the renewal of peace talks between Israel and its Arab interlocutors that were stalled following the massacre.

The TIPH unit was meant to ensure normal life and a sense of security among the Palestinian residents of Hebron in areas that remained under Israeli occupation. On 9 May 1996, following a partial Israeli **redeployment** from Hebron, both sides concluded another agreement which established the framework for the TIPH. Consisting of unarmed volunteers from the six countries, the TIPH was accountable only to a joint Israeli–Palestinian committee and to an ad hoc commission consisting of the participating countries. Though meant to be a temporary measure, the mandate of the TIPH has been periodically extended.

TENET PLAN. In the wake of Israeli reservations and opposition to the **Mitchell Committee Report**, in June 2001 U.S. president **George W. Bush** asked the director of the Central Intelligence Agency, George Tenet (1953–), to work toward establishing and consolidating a significant period of cessation of Palestinian violence to allow Israel to initiate confidence-building measures. While Israel demanded that such a quiet period be extended to six weeks, the **United States** sought a seven-day cessation of violence before a longer "cooling-off" period would begin. The continuation of Palestinian violence and Israeli **targeted killing** ensured that even a limited period of quiet was not possible.

Toward implementing the recommendation of the Mitchell Report and ensuring a temporary cease-fire in the **Al-Aqsa Intifada**, Tenet outlined a security plan on 13 June 2001. It called on both parties to resume security cooperation and work toward establishing an immediate cease-fire. Following the stabilization of the situation, it called for the withdrawal of Israeli forces from the Palestinian areas to positions held prior to 28 September 2000, the lifting of internal closures, and the reopening of border crossings. The plan was not put into practice as neither side would ensure a cessation of hostilities.

TERRORISM. Targeting unarmed civilians for political purposes—the most commonly accepted definition of terrorism—has been an integral part of the Arab–Israeli conflict. Even though the term gained international currency much later, targeting civilians has been in vogue since at least the early 1920s, when the **Zionist** aspirations for a Jewish national home in Palestine gained international recognition through the **Balfour Declaration** and the **League of Nations** award of Palestine as a **mandate** to **Great Britain**. This erupted into widespread violence in Palestine and was manifested in intercommunal riots as highlighted by numerous massacres where innocent Arab and Jewish civilians were killed for explicit political purposes, including the **Western Wall Riots** (1929), the **Hebron Massacre** (1929), and the **Arab Revolt** (1936–1939). This trend increased after the **United Nations** approved the **Partition Plan** on 29 November 1947 and with the onset of the **Arab–Israeli War of 1947–1948**. During this period, scores of civilians were killed, for example, during the **Deir Yassin Massacre** and the ambush of Jewish doctors a few days later in **Jerusalem**.

The 1960s witnessed the beginning of the guerrilla campaign by Palestinian militants and ushered in a new cycle of violence recognized as terrorism. Palestinian militants often entered Israel and carried out numerous acts of terrorism, such as the **Bus 300 Affair** and the **Ma'alot Massacre**. Even though political motives and the struggle for national liberation were used to justify and explain the wanton killing of unarmed civilians, the international community increasingly began to recognize the negative consequences of the new trend. The hijacking of three civilian aircraft by militant Palestinians, widely condemned by the international community, eventually resulted in the military crackdown by **Jordan** commonly known as the **Black September Massacre** of 1970.

International terrorism reached new lows in the **Munich Massacre** of September 1972, when Palestinian guerrillas took hostage and killed Israeli athletes during the Olympic Games in Germany. The hostage taking of Israeli passengers aboard an Air France plane in 1976 resulted in the successful rescue mission known as the **Entebbe Operation**. The frequent actions against civilian aircraft also resulted in a tougher regime against air piracy. International disapproval and countermeasures that are more effective have significantly reduced air piracy since then.

While the **Intifada** (1987–1993) witnessed a popular uprising against the continued Israeli occupation of the **West Bank** and **Gaza Strip**, the onset of the **Oslo Process** increased terrorism. **Suicide attacks** have become the most frequently used terrorist tactic employed by militant Palestinian groups opposed to the peace process, especially **Hamas** and **Islamic Jihad**. The popularity of such attacks among the Palestinians even influenced the nonreligious **Al-Aqsa Martyrs Brigade** to adopt similar tactics against the Israeli civilian population.

The **United States** has designated a number of Palestinian groups as terrorist organizations and imposed a series of sanctions. Likewise, countries such as **Iran**, **Iraq**, Libya, and **Syria** have often faced similar U.S. sanctions due to their suspected "involvement" in various acts of terrorism or their support for militant Palestinian groups.

For their part, the Palestinians have tended to view Israeli reprisal raids and the **targeted killing** of Palestinian leaders as terrorism. Since the 1980s, the **Jewish Underground** and even individuals have conducted a number of terrorist attacks against the Palestinians (for example, the **Hebron Massacre** in 1994 and the **Tel Aviv Massacre**), and they were rarely prosecuted by Israel or were given light sentences.

Recognizing the international disapproval of suicide attacks, during 2002–2003 Egypt sought to mediate with different Palestinian groups with the aim of bringing about a temporary suspension of suicide attacks. This **Cairo Dialogue**, however, failed due to serious differences between Hamas and the **Palestinian National Authority**. *See also* TABA TERROR ATTACK.

TRANSFER. Right-wing extremists in Israel advocate the transfer—that is, expulsion—of Palestinians from the **Occupied Territories** and from Israel as a means of resolving the Israeli–Palestinian conflict. The violent advocacy of this platform led to the proscription of Rabbi Meir Kahane's (1932–1990) **Kach** Party in 1986. Until his **assassination** on 17 October 2001, Rehavam Ze'evi (1926–2001), who founded and led Moledet, advocated a peaceful transfer of Arabs.

TRANSJORDAN. In 1921, in appreciation for the support of Sharif Hussein (1852–1931) of Mecca during the **Arab Revolt** (1916–1918), **Great Britain** partitioned the Palestine **Mandate** and created the semiautonomous Emirate of Transjordan. Abdullah ibn Hussein (later King **Abdullah I**), the son of Sharif Hussein, was installed as the emir. Transjordan was granted independence from Britain in 1946 and became the Hashemite Kingdom of **Jordan** in 1950. *See also* HUSSEIN–MCMAHON CORRESPONDENCE.

TRIPARTITE ARAB FEDERATION. On 29 April 1963, leaders of **Egypt, Iraq**, and **Syria** met in Cairo, signed a treaty of unity, and established the Tripartite Arab Federation. Among other things, the leaders committed themselves "to free the Palestine homeland from the **Zionist** danger." Like many other similar moves, the idea largely remained an unrealized political vision.

TRIPARTITE DECLARATION. In an attempt to stabilize the **armistice agreements** between Israel and its neighbors, endorsed by the **United Nations** Security Council on 11 August 1949, the **United States, Great Britain**, and **France** voluntarily agreed to control the flow of arms to the Middle East. In a public declaration issued on 25 May 1950, these three Western powers committed themselves not to supply arms to any state in the Middle East that had any aggressive designs against its neighbors. By controlling the flow of weapons, they sought to guarantee regional stability. France broke this understanding by clandestinely supplying large quantities of arms to Israel prior to the **Suez War**, and both France and Israel concluded an arms deal in August 1954, long before the **Czech Deal**, that was often seen as a precursor to the Suez War.

TRIPOLI CONFERENCE. Critical of the **Jerusalem** visit of President **Anwar Sadat** of **Egypt**, the leaders of Algeria, **Syria**, South Yemen, and Libya met in the Libyan capital Tripoli, concluding on 5 December 1977. Declaring their determination to fight the Egyptian initiative, they decided to freeze relations with Egypt. In retaliation, Sadat decided to suspend diplomatic ties with these countries as well as **Iraq**, which was also critical of his peace initiatives toward Israel. *See also* CAMP DAVID ACCORDS; REJECTIONIST FRONT.

TRUCE COMMISSION FOR PALESTINE. Continued violence in Palestine during the **Arab–Israeli War of 1947–1948** and the lack of cooperation from the **Mandate** authorities prevented the **Palestine Conciliation Commission** (PCC) of the **United Nations** from fulfilling its mandate in implementing the **Partition Plan** resolution. After the PCC reported to the General Assembly that it was unable to fulfill its assignment because of "the armed hostility of both Palestinian and non-Palestinian Arab elements, the lack of cooperation from the Mandatory Power, the disintegrating security situation in Palestine. . .", the Security Council appointed a Truce Commission composed of the Consuls of Belgium, France, and the United States in Jerusalem "to assist the Security Council in supervising the implementation" of Resolution 46 of 1948. **Syria**, which also had a consular office in Jerusalem, refused to serve in the commission. Besides providing on-the-spot information to the Security Council, the Truce Commission managed to arrange several agreements to limit fighting in Jerusalem as well as supervising relief convoys to the city. The responsibilities of the commission were transferred to the PCC, which was created by the General Assembly on 11 December 1948.

TRUSTEESHIP COUNCIL. On 26 April 1948, less than three weeks before the expiry of the Palestine **Mandate**, the **United Nations** General Assembly voted to establish a Trusteeship Council to prepare a draft statute for **Jerusalem**, which under the **Partition Plan** was to have a special international regime under direct UN administration. As fighting continued in Palestine between the Jews and Arabs in the **Arab–Israeli War of 1947–1948**, the **United States**, which exercised its political, diplomatic, and economic power and influence to secure the UN endorsement of the Partition Plan in November 1949, began to have second thoughts. The decision made by **Great Britain** to abandon the Mandate and to unilaterally withdraw from Palestine on 15 May 1948, followed by Israel's **Declaration of Independence**, made the question irrelevant.

TUNIS RAID. On 25 September 1985, members of **Fatah**, the principal component of the **Palestine Liberation Organization** (PLO), murdered three Israeli tourists in the Cypriot city of Larnaca. In a bid to contain such acts of **terrorism**, Israel conducted an air raid on 1 October against the headquarters of the PLO, which were located in the *Haram al-Sharif* neighborhood of Tunis in Tunisia. Chairman **Yasser Arafat** was not in the office at the time, but more than 60 Palestinians, including some senior members of **Force 17**, the elite force responsible for Arafat's personal security, were killed. In conducting a raid some 4,800 kilometers (3,000 miles) from Israeli shores, Defense Minister **Yitzhak Rabin** declared, "No PLO element anywhere in the world has immunity."

The **United Nations** Security Council condemned the raid and the **United States** abstained when the Council adopted Resolution 573 on 4 October. The violation of Tunisian airspace during the attack also came under international criticism. The direct military attack on Arafat precluded any progress on the **Hussein–Arafat Accord** and the U.S.-led attempts for a joint Jordanian–Palestinian delegation that would negotiate with Israel.

TUNNEL CONTROVERSY. In a midnight operation shortly after the end of Yom Kippur, 23 September 1996, the government of Israeli prime minister **Benjamin Netanyahu** opened a historic tunnel that linked the Western Wall to an exit near the Temple Mount in the Old City of **Jerusalem**. The opening of the 480-meter-long (1,500-foot) Hasmonean Tunnel, which runs under the Muslim quarters in the Old City of Jerusalem and alongside Al-Aqsa Mosque, sparked a wave of violence in **East Jerusalem** that soon spread to the **Occupied**

Territories. As many as 56 Arabs and 14 Israelis were killed in the violence that lasted for five days. For the first time, the Palestinian police force exchanged fire with the **Israel Defense Forces**, which sparked new criticism in Israel over the **Oslo Accords** enabling Palestinians to carry weapons.

TUNNELS. This refers to underground tunnels that link Rafah and **Egypt**. Over the years, Palestinians built underground tunnels in the sand dunes surrounding the Palestinian town of Rafah in the southern **Gaza Strip** and used them to smuggle weapons, explosives, ammunition, and drugs from the **Sinai Peninsula** of **Egypt** into the Strip. Some of the tunnels run more than a kilometer (half a mile) on either side of the border, are well lit, and even contain food and water supplies. Citing smuggling activities, Israel periodically closes the Rafah crossing, the only access point for the residents of Gaza to Egypt and to the outside world. Under the **Oslo Accords**, Israel obtained a small strip of land along the border with Egypt known as the Philadelphi route, which it uses to prevent the illegal movement of people and goods into the Gaza Strip. Under the **Rainbow Operation** of 2004, pursued during the **Al-Aqsa Intifada**, the **Israel Defense Forces** (IDF) demolished a large number of houses along the Philadelphi road and expanded the zone.

TURKEY. The defeat and disintegration of the Ottoman Empire and the division of its Arab-dominated areas by **France** and **Great Britain** brought Turkey into the Arab–Israeli conflict. The Arab resentment of Ottoman rule encouraged **Great Britain** to instigate the **Arab Revolt** (1916–1918) through the **Hussein–McMahon Correspondence**, promising a unified Arab state in return for Arab support for Britain in World War I. When the war ended, most of the Arab areas became **mandate** territories of the two European powers, with Britain taking over Palestine. The defeat and Arab "betrayal" kept Turkey from showing any interest in Palestine until 1940s.

On 29 November 1947, Turkey joined other Arab and Islamic countries and voted against the **Partition Plan** of the **United Nations**. As the Arab–Jewish tensions in Palestine multiplied during the **Arab–Israeli War of 1947–1948**, the United Nations appointed a **Palestine Conciliation Commission** (PCC), with Turkey as one of its members, to reduce the violence and to forestall partition. Though it met periodically, the PCC remained ineffective and was overtaken by events following the establishment of the State of Israel.

In 1949, Turkey granted de facto recognition to Israel, and it has since maintained low-level diplomatic ties with the Jewish state. After the **Suez War**, it reduced its diplomatic representation in Israel. Turkey joined the Arabs in criticizing the Israeli occupation of Arab and Islamic territories in the **June War of 1967**, and the **Jerusalem Law** introduced by Prime Minister **Menachem Begin** in 1980 further eroded the bilateral ties.

The **Kuwait War** and subsequent **Madrid Conference** brought about a strategic shift in the Turkish position, and in December 1991, it upgraded its relations to ambassadorial level. Simultaneously it recognized the **Palestine Liberation Organization**. Since then, Turkey has sought and established a strategic relationship with Israel and concluded a number of defense-related agreements. The close security ties brought about by the military establishment, however, resulted in increased domestic criticism in Turkey, especially from religious elements. *See also* BAGHDAD PACT.

– U –

UNIFIED NATIONAL LEADERSHIP OF THE UPRISING (UNLU). During the 1987 **Intifada**, a number of major Palestinian political factions and groups organized under an umbrella organization and served as the underground leadership. Through periodic leaflets, it evolved a host of strategies to oppose the Israeli occupation, directed the popular struggle, and was in constant contact with the Tunis-based **Palestine Liberation Organization** leadership. The UNLU consisted of the mainstream **Fatah**, the **Popular Front for the Liberation of Palestine**, the **Democratic Front for the Liberation of Palestine**, and the **Palestine People's Party**. The Islamic resistance movement **Hamas** did not join the UNLU and worked independently, but did not challenge it.

UNILATERAL DECLARATION OF INDEPENDENCE (UDI). Since the end of the **mandate** on 15 May 1948, Palestinian independence has been proclaimed on two occasions and the leadership was on the verge of declaring independence for a third time.

On 1 October 1948, the **Arab Higher Committee**, headed by Grand Mufti Hajj Amin al-Husseini (c. 1895–1974), announced the proclamation of Palestinian independence. This announcement, made in Gaza, came days after the formation of the **All Palestine Government**. The State of Palestine was swiftly recognized by **Egypt, Syria**, and **Saudi Arabia**, but was opposed by **Transjordan**, which controlled the **West Bank**. Following the annexation of the West Bank by **Jordan**, the **Arab League**, which backed Palestinian independence, announced the dissolution of the All Palestine Government.

The second occasion came during the first Palestinian **Intifada**, when the Palestine National Council met in Algiers and, on 15 November 1988 after prolonged internal debate, announced the formation of the State of Palestine. Despite lacking the essential component of statehood—namely, effective control over its territories—this move was quickly recognized by most Arab, Islamic, and Third World countries.

In 1999, on the eve of the expiration of the five-year deadline for the interim period set by the **Oslo Accords**, Palestinian leader **Yasser Arafat** threatened to declare a **Palestinian state** once again. To gather support for this proposal, he traveled all over the world and met with more than 50 heads of state and government. However, while agreeing to the need for a Palestinian state, they were unanimous in their disapproval of any unilateral move. Similarly, following the failure of the **Camp David Talks** in the summer of 2000, Chairman Arafat undertook extensive tours, met a number of world leaders, and solicited their support for Palestinian statehood. Compelled by the international disapproval of any unilateral moves, on 9 September 2000 he told the Central Committee of the **Palestine Liberation Organization** of his resolve to postpone the decision and engage in renewed negotiations with Israel. For its part, Israel threatened to retaliate to a UDI by annexing the larger part of the **West Bank**, which is still under its control.

UNION OF SOVIET SOCIALIST REPUBLICS (USSR). *See* RUSSIA; SOVIET UNION.

UNIT 101. A special unit formed in 1953 and led by Col. **Ariel Sharon** to undertake punitive attacks against neighboring Arab states where

Fedayeen forces were operating against Israel. The **Qibya Raid** in October 1953 was carried out by this unit.

UNITED ARAB KINGDOM. Having consolidated his position following the **Black September Massacre**, on 15 March 1972 King **Hussein** of **Jordan** outlined a reconciliatory posture toward the Palestinians. He called for the formation of a United Arab Kingdom comprising two regions: the East Bank—that is, Jordan—and a Palestinian region consisting of "the **West Bank** and any other Palestinian territories which are liberated and whose inhabitants desire to join it." Under this plan, **Jerusalem** would be the capital of the "Palestine region" and Amman the capital of the Jordan region as well as of the kingdom as a whole. Also known as the Federation Plan, it was a redefined version of the pre-1967 situation comprising a confederation between the state of Jordan and the West Bank–based **Palestinian state**. Each region would have executive powers, while the sovereignty would rest with the Hashemite king. There would be a unified armed force, with the king as the commander-in-chief.

This bid by King Hussein to regain the West Bank he had lost in 1967 did not go down well with the Palestinians, who were still furious about the events of Black September, when scores of Palestinians had been killed by the Jordanian army and the **Palestine Liberation Organization** was expelled from Jordan. The idea of a united Jordanian–Palestinian entity has frequently resurfaced and Israel's **Labor Party** long advocated the "**Jordan Option**." **Yasser Arafat** also toyed with the idea of a Jordanian–Palestinian confederation. The decision of King Hussein in July 1988 for **Jordanian disengagement** from the West Bank precluded such an option.

UNITED NATIONS (UN). Ever since the government of **Great Britain** headed by Ernest Bevin referred the Palestine question to it, the United Nations has occupied a prime place in the Arab–Israeli conflict. Acting on the British request, the UN General Assembly convened a special session in April 1947 and, on 15 May, appointed an 11-member **United Nations Special Committee on Palestine** (UNSCOP) to resolve the issue. On 1 September, UNSCOP passed along two different recommendations on the future of Palestine: a seven-member majority report recommending the partition of Palestine and a three-member minority report recommending a **Federal Plan** as the solution. After intense negotiations and lobbying from both sides, on 29 November 1947 the UN General Assembly voted to partition Palestine.

As the British deadline for withdrawal from Palestine neared, Arab–Jewish violence in Palestine was growing. As a result, in April 1948 the United Nations met for a special session to deliberate on a **United States** proposal to postpone the implementation of the **Partition Plan**. However, the Israeli **declaration of independence** and the subsequent outbreak of full-scale hostilities between Israel and its Arab neighbors forced the United Nations to abandon those discussions and to seek a temporary truce between the combatants. By the time the second truce of the **Arab–Israeli War of 1947–1948** came into force on 18 July 1948, Israel had made significant territorial gains and consolidated its military-political position.

Since then, the United Nations has been undertaking numerous efforts to resolve the Arab–Israeli conflict. Its efforts toward securing a peace agreement between Israel and the neighboring Arab states partially succeeded in 1949, when **armistice agreements** were signed. This temporary arrangement, however, did not transform into a lasting peace agreement. As a result, the United Nations sponsored a number of international peacekeeping forces that sought to maintain, monitor, or ensure the compliance of the armistice agreements as well as cease-fire arrangements following the **Suez War**, **June War of 1967**, and **October War of 1973**.

The formation of the **United Nations Relief and Works Agency** in 1950 marked a significant institutional effort by the United Nations to ensure the welfare of Arabs who had become **refugees** following the 1947–1948 war. Through **Resolution 194**, adopted in December 1948, the United Nations recognized the right of the Palestinian refugees to return home or to be paid compensation. UN Security Council **Resolution 242** of 1967 and **Resolution 338** of 1973 eventually emerged as the basic framework for a comprehensive peace in the Middle East that was acceptable to all parties. The United Nations, especially the General Assembly, played a major role in the internationalization of the plight of the Palestinians and the recognition of their right of self-determination. In 1974, **Resolution 3236** accorded observer status to the **Palestine Liberation Organization** (PLO). Continuing with its pro-Arab stance brought about by the growing number of Third World countries, in 1975 the UN General Assembly equated **Zionism** with racism in **Resolution 3379**.

Great Power rivalry, lack of imaginative leadership, absence of influence, and Israeli reservations over the fairness of the world body have impeded the United Nations from playing any significant role in the peacemaking process in the Middle East. The success of its peace initiatives has been negligible. The major peace agreements between Israel and its Arab neighbors, such as the **Camp David Accords, Oslo Agreements, Egypt–Israel Peace Treaty, Israel–Jordan Peace Agreement, Sinai I Agreement, Sinai II Agreement**, and **Israel–Syria Disengagement of Forces Agreement** were all concluded outside the UN framework. Likewise, the United Nations had no role in the **Madrid Conference**, which was cosponsored by the United States and the **Soviet Union**. *See also* BERNADOTTE PLAN; GENEVA CONFERENCE (1971); GENEVA CONFERENCE (1973); GENEVA CONFERENCE (1983); GENEVA UNITED NATIONS SESSION; JARRING MISSION; JENIN CONTROVERSY; MIXED ARMISTICE COMMISSIONS; PALESTINE CONCILIATION COMMISSION; PALESTINIAN COMMITTEE; RESOLUTION 425; RESOLUTION 3210; SPECIAL MUNICIPAL COMMISSIONER FOR JERUSALEM; TRUCE COMMISSION FOR PALESTINE; TRUSTEESHIP COUNCIL; UNITED NATIONS COMMISSION; UNITED NATIONS DISENGAGEMENT OBSERVER FORCE; UNITED NATIONS ECONOMIC SURVEY MISSION FOR THE MIDDLE EAST; UNITED NATIONS EMERGENCY FORCE I; UNITED NATIONS EMERGENCY FORCE II; UNITED NATIONS INTERIM FORCE IN LEBANON; UNITED NATIONS MEDIATOR; UNITED NATIONS MEMBERSHIP; UNITED NATIONS PALESTINE COMMISSION; UNITED NATIONS TRUCE SUPERVISION ORGANIZATION.

UNITED NATIONS COMMISSION. Acting on a request from **Jordan**, on 22 March 1979 the **United Nations** Security Council adopted Resolution 446, which called for a three-member commission "to examine the situation relating to the **settlements** in the Arab territories occupied since 1967." Since this came on the eve of the signing of the **Egypt–Israel Peace Treaty**, the **United States** abstained. Israel, however, refused to cooperate with the commission.

UNITED NATIONS DISENGAGEMENT OBSERVER FORCE (UNDOF). Following the conclusion of the Israel–Syria Disengagement of Forces Agreement of 31 May 1974, the United Nations Security Council adopted Resolution 350 to establish a peacekeeping force to monitor the implementation of the agreement. This paved the way for the formation of the United Nations Disengagement Observer Force, whose jurisdiction extends from Mt. Hermon to the northern Jordan River. Though originally intended for six months, the mandate of UNDOF has been extended periodically. Because of the absence of any skirmishes in its area, it is considered one of the more successful peacekeeping operations undertaken by the United Nations. *See also* OCTOBER WAR OF 1973.

UNITED NATIONS ECONOMIC SURVEY MISSION FOR THE MIDDLE EAST. Following the failure of the May 1949 Lausanne Talks, on 23 August the **Palestine Conciliation Commission** established the Economic Survey Mission, headed by Gordon R. Clapp, the director of the Tennessee Valley Authority, to suggest measures to alleviate the plight of the Palestinian **refugees**. In its 1949 interim report, the Mission suggested a number of public works programs in the Middle East that could provide employment opportunities to the Palestinian refugees. At the same time, it concluded that economic development would be insufficient to bring about peace and progress when "political will to peace is lacking."

UNITED NATIONS EMERGENCY FORCE I (UNEF I). In the aftermath of the **Suez War**, the **United Nations** decided to establish a peacekeeping force between Israel and **Egypt** until a peace settlement could be reached. On 5 November 1956, even before Israel agreed to withdraw from the **Sinai Peninsula**, UN General Assembly Resolution 1000 (ES-1) called for the formation of an emergency force that would act as a buffer between the two sides. The temporary armed police force was asked to secure the cessation of hostilities and supervise the cease-fire; ensure an orderly withdrawal of the forces of **Great Britain, France**, and Israel from Egyptian territory; patrol the Egyptian–Israeli border; and ensure the observance of the Egypt–Israel armistice. On 7 November, the General Assembly defined the scope of the UNEF activities and its composition.

The first UNEF units were deployed along the **Suez Canal** on 15 November 1956 and in the **Gaza Strip** on 7 March 1957, following the Israeli withdrawal. According to the General Assembly resolution, the force was to be deployed on either side of the 233-kilometer (145-mile) Egypt–Israel border, but, because of the Israeli refusal to cooperate, it was confined to the Egyptian side of the border.

In May 1967, President **Gamal Abdul Nasser** of **Egypt** demanded a partial UNEF withdrawal from Sharm al-Sheikh overlooking the Gulf of Aqaba. When the United Nations refused to comply, Egypt on 18 May asked for the complete withdrawal of the force. On the same day, Israel rejected an urgent UN request to reconsider its position and accept the UNEF on its side of the international border. Since the peacekeeping force was not an occupation army, UN secretary-general U Thant (1909–1974) had no option but to comply with the Egyptian request. Even before the UNEF units could be completely withdrawn from the region, the **June War of 1967** broke out, and some UN members were killed in Israeli raids on Gaza. *See also* GOOD FAITH AIDE MEMOIRE.

UNITED NATIONS EMERGENCY FORCE II (UNEF II). On 25 October 1973, following the **October War of 1973**, the **United Nations** Security Council adopted Resolution 340 establishing the second UN Emergency Force to be deployed between the forces of Israel and **Egypt**. Since Israel was still occupying the **Sinai Peninsula**, the deployment was confined to occupied Egyptian territories. Because of the bitter experiences of **United Nations Emergency Force I**, the resolution maintained that any decision concerning the withdrawal of the peacekeeping force could not be made unilaterally by either of the belligerents but must be approved by the Security Council.

On 27 October, the first units of UNEF II were deployed on the west bank of the **Suez Canal**. Following the conclusion of the Egypt–Israel **Disengagement Agreement** signed at **Kilometer 101** on 18 January 1974, the mandate of UNEF II was extended to supervise the agreement.

The Security Council periodically extended the six-month mandate for the peacekeeping force. The conclusion of the U.S.-sponsored **Camp David Accords** generated tension and differences between the **United States** and other members of the Security Council because the security provisions enshrined in the 26 March 1979 agreements undermined the position of UNEF II. As a result, on 24 July 1979, the Security Council declined to extend the mandate of UNEF II and allowed the peacekeeping force to lapse. The Egyptian conclusion of a separate peace with Israel and the exclusion of the **Soviet Union** worked against its renewal. Due to Israeli opposition to the deployment of the **United Nations Truce Supervision Organization** to undertake the functions of UNEF II, as agreed in the Camp David Accords, a U.S.-sponsored multilateral force was created instead.

UNITED NATIONS INTERIM FORCE IN LEBANON (UNIFIL). UNIFIL is an international peacekeeping force created by the **United Nations** in 1978 as a response to Israel's military operations against **Lebanon** code-named the **Litani Operation**. On 15 March 1978, four days after the Israeli invasion, the UN Security Council adopted **Resolution 425**, which called for the formation of an interim international peacekeeping force "for the purpose of confirming the withdrawal of Israeli forces" from southern Lebanon. It also sought to restore international peace and security in the region and to enable the Lebanese government, torn apart by the civil war (1975–1989), to regain effective authority over southern Lebanon, from where Palestinian guerrillas had been carrying out periodic attacks against northern Israel.

Headquartered in Naqura, UNIFIL was originally mandated to monitor the territories bounded by the Israel–Lebanon border in the south, the Litani River in the north, the Mediterranean Sea in the west, and the Lebanon–**Syria** border in the east. Due to Israeli opposition, however, it was never allowed to operate in the Christian-dominated southernmost zone, which in 1985 became Israel's self-declared **security zone**.

A number of factors have impeded the functioning of UNIFIL, including Israeli distrust of the United Nations, Israel's retaliatory tactics against Palestinian violence across the international border, and the weakness of the central authority in Lebanon to enforce its writ in southern Lebanon. Moreover, UNIFIL has neither the mandate nor the ability to respond to the emergence and growth of various paramilitary organizations and militia such as **Amal**, **Hezbollah**, the **Palestine Liberation Organization**, and the **South Lebanon Army**, which operated within the UNIFIL-designated areas.

Composed of military personnel volunteered by various countries, UNIFIL remains one of the largest peacekeeping operations undertaken by the United Nations. While containing the overall situation, it has been unable to prevent periodic escalations of tension in the region. The Israeli invasion of Lebanon in 1982 (**Operation Peace for Galilee**) and its military offensives in 1993 and 1996 (the **Accountability Operation** and **Grapes of Wrath Operation**, respectively) occurred against the backdrop of the UNIFIL presence. During the last of those, an accidental Israeli missile attack on a UNIFIL position in Kfar Kana on 18 April 1996 resulted in the death of more than a hundred Lebanese citizens who had taken refuge at the position in what became known as the **Kfar Kana Massacre**.

Conceived as an "interim" arrangement, UNIFIL has become a permanent fixture in the Middle East, and its original six-month mandate has been renewed numerous times. Its operations continue despite the unilateral Israeli **Lebanese withdrawal** in June 2000, the primary mandate of Resolution 425. However, in August 2001, the strength of the UNIFIL force was reduced from 7,900 to 4,500, and by 2002 it had stabilized at 2,000 troops.

UNITED NATIONS MEDIATOR. On 13 May 1948, during the Second Special Session of the **United Nations** General Assembly, the **United States** suggested the idea of a UN mediator, which was approved the following day. Subsequently, Count Folke Bernadotte (1895–1948), the president of the Swedish Red Cross, was nominated for the position. The UN mediator was entrusted with the task of securing an overall political settlement to the Arab–Israeli conflict and supervising the UN arms embargo. Until the formation of the **United Nations Relief and Works Agency**, he also assumed the responsibility for Arab **refugees**. Following Bernadotte's **assassination** on 18 September, Ralph J. Bunche (1904–1971) was appointed as acting mediator. With the conclusion of the **armistice agreements** between Israel and its neighbors, the functions of the UN mediator lapsed.

UNITED NATIONS MEMBERSHIP. On 15 May 1948, and again on 29 November, Israel applied for **United Nations** membership. However, the Security Council committee on the admission of new states did not take cognizance of the Israeli applications. On 24 February

1949, the day **Egypt** and Israel signed their **armistice agreement**, Israel applied for the UN membership for a third time. Following the approval of Israel's application by the Security Council, the General Assembly asked Israel to clarify its positions on five key issues: the internationalization of **Jerusalem**, borders, Arab **refugees**, the investigation into the **assassination** of **United Nations mediator** Count Folke Bernadotte, and its attitude toward its obligations to the United Nations and the implementation of UN resolutions. Subsequently, on 11 May 1949, the General Assembly approved the Israeli application, with 37 members voting in favor, 12 against, and nine abstaining. Deviating from normal procedure, this decision was accompanied by explicit references to Israel's commitments toward the "implementation" of the Partition Resolution of 29 November 1947 as well as **Resolution 194** of 11 December 1948, which recognized the right of the Palestinians to return or to be paid compensation.

Egypt, Syria, and **Lebanon** have been UN members since its founding in 1945, and **Jordan** became a member in 1955. The **Palestinian National Authority** is not recognized by the United Nations, but **Resolution 3236** granted observer status to the **Palestine Liberation Organization** (PLO).

UNITED NATIONS PALESTINE COMMISSION. On 29 November 1947, following the approval of the **Partition Plan**, the **United Nations** General Assembly voted to establish a Palestine Commission consisting of Bolivia, Czechoslovakia, Denmark, Panama, and the Philippines to implement the consequences of the partition resolution. While the **Jewish Agency** cooperated with the commission, the Arabs and **Great Britain**, the **Mandate** power, were less cooperative with the five-member secretariat, which arrived in Palestine in early March 1948. The commission was adjourned *sine die* on 17 May, three days after Israel proclaimed its establishment.

UNITED NATIONS RELIEF AND WORKS AGENCY (UNRWA). The United Nations Relief and Work Agency is the **United Nations** organization established to assist the Palestinians who became **refugees** due to the **Arab–Israeli War of 1947–1948**. Upon the recommendations of Acting **United Nations mediator** Ralph J. Bunche (1904–1971) on 19 November 1948, the UN General Assembly authorized the secretary-general to establish a special fund and an "administrative organization" toward "the alleviation of conditions of starvation and distress among the Palestine refugees." The General Assembly declared that such an agency would work toward "the relief of Palestine refugees of all communities," but in practice, it was concerned exclusively with the Palestinians who became refugees following the 1947–1948 war. This initial arrangement was intended for nine months between December 1948 and August 1949, but it gradually became permanent due to the prolongation of the conflict.

Immediately after the hostilities, the United Nations sent in the **United Nations Economic Survey Mission for the Middle East**, headed by Gordon Clapp, which proposed the establishment of an organization to temporarily assist the estimated 700,000 Palestinian refugees. Despite the existence of the United Nations High Commissioner for Refugees, the commission called for an exclusive arrangement, and, through Resolution 302 adopted on 8 December 1949, the General Assembly established UNRWA, which began functioning from 1 May 1950.

With its headquarters in Gaza, UNRWA is mandated to provide housing, food, medical services, primary health care, education, essential relief, and vocational training to Palestinian refugees living in the **West Bank** and the **Gaza Strip**, as well as in neighboring Arab countries such as **Jordan**, **Lebanon**, and **Syria**. Altogether, UNRWA operates 59 registered refugee camps in the Middle East, and it also provides these services to other refugees who live outside the camps.

UNRWA originally recognized as refugees anyone who was a resident of Palestine for at least two years before the 1948 conflict and who had fled following the outbreak of hostilities. In 1950, 914,221 refugees were registered with UNRWA. Another 300,000 were made homeless following the **June War of 1967**; by the end of that year, the UNRWA-registered refugee count stood at just under four million. Critics have argued that, since its inception, UNRWA has never conducted any census in the refugee camps and hence the refugee figures are inflated. Contrary to the agency's mandate, some Palestinian militant groups have operated from UNRWA-run refugee camps, a complaint highlighted during the **Jenin Controversy**, an Israeli military campaign in April 2002.

UNITED NATIONS SPECIAL COMMITTEE ON PALESTINE (UNSCOP). Unable to adopt a policy satisfactory to both the Arabs and Jews, on 2 April 1947 **Great Britain** asked the newly formed **United Nations** to find a solution to the Palestine question. Acting on the British request, the United Nations convened the First Special Session of the General Assembly on 28 April to discuss the issue. After prolonged and serious deliberations, the Assembly on 15 May voted 47–7 (with one abstention) to establish an 11-member United Nations Special Committee on Palestine to resolve the issue. The votes against came from the Arab members of the United Nations— **Egypt, Iraq, Lebanon, Saudi Arabia,** and **Syria**—and Islamic Afghanistan and **Turkey**. The new committee consisted of Australia, Canada, Czechoslovakia, Guatemala, India, **Iran**, the Netherlands, Peru, Sweden, Uruguay, and Yugoslavia.

During the visit of UNSCOP to Palestine, the leaders of the *Yishuv* deposed before the committee, but the Palestinian leadership largely boycotted it. The committee also visited Beirut to hear the views of the neighboring Arab states.

On 31 August, UNSCOP submitted its recommendations to the United Nations and unanimously recommended the termination of the British **Mandate** and the granting of independence to Palestine. The committee was divided over the future status of Palestine, however. A seven-member majority advocated partition of Palestine into independent Jewish and Arab states, with international status for **Jerusalem**, while a three-member minority (India, Iran, and Yugoslavia) recommended the formation of a federal Palestine with Arabs and Jews enjoying considerable internal autonomy. The **Partition Plan** was acceptable to the Jewish leadership but was rejected by the Arabs and Palestinians. Both sides rejected the minority **Federal Plan**, and it was dropped from consideration by the United Nations.

Acting on the UNSCOP report, the General Assembly set up two subcommittees, one to draft a viable Partition Plan and the other to consider the Arab counterproposal for a unitary Palestine. On 24 November, the ad hoc committee of the General Assembly rejected the unitary plan proposal and recommended the Partition Plan to the full Assembly. On 29 November, by a two-thirds margin (33–13, with 10 abstentions), Resolution 181, recommending the partition of Palestine, was adopted. *See also* ARAB–ISRAELI WAR OF 1947–1948; ARMISTICE AGREEMENT/S.

UNITED NATIONS TRUCE SUPERVISION ORGANIZATION (UNTSO). On 29 May 1948, within days after the first cease-fire in the **Arab–Israeli War of 1947–1948**, the **United Nations** Security Council adopted Resolution 50 establishing a logistical mechanism to provide advisory and observation support to the **Jerusalem**-based **Truce Commission for Palestine**. In 1948, the United Nations Truce Supervision Organization, consisting of military observers, was sent to the Middle East to supervise the truce and cease-fire arrangements between Israel and neighboring Arab states.

On 11 August 1949, the Security Council mandated UNTSO to "observe and maintain" the cease-fire and to assist the parties "in the supervision of the application and observance of the terms" of the **armistice agreements**. UNTSO thus supervised the implementation of the armistice agreements and chaired the **Mixed Armistice Commissions** between Israel and various Arabs states. Subsequent military conflicts strengthened UNTSO's activities. Following the **Suez War** of 1956, UNTSO personnel patrolled the **Sinai Peninsula** and supported the **United Nations Emergency Force I** (UNEF I), which was deployed along the Egyptian–Israeli border. It became inoperative following the **June War of 1967**. Though ineffective, it continued to monitor cease-fire arrangements following the **October War of 1973**. In 1973, the UNTSO contributed to the formation of the **United Nations Emergency Force II** in the Sinai and the **United Nations Disengagement Observer Force** in the **Golan Heights**. Later in the 1970s, UNTSO was attached to the **United Nations Interim Force in Lebanon**.

With headquarters in Jerusalem, UNTSO observers are located in Beirut and the Golan Heights. Despite the **Camp David Accords** and the presence of the **United States**–led **Multinational Force and Observers**, UNTSO observers are still present in the Sinai.

UNITED STATES. After World War I, the **Zionists** shifted their focus from **Great Britain** to the United States as the principal arena of their diplomatic activities toward establishing a Jewish national home in Palestine. By the time the **Biltmore Program** was outlined in 1942, the *Yishuv*'s strength had grown considerably and the idea of self-determination for the Jews in Palestine seemed a feasible and realistic option.

This strategy proved effective when the United States supported, endorsed, and lobbied for the **Partition Plan** proposed by the **United**

Nations Special Committee on Palestine. The violence in Palestine following the November 1947 General Assembly vote, however, compelled the United States to reconsider its position, and it advocated the suspension of the Partition Plan. On the eve of the British departure, the *Yishuv* leaders met and declared the establishment of the State of Israel. Overriding the advice of the State Department, President Harry S. Truman (1884–1972) recognized the Jewish state within minutes, and this move was followed by other countries.

At least in the initial years, the United States followed a cautious policy and sought to balance its Israel policy within the larger context of its friendly ties with the Arab world. Its desire to exclude Israel from the **Baghdad Pact** and the disapproval of President Dwight D. Eisenhower (1890–1969) of the tripartite aggression against **Egypt** in the **Suez War** were a clear indication of this. Despite its disappointments with President **Gamal Abdul Nasser** of Egypt over the **Czech Deal**, as well as the **nationalization of the Suez Canal**, which precipitated the Suez War, the Eisenhower administration (1953–1961) forced Israel to pull out of the **Sinai Peninsula** and the **Gaza Strip**.

However, things began to change and reached a decisive level on the eve of the **June War of 1967**. Washington began to understand and accommodate the Israeli position. The spectacular military victory consecrated a pro-Israeli bias in U.S. policy. Sidelining the **United Nations**, the United States began to play a greater role in the management of the Arab–Israeli conflict. The adoption of **Resolution 242** of the UN Security Council, despite its built-in ambiguity, was only possible because of strong American efforts.

The preemptive Arab strike and the military setbacks suffered by Israel during the early days of the **October War of 1973** compelled the Richard Nixon administration (1969–1974) to provide massive arms supplies to Israel. This unprecedented move provoked the Arab states to institute an oil embargo against the United States and its allies. The United States not only weathered the **Oil Crisis**, but also succeeded in having Israel accept limited **disengagement agreements** with Egypt and **Syria**. Furthermore, it managed to wean Egypt away from the **Soviet Union** and secure the **Camp David Accords** and the **Egypt–Israel Peace Treaty**. Similar attempts with **Lebanon**, such as the **Israel–Lebanon Agreement**, however, did not last long.

Serious disagreements with Israel over issues such as the status of **Jerusalem**, **settlements** in the **Occupied Territories**, and the rights of

Palestinians did not impede various U.S. administrations from pursuing a policy sympathetic toward the Jewish state. In 1975, Washington even agreed not to recognize or negotiate with the **Palestine Liberation Organization** (PLO) until the latter recognized Israel's right to exist.

The **Kuwait War**, coming on the heels of the end of the Cold War and disintegration of the USSR, offered an opportunity for the United States to monopolize peacemaking in the Middle East through the **Madrid Conference**. Even though Norway played a key role in the formulation of the **Declaration of Principles** (DoP), U.S. president **Bill Clinton** (1946–) offered to host the signing ceremony. Since then, the United States has become the principal force behind the **Oslo Process**, as well as various other peace efforts between Israel and its neighbors. In 1994, the Jordanian track culminated in the **Israel–Jordan Peace Treaty** but the progress on the Syrian (**Shepherdstown Talks**) and Lebanese tracks was minimal.

The failure of the **Camp David Talks** in July 2000 between Prime Minister **Ehud Barak** and Chairman **Yasser Arafat** led to the outbreak of the **Al-Aqsa Intifada**. With the onset of violence, the United States strengthened its efforts to secure a comprehensive peace, promoting the **Clinton Plan**, **Mitchell Committee Report**, and **Sharm al-Sheikh Summit**, of 2000, but was unsuccessful. Following the election of **George W. Bush** in 2000, Washington became less involved in the peace process. However, periodic **suicide attacks** compelled the United States to unveil a number of measures for Israeli–Palestinian reconciliation, including the **Bush Plan**, **Middle East Road Map**, **Tenet Plan**, and **Zinni Plan**.

Since the June War, while not all American efforts were fruitful, any meaningful peace agreements between Israel and its Arab neighbors invariably demanded active U.S. involvement and commitment. The United States also campaigned vigorously for the removal of the **Arab boycott of Israel** and was instrumental in organizing the **Middle East and North Africa Economic Summits**. *See also* ALPHA PLAN; ANGLO-AMERICAN COMMITTEE; AQABA SUMMIT; ASWAN DAM; BAKER PLAN; BYPASS ROADS; CHAMELEON OPERATION; EISENHOWER DOCTRINE; GENEVA UNITED NATIONS SESSION; GRAPES OF WRATH OPERATION; ISRAEL–UNITED STATES MEMORANDUM OF UNDERSTANDING; JOHNSON PLAN; JOHNSTON PLAN; KING–CRANE COMMISSION; LOAN GUARANTEES; MORRISON–GRADY PLAN; MULTILATERAL

TALKS; MULTINATIONAL FORCE AND OBSERVERS; NU-CLEAR NONPROLIFERATION TREATY; OMEGA OPERATION; REAGAN PLAN; ROGERS PLAN; SHARM AL-SHEIKH MEMO-RANDUM; SHARM AL-SHEIKH SUMMIT (1996); SHULTZ PLAN; SHUTTLE DIPLOMACY; SINAI I AGREEMENT; SINAI II AGREEMENT; STOCKHOLM DECLARATION; UNITED STATES INITIATIVE; WYE MEMORANDUM.

UNITED STATES INITIATIVE. Close on the heel of the stalemated **Jarring Mission** and the unsuccessful **Rogers Plan**, the **United States** on 19 June 1970 unveiled another proposal to end the **War of Attrition** and reduce regional tension. This proposal, communicated to Israel, **Egypt**, and **Jordan** as well as the **Soviet Union**, called for **mutual recognition** by the warring parties of "each other's sovereignty, territorial integrity and political independence" and "Israeli withdrawal from territories occupied in the 1967 conflict." After initial hesitation, President **Gamal Abdul Nasser** of Eygpt agreed to a 90-day cease-fire and an 80-kilometer (50-mile) standstill zone on either side of the **Suez Canal** calling for maintenance of the military status quo. This agreement eventually ended the War of Attrition, and hostilities stopped at midnight of 7 August. The deployment of Soviet SA-2 and SA-3 missiles and the commencement of construction on new missile sites inside the standstill zone altered the situation. While the cease-fire continued, Israel suspended its participation in the Jarring Mission on 6 September.

UVDA OPERATION. On 5 March 1949, within days of signing the **armistice agreement** with **Egypt**, Israel launched military operations in the southern Negev and captured additional territory. By the time the Uvda Operation ended on 10 March, Israel had extended its boundaries to the Gulf of Aqaba and secured a sea route from the south. *See also* ARAB–ISRAELI WAR OF 1947–1948.

– V –

VANUNU AFFAIR. Based on information revealed in October 1986 by Mordechai Vanunu (1954–), a former technician at the nuclear research establishment in Dimona, the London *Sunday Times* claimed that Israel had developed thermonuclear weapons. This revelation confirmed long-held suspicions about Israel's nuclear capabilities and the extent of its nuclear arsenal. Shortly after this disclosure, Vanunu was kidnapped from Europe, brought to Israel, and tried for treason. In March 1988, he was given an 18-year prison term for disclosing Israel's nuclear secrets. Until 1998, he was kept in solitary confinement. Vanunu was released on 21 April 2004, still with severe restrictions on his movements and activities; among other things, he was prevented from leaving Israel. In May 2005 fresh charges were filed against Vanunu following a media interview. *See also* NUCLEAR NONPROLIFERATION TREATY; OSIRAQ BOMBING; PLUMBAT OPERATION.

VENICE DECLARATION. On 13 June 1980, the European Council summit meeting in Venice adopted a declaration on the Middle East outlining the council's policy toward finding a "comprehensive solution" to the Arab–Israeli conflict. The conclusion of the **Camp David Accords** and the lack of progress on the Palestinian track provided the backdrop to this declaration, which has since guided European policies toward the region. Recognizing the right of "existence and security" of all the states in the region, the Venice Declaration ruled that the Palestinian problem was more than "simply one of **refugees**" and recognized the right of the Palestinian people "to exercise fully its right to self-determination." All nine members of the council expressed their determination not to accept "any unilateral initiative designed to change the status of **Jerusalem**." The declaration demanded that the **Palestine Liberation Organization** (PLO) be "associated with the negotiations" that seek to establish and promote peace in the Middle East. It also declared the Israeli **settlements** in the **Occupied Territories** to be "illegal under international law."

The Israeli government headed by **Menachem Begin** reacted angrily to the Venice Declaration and dismissed it as an appeasement of the Arabs and a move calculated to undermine the Camp David Accords. Begin referred to the European move as "shameful."

VILLAGE LEAGUE. In an attempt to marginalize the **Palestine Liberation Organization** (PLO) and to encourage an alternative Palestinian leadership that would take control of the civil, economic, and social life of the **Occupied Territories**, Israel in 1977 encouraged the formation of the Village League. Largely drawn from conservative rural figures in the **West Bank**, the league was meant to provide an alternative leadership to the PLO-dominated nationalist leadership. Conceived by Menachem Milson, who in November 1981 took over as the new head of the **civil administration** in the West Bank, the Village League was aimed at creating a pliant Palestinian leadership that would accept, coexist with, and facilitate Israeli occupation. Besides financial incentives, the league members were provided with protection and personal arms. In late 1982, Israel even organized a thinly attended convention of all Village League members in Hebron.

This arrangement, however, failed to function. Perceived by the majority of Palestinians as collaborators, the members of the league lived in perpetual threat and were socially ostracized. In March 1982, **Jordan** threatened to impose the death penalty on league members. Accused of being traitors to the Palestinian cause, they gradually became reluctant to accept Israeli dictates and began to lose their limited influence. As a result, Israel not only disengaged from the Village League but even proscribed it in 1983.

VOLCANO OPERATION. The conclusion of the **Czech Deal** by **Egypt** and bellicose statements by Arab leaders provided an opportunity for Israel to test its new strategy of limited "reprisal raids" aimed at provoking President **Gamal Abdul Nasser** of Egypt into launching an all-out war. Thus, on 2 November 1955, the **Israel Defense Forces** launched an attack on As-Sabha in the Egyptian side of the Al-Auja **Demilitarized Zone**. The limited raid, code-named Volcano, took place far from the **Gaza Strip**, the hotbed of **Fedayeen** attacks, and resulted in the death of 70 Egyptian and seven Israeli soldiers and the wounding of dozens, as well as the capture of 50 Egyptian prisoners of war. Israeli prime minister **David Ben-Gurion** overruled the plans of Gen. **Moshe Dayan** to hold onto the Egyptian position. The attack was the most extensive Israeli operation inside Egypt since the **armistice agreement** of 1949. *See also* SUEZ WAR.

– W –

WAR OF ATTRITION. Amid low-level artillery duels along the **Suez Canal** in July 1969, President **Gamal Abdul Nasser** of **Egypt** declared that "a war of attrition" would be necessary to dislodge Israel from the territories it had occupied during the **June War of 1967**. Following mediation by U.S. secretary of state William Rogers (1913–2001), a three-month-long cease-fire came into force on 7 August 1970, paving the way for indirect Egypt–Israeli negotiations through the **Jarring Mission** of **United Nations** envoy Gunnar Jarring. The negotiations were called off after the first meeting, however, when the Israelis pulled out protesting against the movement of missiles supplied by the **Soviet Union** behind Egyptian lines. The installation of Soviet artillery west of the canal led to tension, and Israel retaliated with a massive air and artillery attack, forcing Egypt to temporarily evacuate Egyptian towns in the Canal Zone. After assuming office, President **Anwar Sadat** of Egypt agreed to a renewed cease-fire after the **United States** promised a $500 million credit to Egypt. *See also* UNITED STATES INITIATIVE.

WASHINGTON DECLARATION. *See* ISRAEL–JORDAN PEACE TREATY.

WEST BANK. On 6 June 1967, within hours after the capture of the former **Jordan**-held territories west of the Jordan River during the **June War of 1967**, Israel removed Jordanian rule, and on the following day, the authority of the **Israel Defense Forces** (IDF) in the West Bank was formally proclaimed. The area was soon brought under the control of the **military administration** based in Beit-el, north of **Jerusalem**. Until the late 1980s, Jordan was satisfied with the **Labor Party**'s desire to circumvent the **Palestine Liberation Organization** in negotiating the fate of the **Occupied Territories** in line with Labor's policy of the **Jordan Option**, which resulted in the **London Agreement** in 1987. This strategy ultimately failed, however, because the right-wing parties, especially **Likud**, viewed the West Bank as part of *Eretz Yisrael* and hence were opposed to any territorial concessions there. Shortly after the outbreak of the **Intifada** (1987–1993), King **Hussein** announced **Jordanian disengagement** in July 1988 and formally renounced any claims to the territories.

The inauguration of the **Oslo Process** and installation of the **Palestinian National Authority** resulted in Palestinian towns of the West Bank coming under Palestinian control. Since the outbreak of **Al-Aqsa**

Intifada, though, the IDF has periodically violated the sanctity of Palestinian rule.

On 21 March 2005, Prime Minister **Ariel Sharon** approved the construction of 3,500 new homes in a neighborhood that would link **Ma'aleh Adumim** in the **West Bank** with **Jerusalem**. Dismissing petitions challenging the **Gaza Withdrawal Plan**, on 9 June 2005, the Israeli Supreme Court ruled that the Occupied Territories were not legally part of Israel and were "seized" during the **June War of 1967**. As part of the Gaza Withdrawal Plan in August, Israel withdrew from four isolated settlements in northern West Bank. *See also* JUDEA AND SAMARIA; SECURITY FENCE.

WESTERN WALL RIOTS, 1929. In September 1928, during Yom Kippur, the Jewish Day of Atonement, Jewish worshippers installed a screen to separate men and women praying at the Western Wall, the last vestige of the biblical Second Temple in **Jerusalem**. They also put in seats and benches for the benefit of the aged and infirm worshippers. Such efforts by Jews to conduct prayers in front of the Western Wall according to Jewish customs were vehemently opposed by the Muslims, who saw them as a violation of the status quo. There were apprehensions among Muslims that the Jews intended to encroach upon the Wall, part of the Temple Mount/*Haram al-Sharif*, which is a *Waqf* (Islamic welfare trust) property. Acting on the complaint from the Waqf authorities, British police the following day forcefully removed these separators, seats, and benches at the Wall. The grand mufti of Jerusalem, Hajj Amin al-Husseini (c. 1895–1974) protested against this purported violation of Muslim rights and thereby caused tensions to run high between Jews and Muslims.

On 14/15 August 1929, a large number of Jews demonstrated in Tel Aviv reiterating Jewish rights, and the following day a group of Jewish youth raised the Jewish flag and sang the Jewish anthem at the Wall. A couple of days later, Muslims burned Jewish prayer books. On 23 August, which was a Friday, the Muslim Sabbath, the Western Wall Riots broke out in Jerusalem and soon spread to other parts of Palestine. In the ensuing violence, 113 Jews and 116 Arabs were killed, the latter mostly from British shooting, and scores of others were wounded. The following month, the **Mandate** administration issued general guidelines for Jewish worshippers at the Western Wall, preventing them from using benches, chairs, or stools for the benefit of worshippers or using screens or curtains to segregate men and women worshippers.

Even though the Jews held the mufti responsible for orchestrating the communal flare-up, his complicity was never established. The small Jewish community in the historic city of Hebron bore the brunt of this violence; more than 50 men, women, and children were killed in the **Hebron Massacre**, and the remaining non-**Zionist** Jews were forced to evacuate the city. Meanwhile **Great Britain** appointed Sir Walter Shaw to investigate the riots and recommend policies to prevent its recurrence. Published in March 1930, the **Shaw Commission** report absolved the mufti of any responsibilities and identified *Aliya* and Jewish land practices as the underlying causes.

Due to the religious controversies, **Great Britain** in 1930, with the consent of the **League of Nations**, appointed an international commission to determine the rights and claims of Jews and Muslims. The report of the commission, headed by Eliel Lofgren, was published in June 1931 and declared Muslims to be the sole owners of the Wall itself, as well as the area in front of and adjacent to it. It granted Jews free access to the Wall, but endorsed the temporary restrictions introduced in September 1929. It also prohibited Jews from blowing the traditional *shofar* (ram's horn) at the Wall. These limitations remained in force during the period of the Mandate.

The Western Wall was inaccessible to Jews from Israel after **Jordan** occupied **East Jerusalem** during the **Arab–Israeli War of 1947–1948**. This situation lasted until 7 June 1967, when Israel captured the Old City during the **June War of 1967**.

WINGATE, ORDE (1903–1944). During the period between the two World Wars, Orde Wingate, a captain in the army of **Great Britain** in the Palestine **Mandate**, commanded a special mixed British-Jewish unit created to protect the **Iraq** Petroleum Company pipeline. The pipeline was used for exporting Iraqi crude through the port city of Haifa and came under repeated attacks from the Arabs. His unconventional military methods had a lasting impact upon military doctrines and tactics of the embryonic Israeli army and its predecessor **Haganah**.

WOODHEAD COMMISSION. Following the submission of the **Peel Commission** report, which recommended the partition of Palestine, **Great Britain** on 5 January 1938 appointed a four-member technical committee headed by Sir John Woodhead to investigate the feasibility of partitioning Palestine. In November, the Woodhead Commission submitted its findings, which reversed the recommendations of the Peel Commission, concluding that the partition of Palestine was impractical and unviable. Although all its members endorsed the idea of a small Jewish state in Palestine, there were strong reservations over its size. While one section suggested a 1,036-square-kilometer (400-square-mile) area, others advocated an even smaller territory; the **Zionist** leadership adamantly rejected both. On 9 November 1938, the British government renounced the partition as "impracticable."

WORLD ZIONIST ORGANIZATION (WZO). Founded by Theodore Herzl (1860–1904), the World Zionist Organization is the official organization of the **Zionist** movement. From the first WZO Congress in Basel, Switzerland, in August 1897, it conducted the political, economic, and settlement activities leading to the establishment of Israel, as outlined in the **Basel Program**. It organized the *Aliya* to Palestine, and promoted the **Balfour Declaration**. In 1923, the **Jewish Agency** was created to coordinate between the *Yishuv* and the **Mandate** administration.

The Zionist General Council, which is elected by the Zionist Congress, functions in the period between congresses and is empowered to deliberate and decide on all matters affecting the WZO and its institutions, including the budget. The Zionist Executive is the executive arm of the WZO and is elected by the Congress for a period of four years. Some of its members are placed in charge of the various departments of the Executive. The WZO Congress met annually until 1901, when it was resolved to meet every two years. Subsequently, until 1939, it met every other year, except during World War I. After the establishment of Israel, in November 1952, the Knesset passed the Zionist Organization–Jewish Agency for Israel Status Law, and later a covenant was signed between the government of Israel and the Zionist Executive defining the major responsibilities of the WZO. Under a revised arrangement worked out in 1970, the WZO was made responsible for immigration from affluent countries, whereas the Jewish

Agency was to take care of *Aliya* from countries where Jews face persecution.

WYE MEMORANDUM. With a view to implementing the **Taba Agreement** of 1995, Israeli prime minister **Benjamin Netanyahu** and **Palestinian National Authority** chairman **Yasser Arafat** signed an agreement on 23 October 1998 at the historic Wye Plantation in Maryland. U.S. president **Bill Clinton** (1946–) also signed the memorandum, which called for a three-phased second **redeployment** (which should have been implemented by April 1997, according to the Taba Agreement). Under this revised plan, Israel agreed to withdraw from 13 percent of the **West Bank** and to transfer another 14 percent of the West Bank from joint Israeli–Palestinian control (Area B) to full Palestinian control (Area A). The memorandum also provided for the opening of the Gaza airport; safe passage between the West Bank and **Gaza Strip**; the release of Palestinian prisoners in Israeli jails; unconditional amendments to those provisions of the **Palestine Liberation Organization** Charter (also known as the PLO Covenant) that were contrary to the **Oslo Process**; and immediate resumption of **Permanent Status Negotiations** covering issues such as **Jerusalem**, **refugees**, water, **settlements**, and the nature and configuration of boundaries between Israel and a future Palestinian entity in the **Occupied Territories**.

Israel subsequently withdrew from 2 percent of the territories near Jenin, facilitated the opening of the Gaza airport, and released a limited number of Palestinian prisoners. The first stage of the third redeployment—which was supposed to be completed by 2 November 1998—was deferred to 16 November due to Knesset nonapproval. After a number of meetings, the cabinet failed to approve the agreement. The Knesset approved it on 17 November by a vote of 75–19; there were 9 abstentions, and as many as 17 Knesset members were absent during the vote, including five ministers (two ministers voted against). This was followed by the approval of the cabinet on 19 November, and Israel completed the first stage of the third redeployment on 20 November, which involved the transfer of 7.1 percent of the West Bank to complete Palestinian control and the transfer of an additional 2 percent of nature reserves from sole Israeli control to joint Israeli–Palestinian control.

Following the decision of the Israeli Knesset in December 1998 to hold an early election, the Wye Memorandum was suspended. It was superseded by the **Sharm al-Sheikh Memorandum** signed on 4 September 1999.

– Y –

YASSIN, SHEIKH AHMED (c. 1933–2004). A Palestinian Islamic scholar, Sheikh Ahmed Yassin was the spiritual leader of the militant Islamic organization **Hamas**. Born in Ashkelon in 1933 or 1934, he became a quadriplegic at a young age due to a serious illness. In 1973, he founded the Gaza wing of the **Muslim Brotherhood**, which originated in **Egypt**. Following the Israeli capture of the **Gaza Strip** in 1967, Yassin became more active in social welfare activities, and in 1979, with Israeli knowledge and partial connivance, he founded the Islamic Society. Devoted to social welfare activities, it sought to Islamize Palestinian society, which had been secularized by **Fatah** and the **Palestine Liberation Organization** (PLO).

In 1984, Yassin was sentenced to 13 years' imprisonment for possession of arms, but he was released a year later in a **prisoner exchange** deal when Israel released 1,000 Palestinian prisoners in return for six Israeli soldiers captured in **Lebanon**. Months after the outbreak of the **Intifada** (1987–1993) in the **Occupied Territories**, Yassin decided to join the political process, and in August 1988, the Islamic Resistance Movement (Hamas) was formed with Yassin as one of its founders.

On 16 October 1991, Yassin was imprisoned on a life term for ordering the kidnapping and killing of four Israeli soldiers. In September 1997, however, after Israel made an **assassination** attempt on the political head of Hamas in Amman (the **Masha'al Affair**), King **Hussein** of **Jordan** pressured Israel to release the visually impaired and invalid cleric, and Yassin was set free from Israeli prison on 1 October 1997. A few days later, Yassin returned to the **Gaza Strip** and continued his opposition to the **Oslo Accords** and the **Palestinian National Authority** headed by Chairman **Yasser Arafat**.

Despite repeated Israeli pressures, Yassin refused to condemn **suicide attacks** or other acts of **terrorism** that increased following the outbreak of the **Al-Aqsa Intifada**. In September 2003, Israel made an unsuccessful assassination attempt on him, but on 22 March 2004, it succeeded. Yassin was briefly replaced by **Abdel Aziz al-Rantisi**, who was soon also killed by Israeli security agents.

YIFTACH OPERATION. During the **Arab–Israeli War of 1947–1948**, Jewish forces on 30 April 1948 launched the Yiftach Operation, an offensive against the town of Safed in Galilee, whose Jewish population had been under siege since February that year. The forces of **Great Britain** had withdrawn from the city on 15 April. After two failed attacks, the forces launched a three-pronged attack on Safed on 10 May, and took it the following day. The capture of the mixed city by Jewish forces resulted in a mass exodus of the Arab population from Safed and neighboring Arab villages. *See also* ARMISTICE AGREEMENT/S; REFUGEE/S.

YISHUV. The Jewish community in Palestine during the **Mandate**. The growth and development of the *Yishuv* was brought about by successive waves of *Aliya* from the Diaspora. The *Yishuv* functioned as an autonomous political body with its own political institutions, educational system, *Histadrut* labor federation, and self-defense forces. The **League of Nations** directed the formation of a **Jewish Agency** in 1929 to provide liaison between the *Yishuv* and the Mandate authorities.

YOAV OPERATION. During the **Arab–Israeli War of 1947–1948**, the second **United Nations**-mandated Arab–Israeli truce came into force on 18 July 1948, lasting longer than the earlier one. It ended on 15 October when the Israeli forces launched an operation on the **Egypt**–Negev front. During this weeklong operation, code-named Yoav, Israeli forces broke through and overran Egyptian lines in the northern Negev, and on 21 October, they captured the city of Beersheba. Encircling the Egyptian forces at al-Faluja, they also expanded and consolidated their hold on parts of the Mediterranean coasts, the Hebron area, and the **Jerusalem** corridor. *See also* ARMISTICE AGREEMENT/S.

YOM KIPPUR WAR. *See* OCTOBER WAR OF 1973.

– Z –

ZINNI PLAN. In November 2001, retired U.S. general Anthony Zinni (1943–) was appointed as the new envoy of President **George W.**

Bush with the explicit purpose of achieving a cease-fire between Israel and the Palestinians. Zinni's long trips to the region and consultations with both sides did not make any headway. He was gradually sidelined by the administration, which forced him to resign from his position in March 2003. *See also* AL-AQSA INTIFADA.

ZIONISM. Zionism can be defined as a political movement that sought the return of the Jewish people to their historic homeland. The name is derived from Zion, a biblical expression for **Jerusalem**. Emerging toward the end of the 19th century, its fortunes rose following the efforts of Theodore Herzl (1860–1904) and the publication of *The Jewish State*. The movement was primarily a response to the increasing anti-Semitism in Europe as well as the outcome of growing nationalist consciousness. It sought to create a Jewish homeland in Palestine through international guarantees that would facilitate the "'return of the Jews" to the Holy Land through migration of Jews from the Diaspora, or *Aliya*. The fulfillment of the Jewish aspiration for a homeland and later statehood in Palestine became problematic because Palestine was not an empty uninhabited land. The movement took the institutional form of the **World Zionist Organization** and other bodies.

Bibliography

CONTENTS

I. INTRODUCTION

Since the late 19th century, the problems of Jewish statelessness, the Jewish desire for a national home, and the establishment of the State of Israel in 1948 have dominated the Middle East and, at times, international politics. As a result, Israel's conflict with the Arab world has been the most widely studied issue in the contemporary world.

Despite the large number of publications on the subject, most of the works have been devoted to a particular conflict, issue, or even a specific war. There are only a handful of works that provide a broad picture of the Arab–Israeli conflict. These include Avi Shlaim's *The Iron Wall*, Alan Dowty's *Israel/Palestine*, and Ritchie Ovendale's *The Origins of the Arab–Israeli Wars*. In *The Arab–Israeli Wars*, Chaim Herzog provides a detailed account of Israel's military campaigns from 1948 to 1982.

The relative availability of archival material in Israel compared to other neighboring states has resulted in a proliferation of scholarship and evolution of the foreign policy of Israel as a fully grown discipline. While most of the works are available in English, a more detailed and nuanced treatment of the problem is generally available in Hebrew only. The lack of available archival materials is a problem in the Arab world. However, access to private papers, as well as personal memoirs by individuals, is slowly providing a nonofficial version of the course of events. Hanan Ashrawi's *This Side of the Peace*, Itamar Rabinovich's *The Brink of Peace*, Uri Savir's *The Process*, and Dennis Ross's *The Missing Peace* offer valuable insights to the Arab–Israeli negotiations.

Since the early 1980s, Israel has witnessed the emergence of scholars known as "New Historians" who have sought to question, challenge, and even rewrite some of the official history in Israel concerning controversial issues such as the refugee problem and the direction and course of the 1948 Arab–Israeli War. This new group of scholars is led by persons such as Simha Flapan, Benny Morris, Avi Shlaim, and Ilan Pappe, and their works have evoked strong rebuttal from others, led by Efraim Karsh.

Autobiographies and biographies of the principal players—David Ben-Gurion, Moshe Sharett, Yitzhak Rabin, Gamal Abdel Nasser, Anwar Sadat, Yasser Arafat, Shimon Peres, King Hussein, and Henry Kissinger, among others—have also contributed to the understanding of the problem. Key individuals such as James Baker, Dennis Ross, and Mahmoud Abbas have described their roles during some aspects of the Arab–Israeli conflict. Scholars like Edward Said and Noam Chomsky have significantly contributed to the greater but often controversial discourse on the Arab–Israeli conflict, especially the role played by the United States.

The conflict is the principle staple for most of the Middle East centers and programs in different parts of the world. The growth of think tanks both in the region and elsewhere has also contributed to the rapidly growing knowledge on the subject. These include the BESA Center for Strategic Studies, the Institute for Palestine Studies, the Jaffee Center for Strategic Studies, PASSIA (Palestinian Academic Society for the Study of International Affairs), and the Washington Institute for Near East Policy, as well as the Middle East programs of the American Enterprise Institute, Brookings Institution, Carnegie Endowment for Peace, and United States Institute for Peace.

Various scholarly journals pertaining to the Middle East such as *International Journal of Middle Eastern Studies*, *Middle Eastern Studies*, *Middle East Insight*, *Middle East Journal*, *Middle East Report*, *Middle East Policy*, *Middle East Quarterly*, and *Mediterranean Quarterly* have prominently covered different aspects of the conflict. Specialized journals such as *Arab Studies Quarterly*, *Israel Affairs*, *Israel Studies*, *Journal of Palestine Studies*, and *Palestine-Israel Journal* have been in the forefront of serious and scholarly debates on the Arab–Israeli conflict. Given the international attention it evokes, the subject of the Arab–Israeli conflict has also been widely commented on in such highly regarded journals as *Orbis, Survivor, New Outlook, Survival, Journal of Democracy, National Interest, Foreign Affairs, Security Dialogue, Journal of Conflict Resolution, Journal of Peace Research*, and *Review of International Affairs*.

The conflict dominates Middle East series brought out by various premier academic publishers, including Cambridge University Press, Oxford University Press, Princeton University Press, Harvard University Press, and State University of New York Press. The conflict has also become the prime focus of various academic societies that deal with the Middle East, such as the Association of Israel Studies, the British Society for Middle Eastern Studies, and the Middle East Studies Association of North America.

With the advent of information technology, the Arab–Israeli conflict has become a major focus of the electronic world. *MERIA* (The Middle East Review of International Affairs), published by the Herzliya-based Interdisciplinary Center, has become the principal vehicle in which Israel's conflict with the outside world is widely discussed, commented, and analyzed. Capitalizing on technological advancements, a number of traditional journals have also gone electronic and thereby reaching a wider audience. Sites such as *Electronic Intifada* have put out periodic bulletins on various aspects of ongoing Israeli–Palestinian violence. The technological advancement has revolutionized the knowledge of the Arab–Israeli conflict, with the result that numerous nongovernmental organizations, political parties, and even known militant groups such as Hamas have periodically publicized their plans and agendas through the Internet.

In recent years, specific groups have been set up to study a particular aspect of the Arab–Israeli conflict. These specialized forums include the Washington-based Foundation for Middle East Peace, which specializes in settlement activities, and the Jerusalem-based *B'tslem*, devoted to Israel's human right violations in the Occupied Territories.

The U.S. State Department, through its Congressional Research Service, periodically publishes and updates some aspects of Arab–Israeli conflict. The official site of the Israel's Ministry of Foreign Affairs provides access to a plethora of official documents pertaining to the Arab–Israeli conflict.

II. HISTORY

Abboushi, W. F. *The Unmaking of Palestine*. Boulder, Colo.: Lynne Rienner, 1985.
Abu-Lughod, Ibrahim, ed. *The Transformation of Palestine: Essay on the Origin and Development of the Arab-Israeli Conflict*. Evanston, Ill.: Northwestern University Press, 1987.

Al-Abid, Ibrahim. *A Handbook to the Palestine Question*. Beirut: Palestine Research Center, 1969.

——, ed. *Selected Essays on the Palestine Question*. Beirut: Palestine Research Center, 1969.

Arab Women's Information Committee. *The ABC of the Palestine Problem*. Part 1, *1896–1949*. Part 2, *1949–1967*. Beirut: Arab Women's Information Committee, 1974.

Arnoni, M. S. *Rights and Wrongs in the Arab-Israel Conflict: To the Anatomy of the Forces of Progress and Reaction in the Middle East*. Passaic, N.J.: Minority of One, 1968.

Aronsfeld, C. C. "The Historical Boundaries of Palestine." *Jewish Frontier* 45, no. 3 (March 1978): 23–28.

Avineri, Shlomo, ed. *Israel and the Palestinians*. New York: St. Martin's, 1971.

Barbour, Neville. *Palestine, Star or Crescent?* New York: Odyssey, 1947.

Bard, Mitchell G., and Joel Himmelfarb. *Myths and Facts: A Concise Record of the Arab-Israeli Conflict*. Washington, D.C.: Near East Report, 1992.

Ben-Gad, Yitschak. *Politics, Lies, and Videotape: 3,000 Questions and Answers on the Mideast Crisis*. New York: Shapolsky, 1991.

Benvenisti, Meron. *Sacred Landscape: The Buried History of the Holy Land since 1948*. Berkeley: University of California Press, 2000.

Ben-Yehuda, Hemda. *The Arab-Israeli Conflict Transformed: Fifty Years of Interstate and Ethnic Crises*. Albany: State University of New York Press, 2002.

Bialer, Uri. *Oil and the Arab-Israeli Conflict, 1948–1963*. Oxford: Macmillan Press, in association with St. Martin's Press, 1999.

Bickerton, Ian J., and Carla L. Klausner. *A Concise History of the Arab-Israeli Conflict*. Englewood Cliffs, N.J.: Prentice Hall, 1989.

Bishop, Donald H. "The Israeli-Palestinian Conflict, Past, Present, and Future." *Scandinavian Journal of Development Alternatives* 9, no. 1 (1990): 5–38.

Buber, Martin. *Israel and Palestine*. New York: Farrar, Straus and Young, 1952.

Buch, Peter. *Burning Issues of the Middle East Crisis*. New York: Pathfinder Press, 1967.

Chiha, Michel. *Palestine*. Beirut: Trident Publications, 1969.

Claiborne, William. *The West Bank: Hostage of History*. Washington, D.C.: Foundation for Middle East Peace, 1980.

Cohen, Michael Joseph. *The Origins and Evolution of the Arab-Zionist Conflict*. Berkeley: University of California Press, 1987.

——. *Palestine to Israel: From Mandate to Independence*. London: Frank Cass, 1988.

Cohen, Richard I., ed. *Vision and Conflict in the Holy Land*. New York: St. Martin's Press, 1985.

Courbage, Youssef. "Reshuffling the Demographic Cards in Israel/Palestine." *Journal of Palestine Studies* 28, no. 4 (1999): 21–39.

Darwaza, Al-Hakam. *The Palestine Question: A Brief Analysis.* Beirut: Palestine Research Center, 1973.

Davis, John H. *The Evasive Peace.* New York: New World Peace, 1968.

Devore, Ronald M. *The Arab-Israeli Conflict: A Historical, Political, Social and Military Bibliography.* Santa Barbara, Calif.: Clio Books, 1976.

Drummond, Dorothy Weitz. *Holy Land, Whose Land? Modern Dilemma, Ancient Roots.* Seattle: Educare Press, 2002.

Dumper, Michael. *The Politics of Sacred Space: The Old City of Jerusalem in the Middle East Conflict.* Boulder, Colo.: Lynne Rienner, 2002.

Duncan, Andrew. *Trouble Spots: The World Atlas of Strategic Information.* Stroud, U.K.: Sutton, 2000.

El-Aref, Aref. *The Tragedy of Palestine.* Sidon, Lebanon: Modern Library, 1962.

Ellis, Marc H. "The Future of Israel/Palestine: Embracing the Broken Middle." *Journal of Palestine Studies* 26, no. 3 (1997): 56–66.

Ferguson, Pamela. *The Palestine Problem.* London: Martin, Brian and O'Keefe, 1973.

Finkelstein, Norman G. *Image and Reality of the Israel-Palestine Conflict.* London: Verso, 1995.

Forrest, A. C. *The Unholy Land.* Toronto: McClelland and Stewart, 1971.

Fraser, Thomas Grant. *The Arab-Israeli Conflict.* London: Macmillan, 1995.

———. *The Middle East, 1914–1979.* London: E. Arnold, 1980.

Friedman, Thomas L. *Beirut to Jerusalem.* New York: Farrar, Straus, Giroux, 1990.

Geddes, Charles L, ed. *A Documentary History of the Arab-Israeli Conflict.* New York: Praeger, 1991.

Gerner, Deborah J. *One Land, Two Peoples: The Conflict over Palestine.* Boulder, Colo: Westview Press, 1994.

Gerson, Joseph. "Legacies of the Storm: Desert Shield, Desert Storm and the Diplomacy of the Israeli-Palestinian-Arab Conflict." *Scandinavian Journal of Development Alternatives* 12, nos. 2–3 (1993): 63–78.

Gilbert, Martin. *The Arab-Israeli Conflict: Its History in Maps.* London: Weidenfeld and Nicolson, 1974.

———. *The Dent Atlas of the Arab-Israeli Conflict: The Complete History of the Struggle and the Efforts to Resolve It.* London: J. M. Dent, 1993.

———. *The Routledge Atlas of the Arab-Israeli Conflict.* London: Routledge, 2002.

Gilboa, Eytan. *The Arab-Israeli Conflict: Sources, Evolution and Prospects for Resolution.* Jerusalem: Academon, 1993.

Glubb, John Bagot. *The Middle East Crisis.* London: Hodder and Stoughton, 1967.

Goldscheider, Calvin. *Cultures in Conflict: The Arab-Israeli Conflict.* Westport, Conn.: Greenwood Press, 2002.

Goodman, Hirsch, and Seth W. Carns. *The Future Battlefield of the Arab-Israeli Conflict*. New Brunswick, N.J.: Transaction, 1990.

Greffenius, Steven. *The Logic of Conflict: Making War and Peace in the Middle East*. Armonk, N.Y.: M. E. Sharpe, 1993.

Hajjar, Lisa. "Human Rights in Israel/Palestine: The History and Politics of Movement." *Journal of Palestine Studies* 30, no. 4 (2001): 21–38.

Hare, William. *The Struggle for the Holy Land: Arabs, Jews, and the Emergence of Israel*. Lanham, Md.: Madison Books, 1995.

Haymson, Albery, H. *Palestine under the Mandate*. Westport, Conn.: Greenwood Press, 1976.

Holliday, Laurel, ed. *Children of Israel, Children of Palestine: Our Own*. New York: Pocket Books, 1998.

Hong, Christopher C. *To Whom the Land of Palestine Belongs*. Hicksville, N.Y.: Exposition Press, 1979.

Hurewitz, J. C. *The Struggle for Palestine*. New York: Schocken Books, 1976.

Ingrams, Doreen. *Palestine Papers, 1917–1922: Seeds of Conflict*. New York: G. Braziller, 1973.

Jiryis, Sabri. "Forty Years since the Seizure of Palestine." *Journal of Palestine Studies* 18, no. 1 (Autumn 1988): 83–95.

John, Robert. *Behind the Balfour Declaration*. Costa Mesa, Calif.: Institute for Historical Review, 1988.

Junod, Dominique-D. *The Imperiled Red Cross and the Palestine-Eretz-Yisrael Conflict, 1945–1952: The Influence of Institutional Concerns on a Humanitarian Operation*. London: Kegan Paul, 1996.

Kadduri, Majdia D., ed. *The Arab-Israeli Impasse*. Washington, D.C.: Robert B. Luce, 1968.

Kapitan, Tomis, ed. *Philosophical Perspectives on the Israeli-Palestinian Conflict*. Armonk, N.Y.: M. E. Sharpe, 1997.

Kerr, Malcolm H. *The Middle East Conflict*. New York: Foreign Policy Association, 1968.

Khalidi, Walid. *From Haven to Conquest: Readings in Zionism and the Palestine Problem until 1948*. Beirut: Institute for Palestine Studies, 1971.

——, ed. "The Palestinian Problem: An Overview." *Journal of Palestine Studies* 21, no. 1 (Autumn 1991): 5–16.

Khouri, Fred J. *The Arab-Israeli Dilemma*. Syracuse, N.Y.: Syracuse University Press, 1985.

Kimmerling, Baruch. *Land, Conflict and Nation Building: A Sociological Study of the Territorial Factors in the Jewish-Arab Conflict*. Jerusalem: Hebrew University, 1976.

Klein, Menachem. *Jerusalem: The Contested City*. New York: New York University Press, in association with the Jerusalem Institute for Israel Studies, 2001.

La Guardia, Anton. *Holy Land, Unholy War: Israelis and Palestinians*. London: John Murray, 2001.

Laqueur, Walter, and Barry Rubin, eds. *The Israel-Arab Reader: A Documentary History of the Middle East Conflict*. New York: Penguin Books, 1984.

Lesch, Ann Mosely, and Dan Tschirgi. *Origins and Development of the Arab-Israeli Conflict*. Westport, Conn.: Greenwood Press, 1998.

Lesch, David W. *1979: The Year That Shaped the Modern Middle East*. Boulder, Colo.: Westview Press, 2001.

Liebes, Tamar. *Reporting the Arab-Israeli Conflict: How Hegemony Works*. London: Routledge, 1997.

Louis, Wm. Roger, and Robert W. Stookey, eds. *The End of the Palestine Mandate*. Austin: University of Texas Press, 1989.

Lukacs, Yehuda, ed. *The Israeli-Palestinian Conflict: A Documentary Record, 1967–1990*. Cambridge: Cambridge University Press, 1992.

Lukacs, Yehuda, and Abdalla M. Battah, ed. *The Arab-Israeli Conflict: Two Decades of Change*. Boulder, Colo.: Westview Press, 1988.

Lustick, Ian. *Unsettled States, Disputed Lands: Britain and Ireland, France and Algeria, Israel and the West Bank-Gaza*. Ithaca, N.Y.: Cornell University Press, 1993.

Mandel, Alisa, and Joshua Obstfeld. *Trends in Israeli-Palestinian Political Fatalities, 1987–1999*. Research Notes no. 8. Washington, D.C.: Washington Institute for Near East Policy, 1999.

Ma'oz, Moshe, and Sari Nusseibeh, eds. *Jerusalem: Points of Friction, and Beyond*. The Hague: Kluwer Law International, 2000.

McDowall, David. *Palestine and Israel: The Uprising and Beyond*. London: I. B. Tauris, 1989.

Mendelsohn, Everett. *A Compassionate Peace: A Future for Israel, Palestine, and the Middle East; A Report Prepared for the American Friends Service Committee*. New York: Hill and Wang, 1989.

Miller, Aaron David. "The Arab-Israeli Conflict, 1967–1987: A Retrospective." *Middle East Journal* 41, no. 3 (Summer 1987): 349–60.

Moore, John Norton, ed. *The Arab-Israeli Conflict*. 4 vols. Princeton, N.J.: Princeton University Press, 1974–1991.

Morris, Benny. *Righteous Victims: A History of the Zionist-Arab Conflict, 1881–1999*. New York: Alfred A. Knopf, 1999.

Moughrabi, Fouad. "Public Opinion, Public Policy and the Israeli-Palestinian Conflict." *American-Arab Affairs*, no. 30 (1989): 40–51.

Mroz, John Edwin. *Beyond Security: Private Perceptions among Arabs and Israelis*. New York: International Peace Academy, 1980.

Nakhleh, Issa. *Encyclopedia of the Palestine Problem*. New York: Intercontinental Books, 1991.

Oz, Amos. "The Israeli-Palestinian Conflict: A Storyteller's Point of View." *Michigan Quarterly Review* 32, no. 2 (Spring 1992): 156–77.

Pappe, Ilan. *The Making of the Arab-Israeli Conflict, 1947–1951.* London: I. B. Tauris, 1992.

Rigby, Andrew. "Unofficial Nonviolent Intervention: Examples from the Israeli-Palestinian Conflict." *Journal of Peace Research* 32, no. 4 (1995): 453–68.

Said, Edward W. *The Question of Palestine.* New York: Times Books, 1980.

Sanders, Ronald. *The High Walls of Jerusalem: A History of the Balfour Declaration, The Birth of the British Mandate for Palestine.* New York: Holt, Rinehart and Winston, 1984.

Sayegh, Fayez Abdullah. *The Arab-Israeli Conflict.* New York: Arab Information Center, 1956.

———. *Zionist Colonization of Palestine.* Beirut: Palestine Research Center, 1965.

Sela, Avraham. *The Decline of the Arab-Israeli Conflict: Middle East Politics and the Quest for Regional Order.* Albany: State University of New York Press, 1998.

———. "The Wailing Wall Riots (1929) as a Watershed in the Palestine Conflict." *Muslim World* 83, nos. 1–2 (January–April 1994): 60–94.

Shaheen, Murad. "Questioning the Water-War Phenomenon in the Jordan Basin." *Middle East Policy* 7, no. 3 (2000): 137–50.

Shapland, Greg. *Rivers of Discord: International Water Disputes in the Middle East.* New York: St. Martin's, 1997.

Sharoni, Simona. *Gender and the Israeli-Palestinian Conflict: The Politics of Women's Resistance.* Syracuse, N.Y.: Syracuse University Press, 1995.

Sheffer, Gabriel, ed. *Dynamics of Conflict: A Re-Examination of the Arab-Israeli Conflict.* Atlantic Highlands, N.J.: Humanities Press, 1975.

Sherman, John, ed. *The Arab-Israeli Conflict, 1945–1971: A Bibliography.* New York: Garland, 1978.

Shipler, David K. *Arab and Jew: Wounded Spirits in a Promised Land.* Harmondsworth, N.Y.: Penguin, 1987.

Stein, Leonard. *The Balfour Declaration.* London: Valentine Mitchell, 1961.

Stetler, Russell, ed. *Palestine, The Arab-Israeli Conflict.* San Francisco: Ramparts Press, 1972.

Taylor, Alan R. *Prelude to Israel, 1943–1947.* Beirut: Institute of Palestine Studies, 1970.

Tessler, Mark Arnold. *A History of the Israeli-Palestinian Conflict.* Bloomington: Indiana University Press, 1994.

Thomas, Baylis. *How Israel Was Won: A Concise History of the Arab-Israeli Conflict.* Lanham, Md.: Lexington Books, 1999.

Van Evera, Stephen. *Causes of War: Power and the Roots of Conflict.* Ithaca, N.Y.: Cornell University Press, 1999.

Waines, David. *The Unholy War: Israel and Palestine, 1897–1971.* Montreal: Chateau Books, 1971.

Warburg, James Paul. *Crosscurrents in the Middle East: A Primer for the General Reader, Including a History of the Region, a Survey of Recent Developments, an Appraisal of Western Responsibility, and the Prospects for Peace.* London: V. Gollancz, 1969.

Warner, Jeroen. "Kicking the Water Habit: Israel, Palestine and the New Water Order." *Amsterdam Middle East Papers*, no. 8 (1996).

Wasserstein, Bernard. *Divided Jerusalem: The Struggle for the Holy City.* New Haven, Conn.: Yale University Press, 2001.

Wolf, Aaron T. *Hydropolitics along the Jordan River: Scarce Water and Its Impact on the Arab-Israeli Conflict.* Tokyo: United Nations University Press, 1995.

Wright, Clifford A. *Facts and Fables: The Arab-Israeli Conflict.* New York: Routledge, Chapman and Hall, 1989.

Wright, Martin ed. *Israel and the Palestinians.* Harlow, Essex, England: Longman, 1989.

Zu'iter, Akram. *The Palestine Question.* Damascus: Palestine Arab Refugee Institution, 1958.

III. ARAB–ISRAELI WARS

Abu-Lughod, Ibrahim, ed. *The Arab-Israeli Confrontation of June 1967: An Arab Perspective.* Evanston, Ill.: Northwestern University Press, 1970.

Aker, Frank. *October 1973: The Arab-Israeli War.* Hamden, Conn.: Archon Books, Shoe String Press, 1985.

Alami, Musa. "The Lesson of Palestine." *Middle East Journal* 3 (October 1949): 373–405.

Aronson, Shlomo. *Israel's Nuclear Programme, the Six-Day War and Its Ramifications.* London: King's College, n.d.

Aruri, Naseer H. *Middle East Crucibles: Studies on the Arab-Israeli War of 1973.* Wilmette, Ill.: Medina University Press, 1975.

Bailey, Sydney Dawson. *Four Arab-Israeli Wars and the Peace Process.* London: Macmillan, 1990.

Bregman, Ahron. *Israel's Wars: A History since 1947.* London: Routledge, 2002.

———. *Israel's Wars, 1947–1993.* London: Routledge, 2000.

Cattan, Henry. *The Dimensions of the Palestine Problem, 1967.* Beirut: Institute for Palestine Studies, 1967.

Dupuy, Trevor N. *Elusive Victory: The Arab-Israeli Wars, 1947–1974.* New York: Harper and Row, 1978.

El-Ayonty, Y. "The Palestinians and the Fourth Arab-Israeli War." *Current History* 66, no. 390 (February 1974): 74–78.

El-Jamasi, Muhammad Abd Al-Ghani. *The October War: Memoirs of Field Marshal El-Gamasy of Egypt.* Cairo: American University in Cairo Press, 1993.

El-Khalidi, Ahmad Samih. *The Arab-Israeli War, 1967.* Beirut: Arab Women's Information Committee, 1969.

Eshel, David. *The Lebanon War, 1982.* Hod Hasharon, Israel: Eshel-Dramit, 1983.

Gabriel, Richard A. *Operation Peace for Galilee: The Israeli-PLO War in Lebanon.* New York: Hill and Wang, 1984.

Golan, Galia. *The Soviet Union and the Arab-Israel War of October 1973.* Jerusalem: Leonard Davis Institute for International Relations, Hebrew University, 1974.

———. *Yom Kippur and After.* Cambridge: Cambridge University Press, 1977.

Handel, Michael I. *Perception, Deception, and Surprise: The Case of the Yom Kippur War.* Jerusalem: Leonard Davis Institute for International Relations, Hebrew University, 1976.

Harkavy, Robert E. *Preemption and Two-Front Conventional Warfare: A Comparison of 1967 Israeli Strategy with the Pre-World War I German Schlieffen Plan.* Jerusalem: Leonard Davis Institute for International Relations, Hebrew University, 1977.

Herzog, Chaim. *The Arab-Israeli Wars: War and Peace in the Middle East from the War of Independence to Lebanon.* London: Arms and Armour Press, 1985.

Karmi, Ghada, "The 1948 Exodus: A Family Story." *Journal of Palestine Studies* 23, no. 2 (Winter 1994): 31–40.

Khalidi, Walid. "Plan Dalet: Master Plan for the Conquest of Palestine." *Journal of Palestine Studies* 18, no. 1 (Autumn 1988): 3–70.

Kumaraswamy, P R, ed. *Revisiting the Yom Kippur War.* London: Frank Cass, 2000.

Kurzman, Dan. *Genesis 1948: The First Arab-Israeli War.* New York: World Publishing, 1970.

Love, Kennett. *Suez: The Twice-Fought War.* New York: McGraw-Hill, 1969.

Morris, Benny. *1948 and After: Israel and the Palestinians.* Oxford: Oxford University Press, 1994.

Nazzal, Nafez. "The Zionist Occupation of Western Galilee, 1948." *Journal of Palestine Studies* 11, no. 3 (Spring 1974): 58–76.

Nutting, Anthony. *No End of a Lesson: The Story of Suez.* New York: Clarkson Potter, 1967.

Ovendale, Ritchie. *The Origins of the Arab-Israeli Wars.* New York: Longman, 1992.

Parker, Richard B. "The June 1967 War: Some Mysteries Explored." *Middle East Journal* 46, no. 2 (Spring 1992): 177–97.

——, ed. *The Six Day War: A Retrospective*. Gainesville: University Press of Florida, 1996.

Rabinovich, Itamar. *The War for Lebanon, 1970–1983*. Ithaca, N.Y.: Cornell University Press, 1984.

Richards, Martin. "The Israeli-Lebanese War of 1982." *Army Quarterly and Defense Journal* 113 (1983): 9–19.

Roth, Stephen J., ed. *The Impact of the Six-Day War: A Twenty-Year Assessment*. New York: St. Martin's Press, in association with Institute of Jewish Affairs, 1988.

Rubinstein, C. L. "The Lebanon War: Objectives and Outcomes." *Australian Outlook* 37 (1983): 10–17.

Samo, Elias, ed. *The June 1967 Arab-Israeli War: Miscalculation or Conspiracy?* Wilmette, Ill.: Medina University Press, 1971.

IV. THE ARAB–ISRAELI PEACE PROCESS

Abed, George T. "The Palestinians in the Peace Process: The Risks and the Opportunities." *Journal of Palestine Studies* 22, no. 1 (Autumn 1992): 5–17.

Abu-Nimer, Muhammad. *Dialogue, Conflict Resolution, and Change: Arab-Jewish Encounters in Israel*. Albany: State University of New York Press, 1999.

Abu-Odeh, Adnan. *Jordanians, Palestinians and the Hashemite Kingdom in the Middle East Peace Process*. Washington, D.C.: United States Institute of Peace Press, 1999.

Adwan, Sami. "Reflections on Joint Israeli-Palestinian Cooperation Projects." *Palestine-Israel Journal* 7, nos. 1–2 (2000): 89–96.

Aggestam, Karin. *Two-Track Diplomacy: Negotiations between Israel and the PLO through Open and Secret Channels*. Jerusalem: Leonard Davis Institute for International Relations, Hebrew University, 1998.

Alin, Erika G. "West Bank and Gaza Palestinians and the Peace Process." *Critique*, no. 3 (Fall 1993): 13–34.

Allen Brian, Elyse Aronson, and Monica Neal, eds. *Countdown to May 1999: Oslo and the U.S.-Israeli-Palestinian Triangle*. Washington, D.C.: Washington Institute for Near East Policy, 1999.

Al-Madfai, Madiha Rashid. *Jordan, the United States, and the Middle East Peace Process, 1974–1991*. Cambridge: Cambridge University Press, 1993.

Amery, H. M. "The PLO-Israel Agreement: Implications and Opportunities." *Middle Eastern Times* 1, no. 3 (October 1993): 4–14.

Amery, Hussein A., and Aaron T. Wolf, eds. *Water in the Middle East: A Geography of Peace*. Austin: University of Texas Press, 2000.

Amit, Daniel J. "Strategies for Struggle, Strategies for Peace." *Journal of Palestine Studies* 12, no. 3 (Spring 1983): 23–30.

Arad, Ruth W. *The Economics of Peacemaking: Focus on the Egyptian-Israeli Situation*. London: Macmillan, 1983.

Aronson, Geoffrey. *Settlement and the Israel-Palestinian Negotiations: An Overview*. Final Status Issues Paper no. 3, Institute for Palestine Studies, 1996.

Ashrawi, Hanan. *This Side of Peace: A Personal Account*. New York: Simon and Schuster, 1995.

Awartani, Hisham. "Economic Interactions among Participants in the Middle East Peace Process." *Middle East Journal* 51, no. 2 (1997): 215–29.

Bahiri, Simcha. "Economic Aspects of an Israeli-Palestinian Interim Settlement." *Israel-Palestine: Issues in Conflict, Issues for Cooperation* 2, no. 5 (1993).

———. *Peace Pays*. Jerusalem: Israel/Palestine Center for Research and Information, 1993.

Bailey, Sydney. *Four Arab-Israeli Wars and the Peace Process*. London: Macmillan, 1990.

Barder, Christopher. *Oslo's Gift of "Peace": The Destruction of Israel's Security*. Shaarei Tikva, Israel: Ariel Center for Policy Research, 2001.

———. *A Statistically Based Survey of the Oslo Process, Its Agreements and Results*. Shaarei Tikva, Israel: Ariel Center for Policy Research, 2002.

Bar-On, Mordechai. *In Pursuit of Peace: A History of the Israeli Peace Movement*. Washington, D.C.: United States Institute of Peace, 1996.

———. *Peace Politics in Israel from Sadat to Hussein*. Tel Aviv: International Center for Peace in the Middle East, 1986.

Bar-Siman-Tov, Yaacov. "The Arab-Israeli Conflict: Learning Conflict Resolution." *Journal of Peace Research* 31, no. 1 (February 1994): 75–92.

Bar-Tal, Daniel. *Ethos as an Expression of Identity: Its Changes in Transition from Conflict to Peace in the Israeli Case*. Jerusalem: Leonard Davis Institute for International Relations, Hebrew University, 2000.

Beckerman, Chaia, ed. *Negotiating the Future*. Jerusalem: Israel/Palestine Center for Research and Information, 1996.

Beilin, Yossi. *Touching Peace: From the Oslo Accord to a Final Agreement*. London: Weidenfeld and Nicolson, 1999.

Ben-Dor, Gabriel, and David B. Dewitt, ed. *Confidence-Building Measures in the Middle East*. Boulder, Colo.: Westview Press, 1994.

Ben-Meir, Alon. *A Framework for Arab-Israeli Peace*. St. Louis: Robert, 1993.

Ben-Shahar Haim, Gideon Fishelson, and Zeev Hirsch. *Economic Cooperation and Middle East Peace*. London: Weidenfeld and Nicolson, 1989.

Bentsur, Eytan. *Making Peace: A First-Hand Account of the Arab-Israeli Peace Process*. Westport, Conn.: Praeger, 2001.

Bercovitch, Jacob. "Conflict Management and Israeli-Palestinian Conflict: The Importance of Capturing the Right Moment." *Asia-Pacific Review* 9, no. 2 (2002): 113–29.

Bercovitch, Jacob, and Richard Jackson. *International Conflict: A Chronological Encyclopedia of Conflicts and Their Management.* Washington, D.C.: Congressional Quarterly, 1997.

Berton, Peter, Hiroshi Kimura, and William I. Zartman. *International Negotiation: Actors, Structure/Process, Values.* New York: St. Martin's, 1999.

Blum, Yehuda Zvi. *Secure Boundaries and Middle East Peace: In the Light of International Law and Practice.* Jerusalem: Faculty of Law, Institute for Legislative Research, and Computative Law, Hebrew University, 1971.

Bornstein, Avram S. *Crossing the Green Line between Palestine and Israel.* Philadelphia: University of Pennsylvania Press, 2001.

Bowker, Robert. *Beyond Peace: The Search for Security in the Middle East.* Boulder, Colo.: Lynne Rienner, 1996.

Breger, Marshall J. *Jerusalem's Holy Places and the Peace Process.* Washington, D.C.: Washington Institute for Near East Policy, 1998.

Breger, Marshall J., and Ora Ahimeir, eds. *Jerusalem: A City and Its Future.* Syracuse, N.Y.: Syracuse University Press, 2002.

Bruton, Henry Jackson. *The Promise of Peace: Economic Cooperation between Egypt and Israel.* Washington, D.C.: Brookings Institution, 1981.

Caplan, Neil. *The Lausanne Conference, 1949: A Case Study in Middle East Peacemaking.* Tel Aviv: Moshe Dayan Center for Middle East and African Studies, Tel Aviv University, 1993.

Cattan, Henry. *Palestine: The Road to Peace.* London: Longman, 1970.

Center for Palestine Research and Studies. "The Declaration of Principles: What's in It for the Palestinians." *Palestine-Israel Journal of Politics, Economics and Culture* 1 (Winter 1994): 39–55.

Chacour, Elias. *We Belong to the Land: The Story of a Palestinian Israeli Who Lives for Peace and Reconciliation.* Notre Dame, Ind.: University of Notre Dame Press, 2001.

Chomsky, Naom. *Peace in the Middle East: Reflections on Justice and Nationhood.* New York: Vintage Books, 1974.

Cobban, Helena. *The Israeli-Syrian Peace Talks: 1991–1996 and Beyond.* Washington, D.C.: United States Institute of Peace Press, 1999.

Cohen, Renae. *The Israeli Peace Initiative and the Israel-PLO Accord: A Survey of American Jewish Opinion in 1994.* New York: American Jewish Committee, 1995.

Cohen, Stuart A. *Military, Economic and Strategic Aspects of the Middle East Peace Process.* Ramat Gan, Israel: BESA Center for Strategic Studies, Bar Ilan University, 1995.

Corbin, Jane. *Gaza First: The Secret Norway Channel to Peace between Israel and the PLO*. London: Bloomsbury Press, 1994.

Cordesman, Anthony H. *Perilous Prospects: The Peace Process and the Arab-Israeli Military Balance*. Boulder, Colo.: Westview Press, 1996.

Cortright, David. *The Price of Peace: Incentives and International Conflict Prevention*. Lanham, Md.: Rowman and Littlefield, 1997.

Curtis, Michael. *People and Politics in the Middle East: Proceedings of the Annual Conference of the American Academic Association for Peace in the Middle East*. New Brunswick, N.J: Transaction Books, 1971.

——. "The Uprising's Impact on the Options for Peace." *Middle East Review* 21, no. 2 (Winter 1988/89): 3–12.

Dajani, Burhan. "The September 1993 Israeli-PLO Document: A Textual Analysis." *Journal of Palestine Studies* 23, no. 3 (Spring 1994): 5–23.

Davis, John Herbert. *The Evasive Peace: A Study of the Zionist-Arab Problem*. London: J. Murray, 1968.

Dayan, Moshe. *Breakthrough: A Personal Account of the Egypt-Israel Peace Negotiations*. London: Weidenfeld and Nicolson, 1981.

Demant, Peter. "Israeli-Palestinian Dialogue: Pitfalls and Promises—The Jewish Side from the Gulf Crisis to the 1992 Election." *Shofar* 12, no. 2 (1994): 1–36.

D'estree, Tamra Pearson. "Women and the Art of Peacemaking: Data from Israeli-Palestinian Interactive Problem-Solving Workshops." *Political Psychology* 19, no. 1 (1998): 185–209.

Doron, Gideon. "Two Guiding Principles for a Just Resolution of the Israeli-Palestinian Conflict." *International Problems* 32, nos. 3–4 (1993): 29–36.

Drysdale, Alasdair. *Syria and the Middle East Peace Process*. Ann Arbor, Mich.: UMI Books on Demand, 2000.

Duncan, Andrew. "The Israeli-Palestinian Permanent-Status Agreement." *Jane's Intelligence Review* 8, no. 5 (1996): 213–17.

Eban, Abba Solomon. *Israel's Call for a Negotiated Peace*. New York: Israel Information Services, 1967.

Eisenberg, Laura Zittrain. *Negotiating Arab-Israeli Peace: Patterns, Problems, Possibilities*. Bloomington: Indiana University Press, 1998.

El-Ayouty, Yassin. *Egypt, Peace and the Inter-Arab Crisis*. Amherst: Council on International Studies, State University of New York at Buffalo, 1979.

Elazar, Daniel Judah. *The Camp David Framework for Peace: A Shift toward Shared Rule*. Washington, D.C.: American Enterprise Institute for Public Policy Research, 1979.

——. *Federal-Confederal Solutions to the Israeli-Palestinian-Jordanian Conflict: Concepts and Feasibility*. Working Papers Series, no. 6. Israeli-Palestinian Peace Research Project, 1991/92.

Elmusa, Sharif S. "The Israeli-Palestinian Water Dispute Can Be Resolved." *Palestine-Israel Journal* 3 (1994): 18–26.

———. "The Land-Water Nexus in the Israeli-Palestinian-Conflict." *Journal of Palestine Studies* 25, no. 3 (1996): 69–78.

El-Nawawy, Mohammed. *The Israeli-Egyptian Peace Process in the Reporting of Western Journalists*. Westport, Conn.: Ablex, 2002.

Emmett, Ayala H. *Our Sisters' Promised Land: Women, Politics and Israeli-Palestinian Coexistence*. Ann Arbor: University of Michigan Press, 1996.

Endresen, Lena C. *Contact and Cooperation*. Oslo: Institute for Applied Social Science, 2001.

Evan, William M. "Toward a Confederation of Israel-Palestine and Jordan." *Palestine-Israel Journal* 6, no. 4 (1999–2000): 80–89.

Fellman, Gordon. *Peace in the World; or, The World in Pieces*. Jerusalem: Leonard Davis Institute for International Relations, Hebrew University, 1989.

Fernea, Elizabeth Warnock, and Mary Evelyn Hocking, eds. *The Struggle for Peace: Israelis and Palestinians*. Austin: University of Texas Press, 1992.

Feste, Karen A. *Plans for Peace: Negotiation and the Arab-Israeli Conflict*. New York: Praeger, 1991.

Fisher, Roger. *Dear Israelis, Dear Arabs: A Working Approach to Peace*. New York: Harper and Row, 1972.

Fisher, Ronald J. *Interactive Conflict Resolution*. Syracuse, N.Y.: Syracuse University Press, 1997.

Flamhaft, Ziva. *Israel on the Road to Peace: Accepting the Unacceptable*. Boulder, Colo.: Westview Press, 1996.

Flapan, Simha, ed. *When Enemies Dare to Talk: An Israeli-Palestinian Debate*. London: Croom Helm, 1979.

Freedman, Robert O. *The Middle East and the Peace Process: The Impact of the Oslo Accords*. Gainesville: University Press of Florida, 1998.

Friedlander, Melvin Alan. *Sadat and Begin: The Domestic Politics of Peacemaking*. Boulder, Colo.: Westview Press, 1983.

Garfinkle, Adam. "Israeli and Palestinian Proposals for the West Bank." *Orbis* 36, no. 3 (Summer 1992): 429–42.

Gazit, Mordechai. *Israeli Diplomacy and the Quest for Peace*. Portland, Ore.: Frank Cass, 2002.

———. *The Peace Process, 1969–1973: Efforts and Contacts*. Jerusalem: Magnes Press, Hebrew University, 1983.

Gershon, Baskin, and Al-Qaq Zakaria, eds. *Creating a Culture of Peace*. Jerusalem: Israel/Palestine Center for Research and Information, 1999.

Giacaman, George, and Dag Jorund Lonning, eds. *After Oslo: New Realities, Old Problems*. London: Pluto Press, 1998.

Gidron, Benjamin, Stanley N. Katz, and Yeheskel Hasenfeld, eds. *Mobilizing for Peace: Conflict Resolution in Northern Ireland, Israel/Palestine and South Africa*. New York: Oxford University Press, 2002.

Gilboa, Eytan. *Simulation of Conflict and Conflict Resolution in the Middle East*. Jerusalem: Magnes Press, 1980.

Ginat, Joseph, and Onn Winckler. *Jordanian-Palestinian-Israeli Triangle: Smoothing the Path to Peace*. Portland, Ore.: Sussex Academic Press, 1998.

Giniewski, Paul. "The Israeli-Palestinian "Peace": Root Causes and Prospects." *Midstream* 43, no. 6 (1997): 18–20.

Gopin, Marc. *Holy War, Holy Peace: How Religion Can Bring Peace to the Middle East*. New York: Oxford University Press, 2002.

Guyatt, Nicholas. *The Absence of Peace: Understanding the Israeli-Palestinian Conflict*. London: Zed Books, 1998.

———. "The Real Lesson of the Oslo Accord: Localize the Arab-Israeli Conflict." *Foreign Policy Briefing* 31, no. 9 (May 1994): 1–15.

Haddad, George Meri. *Arab Peace Efforts and the Solution of the Arab-Israeli Problem*. Detroit: Association of Arab-American University Graduates, 1976.

Haddadin, Munther J. *Diplomacy on the Jordan: International Conflict and Negotiated Resolution*. Boston: Kluwer Academic, 2001.

Hall-Cathala, David. *The Peace Movement in Israel, 1967–1987*. London: Macmillan, 1990.

Hammami, S. "A Palestinian Strategy for Peaceful Coexistence." *New Outlook* 18, no. 3 (March–April 1975): 56–61.

Hareven, Alouph, ed. *If Peace Comes: Risks and Prospects*. Jerusalem: Van Leer Jerusalem Foundation, 1978.

Hassan, Bin-Talal. *Search for Peace: The Politics of the Middle Ground in the Arab East*. New York: St. Martin's, 1984.

Hassassian, Manuel. "From Armed Struggle to Negotiation." *Palestine-Israel Journal* 1 (Winter 1994): 15–22.

Heller, Mark. *The Israeli-PLO Agreement: What If It Fails? How Will We Know?* Tel Aviv: Tel Aviv University, Jaffee Center for Strategic Studies, 1994.

———. *A Palestinian State: The Implications for Israel*. Cambridge, Mass.: Harvard University Press, 1983.

Heller, Mark, and Sari Nusseibeh. *No Trumpets, No Drums: A Two-State Settlement of the Israel-Palestinian Conflict*. New York: Hill and Wang, 1991.

Hermann, Tamar. "A Path Strewn with Thorns: Along the Difficult Road of Israeli-Palestinian Peacemaking." In *The Management of Peace Processes*, edited by John Darby and Roger MacGinty, 107–53. New York: Palgrave, 2000.

Herring, Eric. *Danger and Opportunity: Explaining International Crisis Outcomes*. Manchester, England: Manchester University Press, 1995.

Hess, Arieh. *Trilateral Confederation: A New Political Vision for Peace*. Final Status Publications Series. Jerusalem: IPCRI, 1999. Available at www.ipcri.org/files/publications_files/trilateral%20confideration.pdf.

Hollis, Rosemary, and Nadim Shehadi, eds. *Lebanon on Hold: Implications for Middle East Peace*. Oxford, England: Royal Institute of International Affairs, in association with the Centre for Lebanese Studies, 1996.

Hopmann, P. Terrence. *The Negotiation Process and the Resolution of International Conflicts*. Columbia: University of South Carolina Press, 1996.

Hussaini, H. I., ed. *Toward Peace in Palestine*. Washington, D.C.: Palestine Information Office, 1978.

Isaac, H. Shuval, ed. *Water and Peace in the Middle East*. Amsterdam: Elsevier, 1994.

Jackson, Elmore. *Middle East Mission: The Story of a Major Bid for Peace in the Time of Nasser and Ben-Gurion*. New York: W. W. Norton, 1983.

Jaffee Center for Strategic Studies, Study Group. *Israel, the West Bank and Gaza: Toward a Solution*. Tel Aviv: Tel Aviv University, Jaffee Center for Strategic Studies, 1989.

Joffe, Lawrence. *Keesing's Guide to the Mid-East Peace Process*. London: Cartermill, 1996.

Kadi, Leila S. *The Arab-Israeli Conflict: The Peaceful Proposals*. Beirut: Palestine Research Center, 1973.

Kally, Elisha. *Water and Peace: Water Resources and the Arab-Israeli Peace Process*. Westport, Conn.: Praeger, 1993.

Kaminer, Reuven. *The Politics of Protest: The Israeli Peace Movement and the Palestinian Intifada*. Brighton, England: Sussex Academic Press, 1996.

Kanovsky, Eliyahu. "Will Arab-Israeli Peace Bring Prosperity?" *Middle Eastern Quarterly* 1 (1994): 3–10.

Karmi, Ghada. *Jerusalem Today: What Future for the Peace Process?* Reading, England: Ithaca Press, 1996.

Kass, Ilana. *The Deadly Embrace: The Impact of Israeli and Palestinian Rejectionism on the Peace Process*. Lanham, Md.: University Press of America, 1997.

Kaufman, Edy. "Bringing Human Rights into the Israeli-Palestinian Peace Process." *Palestine-Israel Journal* 6, no. 1 (1999): 8–13.

———. "Human Rights and Conflict Resolution: Searching for Common Ground between Justice and Peace in the Israeli/Palestinian Conflict." *Nidr Forum* (December 1998): 16–23.

———. "Israel-Palestinian Coauthoring: A New Development toward Peace?" *Journal of Palestine Studies* 22, no. 4 (1993): 32–44.

Kaufman, Edy, Abed B. Shukri, and Robert L. Rothstein, eds. *Democracy, Peace and the Israeli-Palestinian Conflict*. Boulder, Colo.: Lynne Rienner, 1993.

Kaye, Dalia Dassa. *Beyond the Handshake: Multilateral Cooperation in the Arab-Israeli Peace Process*. New York: Columbia University Press, 2001.

Kelman, Herbert C. "Acknowledging the Other's Nationhood: How to Create a Momentum for the Israeli-Palestinian Negotiations." *Journal of Palestine Studies* 22, no. 1 (1992): 18–38.

———. "Building a Sustainable Peace: The Limits of Pragmatism in the Israeli-Palestinian Negotiations." *Journal of Palestine Studies* 28, no. 1 (1998): 36–50.

———. *Creating the Conditions for Israeli-Palestinian Negotiations.* Washington, D.C.: Wilson Center, 1981.

———. "Overcoming the Barriers to Negotiation of the Israeli-Palestinian Conflict." *Journal of Palestine Studies* 16, no. 1 (1986): 13–28.

Kemp, Geoffrey, and Jeremy Pressman. *Point of No Return: The Deadly Struggle for Middle East Peace.* Washington, D.C.: Carnegie Endowment for International Peace, in cooperation with Brookings Institution Press, 1997.

Khalidi, Rashid. "A Palestinian View of the Accord with Israel." *Current History* 93, no. 580 (February 1994): 67–71.

———. "Toward Peace in the Holy Land." *Foreign Affairs* 66, no. 4 (Spring 1988): 771–89.

Khashan, Hilal. *Partner or Pariah? Attitudes toward Peace with Israel in Syria, Lebanon and Jordan.* Washington, D.C.: Washington Institute for Near East Policy, 1996.

Khatchadourian, Haig. *The Quest for Peace between Israel and the Palestinians.* New York: Peter Lang, 2000.

Kimche, David. *The Last Option: After Nasser, Arafat and Saddam Hussein, the Quest for Peace in the Middle East.* New York: Charles Scribner's Sons, 1991.

Kimche, Jon. *There Could Have Been Peace.* New York: Dial Press, 1973.

King, John. *Handshake in Washington: The Beginning of Middle East Peace?* Reading, England: Ithaca Press, 1994.

Kleiman, Aaron S. *Compromising Palestine: A Guide to Final Status Negotiations.* New York: Columbia University Press, 2000.

———. *Constructive Ambiguity in Middle East Peace-Making.* Tel Aviv: Tel Aviv University, 1999.

———. *Israel, Jordan, Palestine: The Search for a Durable Peace.* Beverly Hills, Calif.: Sage, 1981.

Korzenny, Felipe, ed. *Communicating for Peace: Diplomacy and Negotiation.* Newbury Park, Calif.: Sage, 1990.

Kriesberg, Louis. *International Conflict Resolution: The U.S.-USSR and Middle East Cases.* New Haven, Conn.: Yale University Press, 1992.

Lapidoth, Ruth Eschelbacher. *Autonomy: Flexible Solutions to Ethnic Conflicts.* Washington, D.C.: United States Institute of Peace Press, 1997.

Lapidoth, Ruth, and Moshe Hirsch, eds. *The Arab-Israeli Conflict and Its Resolution: Selected Documents.* Dordrecht, The Netherlands: Martinus Nijhoff, 1992.

Laqueur, Walter. "Is Peace Still Possible in the Middle East? The View from Tel Aviv." *Commentary* 66, no. 1 (July 1978): 29–36.

Lefebvre, Jeffrey A. "Historical Analogies and the Israeli-Palestinian Peace Process: Munich, Camp David and Algeria." *Middle East Policy* 3, no. 1 (1994): 84–101.

Lesch, Ann Mosely. *Transition to Palestinian Self-Government: Practical Steps toward Israeli-Palestinian Peace*. Report of a Study of the Middle East Program Committee on International Security Studies, American Academy of Arts and Sciences, Cambridge, Mass. Bloomington: Indiana University Press, 1992.

Lesch, Ann Mosely, and Mark Tessler. *Israel, Egypt, and the Palestinians: From Camp David to Intifada*. Bloomington: Indiana University Press, 1988.

Lieberfeld, Daniel. "Post-Handshake Politics: Israel/Palestine and South Africa Compared." *Middle East Policy* 6, no. 3 (1999): 131–40.

———. *Talking with the Enemy: Negotiation and Threat Perception in South Africa and Israel/Palestine*. Westport, Conn.: Praeger, 1999.

Lukacs, Yehuda. *Israel, Jordan, and the Peace Process*. Syracuse, N.Y.: Syracuse University Press, 1997.

Lustick, Ian S. *From Wars toward Peace in the Arab-Israeli Conflict, 1969–1993*. New York: Garland, 1994.

———. "Necessary Risks: Lessons for the Israeli-Palestinian Peace Process from Ireland and Algeria." *Middle East Policy* 3, no. 3 (1994): 41–59.

Makovsky, David. *Making Peace with the PLO: The Rabin Government's Road to the Oslo Accord*. Boulder, Colo.: Westview Press, 1995.

Malik, Habib C. *Between Damascus and Jerusalem: Lebanon and the Middle East Peace*. Washington, D.C.: Washington Institute for Near East Policy, 1997.

Mansur, Camille. "The Palestinian-Israeli Peace Negotiations: An Overview and Assessment." *Journal of Palestine Studies* 22, no. 3 (Spring 1993): 5–31.

Ma'oz, Ifat. *Identities, Identifications, and Evaluation of Concessions in the Israeli-Palestinian Negotiations*. Jerusalem: Leonard Davis Institute for International Relations, Hebrew University, 2000.

Ma'oz, Moshe. *Syria and Israel: From War to Peacemaking*. Oxford: Clarendon Press, 1995.

Marantz, Paul, and Janice Gross Stein, eds. *Peace-Making in the Middle East: Problems and Prospects*. London: Croom Helms, 1985.

Mazzawi, Musa E. *Palestine and the Law: Guidelines for the Resolution of the Arab-Israel Conflict*. Reading, England: Ithaca Press, 1997.

Mehdi, Mohammad Taki. *Peace in the Middle East*. New York: New World Press, 1967.

Meital, Yoram. *Egypt's Struggle for Peace: Continuity and Change*. Gainesville: University Press of Florida, 1997.

Miall, Hugh. *Contemporary Conflict Resolution: The Prevention, Management and Transformation of Deadly Conflicts*. Malden, Mass.: Polity Press, 1999.

Mishal, Shaul. *Investment in Peace: Politics of Economic Cooperation between Israel, Jordan, and the Palestinian Authority*. Portland, Ore.: Sussex Academic Press, 2001.

Montell, Jessica. *Prisoners of Peace: Administrative Detention during the Oslo Process*. Jerusalem: B'tselem, 1997.

Moughrabi, Fouad, et al. "Palestinians and the Peace Process." *Journal of Palestine Studies* 21, no. 1 (Autumn 1991): 36–53.

Nachmias, Nitza. *Transfer of Arms, Leverage, and Peace in the Middle East*. New York: Greenwood Press, 1988.

Nakhleh, Emile A. "Palestinians and Israelis: Options for Coexistence." *Journal of Palestine Studies* 22, no. 2 (Winter 1989): 3–15.

Nasrallah, Hassan. "Peace Requires Departure of the Palestinians." *Middle East Insight* 15, no. 2 (2000): 29–34.

Peres, Shimon. *Battling for Peace: A Memoir*. Edited by David Landau. New York: Random House, 1995.

Peretz, Don. *Palestinian Refugees and the Middle East Peace Process*. Washington, D.C.: United States Institute of Peace, 1993.

Perry, Mark. *A Fire in Zion: The Israeli-Palestinian Search for Peace*. New York: William Morrow, 1994.

Peters, Joel. *Pathways to Peace: The Multilateral Arab-Israeli Peace Talks*. London: Royal Institute of International Affairs, 1996.

Quandt, William B. *Camp David: Peacemaking and Politics*. Washington, D.C.: Brookings Institution, 1986.

———. *The Middle East: Ten Years after Camp David*. Washington, D.C.: Brookings Institution, 1988.

———. *Peace Process: American Diplomacy and the Arab-Israeli Conflict since 1967*. Washington, D.C.: Brookings Institution, 1993.

Quigley, John B. *Flight into the Maelstrom: Soviet Immigration to Israel and Middle East Peace*. Reading, England: Ithaca Press, 1997.

Rabinovich, Itamar. *The Brink of Peace: The Israeli-Syrian Negotiations*. Princeton, N.J.: Princeton University Press, 1998.

———. *The Road Not Taken: Early Arab-Israeli Negotiations*. New York: Oxford University Press, 1991.

———. *Waging Peace: Israel and the Arabs at the End of the Century*. New York: Farrar, Straus, Giroux, 1999.

Reich, Bernard, ed. *Arab-Israeli Conflict and Conciliation: A Documentary History*. Westport, Conn.: Praeger, 1995.

Rice, Michael. *False Inheritance: Israel in Palestine and the Search for a Solution*. London: Kegan Paul International, 1994.

Rifai, Omar. *Remarks upon the Fifth Anniversary of Jordan-Israel Peace.* Jerusalem: American Jewish Committee, 1999.

Riyad, Mahmud. *The Struggle for Peace in the Middle East.* London: Quartet Books, 1981.

Rosenwasser, Penny. *Voices from a "Promised Land": Palestinian and Israeli Peace Activists Speak Their Heart.* Willimantic, Conn.: Curbstone Press, 1992.

Ross, Dennis. *The Missing Peace: The Inside Story of the Fight for the Middle East Peace.* New York: Farrar, Straus, Giroux, 2004.

Rothman, Jay Manuel. "The Human Dimension in Israeli-Palestinian Negotiations." *Jerusalem Journal of International Relations* 14, no. 3 (1992): 69–81.

———. "Negotiation as Consolidation: Prenegotiation in the Israeli-Palestinian Conflict." *Jerusalem Journal of International Relations* 13, no. 1 (1991): 22–44.

Rothstein, Robert L. *After the Peace: Resistance and Reconciliation.* Boulder, Colo.: Lynne Rienner, 1999.

Rouyer, Alwyn Rudolf. *Turning Water into Politics: The Water Issue in the Palestinian-Israeli Conflict.* New York: St. Martin's, 2000.

———. "The Water Issue in the Israeli-Palestinian Peace Process." *Survival* 39, no. 2 (1997): 57–81.

Rubin, Barry, and Joseph Ginat, eds. *From War to Peace: Arab-Israeli Relations, 1973–1993.* Brighton, England: Sussex Academic Press, 1994.

Rutherford, Evan L. *Palestinians and Israelis on Peace.* Derby, England: E. Rutherford, 1978.

Said, Edward W. *The End of the Peace Process: Oslo and After.* London: Granta Books, 2000.

———. *Peace and Its Discontents: Essays on Palestine in the Middle East Peace Process.* New York: Vintage Books, 1996.

Sanders, Jacinta. "Honest Brokers? American and Norwegian Facilitation of Israeli-Palestinian Negotiations, 1991–1993." *Arab Studies Quarterly* 21, no. 2 (1999): 47–70.

Saunders, Harold H. "An Israeli-Palestinian Peace." *Foreign Affairs* 61, no. 1 (Fall 1982): 100–121.

———. *The Other Walls: The Politics of the Arab-Israeli Peace Process.* Washington, D.C.: American Enterprise Institute for Public Policy Research, 1985.

Savir, Uri. *The Process.* New York: Random House, 1998.

Sayegh, Fayez. "The Camp David Agreement and the Palestinians." *Journal of Palestine Studies* 8, no. 2 (Winter 1979): 3–54.

———. *Camp David and Palestine: A Preliminary Analysis.* New York: Americans for Middle East Understanding, 1978.

——. *Palestine, Israel and Peace*. Beirut: Palestine Research Center, 1970.

Schaeffner, Christina, and Anita Wenden, eds. *Language and Peace*. Aldershot, England: Dartmouth, 1995.

Schoepflin, Julia. *The Arab Boycott of Israel: Can It Withstand the Peace Process?* London: Institute of Jewish Affairs, 1994.

Shalev, Aryeh. *Security Arrangements in Sinai within the Framework of a Peace Treaty with Egypt*. Tel Aviv: Center for Strategic Studies, Tel Aviv University, 1978.

Shamir, Shimon. *Two Years after the Signing of the Peace Treaty between Israel and Egypt*. Tel Aviv: Tel Aviv University, 1981.

Shlaim, Avi. "The Oslo Accords." *Journal of Palestine Studies* 23, no. 3 (Spring 1994): 24–40.

Shuval, Hillel I. "A Water for Peace Plan: Reaching an Accommodation on the Israeli-Palestinian Shared Use of the Mountain Aquifer." *Palestine-Israel Journal* 3, nos. 3–4 (1996): 74–83.

Spiegal, Steven L., ed. *The Arab-Israeli Search for Peace*. Boulder, Colo.: Westview Press, 1993.

Spielmann, Miriam. *If Peace Comes: The Future Expectations of Jewish and Arab Israeli Children and Youth*. Stockholm: Almqvist and Wiksell International, 1984.

Sprinzak, Ehud. *The Israeli Right and the Peace Process, 1992–1996*. Jerusalem: Leonard Davis Institute for International Relations, Hebrew University, 1998.

Stanly, Bruce. "Raising the Flag over Jerusalem: The Search for a Palestinian Government." *American-Arab Affairs* 26 (Fall 1988): 9–27.

Stebbing, John. *A Structure of Peace: The Arab-Israeli Conflict*. Oxford, England: New Cherwell Press, 1993.

Stein, Kenneth W. *Heroic Diplomacy: Sadat, Kissinger, Carter, Begin and the Quest for Arab-Israeli Peace*. New York: Routledge, 1999.

——. *Making Peace among Arabs and Israelis: Lessons from Fifty Years of Negotiating Experience*. Washington, D.C.: United States Institute of Peace, 1991.

Touval, Saadia. *The Peace Brokers: Mediators in the Arab-Israeli Conflict, 1948–1979*. Princeton, N.J.: Princeton University Press, 1982.

Usher, Graham. *Palestine in Crisis: The Struggle for Peace and Political Independence after Oslo*. London: Pluto Press, in association with the Transnational Institute (TNI) and Middle East Research and Information Project (MERIP), 1997.

Wolfsfeld, Gadi. *Constructing News about Peace: The Role of the Israeli Media in the Oslo Peace Process*. Tel Aviv: Tami Steinmetz Center for Peace Research, Tel Aviv University, 1997.

Wright, J. W., Jr., ed. *The Political Economy of Middle East Peace: The Impact of Competing Trade Agendas*. London: Routledge, 1999.

Zittrain-Eisenberg, Laura, and Neil Caplan. *Negotiating Arab-Israeli Peace: Patterns, Problems, Possibilities.* Bloomington: Indiana University Press, 1998.

V. THE POLITICS OF ISRAEL

Abir, Mordechai. *Sharm Al-Sheikh–Bab Al-Mandeb: The Strategic Balance and Israel's Southern Approaches.* Jerusalem: Leonard Davis Institute for International Relations, Hebrew University, 1974.

Abu-Lughod, Janet. "Israeli Settlements in the Occupied Arab Land: Conquest to Colony." *Journal of Palestine Studies* 10, no. 2 (Winter 1982): 16–54.

Alpher, Joseph. *Israel's Lebanon Policy: Where To?* Memorandum no. 12. Tel Aviv: Jaffee Center for Strategic Studies, Tel Aviv University, 1984.

Amnesty International. *Israel and the Occupied Territories: Amnesty International Concerns in 1988.* New York: Amnesty International, 1989.

Arian, Asher. *Security Threatened: Surveying Israeli Opinion on Peace and War.* Cambridge: Jaffee Center for Strategic Studies, Tel Aviv University, and Cambridge University Press, 1995.

Arian, Asher, et al. "Public Opinion and Political Change: Israel and the Intifadah." *Comparative Politics* 24, no. 3 (April 1992): 317–34.

Aronson, Shlomo. *Making Peace with the Land: Designing Israel's Landscape.* Washington, D.C.: Spacemaker, 1998.

Aruri, Nasser, ed. *Occupation: Israel over Palestine.* Belmont, Mass.: Association of Arab-American University Graduates, 1989.

Avnery, Uri. *Israel without Zionism: A Plan for Peace in the Middle East.* New York: Collier Books, 1971.

——. *My Friend, the Enemy.* London: Zed Books, 1985.

Bar-On, Mordechai. "The Israeli-Palestinian Conflict—A Zionist Perspective." *New Outlook* 34, no. 2 (1991): 33–35.

Bar-Siman-Tov, Yaacov. *Israel and the Peace Process, 1977–1982: In Search of Legitimacy for Peace.* Albany: State University of New York Press, 1994.

——. *Peace Policy as Domestic and as Foreign Policy: The Israeli Case.* Jerusalem: Leonard Davis Institute for International Relations, Hebrew University, 1998.

——. *Uncertainty and Risk-Taking in Peacemaking: The Israeli Experience.* Jerusalem: Leonard Davis Institute of International Relations, Hebrew University, 1999.

Barzilai, Gad. *Wars, Internal Conflict and Political Order: A Jewish Democracy in the Middle East.* Albany: State University of New York Press, 1996.

Bawly, Dan, and Eliahu Salpeter. *Fire in Beirut: Israel's War in Lebanon with the PLO*. New York: Stein and Day, 1984.

Beinin, Joel. *The Dispersion of Egyptian Jewry: Culture, Politics, and the Formation of a Modern Diaspora*. Berkeley: University of California Press, 1998.

Ben-Eliezer, Uri. *The Making of Israeli Militarism*. Bloomington: Indiana University Press, 1998.

Bialer, Uri. *Our Place in the World: Mapai and Israel's Foreign Policy Orientation, 1947–1952*. Jerusalem: Magnes Press, 1981.

Black, Ian. *Israel's Secret Wars: A History of Israel's Intelligence Services*. New York: Grove Weidenfeld, 1991.

Bloch-Tzemach, Dalit. *"Dwelling-Tourism": The Case of Israelis in Japan*. Jerusalem: Harry S. Truman Research Institute for the Advancement of Peace, Hebrew University, 2002.

Brecher, Michael. *Decisions in Israel's Foreign Policy*. New Haven, Conn.: Yale University Press, 1975.

Coates, Ken, ed. *Israel and Palestine: Human Rights in Israel and in the Occupied Territories*. Nottingham, England: Bertrand Russell Peace Foundation, 1985.

Cohen, Avner. *Israel and the Bomb*. New York: Columbia University Press, 1998.

Curtis, Michael, ed. *Israel: Social Structure and Change*. New Brunswick, N.J.: Transaction Books, 1973.

Dan, Uri. *To the Promised Land: The Bird of Israel*. New York: Doubleday, 1988.

DeGaury, Gerald. *The New State of Israel*. New York: Praeger, 1952.

Diskin, Abraham. *Voters' Attitudes on the Arab-Israeli Conflict and the 1996 Elections*. Jerusalem: Leonard Davis Institute for International Relations, Hebrew University, 1999.

Elath, Eliahu. *Israel and Her Neighbors*. London: James Barrie, 1956.

Elizur, Yuval. "Israel Banks on a Fence." *Foreign Affairs* 82, no. 2 (2003): 106–19.

Elston, D. R. *Israel: The Making of a Nation*. Oxford: Oxford University Press, 1963.

Eshkol, Levi. *Israel's Peace Plan: A Statement by Mr. Levi Eshkol, Prime Minister of Israel in the Knesset, 17 May 1965*. Jerusalem: Israel Ministry for Foreign Affairs, 1965.

Fein, Leonard J. *Israel: Politics and People*. Boston: Little, Brown, 1968.

Feldman, Shai, and Heda Rechnitz-Kijner. *Deception, Consensus and War: Israel in Lebanon*. Paper no. 27. Tel Aviv: Jaffee Center for Strategic Studies, Tel Aviv University, 1984.

Gordon, Haim. *Dance, Dialogue, and Despair: Existentialist Philosophy and Education for Peace in Israel*. University: University of Alabama Press, 1986.

Haidar, Aziz. *The Arab Population in the Israeli Economy*. Tel Aviv: International Center for Peace in the Middle East, 1990.

------. *Social Welfare Services for Israel's Arab Population*. Boulder, Colo.: Westview Press, 1991.

Haj, Majid. *Arab Local Government in Israel*. Boulder, Colo.: Westview Press, 1990.

Harkabi, Yehoshafat. *Israel's Fateful Decisions*. London: I. B. Tauris, 1988.

Harris, William Wilson. *Taking Roots: Israeli Settlements in the West Bank, the Golan and Gaza-Sinai, 1967–1980*. Letchworth, England: John Wiley and Sons, 1980.

Hazan, Reuven Y. *The Labor Party and the Peace Process: Partisan Disintegration amid Political Cohesion*. Jerusalem: Leonard Davis Institute for International Relations, Hebrew University, 1998.

Hilterman, Joost. "Israel's Strategy to Break the Uprising." *Journal of Palestine Studies* 19, no. 2 (Winter 1990): 87–98.

Hollis, Rosemary. *Israel on the Brink of Decision: Division, Unity and Crosscurrents in the Israeli Body Politic*. London: Research Institute for the Study of Conflict and Terrorism, 1990.

Horowitz, Dan. *Israel's Concept of Defensible Borders*. Jerusalem: Leonard Davis Institute for International Relations, Hebrew University, 1975.

Hunter, Jane. *Israeli Foreign Policy: South African and Central America*. Nottingham, England: Spokesman for the Bertrand Russell Peace Foundation, 1987.

IDF Journal. *Peace for Galilee*. Tel Aviv: Israel Defense Forces, 1982.

Inbar, Efraim. "Israel and Lebanon, 1975–1982." *Crossroads*, no. 10 (1983): 39–80.

------. *Israel in the Region*. Ramat Gan, Israel: BESA Center for Strategic Studies, Bar Ilan University, 2001.

------. *Rabin and Israel's National Security*. Washington, D.C.: Woodrow Wilson Center Press, 1999.

------, ed. *Regional Security Regimes: Israel and Its Neighbors*. Albany: State University of New York Press, 1995.

------. *War and Peace in Israeli Politics: Labor Party Positions on National Security*. Boulder, Colo.: Lynne Rienner, 1991.

Jansen, Michel E. *The Battle of Beirut: Why Israel Invaded Lebanon*. Boston: South End, 1983.

Jastrow, Morris. *Zionism and the Future of Palestine: The Fallacies and Dangers of Political Zionism*. New York: Macmillan, 1919.

Karsh, Efraim, ed. *Between War and Peace: Dilemmas of Israeli Security*. London: Frank Cass, 1996.

------, ed. *From Rabin to Netanyahu: Israel's Troubled Agenda*. London: Frank Cass, 1997.

——, ed. *Israel: The First Hundred Years.* 4 vols. London: Frank Cass, 2000–2004.

Kieval, Gershan R. *Party Politics in Israel and the Occupied Territories.* Westport, Conn.: Greenwood Press, 1983.

Kimmerling, Baruch. *A Conceptual Framework for the Analysis of Behavior in a Territorial Conflict: The Generalization of the Israeli Case.* Jerusalem: Leonard Davis Institute for International Relations, Hebrew University, 1979.

Kishtainy, Khalid. *Whither Israel? A Study of Zionist Expansionism.* Beirut: Palestine Research Center, 1970.

Klein, Yitzhak. *Israel's War with the Palestinians: Sources, Political Objectives, and Operational Means.* Shaarei Tikva, Israel: Ariel Center for Policy Research, 2001.

Kop, Yaakov. *Sticking Together: The Israeli Experiment in Pluralism.* Washington, D.C.: Brookings Institution Press, 2002.

Kretzmer, David. *The Legal Status of the Arabs in Israel.* Tel Aviv: International Center for Peace in the Middle East, 1987.

Kumaraswamy, P R. *Beyond the Veil: Israel-Pakistan Relations.* Memorandum no. 55. Tel Aviv: Jaffee Centre for Strategic Studies, 2000.

——. *Political Legitimacy of the Minorities: Israeli Arabs and the 1996 Knesset Elections.* Emirates Occasional Paper no. 20. Abu Dhabi: Emirates Centre for Strategic Studies Research, 1998.

Kurzman, Dan. *Soldier of Peace: The Life of Yitzhak Rabin.* New York: HarperCollins, 1998.

Lesch, Ann. "Israeli Settlements in the Occupied Territories." *Journal of Palestine Studies* 8, no. 1 (Autumn 1978): 100–119.

Levey, Zach. *Israel and the Western Powers, 1952–1960.* Chapel Hill: University of North Carolina Press, 1997.

Levran, Aharon. *The Decline of Israeli Deterrence.* Shaarei Tikva, Israel: Ariel Centre for Policy Research, 2001.

Levy, Yagil. *Trial and Error: Israel's Route from War to De-Escalation.* Albany: State University of New York Press, 1997.

Lilienthal, Alfred M. *The Zionist Connection: What Price Peace?* New York: Dodd Mead, 1978.

Lopes, Cardozo, and T. Nathan. *Between Silence and Speech: Essays on Jewish Thought.* Northvale, N.J.: Jason Aronson, 1995.

Mandelbaum, Michael. *Israel and the Occupied Territories: A Personal Report on the Uprising.* New York: Council on Foreign Relations, 1988.

Masalha, Nur. *Imperial Israel and the Palestinians: The Politics of Expansion, 1967–2000.* Sterling, Va.: Pluto Press, 2000.

Matar, Ibrahim. "Israeli Settlements in the West Bank and Gaza Strip." *Journal of Palestine Studies* 11, no. 1 (Autumn 1981): 93–110.

McCormack, Timothy L. H. *Self-Defense in International Law: The Israeli Raid on the Iraqi Nuclear Reactor.* New York: St. Martin's, 1996.

Milgram, Norman A., ed. *Stress and Coping in Time of War: Generalizations from the Israeli Experience.* New York: Brunner/Mazel, 1986.

Milson, Menahem. *Israel's Policy in the West Bank and Gaza Strip.* Washington, D.C.: Wilson Center, 1986.

Navon, Emmanuel. *The Foreign Policy of Israel from the Yom Kippur War to the Oslo Agreements (1973–1993): Between National Identity and Political Interest.* Jerusalem: Hebrew University, 2000.

Nazzal, Nafez. *Policies of the Israeli Occupation in the West Bank.* Working Papers no. 46. Washington, D.C.: Woodrow Wilson Center, 1983.

Netanyahu, Binyamin. *A Place among the Nations: Israel and the World.* New York: Bantam Books, 1993.

Newman, David, ed. *The Impact of Gush Emunim: Politics and Settlement in the West Bank.* London: Croom Helm, 1985.

——. *Jewish Settlements in the West Bank: The Role of Gush Emunim.* Durham, England: Centre for Middle Eastern Studies, University of Durham, 1982.

——. *Population, Settlement and Conflict: Israel and the West Bank.* Cambridge: Cambridge University Press, 1991.

Nisan, Mordechai. *Toward a New Israel: The Jewish State and the Arab Question.* New York: Ams Press, 1992.

Norton, Augustus Richard. "Israel and South Lebanon." *American-Arab Affairs,* no. 100 (1984): 23–31.

——. "Occupation Risks and Planned Retirement: The Israeli Withdrawal from South Lebanon." *Middle East Insight* 4 (1985): 14–18.

O'Brien, William V. "Israel in Lebanon." *Middle East Review* 15 (1982–83): 5–14.

Peretz, Don. *Israel and the Palestine Arabs.* Washington, D.C.: Middle East Institute, 1958.

Peri, Yoram. *The Israeli Military and Israel's Palestinian Policy: From Oslo to the Al Aqsa Intifada.* Washington, D.C.: United States Institute of Peace, 2002.

Podeh, Elie. *The Arab-Israeli Conflict in Israeli History Textbooks, 1948–2000.* Westport, Conn.: Bergin and Garvey, 2001.

Portugali, Juval. "Jewish Settlement in the Occupied Territories: Israel's Settlement Structure and the Palestinians." *Political Geography Quarterly* 10, no. 1 (January 1991): 26–53.

Posner, Steve. *Israel Undercover: Secret Warfare and Hidden Diplomacy in the Middle East.* Syracuse, N.Y.: Syracuse University Press, 1987.

Rabin, Yitzhak. *The Rabin Memoir.* Berkeley: University of California Press, 1996.

Rafael, Gideon. *Destination Peace: Three Decades of Israeli Foreign Policy; A Personal Memoir*. London: Weidenfeld and Nicolson, 1981.

Rejwan, Nissim. *Israel in Search of Identity: Reading the Formative Years*. Gainesville: University Press of Florida, 1999.

———. *Israel's Place in the Middle East: A Pluralist Perspective*. Gainesville: University Press of Florida, 1998.

Rodinson, Maxime. *Israel and the Arabs*. New York: Pantheon Books, 1968.

Rouhana, Nadim. "The Intifada and the Palestinians of Israel: Resurrecting the Green Line." *Journal of Palestine Studies* 19, no. 3 (Spring 1990): 58–75.

Ryan, Sheila. "Israel's Invasion of Lebanon: Background to the Crisis." *Journal of Palestine Studies* 11 (1982): 23–37.

Sabella, Bernard. "Russian Jewish Immigration and the Future of Israeli–Palestinian Conflict." *Middle East Report* 182 (1993): 36–40.

St. John, Robert. *Shalom Means Peace*. Garden City, N.Y.: Doubleday, 1949.

Schiff, Ze'ev, and Ehud Ya'ari. *Intifada: The Palestinian Uprising—Israel's Third Front*. New York: Simon and Schuster, 1990.

———. *Israel's Lebanon War*. New York: Simon and Schuster, 1984.

Sefer, Sasson, ed. *Peacemaking in a Divided Society: Israel after Rabin*. Portland, Ore.: Frank Cass, 2001.

Sella, Amnon. *Israel the Peaceful Belligerent, 1967–1979*. New York: Macmillan, 1986.

Shafir, Gershon, and Yoav Peled, eds. *The New Israel: Peacemaking and Liberalization*. Boulder, Colo.: Westview Press, 2000.

Shalom, Zaki. *David Ben-Gurion, The State of Israel and the Arab World, 1949–1956*. Portland, Ore.: Sussex Academic Press, 2002.

Shamir, Jacob. *The Dynamics of Israeli Public Opinion on Peace and the Territories*. Tel Aviv: Tami Steinmetz Center for Peace Research, Tel Aviv University, 1993.

Sherman, Martin. *The Politics of Water in the Middle East: An Israeli Perspective on the Hydro-Political Aspects of the Conflict*. New York: St. Martin's, 1999.

Shindler, Colin. *Ploughshares into Swords? Israelis and Jews in the Shadow of the Intifada*. London: I. B. Tauris, 1991.

Slater, Robert. *Rabin of Israel: Warrior for Peace*. London: Robson, 1996.

Stav, Arieh, ed. *Israel and a Palestinian State: Zero-Sum Game?* Tel Aviv: Zmora-Bitan, 2001.

Tekoah, Yosef. *In the Face of the Nations: Israel's Struggle for Peace*. New York: Simon and Schuster, 1976.

Teveth, Shabtai. *Ben-Gurion's Spy: The Story of the Political Scandal That Shaped Modern Israel*. New York: Columbia University Press, 1996.

Timerman, Jacob. *The Longest War: Israel in Lebanon*. New York: Knopf, 1982.

Uri, Pierre Emmanuel. *Israel and the Common Market.* Jerusalem: Weidenfeld and Nicolson, 1971.

Verrier, June. *Israel's Lebanon War and Its Aftermath.* Basic Paper no. 11. Canberra, Australia: Department of Parliamentary Library, 1982.

Yaniv, Avner. *Dilemmas of Security: Politics, Strategy and the Israeli Experience in Lebanon.* New York: Oxford University Press, 1987.

Yishai, Yael. *Land or Peace: Whither Israel?* Stanford, Calif.: Hoover Institution Press, 1987.

Yorke, Valerie. *Domestic Politics and Regional Security: Jordan, Syria and Israel—The End of an Era?* Aldershot, England: Gower, for the International Institute for Strategic Studies, 1988.

Yuchtman-Yaar, Ephraim. *Between Consent and Dissent: Democracy and Peace in the Israeli Mind.* Lanham, Md.: Rowman and Littlefield, 2000.

VI. PALESTINIAN POLITICS

Abdul Hamid, Ra'ed. *Legal and Political Aspects of Palestinian Elections.* Jerusalem: Israel/Palestine Center for Research and Information, Law and Development Program, 1995.

Abed Rabbo, Samir, and Doris Safi, eds. *The Palestinian Uprising.* Belmont, Mass.: Association of Arab-American University Graduates, 1990.

Abu-Amr, Ziad. "Hamas: A Historical and Political Background." *Journal of Palestine Studies* 22, no. 4 (Summer 1993): 5–19.

——. *The Intifada: Causes and Factors of Continuity.* Jerusalem: PASSIA, 1989.

——. *Islamic Fundamentalism in the West Bank and Gaza: Muslim Brotherhood and Islamic Jihad.* Bloomington.: Indiana University Press, 1994.

——. "The Palestinian Uprising in the West Bank and Gaza Strip." *Arab Studies Quarterly* 10 (1988): 384–405.

Ahmad, Hisham H. *From Religious Salvation to Political Transformation: The Rise of Hamas in Palestinian Society.* Jerusalem: PASSIA, 1994.

al-Jarbawi, Ali. "The Position of Palestinian Islamists on the Palestine-Israel accord." *Muslim World* 83, nos. 1–2 (January–April 1994): 127–54.

Al-Khalidi, Walid. *Palestine Reborn.* London: I. B. Tauris, 1992.

Amos, John W. *Palestinian Resistance: Organization of a Nationalist Movement.* New York: Pergamon Press, 1980.

Andoni, Lamis. "The PLO at the Crossroad." *Journal of Palestine Studies* 21, no. 1 (Autumn 1991): 54–65.

Aruri, Nasser. *The Intifada.* Brattleboro, Vt.: Amana Books, 1989.

——, ed. *Palestinian Refugees: The Right of Return.* Sterling, Va.: Pluto Press, 2001.

————. *The Palestinian Resistance to Israeli Occupation*. Wilmette, Ill.: Medina University Press International, 1970.

Aruri, Nasser H., and John J. Carroll. "A New Palestinian Charter." *Journal of Palestine Studies* 23, no. 4 (Summer 1994): 5–17.

Arzt, Donna E. *Refugees into Citizens: Palestinians and the End of the Arab-Israeli Conflict*. New York: Council on Foreign Relations, 1997.

Aumann, Moshe. *The Palestinian Labyrinth: A Way Out*. Jerusalem: Israel Academic Committee on the Middle East, 1982.

Bahiri, Simcha. "Palestinian Industrial Development and Israeli-Palestinian Attitudes to Cooperation." *Palestine-Israel Journal* 4 (1994): 74–81.

Bailey, Clinton. *Hamas: The Fundamentalist Challenge to the PLO*. Washington, D.C.: Institute for Near East Policy Research, 1992.

Bassiouni, M. Cherif, and Louise Cainkar, eds. *The Palestinian Intifada, December 9, 1987–December 8, 1988: A Record of Israeli Repression*. Chicago: Data Base Project on Palestinian Human Rights, 1989.

Becker, Jillian. *The PLO: The Rise and Fall of the Palestine Liberation Organization*. New York: St. Martin's, 1984.

Ben-Dor, Gabriel ed. *The Palestinians and the Middle East Conflict: Studies in Their History, Sociology and Politics*. Ramat Gan, Israel: Turtledove, 1979.

Bennis, Phyllis, and Neal Cassidy. *From Stones to Statehood: The Palestinian Uprising*. London: Zed Books, 1990.

Ben-Ze'ev, Efrat. *Narratives of Exile: Palestinian Refugee Reflections on Three Villages—Tirat Haifa, Ein Hawd and Ijzim*. Oxford, England: Efrat Ben-Ze'ev, 2000.

Bishara, Azmy. "The Israeli-Palestinian Conflict—A Palestinian Perspective." *New Outlook* 34, no. 2 (1991): 33–35.

Bowden, T. "The Politics of the Arab Rebellion in Palestine, 1936–1939." *Middle East Studies* 11, no. 2 (March 1975): 147–74.

Brynen, Rex. "PLO Policy in Lebanon: Legacies and Lessons." *Journal of Palestine Studies* 18, no. 2 (Winter 1989): 48–70.

————. *Sanctuary and Survival: The PLO in Lebanon*. Boulder, Colo.: Westview Press, 1990.

Carey, Roane, ed. *The New Intifada: Resisting Israel's Apartheid*. London: Verso, 2001.

Cattan, Henry. *The Palestine Question*. London: Croom Helm, 1987.

Chaliand, Gerard. *The Palestinian Resistance*. Baltimore: Penguin Books, 1972.

Cheal, Beryle. "Refugees in the Gaza Strip, December 1948–May 1950." *Journal of Palestine Studies* 18, no. 1 (Autumn 1988): 138–57.

Cobban, Helena. *The Palestinian Liberation Organization: People, Power and Politics*. New York: Columbia University Press, 1984.

————. "The PLO and the Intifada." *Middle East Journal* 44, no. 2 (Spring 1990): 207–33.

Cooley, John K. *Green March, Black September: The Story of the Palestinian Arab*. London: Frank Cass, 1973.

Cossali, Paul, and Clive Robson. *Stateless in Gaza*. London: Zed Press, 1986.

Crowers, Andrew, and Tony Walker. *Behind the Myth: Yassir Arafat and the Palestinian Revolution*. Brooklyn, N.Y.: Olive Branch Press, 1991.

Cubert, Harold M. *The PFLP's Changing Role in the Middle East*. London: Frank Cass, 1997.

Curtis, Michael, Joseph Neyer, Chaim I. Waxman, and Allen Pollack, eds. *The Palestinians: People, History, Politics*. New Brunswick, N.J.: Transaction Books, 1975.

Diwan, Ishac. "Palestine between Israel and Jordan: The Economics of an Uneasy Triangle." *Beirut Review* 8 (1994): 21–44.

Dobson, Christopher. *Black September: Its Short, Violent History*. New York: Macmillan, 1974.

Dodd, Peter, and Halim Barakat. *River without Bridges: A Study of the Exodus of the 1967 Palestinian Arab Refugees*. Beirut: Institute for Palestine Studies, 1969.

Elpeleg, Z. *The Grand Mufti: Haj Amin al-Hussaini, Founder of the Palestinian National Movement*. London: Frank Cass, 1993.

Emerson, Gloria J. *Gaza: A Year in the Intifada—A Personal Account from an Occupied Land*. New York: Atlantic Monthly Press, 1991.

Emery, Michael. "Press Coverage of the Palestinian Intifada." *Journal of Arab Affairs* 7 (Fall 1988): 199–205.

Epp, Frank H. *Palestinians: Portrait of a People in Conflict*. Toronto: McClelland and Stewart, 1976.

Farsoun, Samih Khalil, and Christina E. Zacharia. *Palestine and the Palestinians*. Boulder, Colo.: Westview Press, 1997.

Ferber, Elizabeth. *Yasir Arafat: A Life of War and Peace*. Brookfield, Conn.: Millbrook, 1995.

Finkelstein, Norman. "Reflections on Palestinian Attitudes during Gulf War." *Journal of Palestine Studies* 21, no. 3 (Spring 1992): 54–70.

Flapan, Simha. "The Palestinian Exodus, 1948." *Journal of Palestine Studies* 16, no. 4 (Summer 1987): 3–26.

———. *Zionism and the Palestinians*. New York: Barnes and Noble, 1979.

Frangi, Abdallah. *The PLO and Palestine*. London: Zed Books, 1983.

Freedman, Robert O., ed. *The Intifada: Its Impact on Israel, the Arab World and the Superpowers*. Miami: Florida International University Press, 1991.

Friedman, Robert I. "The Palestinian Refugees." *New York Review of Books* 37 (29 March 1990): 36–44.

Frisch, Hillel. *Countdown to Statehood: Palestinian State Formation in the West Bank and Gaza*. Albany: State University of New York Press, 1998.

Genet, Jean. "The Palestinians." *Journal of Palestine Studies* 9, no. 1 (Autumn 1973): 3–34.

Gilmour, David. *Dispossessed: The Ordeal of the Palestinians, 1917–1980.* London: Sidgwick and Jackson, 1980.

Gowers, Andrew. *Behind the Myth: Yasser Arafat and the Palestinian Revolution.* Brooklyn, N.Y.: Olive Branch Press, 1992.

Gresh, Alain. *The PLO: The Struggle Within; Towards an Independent Palestinian State.* London: Zed Books, 1988.

Groth, Alon. *The PLO's Road to Peace: Processes of Decision-Making.* London: Royal United Services Institute for Defence Studies, 1995.

Haj-Yahya, Yusuf Mahmud. *Alleged Palestinian Collaborators with Israel and Their Families: A Study of Victims of Internal Political Violence.* Jerusalem: Harry S. Truman Research Institute for the Advancement of Peace, Hebrew University, 1999.

Hallaj, Muhammad. "Palestinians after the Gulf War." *American-Arab Affairs*, no. 35 (Winter 1990–91): 117–25.

———. "Taking Sides: Palestinians and the Gulf Crisis." *Journal of Palestine Studies* 20, no. 3 (Spring 1991): 41–47.

Hanf, Theodor. *A Date with Democracy: Palestinians on Society and Politics; An Empirical Survey.* Bernard Sabella; in Collaboration With Petra Bauerle; Translated From German By John Richardson. Freiburg, Germany: Arnold Bergstraesser Institut, 1996.

Harkabi, Yehoshafat. *The Position of the Palestinians in the Israeli-Arab Conflict and Their National Covenant (1968): An Israeli Commentary.* New York: S. N., 1970.

Hart, Alan. *Arafat: A Political Biography.* Bloomington: Indiana University Press, 1989.

———. *Arafat: Terrorist or Peacemaker?* London: Sidgwick and Jackson, 1984.

Harub, Khalid. *Hamas: Political Thought and Practice.* Washington, D.C.: Institute for Palestine Studies, 2000.

Hilal, Jamil. "PLO Institutions: The Challenge Ahead." *Journal of Palestine Studies* 23, no. 1 (Autumn 1993): 46–60.

Hunter, Robert. *The Palestinian Uprising: A War by Other Means.* Berkeley: University of California Press, 1991.

Inbar, Efraim, and Shmuel Sandler. *The Risks of Palestinian Statehood.* Ramat Gan, Israel: BESA Center for Strategic Studies, Bar Ilan University, 1997.

Institute for Palestine Studies. *The Palestinian Refugees: A Collection of United Nations Documents.* Beirut: Institute of Palestine Studies, 1970.

Israeli, Raphael. *Palestinians between Israel and Jordan: Squaring the Triangle.* New York: Praeger, 1991.

———, ed. *PLO in Lebanon: Selected Documents*. New York: St. Martin's, 1983.

Iyad, Abu, with Eric Rouleau. *My Home, My Land: A Narrative of Palestinian Struggle*. New York: Times Books, 1981.

Jbara, Taysir. *Palestinian Leader Hajj Amin al-Husayni, Mufti of Jerusalem*. Princeton, N.J.: Kingston Press, 1985.

Kamin, J. "The PLO in the Aftermath of Rebellion." *SAIS Review* 5, no. 1 (Winter–Spring 1985): 91–105.

Kawar, Amal. *Daughters of Palestine: Leading Women of the Palestinian National Movement*. Albany: State University of New York Press, 1996.

Kelman, Herbert. *Understanding Arafat*. Tel Aviv: International Center for Peace in the Middle East, 1983.

Khalidi, Rashid. "The Palestinians in Lebanon: Social Repercussions of Israel's Invasion." *Middle East Journal* 38 (1984): 255–66.

———. *Under Siege: PLO Decision Making during the 1982 War*. New York: Columbia University Press, 1986.

———. "The Uprising and the Palestine Question." *World Policy Journal* 5, no. 3 (Summer 1998): 497–518.

Khalidi, Walid. *Palestine Reborn*. London: I. B. Tauris, 1992.

Khoury, Laura Giries. *Variations in the Tendencies toward Cultural Normalization among the Palestinians Living in the West Bank and Gaza Strip after the Peace Process*. Ann Arbor, Mich.: UMI, 2001.

Kimmerling, Baruch. *The Palestinian People: A History*. Cambridge, Mass.: Harvard University Press, 2003.

Laffin, John. *The PLO Connections*. London: Coegi Books, 1982.

Lalor, Paul. *Towards a Palestinian Entity*. London: Royal Institute of International Affairs, 1989.

Lederman, Jim. "Dateline West Bank: Interpreting the Intifada." *Foreign Policy* 72 (Fall 1998): 230–46.

Lehn, Walter. *The Development of Palestinian Resistance*. North Dartmouth, Mass.: Association of Arab-American Graduates, 1974.

Lesch, Ann Mosely. "Prelude to the Uprising in the Gaza Strip." *Journal of Palestine Studies* 20, no. 1 (Autumn 1990): 1–23.

———. *Transition to Palestinian Self-Government*. Bloomington: Indiana University Press, 1992.

Levitt, Wendy. *Intifada: The Palestinians Popular Uprising*. London: Kegan Paul International, 1989.

Litvak, Meir. "Palestinian Leadership in the Territories during the Intifada, 1987–1992." *Orient* 34, no. 2 (June 1993): 199–220.

Lockman, Zachary, and Joel Beinin, eds. *Intifada: The Palestinian Uprising against Israeli Occupation*. Boston: South End Press, 1989.

Lustick, Ian S. "Writing the Intifada: Collective Action in the Occupied Territories." *World Politics* 45, no. 4 (July 1993): 560–94.

Maksoud, Clovis. "The Implications of the Palestinian Uprising: Where from Here?" *American-Arab Affairs* 26 (Fall 1988): 50–55.

Ma'oz, Moshe, ed. *Palestinian Arab Politics*. Jerusalem: Academic Press, 1975.

——. *Palestinian Leadership on the West Bank*. London: Frank Cass, 1984.

Marshall, Phil. *Intifada, Zionism, Imperialism and the Palestinian Resistance*. Chicago: Bookmarks, 1989.

Marx, Emanuel. "Palestinian Refugee Camps in the West Bank and the Gaza Strip." *Middle Eastern Studies* 28, no. 2 (April 1992): 281–94.

Mattar, Philip. "The PLO and the Gulf Crisis." *Middle East Journal* 48, no. 1 (Winter 1994): 31–46.

McDowall, David. *Palestine and Israel: The Uprising and Beyond*. Berkeley: University of California Press, 1989.

Miller, Aaron David. "The Future of Palestinian Nationalism." *Middle East Insight* 3, no. 5 (July–August 1984): 23–29.

——. "Palestinians and the Intifada: One Year Later." *Current History* 88 (February 1989): 73–76, 106–7.

——. "The PLO and Peace Process: The Organizational Imperative." *SAIS Review* 7, no. 1 (Winter–Spring 1987): 95–109.

——. *The PLO and the Politics of Survival*. New York: Praeger Publications, with the Center for Strategic and International Studies, Georgetown University, 1983.

Milton-Edwards, Beverley. *Islamic Politics in Palestine*. London: I. B. Tauris, 1999.

Mishal, Shaul. *The PLO under Arafat: Between Gun and Olive Branch*. New Haven, Conn.: Yale University Press, 1986.

Mishal, Shaul, and Avraham Sela. *The Palestinian Hamas: Vision, Violence and Coexistence*. New York: Columbia University Press, 2000.

Morris, Benny. *The Birth of the Palestinian Refugee Problem, 1947–1949*. Cambridge: Cambridge University Press, 1988.

Musallem, Sami. *The Palestine Liberation Organization: Its Structure and Function*. Brattleboro, Vt.: Amana Books, 1988.

Muslih, Muhammad. "The Shift in Palestinian Thinking." *Current History* 91, no. 561 (January 1992): 22–28.

Nakhleh, Emile A. "The West Bank and Gaza: People, Perceptions and Policies." *American-Arab Affairs*, no. 1 (Summer 1982): 95–103.

——. *The West Bank and Gaza: Toward the Making of a Palestinian State*. Washington, D.C.: American Enterprise Institute, 1979.

——. "The West Bank and Gaza: Twenty Years Later." *Middle East Journal* 42, no. 2 (Spring 1988): 209–26.

Nakhleh, Khalil. *Palestinian Struggle under Occupation*. Belmont, Mass.: Association of Arab-American University Graduates, 1980.

Nassar, Jamal R. *The Palestine Liberation Organization: From Armed Struggle to Declaration of Independence.* London: Eurospan, 1992.

Nassar, Jamal R., and Roger Heacock, eds. *Intifada: Palestine at the Crossroads.* New York: Praeger, 1990.

Nazzal, Nafez, and Laila Nazzal. *A Historical Dictionary of Palestine.* Lanham, Md.: Scarecrow Press, 1997.

Nuesse, Andrea. *Muslim Palestine: The Ideology of Hamas.* London: Routledge Curzon, 2002.

O'Ballance, Edgar. *The Palestinian Intifada.* New York: St. Martin's, 1998.

Palumbo, Michael. *The Palestinian Catastrophe: The 1948 Expulsion of a People from Their Homeland.* London: Faber and Faber, 1987.

Peretz, Don. "Arab Palestine: Phoenix or Phantom?" *Foreign Affairs* 48, no. 2 (January 1970): 322–33.

——. *Intifada: The Palestinian Uprising.* Boulder, Colo.: Westview Press, 1990.

——. *The Palestine Arab Refugee Problem.* Santa Monica, Calif.: Rand, 1969.

——. *The West Bank: History, Politics, Society and Economy.* Boulder, Colo.: Westview Press, 1986.

Pipes, Daniel. "Declaring Statehood: Israel and the PLO." *Orbis* 33, no. 2 (Spring 1989): 247–59.

Plascov, Avi. *The Palestinian Refugees in Jordan, 1948–1957.* London: Frank Cass, 1981.

——. *A Palestinian State? Examining the Alternative.* Adelphi Papers, no. 163. London: International Institute for Strategic Studies, 1981.

Porath, Yehoshua. *The Emergence of the Palestinian National Movement, 1918–1929.* London: Frank Cass, 1973.

Pressberg, Gail. "The Uprising: Causes and Consequences." *Journal of Palestine Studies* 17, no. 3 (Spring 1988): 38–50.

Price, D. "Jordan and Palestinians: The PLO's Prospects" *Conflict Studies* 66 (December 1975): 525–56.

Quandt, William. "The Uprising: Breaking a Ten-Year Deadlock." *American-Arab Affairs* 27 (Winter 1988–89): 18–28.

Reische, Diana L. *Arafat and the Palestine Liberation Organization.* New York: F. Watts, 1991.

Roy, Sara. "From Hardship to Hunger: The Economic Impact of the Intifada on the Gaza Strip." *American-Arab Affairs* 3 (1990): 109–32.

Rubenstein, Danny. "The Political and Social Impact of the Intifada on Palestinian Arab Society." *Jerusalem Quarterly*, no. 52 (Autumn 1989): 3–17.

Rubin, Barry M. *Revolution until Victory? The Politics and History of the PLO.* Cambridge, Mass.: Harvard University Press, 1994.

——. *The Transformation of Palestinian Politics: From Revolution to State-Building.* Cambridge, Mass.: Harvard University Press, 1999.

Rubinstein, Danny. *The Mystery of Arafat*. South Royalton, Vt.: Steerforth Press, 1995.
Sahliyeh, Emile. *In Search of Leadership: West Bank Politics since 1967*. Washington, D.C.: Brookings Institution, 1988.
———. *The PLO after the Lebanon War*. Boulder, Colo.: Westview Press, 1986.
Said, Edward W. *The Politics of Dispossession: The Struggle for Palestinian Self-Determination, 1969–1994*. London: Chatto and Windus, 1994.
Sayigh, Yezid. "Struggle Within, Struggle Without: The Transformation of PLO Politics since 1982." *International Affairs* 65, no. 2 (Spring 1989): 247–65.
Schenker, David Kenneth. *Palestinian Democracy and Governance: An Appraisal of the Legislative Council*. Washington, D.C.: Washington Institute for Near East Policy, 2000.
Schenker, Hillel, ed. *After Lebanon: The Israeli-Palestinian Connection*. New York: Pilgrim Press, 1983.
Schoch, Bernd. *The Islamic Movement: A Challenge for Palestinian State-Building*. Jerusalem: PASSIA, 1999.
Sela, Avraham. "The PLO, the West Bank and the Gaza Strip." *Jerusalem Quarterly*, no. 8 (Summer 1978): 66–77.
Shadid, Mohammad K. "The Muslim Brotherhood Movement in the West Bank and Gaza." *Third World Quarterly* 10, no. 2 (April 1988): 54–69.
Sharabi, Hisham. *Palestine Guerillas: Their Credibility and Effectiveness*. Beirut: Institute for Palestine Studies, 1970.
Shemesh, Moshe. *The Palestinian Entity, 1959–1974: Arab Politics and the PLO*. London: Frank Cass, 1996.
Shlaim, Avi. "The Rise and Fall of the All-Palestine Government in Gaza." *Journal of Palestine Studies* 20, no. 1 (Autumn 1990): 37–53.
Smith, Charles D. *Palestine and the Arab-Israeli Conflict*. Boston: St. Martin's, 2001.
Stein, Kenneth W. "The Intifada and the 1936–39 Uprising: A Comparison." *Journal of Palestine Studies* 19, no. 4 (Summer 1990): 64–85.
Suleiman, Michael. "Intifada: The Latest Uprising for Palestinian Independence." *Journal of Arab Affairs* 8, no. 1 (Spring 1989): 1–9.
Trottier, Julie. *Hydropolitics in the West Bank and Gaza Strip*. Jerusalem: PASSIA, 1999.
Waart, Paul Jacobus Ignatius Maria de. *Dynamics of Self-Determination in Palestine: Protection of Peoples as a Human Right*. Leiden, The Netherlands: Brill, 1994.
Weingrod, Alex. "Living along the Seam: Israeli Palestinians in Jerusalem." *International Journal of Middle East Studies* 30, no. 3 (1998): 369–87.

Yaniv, Avner. *PLO: A Profile*. Jerusalem: Israel Universities Study Group for Middle Eastern Affairs, 1974.
Yodfat, Aryeh. *PLO Strategy and Politics*. New York: St. Martin's, 1981.

VII. TERRORISM AND VIOLENCE

Alexander, Yonah, and Joshua Sinai. *Terrorism: PLO Connection*. Bristol, Pa.: Crane Russak, 1989.
Aronson, Geoffrey. *Israel, Palestinians and the Intifada*. London: Kegan Paul International, 1990.
Charny, Israel W. *Strategies against Violence: Design for Nonviolent Change*. Boulder, Colo.: Westview Press, 1978.
Chomsky, Noam. *Pirates and Emperors: International Terrorism in the Real World*. Montreal: Black Rose Books, 1987.
Guelke, Adrian. *The Age of Terrorism and the International Political System*. London: I. B. Tauris, 1995.
Harmon, Christopher C. *Terrorism Today*. London: Frank Cass, 2000.
Korn, David A. *Assassination in Khartoum*. Bloomington: Indiana University Press, 1993.
Kushner, Harvey W., ed. *The Future of Terrorism: Violence in the New Millennium*. Thousand Oaks, Calif.: Sage, 1998.
A License to Kill: Israeli Operations against "Wanted" and Masked Palestinians. New York: Human Rights Watch, 1993.
O'Ballance, Edgar. *Islamic Fundamentalist Terrorism, 1979–1995: The Iranian Connection*. New York: New York University Press, 1997.
Stork, Joe. *Erased in a Moment: Suicide Bombing Attacks against Israeli Civilians*. New York: Human Rights Watch, 2002.
Tanter, Raymond. *Rogue Regimes: Terrorism and Proliferation*. New York: St. Martin's, 1998.

VIII. THE ARAB WORLD

Abboushi, W. F. *The Angry Arabs*. Philadelphia: Westminster Press, 1974.
Abu-Lughod, Ibrahim, and Ahmad Eqbal, eds. *The Invasion of Lebanon*. Washington, D.C.: Institute for Policy Studies, 1983.
Aburish, Said K. *A Brutal Friendship: The West and the Arab Elite*. London: Victor Gollancz, 1997.

Armstrong, Tony. *Breaking the Ice: Rapprochement between East and West Germany, the United States and China, and Israel and Egypt.* Washington, D.C.: United States Institute of Peace Press, 1993.

Avi-Ran, Reuvan. "The Syrian-Palestinian Conflict in Lebanon." *Jerusalem Quarterly*, no. 42 (Spring 1987): 57–82.

Bailey, C. "Changing Attitudes towards Jordan in the West Bank." *Middle East Journal* 32, no. 2 (Spring 1978): 155–66.

Bishara, Ghassan. "Impotence in the Face of Adversity: Arab Regimes and the Palestine Question." *Arab Studies Quarterly* 2, nos. 2–3 (Spring–Summer 1989): 303–14.

Brand, Laurie A. *Palestinians in the Arab World: Institution Building and the Search for State.* New York: Columbia University Press, 1988.

Brynen, Rex, ed. *Echoes of the Intifada: Regional Repercussions of the Palestinian-Israeli Conflict.* Boulder, Colo.: Westview Press, 1991.

Buheiry, Marwan R. *The Formation and Perception of the Modern Arab World.* Princeton, N.J.: Darwin Press, 1989.

Caplan, Neil, and Jon Black. "Israel and Lebanon: Origins of a Relationship." *Jerusalem Quarterly*, no. 27 (1983): 48–58.

Cordesman, Anthony H. *Saudi Arabia: Guarding the Desert Kingdom.* Boulder, Colo.: Westview, 1997.

Doran, Michael Scott. *Pan-Arabism before Nasser: Egyptian Power Politics and the Palestine Question.* New York: Oxford University Press, 1999.

Faour, Muhammad. *The Arab World after Desert Storm.* Washington, D.C.: United States Institute of Peace Press, 1993.

Fisk, Robert. *Pity the Nation: Lebanon at War.* Oxford: Oxford University Press, 1992.

Gabriel, Richard A. *Operation Peace for Galilee: The Israeli-PLO War in Lebanon.* New York: Hall and Wang, 1984.

Garfinkle, Adam M. *Israel and Jordan in the Shadow of War: Functional Ties and Futile Diplomacy in a Small Place.* New York: St. Martin's, 1992.

Gordon, Shmuel. *The Vulture and the Snake: Counter-Guerrilla Air Warfare; The War in Southern Lebanon.* Ramat Gan, Israel: BESA Center for Strategic Studies, Bar-Ilan University, 1998.

Hudson, Michael. "The Palestinian Factor in the Lebanese Civil War." *Middle East Journal* 32, no. 3 (Summer 1978): 261–78.

Hussein. "The Jordanian-Palestinian Initiative: Mutual Recognition and Territory for Peace." *Journal of Palestine Studies* 14, no. 4 (Summer 1985): 11–22.

Israeli, Raphael. *"I, Egypt": Aspects of President Anwar al-Sadat's Political Thought.* Jerusalem: Magnes Press, Hebrew University, 1981.

Kadi, Leila S. *Arab Summit Conferences and the Palestinian Problem, 1936–1950 and 1964–1966.* Beirut: PLO Research Center, 1966.

Kapelionk, Amnon. "New Light on the Arab-Israeli Conflict and Refugee Problems and Its Origin." *Journal of Palestine Studies* 16, no. 3 (Spring 1987): 16–24.

Karsh, Efraim, and P R Kumaraswamy, eds. *Israel, the Hashemites and the Palestinians: The Fateful Triangle.* London: Frank Cass, 2003.

Kazziha, Walid. *Palestine in the Arab Dilemma.* New York: Barnes and Noble, 1979.

Khalidi, R. "The Palestinians in Lebanon: Social Repercussions of Israel's Invasion." *Middle East Journal* 38, no. 2 (Spring 1984): 255–66.

Lawson, Fred Haley. *Why Syria Goes to War: Thirty Years of Confrontation.* Ithaca, N.Y.: Cornell University Press, 1996.

Lesch, Ann Mosley. *Arab Politics in Palestine, 1917–1936: The Frustration of a Nationalist Movement.* Ithaca, N.Y.: Cornell University Press, 1979.

Lesch, Ann Mosley, and Mark Tesslar. *Israel, Egypt and the Palestinians: From Camp David to Intifada.* Bloomington: Indiana University Press, 1989.

Mackey, Sandra. *Passion and Politics: The Turbulent World of the Arabs.* New York: Dutton, 1992.

Mayer, Thomas. *Egypt and the Palestine Question, 1936–1945.* Berlin: K. Schwars, 1983.

Miller, Aaron David. *The Arab States and the Palestine Question: Between Ideology and Self-Interest.* New York: Praeger, 1986.

Mishal, Saul. *West Bank, East Bank: The Palestinians in Jordan, 1949–1967.* New Haven, Conn.: Yale University Press, 1976.

Mufti, Malik. *Sovereign Creations: Pan-Arabism and Political Order in Syria and Iraq.* Ithaca, N.Y.: Cornell University Press, 1996.

Queen Noor. *Leap of Faith: Memoirs of an Unexpected Life.* New York: Miramax Books, 2003.

Quilliam, Neil. *Syria and the New World Order.* Reading, England: Ithaca, 1999.

Rabil, Robert G. *Embattled Neighbors: Syria, Israel, Lebanon.* London: Lynne Rienner, 2003.

Rejwan, Nissim. *Arab Aims and Israeli Attitudes: A Critique of Yehoshafat Harkabi's Prognosis of the Arab-Israeli Conflict.* Jerusalem: Leonard Davis Institute for International Relations, Hebrew University, 2000.

Rubin, Barry. *The Arab States and the Palestine Conflict.* Syracuse, N.Y.: Syracuse University Press, 1981.

Sayigh, Anis. *Palestine and Arab Nationalism.* Beirut: PLO Research Center, 1970.

Shlaim, Avi. *The Iron Wall: Israel and the Arab World.* London: A. Lane, 1999.

Tessler, Mark Arnold. *Israel at Peace with the Arab World.* Abu Dhabi: Emirates Center for Strategic Studies and Research, 1996.

Wurmser, Meyrav. *The Schools of Ba'athism: A Study of Syrian Schoolbooks.* Washington, D.C.: Middle East Media Research Institute, 2000.

Yaari, Ehud. *Peace by Piece: A Decade of Egyptian Policy toward Israel*. Washington, D.C.: Washington Institute for Near East Policy, 1998.

IX. THE ARAB–ISRAELI CONFLICT AND THE UNITED STATES

Ahmad, H. "From the Balfour Declaration to World War II: The US Stand on Palestinian Self-Determination." *Arab Studies Quarterly* 12, nos. 1–2 (Winter–Spring 1990): 9–41.

Aruri, Nasser. "The United States and Palestine: Reagan's Legacy to Bush." *Journal of Palestine Studies* 18, no. 3 (Spring 1989): 3–21.

Ben-Zvi, Abraham. *The United States and the Palestinians: The Carter Era*. Tel Aviv: Center for Strategic Studies, 1981.

Chomsky, Noam. *The Fateful Triangle: The United States, Israel, and the Palestinians*. Boston: South End Press, 1984.

Clawson, Patrick, and Gedal Zoe Danon. *Dollars and Diplomacy: The Impact of U.S. Economic Initiatives on Arab-Israeli Negotiations*. Washington, D.C.: Washington Institute for Near East Policy, 1999.

Cordesman, Anthony H. *U.S. Forces in the Middle East: Resources and Capabilities*. Boulder, Colo: Westview Press, 1997.

Druks, Herbert. *The Uncertain Alliance: The U.S. and Israel from Kennedy to the Peace Process*. Westport, Conn.: Greenwood Press, 2001.

Farsoun, S. "The Palestinians, the PLO and US Foreign Policy." *American-Arab Affairs*, no. 1 (Summer 1982): 81–95.

Fraser, Thomas Grant. *The USA and the Middle East since World War II*. New York: St. Martin's, 1989.

Hurst, Steven. *The Foreign Policy of the Bush Administration: In Search of a New World Order*. New York: Cassell, 1999.

Kuniholm, Bruce R., and Michael Rubner. *The Palestinian Problem and United States Policy: A Guide to Issues and References*. Claremont, Calif.: Regina Books, 1986.

Lesch, David W. *The Middle East and the United States: A Historical and Political Reassessment*. Boulder, Colo.: Westview, 1999.

Lieber, Robert J., ed. *Eagle Adrift: American Foreign Policy at the End of the Century*. New York: Longman, 1996.

Little, Douglas. *American Orientalism: The United States and the Middle East since 1945*. Chapel Hill: University of North Carolina Press, 2002.

Nordlinger, Eric A. *Isolationism Reconfigured: American Foreign Policy for a New Century*. Princeton, N.J.: Princeton University Press, 1995.

Payne, Richard J. *The Clash with Distant Cultures: Values, Interests and Force in American Foreign Policy*. Albany: State University of New York Press, 1995.

Peck, Juliana S. *The Reagan Administration and the Palestinian Question: The First Thousand Days.* Washington, D.C.: Institute for Palestine Studies, 1984.

Quandt, William B. "After the Israeli-PLO Breakthrough: Next Steps for the United States." *Brookings Review* 12, no. 1 (Winter 1994): 28–35.

———. *Decades of Decisions: American Policy toward the Arab-Israeli Conflict. 1967–1976.* Berkeley: University of California Press, 1977.

Reich, Bernard. *Quest for Peace: United States–Israel Relations and the Arab-Israeli Conflict.* New Brunswick, N.J.: Transaction Books, 1977.

Rubenberg, Cheryl. "U.S. Policy toward the Palestinians: A Twenty-Year Assessment." *Arab Studies Quarterly* 10, no.1 (Winter 1988): 1–43.

Slonim, Shlomo. *United States–Israel Relations, 1967–1973: A Study in the Convergence and Divergence of Interests.* Jerusalem: Leonard Davis Institute for International Relations, Hebrew University, 1974.

Sohar, Ezra. *A Concubine in the Middle East: American-Israeli Relations.* Jerusalem: Ariel Center for Policy Research, 1999.

Stein, Kenneth W. "The Palestinian Uprising and the Shultz Initiative." *Middle East Review* 21 (Winter 1988–89): 13–20.

Steinbruner, John D., ed. *Restructuring American Foreign Policy.* Washington, D.C.: Brookings Institution, 1989.

Thorpe, Merle, Jr. "Notes of a Bit Player in the Israeli-Palestinian Conflict Settlements in the U.S. Policy." *Journal of Palestine Studies* 23, no. 3 (1994): 41–52.

Weinstein, Allen, and Moshe Ma'oz, eds. *Truman and the American Commitment to Israel: A Thirtieth Anniversary Conference.* Jerusalem: Magnes Press, Hebrew University, 1981.

Zunes, Stephen. "The United States and the Breakdown of the Israeli–Palestinian Peace Process." *Middle East Policy* 8, no. 4 (2001): 66–85.

X. THE ARAB–ISRAELI CONFLICT AND THE INTERNATIONAL COMMUNITY

Avineri, Shlomo. "The Impact of Changes in the Soviet Union and Eastern Europe on the Arab-Israeli Conflict." *Mediterranean Quarterly* 2, no. 1 (Winter 1991): 45–57.

Beinin, Joel. *Was the Red Flag Flying There? Marxist Politics and the Arab-Israeli Conflict in Egypt and Israel, 1948–1965.* Berkeley: University of California Press, 1990.

Beloff, Max. *The Role of the Palestine Mandate in the Period of Britain's Imperial Decline.* Haifa, Israel: University of Haifa, 1981.

Ben-Zvi, Abraham. *Between Lausanne and Geneva: International Conferences and the Arab-Israel Conflict.* Boulder, Colo.: Westview Press, 1989.

Brook, David. *Preface to Peace: The United Nations and the Arab-Israel Armistice System*. Washington, D.C.: Public Affairs Press, 1964.

Brown, Michael E. *The International Dimensions of Internal Conflict*. Cambridge, Mass.: MIT Press, 1996.

Caplan, Neil. *The Limitations of Third-Party Intervention in the Arab-Israeli Conflict: Lessons from Selected Episodes, 1949–1956*. Jerusalem: Leonard Davis Institute for International Relations, Hebrew University, 1999.

Cattan, Henry. *Palestine and International Law: The Legal Aspects of the Arab-Israeli Conflict*. New York: Longman, 1976.

Cohen, Esther Rosalind. *International Criticism of Israeli Security Measures in the Occupied Territories*. Jerusalem: Magnes Press, Hebrew University, 1984.

Cohen, Michael J. *Palestine: Retreat from the Mandate; The Making of British Policy, 1936–1945*. New York: Holmes and Meier, 1978.

——. *Palestine and the Great Powers, 1945–1948*. Princeton, N.J.: Princeton University Press, 1982.

Comay, Michael Saul. *U.N. Peace-Keeping in the Israel-Arab Conflict, 1948–1975: An Israel Critique*. Jerusalem: Leonard Davis Institute for International Relations, Hebrew University, 1976.

Esman, Milton J., and Shibley Telhami, eds. *International Organizations and Ethnic Conflict*. Ithaca, N.Y.: Cornell University Press, 1995.

Gerges, Fawaz A. *The Superpowers and the Middle East: Regional and International Politics, 1955–1967*. Boulder, Colo.: Westview Press, 1994.

Golan, Galia. *The Soviet Union and the Palestine Liberation Organization: An Uneasy Alliance*. New York: Praeger, 1980.

Gruen, George E. "Turkey's Relations with Israel and Its Neighbors." *Middle East Review* 17, no. 3 (Spring 1985): 33–43.

Hanna, Paul L. *British Policy in Palestine*. Washington, D.C.: American Council on Public Affairs, 1942.

Jones, Martin. *Failure in Palestine: British and United States Policy after the Second World War*. New York: Mansell, 1986.

Kreutz, Andrej. *Vatican Policy on the Palestinian-Israeli Conflict: The Struggle for the Holy Land*. New York: Greenwood Press, 1990.

Kuroda, Yasumasa. *Japan in a New World Order: Contributing to the Arab-Israeli Peace Process*. Commack, N.Y.: Nova Science Publishers, 1994.

Mackinlay, John. *The Peacekeepers: An Assessment of Peacekeeping Operations at the Arab-Israel Interface*. Boston: Unwin Hyman, 1989.

Nir, Yeshayahu. *The Israeli-Arab Conflict in Soviet Caricatures, 1967–1973: A Research Monograph in Visual Communication*. Tel Aviv: Tcherikover, 1976.

Oded, Arye. *Africa and the Middle East Conflict*. Boulder, Colo.: Lynne Rienner, 1987.

Pelcovitz, Nathan Albert. *Peacekeeping on Arab-Israeli Fronts: Lessons from the Sinai and Lebanon*. Boulder, Colo.: Westview Press, with the Foreign Policy Institute, School of Advanced International Studies, Johns Hopkins University, 1984.

Taras, David, and David H. Goldberg, eds. *The Domestic Battleground: Canada and the Arab-Israeli Conflict*. Kingston, Ont.: McGill-Queen's University Press, 1989.

Tibi, Bassam. *Conflict and War in the Middle East, 1967–1991: Regional Dynamic and the Superpowers*. London: Macmillan, 1993.

Wehling, Fred. *Irresolute Princes: Kremlin Decision Making in Middle East Crises, 1967–1973*. New York: St. Martin's, 1997.

Wood, Pia Christina. "France and the Israeli-Palestinian Conflict: The Mitterrand Policies, 1981–1992." *Middle East Journal* 47, no. 1 (1993): 21–40.

Woods, Ngaire. *Explaining International Relations since 1945*. Oxford: Oxford University Press, 1996.

Younis, Mona. *Liberation and Democratization: The South African and Palestinian National Movements*. Minneapolis: University of Minnesota Press, 2000.

XI. MISCELLANEOUS

Aharon, Ada. *Women: Creating a World beyond War and Violence*. Haifa: New Horizon, 2001.

Albright, David. *Plutonium and Highly Enriched Uranium, 1996: World Inventories, Capabilities and Policies*. Oxford: Oxford University Press, 1997.

Aliboni, Roberto, George Joffé, and Tim Niblock, eds. *Security Challenges in the Mediterranean Region*. London: Frank Cass, 1996.

Bar-Tal, Daniel, and Staub Ervin, eds. *Patriotism in the Lives of Individuals and Nations*. Chicago: Nelson-Hall, 1997.

Bunzl, John. *Between Vienna and Jerusalem: Reflections and Polemics on Austria, Israel and Palestine*. Frankfurt am Main: Peter Lang, 1997.

Bercovitch, Jacob, ed. *Resolving International Conflicts: The Theory and Practice of Mediation*. Boulder, Colo.: Lynne Rienner, 1996.

Beres, Louis René. "After the Gulf War: Israel, Palestine and the Risk of Nuclear War in the Middle East." *Strategic Review* 19, no. 4 (1991): 48–55.

———. "Israel, Palestine and Regional Nuclear War." *Bulletin of Peace Proposals* 22, no. 2 (1991): 227–34.

———. "Israel, Palestinian Demilitarization and International Law." *Midstream* 43, no. 5 (1997): 4–6.

Bialer, Uri. *Armed Forces in Foreign Territories under the Terms of Peace Agreements: Historical Implications*. Tel Aviv: Center for Strategic Studies, Tel Aviv University, 1979.

Bill, James Alban. *Politics in the Middle East*. New York: HarperCollins, 1994.

Blum, Yehuda Zvi. *The Juridical Status of Jerusalem*. Jerusalem: Leonard Davis Institute for International Relations, Hebrew University, 1974.

Bond, Brian. *The Pursuit of Victory: From Napoleon to Saddam Hussein*. Oxford: Oxford University Press, 1996.

Breslauer, George W., Harry Kreisler, and Benjamin Ward, eds. *Beyond the Cold War: Conflict and Cooperation in the Third World*. Berkeley, Calif.: International and Area Studies, Institute of International Studies, 1991.

Chomsky, Noam. *Powers and Prospects: Reflections on Human Nature and the Social Order*. London: Pluto Press, 1996.

Christopher, Warren. *In the Stream of History: Shaping Foreign Policy for a New Era*. Stanford, Calif.: Stanford University Press, 1998.

Ciment, James. *Encyclopedia of Conflicts since World War II*. Armonk, N.Y.: Sharpe Reference, 1999.

Cockburn, Cynthia. *The Space between Us: Negotiating Gender and National Identities in Conflict*. London: Zed Books, 1998.

Cooke, Miriam, and Rustomji-Kerns Roshni, eds. *Blood into Ink: South Asian and Middle Eastern Women Write War*. Boulder, Colo.: Westview Press, 1994.

Cordesman, Anthony H. *Peace and War: The Arab-Israeli Military Balance Enters the 21st Century*. Westport, Conn: Praeger, 2002.

Corm, Georges G. *Fragmentation of the Middle East: The Last Thirty Years*. London: Hutchinson, 1988.

Curtis, Michael, ed. *Religion and Politics in the Middle East*. Boulder, Colo.: Westview Press, 1981.

Danspeckgruber, Wolfgang, and Arthur Watts, eds. *Self-Determination and Self-Administration: A Sourcebook*. Boulder, Colo.: Lynne Rienner, 1997.

Davis, M. Jane. *Politics and International Relations in the Middle East: Continuity and Change*. Aldershot, England: Edward Elgar, 1995.

Donahue, John M., and Barbara Rose Johnston, eds. *Water, Culture and Power: Local Struggles in a Global Context*. Washington, D.C.: Island Press, 1998.

Eban, Abba Solomon. *Diplomacy for the Next Century*. New Haven, Conn.: Yale University Press, 1998.

El-Hindi, Jamal L. "Compensation as Part of Equal Utilization in the Israeli-Palestinian Water Context." *Arab Studies Quarterly* 22, no. 2 (2000): 113–46.

Elizur, Judith Neulander. *Images in Situations of Protracted Conflict*. Jerusalem: S. N., 1998.

Elmusa, Sharif S. "Power and Trade: The Israeli-Palestinian Economic Protocol." *Journal of Palestine Studies* 24, no. 2 (1995): 14–32.

Evron, Yair. *The Demilitarization of Sinai*. Jerusalem: Leonard Davis Institute for International Relations, Hebrew University, 1975.

Farra, Muhammad. *Years of No Decision*. London: KPI, 1987.

Feldman, Shai. *Nuclear Weapons and Arms Control in the Middle East*. Cambridge, Mass.: MIT Press, 1997.

Fry, Michael, ed. *History, the White House, and the Kremlin: Statesmen as Historians*. London: Pinter, 1991.

Fuller, Graham E., and Ian O. Lesser. *A Sense of Siege: The Geopolitics of Islam and the West*. Boulder, Colo.: Westview Press, 1995.

Goldberg, Bernard. *Bias: A CBS Insider Exposes How the Media Distorts the News*. Washington, D.C.: Regnery, 2001.

Gordon, Philip H. *The Transatlantic Allies and the Changing Middle East*. Oxford: Oxford University Press, 1998.

Gorman, Robert F. *Historical Dictionary of Refugee and Disaster Relief Organizations*. 2nd ed. Metuchen, N.J.: Scarecrow Press, 2000.

Greenstein, Ran. *Genealogies of Conflict: Class, Identity and State in Palestine/Israel and South Africa*. Hanover, N.H.: Wesleyan University Press, 1995.

Guazzone, Laura, ed. *The Middle East in Global Change: The Politics and Economics of Interdependence versus Fragmentation*. New York: St. Martin's, 1997.

Harvey, Frank P., and Ben D. Mor, eds. *Conflict in World Politics: Advances in the Study of Crisis, War and Peace*. New York: St. Martin's, 1997.

Heper, Metin, and Raphael Israeli, eds. *Islam and Politics in the Modern Middle East*. London: Leaper, 1984.

Herman, Michael. *Intelligence Power in Peace and War*. Cambridge: Cambridge University Press, 1996.

Homer-Dixon, Thomas, and Jessica Blitt, eds. *Ecoviolence: Links among Environment, Population and Security*. Lanham, Md.: Rowman and Littlefield, 1998.

Huth, Paul K. *Standing Your Ground: Territorial Disputes and International Conflict*. Ann Arbor: University of Michigan Press, 1996.

Inbar, Efraim, and Gabriel Sheffer, eds. *The National Security of Small States in a Changing World*. London: Frank Cass, 1997.

Israeli, Raphael. *Peace Is in the Eye of the Beholder*. Berlin: Mouton, 1985.

Katzenstein, Peter J., ed. *The Culture of National Security: Norms and Identity in World Politics*. New York: Columbia University Press, 1996.

Kershenovich, Paulette. *A Case Study of the Jerusalem Link as a Women's Dialogue Group*. Tel Aviv: Paulette Kershenovich, 2000.

Kolodziej, Edward A., and Roger E. Kanet, eds. *Coping with Conflict after the Cold War*. Baltimore: Johns Hopkins University Press, 1996.

Kriesberg, Louis. *Constructive Conflicts: From Escalation to Resolution*. Lanham, Md.: Rowman and Littlefield, 1998.

Lavy, Victor. *Regional Conflict, Country Risk and Foreign Direct Investment in the Middle East*. Jerusalem: Leonard Davis Institute for International Relations, Hebrew University, 1999.

Lebow, Richard Ned. *The Art of Bargaining*. Baltimore: Johns Hopkins University Press, 1996.

———. *We All Lost the Cold War*. Princeton, N.J.: Princeton University Press, 1994.

Leng, Russell J. *Bargaining and Learning in Recurring Crises: The Soviet-American, Egyptian-Israeli, and Indo-Pakistani Rivalries*. Ann Arbor: University of Michigan Press, 2000.

Lipsey, Roderick K. Von. *Breaking the Cycle*. New York: St. Martin's, 1997.

Ma'oz, Ze'ev, ed. *Regional Security in the Middle East: Past, Present, and Future*. London: Frank Cass, 1997.

McClellan, Grant S. *The Middle East in the Cold War*. New York: Wilson, 1956.

Miller, Benjamin. *The Global Sources of Regional Transitions from War to Peace: The Case of the Middle East*. Jerusalem: Leonard Davis Institute for International Relations, Hebrew University, 1999.

———. *When Opponents Cooperate: Great Power Conflict and Collaboration in World Politics*. Ann Arbor: University of Michigan Press, 1995.

Milstein, Uri. *The General Theory of Security: The Survival Principle*. Tel Aviv: Survival, 1991.

Mitchell, Thomas G. *Native vs. Settler: Ethnic Conflict in Israel/Palestine, Northern Ireland, and South Africa*. Westport, Conn.: Greenwood Press, 2000.

Moller, Bjorn. *Dictionary of Alternative Defense*. Boulder, Colo.: Lynne Rienner, 1995.

Moore, Dahlia. *Social Identities of Young Jews, Arabs and Palestinians*. Jerusalem: Harry S. Truman Research Institute for the Advancement of Peace, Hebrew University, 2001.

Mudimbe, V. Y., ed. *Nations, Identities, Cultures*. Durham, N.C.: Duke University Press, 1995.

Mushkat, Marionm. *The Third World and Peace: Some Aspects of the Interrelationship of Underdevelopment and International Security*. New York: St. Martin's, 1982.

Muslih, Muhammad Y. *The Golan: The Road to Occupation*. Washington, D.C.: Institute for Palestine Studies, 1999.

Mutalib, Hussin, and Taj Ul-Islam Hashmi, ed. *Islam, Muslims, and the Modern State: Case Studies of Muslims in Thirteen Countries*. New York: St. Martin's, 1994.

Neff, Donald. *Warriors against Israel*. Brattleboro, Vt.: Amana Books, 1988.

Nester, William R. *International Relations: Geopolitical and Geoeconomic Conflict and Cooperation*. New York: HarperCollins College, 1995.

Newman, David, ed. *Boundaries, Territory and Postmodernity*. London: Frank Cass, 1999.

O'Neill, Robert, ed. *Prospects for Security in the Mediterranean*. Hamden, Conn.: Archon Books, 1988.

Palsson, Gisli. *Beyond Boundaries: Understanding, Translation, and Anthropological Discourse*. Oxford: Berg, 1993.

Peres, Shimon, with Naor Arye. *The New Middle East*. New York: H. Holt, 1993.

Resnick, Uri. *Palestinian and Israeli Political Behavior, 1993–1996: The Effects of Ambiguity on Strategic Interaction*. Jerusalem: Hebrew University, 1998.

Rikhye, Inder Jit. *The Middle East and the New Realism*. New York: International Peace Academy, 1975.

Shamir, Jacob. *The Anatomy of Public Opinion*. Ann Arbor: University of Michigan Press, 2000.

Smock, David R. *Making War and Waging Peace: Foreign Intervention in Africa*. Washington, D.C.: United States Institute of Peace Press, 1993.

Snow, Donald M. *Uncivil Wars: International Security and the New Internal Conflicts*. Boulder, Colo.: Lynne Rienner, 1996.

Spielberger, Charles S., and Irwin G. Sarason, eds. *Stress and Anxiety*. Washington, D.C.: Hemisphere Publication, 1975.

Tessler Mark, Jodi Nachtwey, and Anne Banda. *Area Studies and Social Science: Strategies for Understanding Middle East Politics*. Bloomington: Indiana University Press, 1999.

Urian, Dan. *Palestinians and Israelis in the Theatre*. London: Hardwood Academic Press, 1995.

Weiner, Eugene. *The Handbook of Interethnic Coexistence*. New York: Continuum, 1998.

Weldes, Jutta, et al., eds. *Cultures of Insecurity: States, Communities, and the Production of Danger*. Minneapolis: University of Minnesota Press, 1999.

Whittaker, David J. *Conflict and Reconciliation in the Contemporary World*. London: Routledge, 1999.

Wiseman, Henry, ed. *Peacekeeping: Appraisals and Proposals*. New York: Pergamon Press, 1983.

Zartman, William I., and Victor A. Kremenyuk, eds. *Cooperative Security: Reducing Third World Wars*. Syracuse, N.Y.: Syracuse University Press, 1995.

About the Author

P R Kumaraswamy is an associate professor of Middle Eastern studies at Jawaharlal Nehru University (JNU) in New Delhi, India. He obtained a Ph.D. from the same university for his thesis "India's Policy towards Israel, 1948–1980." From 1992 to 1999, he was a research fellow in Jerusalem at the Harry S. Truman Research Institute for the Advancement of Peace. He was also briefly associated with the Institute for Defence Studies and Analyses (IDSA), New Delhi.

Since joining the faculty of JNU in September 1999, Dr. Kumaraswamy has been researching, teaching, and writing on various aspects of the Middle East. His publications include *Security beyond Survival: Essays for K Subrahmanyam* (editor, 2004), *The Fateful Triangle: Israel Hashemites and Palestinians* (coeditor with Efraim Karsh, 2000), *Israel and the Islamic World* (coeditor with Efraim Karsh, 2006), *Revisiting the Yom Kippur War* (editor, 2000), *China and the Middle East* (editor, 1999), *Beyond the Veil: Israel–Pakistan Relations* (2000), *India and Israel: Evolving Strategic Partnership* (1998), *Political Legitimacy of the Minorities: Israeli Arabs and the 1996 Knesset Elections* (1998), and *Israel's China Odyssey* (1994).

Dr. Kumaraswamy has published research articles in a number of journals, including *Arab Studies Quarterly, Asian and African Studies, Asian Studies Review, Contemporary South Asia, Israel Affairs, Issues and Studies, Jane's Intelligence Review, Journal of Indo-Judaic Studies, Journal of South Asian and Middle Eastern Studies, MERIA Journal, Mediterranean Quarterly, Middle East International, Middle East Policy, Middle East Quarterly, Middle Eastern Studies, Security Dialogue,* and *The Bulletin of Atomic Scientists.*